THE COLUMBIA GUIDE TO
AMERICAN INDIANS OF THE SOUTHWEST

The Columbia Guides to American Indian History and Culture

COLUMBIA GUIDES TO
AMERICAN INDIAN HISTORY AND CULTURE

The Columbia Guide to American Indians of the Southeast
Theda Perdue and Michael D. Green

The Columbia Guide to American Indians of the Northeast
Kathleen J. Bragdon

The Columbia Guide to American Indians of the Great Plains
Loretta Fowler

THE COLUMBIA GUIDE TO
AMERICAN INDIANS
OF THE SOUTHWEST

Trudy Griffin-Pierce

COLUMBIA UNIVERSITY PRESS

NEW YORK

Columbia University Press
Publishers Since 1893
New York   Chichester, West Sussex
Copyright © 2010 Columbia University Press
All rights reserved

Library of Congress Cataloging-in-Publication Data
Griffin-Pierce, Trudy, 1949–2009.
The Columbia guide to American Indians of the Southwest /
Trudy Griffin-Pierce.
p.   cm. — (Columbia guides to American Indian history and culture)
Includes bibliographical references and index.
ISBN 978-0-231-12790-5 (cloth : alk. paper)
1. Indians of North America—Southwest, New—History. 2. Indians of
North America—Southwest, New—Social life and customs. I. Title. II. Series.
E78.S7G75   2009
979.004'97—dc22
2009005489

Columbia University Press books are printed on permanent and durable acid-free paper.
This book was printed on paper with recycled content.
Printed in the United States of America

c 10 9 8 7 6 5 4 3 2 1

References to Internet Web sites (URLs) were accurate at the time of writing.
Neither the author nor Columbia University Press is responsible for URLs
that may have expired or changed since the manuscript was prepared.

CONTENTS

The hogan and cornfield outside the Chinle Hospital, Chinle, Arizona. At the far left is the hospital; at the right is the housing compound for Indian Health Service physicians and personnel.

PREFACE

As I look at photographs from a trip to visit my Navajo family in Chinle, Arizona, I see images of the past and present blended within every frame. Each photo depicts some aspect of the ongoing processes that make up contemporary Indian life in today's American Southwest; each one is dense with meaning.

The photograph facing this page juxtaposes the Chinle Hospital and a hogan; a cornfield stands behind the hogan, and in the background are the houses in the living compound for Indian Health Service (IHS) physicians and their families. This image represents the ongoing collaboration between medicine people and IHS personnel. Since its inception in 2000, the Office of Native Medicine (ONM) has been located within the Chinle Hospital, with a hogan facility for traditional healing activities. In keeping with its goal of bridging the gap in understanding between physicians and Navajo people, the medicine men who work at ONM provide a wide array of services, including but not limited to giving prayers and short ceremonies for Navajo patients in the hospital; connecting Navajos who seek traditional healing but are not patients at the hospital with appropriate medicine people for their diseases; conducting classes for medicine people about such topics as recognizing the symptoms of diabetes; and giving formal lectures on Navajo medicine beliefs and practices for non-Navajo hospital staff. There are actually two hogans at Chinle: one that is entered through the doorway of ONM and is part of the physical structure of the hospital and the one shown in the photograph. This accommodation reflects Navajo beliefs about the dead: because ceremonies should not be conducted in the same structure where death has occurred, many medicine people refuse to perform them within the hospital. While such basic concepts are shared, specific beliefs regarding traditional healing differ among individual medicine people.

The cornfield that is visible in the photograph just behind the hogan can be understood on several levels. First, corn represents traditional Navajo food, a gift from Mother Earth, and reminds patients who come to the hospital to replace processed foods with healthier choices. Corn is also a metaphor for the proper way to live; it stands as a visual reminder of the restoration of order, and therefore health, in a person's life. Just as corn plants grow from the ground upward, medicine people perform ritual actions from the feet upward. Corn plants also produce corn pollen, *tádidíín*, the sacred substance of life, an essential component of ceremonies because the Pollen Path, *Tádidíín bee Ké'ehaschíín*, is a metaphor for moving along one's life trail. This means living each day in a way that is guided by ideals of harmony and balance.[1]

Finally, the living compound for Indian Health Service physicians and their families reflects another facet of American Indian life: the relative isolation of doctors from the Indian communities they have come to serve. Individuals who enjoy health insurance in the United States usually have primary care physicians; however, the two-year rotation period for IHS physicians precludes the development of such in-depth relationships. This is particularly alienating for Native patients because relationships are the basis from which American Indian people experience life. Even doctors who prioritize relationship building and want to raise their families on the reservation are unable to do so because of the existing institutional framework.

My intention in this book is to extend the scope of the written information through the photographs and their accompanying captions. As part of *The Columbia Guides to American Indian History and Culture* series, this book was written with specific guidelines for consistency to make the material more accessible for its intended audience. In a field of ever burgeoning literature—arguably, the Native peoples of the Southwest have the largest corpus of literature written by and about them, in contrast to the indigenous peoples of other regions in the United States—it is impossible to include everything that has been published on this topic. Therefore, I encourage readers to use the sources listed in part IV as a starting point from which to seek out the sources cited *within* these resources for further research.

Above all, through the visual images that accompany the text, I seek to convey the vitally important fact that American Indians are contemporary peoples. Duane Champagne, the noted Chippewa professor of sociology and American

Indian Studies at UCLA, speaks to the contemporary nature of Indian life when he says that indigenous peoples are choosing a path to the future that emphasizes social change rather than assimilation, race, or ethnicity, and is grounded in their own traditions. "Having been independent nations in the sense of managing land and having autonomous political, cultural, and economic institutions," he says, today's indigenous nations are striving "to maintain . . . recover, and restore powers and institutions of government and society."[2] It is not that they do not want to cooperate with the federal government in the pursuit of these goals, "but because their religions and founding institutional teachings inform them that they have a sacred purpose to accomplish in the world," indigenous nations often come into conflict with the government.[3] In reading the narrative sections of this book, it is important to remember that Native peoples have always been active participants, creating their own patterns of change even within the constraints of colonial contexts. The choices they make are informed by their own models of cultural order.

Respected anthropologist Louise Lamphere[4] describes the long tradition of anthropologists in the Southwest establishing close relationships with families in the communities where they conducted fieldwork. My path differed somewhat from this tradition because I became an anthropologist in an effort to better understand the cultural, social, economic, and historical context in which my first Navajo family lived. In 1968, when I was earning my undergraduate degree at Florida State University, I wrote to Navajo Tribal Chairman Raymond Nakai, asking him to find a traditional Navajo family that I could join as a daughter. Two years later, we were living about five miles from Many Farms, Arizona, in their hogan without electricity, running water, or a pickup truck; each morning, we took the sheep and goats out, returning in the late afternoon. In large part, this book reflects my desire to go back and examine more systematically and with greater comparative depth issues that I was aware of but could not yet articulate when I came to live with this elderly Navajo couple. In 1971, I moved to Arizona permanently, choosing the University of Arizona for graduate work because it was relatively near my Navajo family.

I developed a close and ongoing relationship with another family during my dissertation research. Avery Denny, my Navajo brother, helped me enormously as I worked with his father, a well-known Male Shootingway chanter. Both of his parents have given ceremonies for me at different times in my life. I am also close to Avery's wife, Pat, a respected educator, and to their children as well as to Avery's sisters. Over the course of the last thirty-eight years, I have watched their children grow up and have children of their own, and I have shared Avery's path from electrician to Nightway chanter and spokesperson for the Navajo Nation. As he develops the statement of philosophy for education at Diné College, where he teaches, I am seeing the processes identified by Duane Champagne in action.

This book also draws from my ongoing work with tribal communities in the context of biomedicine and traditional medicine, and especially what I have learned from Native students in my anthropology classes at the University of Arizona. They include a female White Mountain Apache wildland firefighter, the granddaughter of a Navajo Code Talker, the son of a well-known Hopi jewelry maker who is following in his father's footsteps, and a Zuni trying to reconcile his traditional beliefs with what he was being taught in an evolutionary biology class; his goal, upon earning his degree, was to return to Zuni to serve in tribal government and to make informed decisions that would help his people negotiate an acceptable and productive path to social change. One of the most memorable students was Raymond Nakai's niece, who approached me at the end of the class in which I told the story of my letter to her uncle seeking a Navajo family. "*Now* I understand the letter I found last summer in my uncle's archives!" she told me, some thirty-six years later.

The chapters in this volume are divided into four topical areas, although the content in each part is not mutually exclusive. The first four chapters form part I, "History and Culture," and provide the reader with an archaeological/ethnographic perspective and a greatly condensed account of history as it affected Native peoples in the Southwest. For the sake of consistency with the other volumes in this series, I have taken a traditional scholarly approach. I stress that this is only one perspective among many, and I direct readers to Champagne's[5] focus on the Native experience of colonialism (including but not limited to the Southwest), Ferguson and Colwell-Chanthaphonh's[6] and Whiteley's[7] emphasis on collaboration, contemporary accounts in one of my previous books,[8] and a wide range of oral traditions noted in section 4 of part IV of this book. Part II serves as a selected list of important individuals, places of significant cultural or historical meaning, and key events in the history of Native peoples of the Southwest. Part III provides a chronology of major events. The selected resources guide in part IV begins with an account of the methods and history of research in southwestern archaeology and ethnology and goes on to present annotated bibliographies under specific topics, museum and tribal Internet sites, and films.

Finally, I want to point out that the divisions of this book are a heuristic device structured to help readers more easily locate the topics that interest them. My intent is to make this information accessible to a wider audience so that they can seek out sources far beyond the scope of this book. I ask readers to keep in mind that this is a Westernized presentation that violates the holistic sense of spiritual connectedness that underlies all American Indian worldviews. . . . As though to remind me of this perspective of interconnection, at this very moment, a hawk has landed on a limb of the eucalyptus tree just outside my office window on the third floor of the anthropology building. He is swiveling his head in my direction, peering at me through hooded eyes. . . .

NOTES

1. Trudy Griffin-Pierce, *Earth Is My Mother, Sky Is My Father: Space, Time, and Astronomy in Navajo Sandpainting* (Albuquerque: University of New Mexico Press, 1992), 192–193.
2. Duane Champagne, *Social Change and Cultural Continuity Among Native Nations* (Lanham, Md.: AltaMira Press, 2007), 1.
3. Ibid.
4. Louise Lamphere with Eva Price, Carole Cadman, and Valerie Darwin, *Weaving Women's Lives: Three Generations in a Navajo Family* (Albuquerque: University of New Mexico Press, 2007), 11.
5. Champagne, *Social Change and Cultural Continuity*.
6. T. J. Ferguson and Chip Colwell-Chanthaphonh, *History Is in the Land: Multivocal Tribal Traditions in Arizona's San Pedro Valley* (Tucson: University of Arizona Press, 2006).
6. Peter M. Whiteley, "Archaeology and Oral Tradition: The Scientific Importance of Dialogue," *American Antiquity* 67 (3) (2002): 405.
7. Trudy Griffin-Pierce, *Native Peoples of the Southwest* (Albuquerque: University of New Mexico Press, 2000).

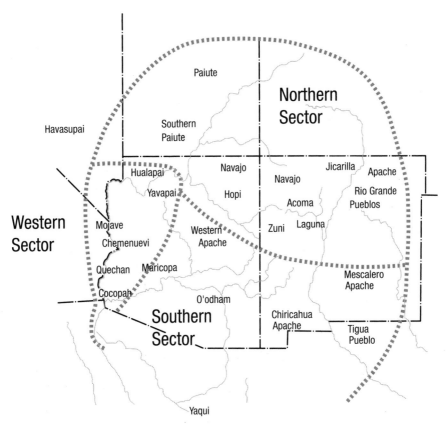

Map 1. Location of Southwestern Indian Tribes

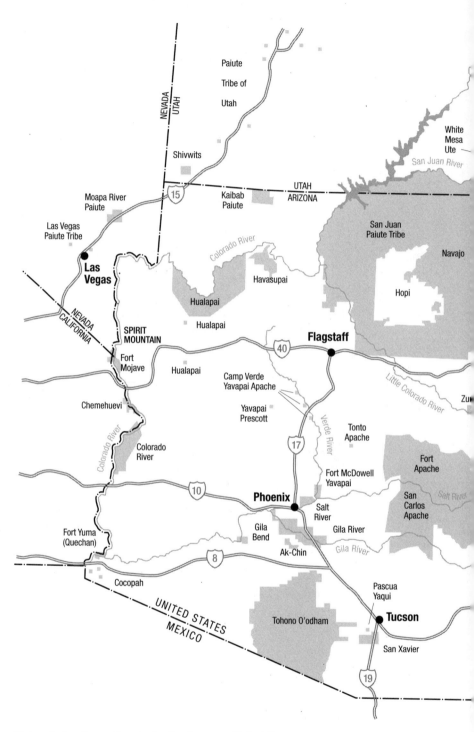

Map 2. Indian Reservations in the Southwestern United States

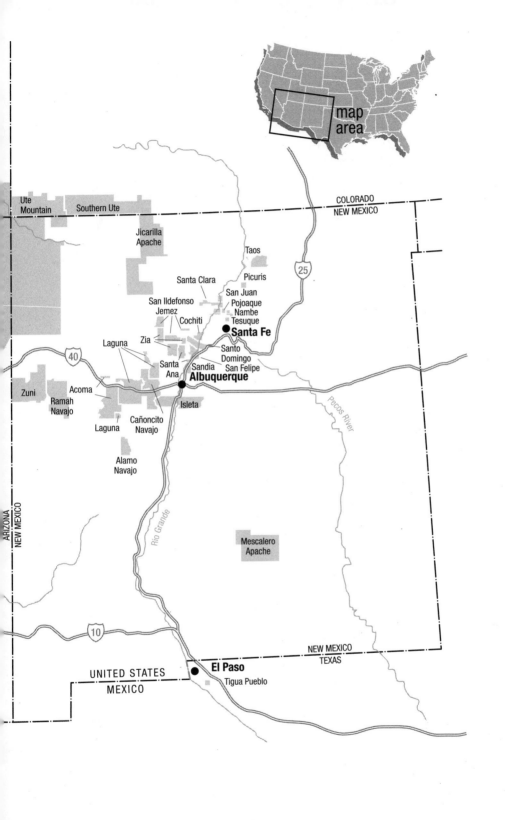

map
area

COLORADO
NEW MEXICO

Ute Mountain

Southern Ute

Jicarilla Apache

Taos

Picuris

Santa Clara

San Juan
Pojoaque
Nambe
Tesuque

San Ildefonso
Jemez

Cochiti

Santa Fe

Zia

Laguna

Santo Domingo
San Felipe

Santa Ana

Sandia

Albuquerque

Acoma

Isleta

Zuni

Ramah Navajo

Laguna

Cañoncito Navajo

Alamo Navajo

Rio Grande

Pecos River

Mescalero Apache

ARIZONA
NEW MEXICO

NEW MEXICO
TEXAS

El Paso

Tigua Pueblo

UNITED STATES
MEXICO

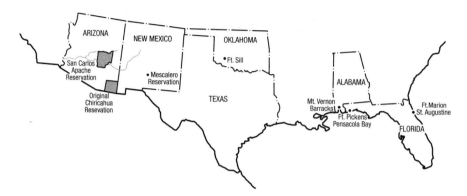

Map 3. Territory of the Chiricahua Apache Bands

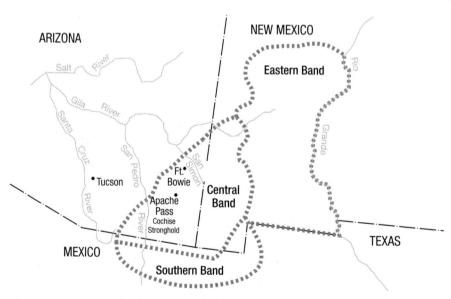

Map 4. Places Associated with the Removal of the Chiricahua Apache from Arizona to Oklahoma

The Columbia Guide to American Indians of the Southwest

Part I

History and Culture

CHAPTER 1

Introduction

The rugged landscape of the Southwest resonates with stories and meanings from the past that are vitally alive for the tribal peoples who live there today. With the oldest continuous record of human habitation on the continent outside of Mesoamerica,[1] the Southwest has an unbroken cultural continuity that connects the Native peoples of this region to their land in concrete and tangible ways. So powerful is the land that specific mountains, rivers, mesas, and canyons—and the stories from the past that they anchor—are able to provide wisdom for negotiating present-day problems.[2]

Spatially as well as temporally, the Southwest is immense, with vast distances, brilliant colors, and dazzling light that amaze the eye. When the Europeans arrived, they could not alter the landscape to the degree that they did in other areas. Forested mountain ranges and expanses of desert and plateau lands remain much as they have been for centuries, despite the damming of rivers and the construction of metropolitan areas. Anglo-Americans may have drastically changed their lives, but Native peoples of the Southwest have taken control over their own destiny as they continue to practice their traditions today and pass them on to new generations.

Although Mesoamerican influence—cultigens, pottery making, and belief systems—gives the Southwest a certain underlying continuity that distinguishes it from other areas, this region is not a frontier of Mesoamerica.[3] The various peoples of the Southwest blended that influence with their own cultural traditions, creating unique syntheses as they also adapted to the demands of their specific territories. Most of the archaeological evidence centers around three primary cultural divisions: the **Ancestral Pueblo** (Anasazi) and **Mogollon**, the forebearers of contemporary **Pueblo** peoples, and the **Hohokam**, almost certainly the ancestors of the **O'odham**. Each of these precontact traditions has descendants who live in the region today. The **Patayan**, another precontact people with living descendants, left much less in the form of cultural remains and will be described near the end of this chapter. The **Athapaskan** speakers entered the Southwest at least a century before European arrival,[4] bringing their own cultural patterns as they moved into areas that were unsuitable for intensive agriculture. (It is important to note that Athapaskan speakers believe that they originated in the Southwest.)

The Native peoples of the region were especially fortunate because their land was not as desirable to Europeans as were other areas of North America. Although some groups, especially the Puebloans of the Rio Grande Valley, felt the brunt of Spanish contact, most did not experience such direct impact on their ways of life until much later. This delay enabled them to adapt more gradually to Anglo-American contact than groups farther east had to when forcibly removed from their homelands.

In a region with limited permanent water sources, short growing seasons in the higher plateaus, and rugged terrain without large areas suitable for farming, it is remarkable that southwestern cultures developed as they did. The precontact peoples who lived there established technologically advanced cultures based on **agriculture**, some with extensive canal irrigation systems. The Yavapais practiced horticulture, which meant leaving the gardens that they had planted during periods of hunting and gathering, returning intermittently to tend to and finally to harvest their crops. In contrast, Pueblo culture, with its permanent compact villages, depended upon agriculture.

Water makes the difference between life and death in the arid and semi-arid Southwest. In addition to two major river systems, the Colorado River and the Rio Grande, the Pecos River leads south near the eastern boundary of the Southwest; the Salt and Gila rivers flow through southern Arizona; the Rio Alisos, the Rio Sonora, and the Rio Yaqui flow west of the Sierra Madre Occidental in northwestern Mexico; the Rio Conchos joins the Rio Grande, as does the Pecos River, in northern Mexico; and the Rio Salado flows east of the Sierra Madre Occidental and north of the Sierra Madre Oriental.

The Southwest can be divided into six major regions on the basis of environmental conditions.[5] The southern Rocky Mountains, which extend south through central Colorado into north central New Mexico, are characterized by high, forested mountain ranges; sparsely inhabited, except for lower elevations, because of a short growing season and lack of arable land, this region did provide large game animals and heavy stands of coniferous trees. The Colorado Plateau, in western Colorado, eastern and southern Utah, the northern half of Arizona, and northwestern New Mexico, features sandstone mesas, mountains with pine forests, and deep canyons cut by rivers, most notably the Grand Canyon. The rugged terrain of the plateau ranges from 5,000 feet to 6,750 feet in elevation, with pine forests in the mountains and dense stands and scattered clumps of pinyon pine and juniper on the mesas. The Basin and Range region includes the southern half of Arizona, southern New Mexico, Sonora, eastern Chihuahua, Coahuila, and the Mexican states to the southeast; its name comes from parallel mountain ranges separated by alluvial material that washes off the mountains during rainstorms to form basins. Low, hot, broad desert fills most of this zone, and rainfall varies with altitude and temperature: the western area receives less than 5 inches of precipitation annually, while the east averages about twice that amount. Covered by cactus, mesquite, and palo verde, the Basin and Range area includes the Sonoran Desert, home to the giant saguaro cactus. The southwestern edge of the High Plains is a vast, semi-arid grassland that extends into eastern New Mexico. The last two regions, located south of the international border, include two major mountain systems: the Sierra Madre Occidental, along the Sonora–Chihuahua border and the Sinaloa–Durango border; and the Sierra Madre Oriental to the east and south. These mountains are cut by deep canyons that open into adjacent desert lands; the southern extension of the Basin and Range zone lies between the two high, rugged mountain systems.

The boundaries of the Southwest have long been debated because of the region's geographic and cultural continuity with other regions, especially southward into Mexico. The term "the Greater Southwest"[6] emphasizes the fact of cultural unity that extends from New Mexico in the United States to the Mexican state of Nayarit and includes the peoples who lived north of the urban civilizations of central Mexico. Even without horses, precontact southwesterners traveled to northern Texas and Oklahoma and into Mexico to trade for copper, bison hides, shells, and the feathers of the brightly colored macaw.[7] Some Native peoples, such as the Tohono O'odham (once known as Papagos) traveled annually between their homes in Mexico and southern Arizona; today, their mobility has become a highly contested issue with the increase in border security. When the Mexican government waged military campaigns in the late 1800s, followed by a program of systematic deportation, Yaquis fled northward, eventually gaining recognition and land in southern Arizona from the U.S. government; today, some have chosen to return to their ancestral homeland. Within the United States, Yuman peoples continue to live on both sides of the Colorado River, in Arizona and California, and they share many traditions with California Indians. In northern

New Mexico, Jicarilla Apaches and the people of Taos Pueblo share aspects of dress and customs with Plains peoples. A tribe formerly known as the Kiowa-Apaches because of their early alliance with the Kiowas is officially known today as the Plains Apache Tribe of Oklahoma, and still recognizes kinship with the southwestern Apaches. All the American Indian people of this region believe that they originated in the Southwest, and each group has its own origin narrative explaining how they came to be in their homeland.

The first occupants of the Southwest encountered a very different environment than exists today. Although the North American ice sheets never reached the Southwest, they did cover much of the continent during the last ice age, the **Pleistocene**. Lower sea levels exposed a land bridge between Asia and Alaska, enabling the first Americans to enter North America. The timing of this crossing remains hotly debated: the first settlement of Alaska has been documented archaeologically as 10,000–9500 B.C. with widespread occupation of North America within 500 years,[8] but radiocarbon dates from Monte Verde in southern Chile provide some evidence for human settlement several thousand years earlier.[9] In the Southwest, the ice age created woodlands, marshes, and lush grasslands that supported herds of huge mammals, such as the mammoth (*Mammuthus columbi*), American camel (*Camelops* sp.), Shasta ground sloth (*Northrotheriops shastensis*), lion (*Panthera leo atrox*), and horse (*Equus* sp.). Mammoths may have weighed two and a half times as much as the modern elephant, while lions weighed about 50 percent more than modern forms.[10] Considerable evidence supports the presence of humans in the Southwest after 9500 B.C. and for the remaining four millennia of the Paleo-Indian period. The most famous Paleo-Indian sites in the Southwest, Clovis and Folsom, characteristic of the periods 9500–9000 B.C. and 9000–8500/8000 B.C., respectively, have provided the names for the oldest spear points found across North America. Clovis points, which have a long indentation called a flute that runs from the base partway to the tip and allows the tip to be attached to a spear, are generally associated with remains of large, now-extinct Pleistocene animals. Folsom points, with a longer flute and shorter spear point, are associated with the remains of smaller animals, as well as a smaller type of bison that lived during the post–Pleistocene geological period known as the Holocene. From the Folsom era to the end of the Paleo-Indian period, drier climatic conditions led to major habitat change for big game animals, including a reduction in the number of water holes, where most hunters ambushed their prey.

Spanning the millennia from 6000/5500 to 200 B.C., the **Archaic** period encompassed the decline of big game hunting, the establishment of an economy based on plant gathering, and the beginning of corn cultivation. The low density of artifacts in Archaic sites as well as the difficulty in locating these sites accounts for a paucity of archaeological evidence. While most Paleo-Indians lived near areas where big game animals watered, Archaic peoples settled in a much wider range of environments so that they could take advantage of a greater variety of animals, such as deer, antelope, rabbits, squirrels, and rodents. Wild plant foods provided some 75 to 80 percent of their diet. As in hunting and gathering societies throughout time, women, who gathered and processed plant foods, made a far greater contribution to overall subsistence than men.

In contrast to Paleo-Indian spear point styles in use across vast areas of the United States, spear point styles became increasingly more regional during the Archaic period. Stylistic patterns seem to have been a means of communicating important social information within and outside of a group. Archaeologists group spear points into distinct "style zones" based on similarities in shape and design within each area.[11] By using tools and weapons of a certain design, hunters showed that they belonged to a specific group. As regional population density increased and groups became more closely tied to particular areas, they relied more heavily on plant foods and raw materials. The use of stone tools that were made from materials in that area and bearing the stylistic imprint of local hunters demonstrated to others that they were hunting within their home territory.

The introduction of corn, beans, and squash from Mexico was the most significant event of the Late Archaic Period. However, the origin of agriculture was probably more of a process that occurred over time than a single event. According to widespread archaeological evidence, by 1000 B.C., people were cultivating corn in an area that spanned southern Arizona to northwestern New Mexico. In at least part of the Southwest, people had probably begun raising cultigens by about 1500 B.C.[12]

As population increased, Archaic groups had less access to certain resources and felt greater pressure to find sufficient food within their territories. Agriculture was a way to ensure that food would be available. However, plant cultivation constrained the movement of groups because maize and squash from Mexico were unsuited to the aridity and shorter growing seasons of the southwestern United States and needed to be cared for and protected to yield an abundant harvest. This meant that farming required a repetitive pattern of seasonal movement around a particular locality. Archaic peoples probably adopted farming not as an alternative way of life, but rather as a way to enhance the effectiveness of their hunting and gathering way of life.

When southwestern groups began to stay longer in the same settlements or to revisit them annually, they began to construct permanent dwellings at these sites. Archaeologists have found three pit houses, several subterranean storage pits, and some of the earliest evidence of agriculture in the Southwest at the site of Milagro in Tucson.[13] Not only did storing food for winter consumption protect them against fluctuations in hunted and gathered resources, but a more sedentary lifestyle also made possible greater complexity in social and ritual life. Cross-cultural studies of agricultural and hunting and gathering groups have shown that burials reinforce rights of ownership and inheritance and are associated with more formalized ties to particular areas of specific social groups.[14]

By the end of the Archaic, around 200 B.C., southwestern peoples were burying their dead, storing food in pits, and building permanent dwellings and had begun to be less mobile, but it was not until about 600 to 800 A.D. that groups started to reside in individual villages throughout the year. Although farming provides a more secure food supply, dependence on a small range of plants can lead to malnutrition and even the risk of starvation. When environmental conditions are favorable, agricultural fields can be very productive, but when conditions are poor, they can fail completely. Local plant and animal communities include species that have evolved in that environment over thousands of years, developing drought resistance through such characteristics as root systems that can tap water from deep underground. Imported cultigens, however, developed outside the region and require human manipulation of the environment in order to survive. Humans need protein for health, and the initial cultigens in the Southwest—corn and squash—were incomplete proteins because they did not contain the amino acid lysine. It is also possible that planting and harvesting coincided with and took precedence over the peak periods for hunting large animals, which lowered intake of meat, an important source of complete protein. Furthermore, as groups began to settle permanently in given territories, they had far less access to other areas than they had had as hunters and gatherers.

Late Archaic groups also began to construct communal buildings that were considerably larger than average houses of that time. By 700 to 900 A.D., such structures had become regular features of a standardized settlement plan. In many agricultural societies, communal buildings are ceremonial structures where calendrical rituals are held. Dependence on agriculture and the need to ensure an abundant harvest for the survival of the community increase the need to understand and predict environmental fluctuations, both seasonally and over longer periods of time. Communal rituals also reinforce a sense of community that centers on the well-being of the entire village. Another benefit of such rituals is the redistribution of food and other resources among groups in different areas. Such sharing can reduce the risk of starvation.

Two important innovations paved the way for sedentary life. First, beans were introduced; this cultigen contains lysine, the missing amino acid that makes corn and squash into complete proteins. Second, the production of ceramic vessels changed methods of food processing, which also improved nutrition. These containers allowed food to be boiled efficiently and for longer intervals; boiling dried foods, such as corn, enables more of the carbohydrates to be metabolized into glucose, which is more easily digested. Beans can be dried, stored, and cooked later. Ceramic vessels stored foods more efficiently and made possible a broader range of food preparation methods, which meant that more nutrients could be extracted from dried and stored foods. The first ceramic vessels appeared around 200 A.D. and had become widespread by 500 A.D.

One of the most intriguing and unparalleled periods in the precontact Southwest began in 700 A.D. and lasted until about 1130 A.D. This time of exceptional change saw the most dramatic rise in population and the widest range of settlements in the most varied landscapes in the region.[15] The surge in population probably occurred because of increased fertility due to innovations in food storage and preparation, as well as a more settled way of life, rather than decreased mortality, which is supported by skeletal evidence.[16] At the same time, a period of above-average rainfall favorable to agriculture made more food available.

As the population continued to climb, Ancestral Pueblo, Hohokam, and Mogollon peoples must have been forced to settle in less desirable terrain. To counter the greater unpredictability of harvests, people developed more localized cooperative networks. Subregional stylistic pottery traditions from the middle of the eleventh century contrast with the considerable similarity across broad areas seen in pottery traditions from the ninth and tenth centuries, providing evidence for such networks.[17] People were also trading tools and basic materials, such as chert, within subregions and occasionally over great distances. Ceramic vessels ranging from decorated wares to simple cooking containers were also exchanged, which indicates that this trade was a means of establishing and maintaining social ties rather than simply an effort to obtain locally unavailable goods. From agricultural societies, archaeologists have found that people trade a variety of goods to create and strengthen trade partnerships or fictional kinship ties that will then allow access to surplus food during local shortages. Group leaders probably controlled the exchange of more precious goods, such as shells from the Gulf of California, copper bells from northern or western Mexico, and macaw feathers from Mexico.

The major sites during this period were Chaco (Ancestral Pueblo), near the convergence of the Rio Grande, Little Colorado, and San Juan rivers in northern New Mexico, and Snaketown (Hohokam), near the terminus of the Salt River where it intersects with the Gila River in southern Arizona. Both locations were well situated in relation to long-distance trade routes, and archaeologists have found a high frequency of trade goods in both areas. In addition to these large towns with their commanding public architecture, small villages spread across the landscape.

In the late eleventh and early twelfth centuries throughout the Southwest, people began moving into neighboring valleys or settlements as they abandoned or reorganized sites. Construction activity ceased at the largest population centers, such as Snaketown. At both Snaketown and Chaco, people stopped making many of the objects that had characterized their cultures, such as stone palettes and effigies at Snaketown and cylinder vessels and massive Great Houses at Chaco. By 1130–1150 A.D., many of the towns and smaller settlements from this period were completely abandoned.

The most common explanations for the abandonment of Chaco and other major sites have been climatic change and reduced agricultural productivity. However, archaeologists have found little correlation between abandonment and climate change because the periods of low rainfall occurred well after most of the people had left or stopped constructing new buildings. People had suffered from infectious and nutritional diseases for centuries before the abandonment, and where health information does exist, such as on Black Mesa, death rates do not suggest that groups were near extinction.[18]

Two key factors probably played a role in the scale of population movement throughout the Southwest at this time. To support a concentration of people and to construct such massive buildings, Chacoans harvested huge quantities of wood, which may have resulted in the almost treeless landscape at Chaco today. This deforestation was not the only cause of depopulation, but it probably contributed, especially in locations with such great numbers of people.

The other factor relates to the nature of social groups. The fact that people abandoned entire regions and many settlements completely rather than partly highlights the importance of the entire social network within and between communities.[19] Anthropologist Peter Whiteley points out that from a Hopi perspective, climate change and devastating epidemics were considered to be "inextricable from the political administration of society" rather than random events.[20] In Puebloan societies, one of the ways that leaders maintained authority was by instilling fear of their supernatural powers; events that made people question their leaders' power could be extremely disruptive.

Against the background of these overall trends in the period between 700 and 1130 A.D., different cultures existed with fully developed village life. The major cultural divisions that have left the most archaeological evidence are the Mogollon and Ancestral Pueblo, the forebearers of contemporary Pueblo peoples, and the Hohokam, the probable ancestors of the O'odham.

The Mogollon people lived in the mountains of east central Arizona and west central New Mexico, hunting deer and turkey and gathering wild plants. They cultivated small garden plots of corn, beans, and squash in the small grassy meadows that lie between hillsides covered with pines. Their culture was first found in the Mogollon Rim and Plateau, named after Juan Ignacio Flores Mogollon, a governor of New Mexico.

The Mogollon Rim, an escarpment where the highlands meet the Colorado Plateau, marks the northern boundary of a zone of mountains that runs diagonally between the plateau to the north and the Basin and Range deserts to the south. Steep canyons, narrow valleys, and high elevations characterize this region. Below 3,500 feet, desert shrubs and cactus flourish, while brushy chaparral and evergreen woodlands of juniper, pinyon, and oak stand at intermediate elevations above 3,500 feet. Above 6,000 feet, western yellow pine dominates. Precipitation, in the form of rain and snow, is highly variable, making it difficult to predict where certain foods will be abundant in any given year. The lack of flat land as well as spotty precipitation and a short growing season made agriculture more difficult in this region, and the Mogollon probably practiced a mixed hunting, gathering, and farming subsistence strategy. Their flexibility in social organization enabled them to join others in times of abundance and to split into smaller groups during times of scarcity. The earliest Mogollon lived in pit houses, but in the late tenth and early eleventh centuries, they began to build contiguous above-ground rooms similar to those in which the Pueblos live today. Mogollon ceremonies took place in subterranean structures called **kivas**.

The Ancestral Pueblo, who left behind dramatic cliff dwellings and multistoried pueblos, occupied a vast area in northeastern Arizona, northwestern New Mexico, southeastern Utah, and southwestern Colorado (often referred to as the Four Corners region) and extending into Nevada during some periods. Archaeologists divide them into the Eastern and Western Anasazi, just as ethnologists speak of the Eastern and Western Puebloans, who are their descendants, today. The Eastern Anasazi—whose homeland was present-day New Mexico along its northern border with Colorado—created **Chaco**, while the Western Anasazi lived in present-day Arizona and southeastern Utah. Both groups are further divided into smaller groups, such as the Western Pueblo *Hisatsinom*, the ancestors of the Hopi.

Remarkable settlements such as Chaco, however, were the exceptions within the Ancestral Pueblo region. Through much of the precontact period, the Mogollon and the Ancestral Pueblo lived in small groups of a few families rather than in the more densely populated postcontact Pueblo villages. About ten to twenty-five people lived together, farming fields along drainages, collecting wild plants, and hunting a range of animals.

The desert farmers of the Southwest, the Hohokam, lived in southern Arizona south of the Mogollon Rim and in extreme northern Mexico, with settlements that extended north toward present-day Flagstaff during some periods. Their ball courts and platform mounds were sites of ritual activity. Snaketown, the best-known and largest Hohokam site, lies at the confluence of the Gila and Salt rivers. In the early to mid-eleventh century, it was home to three to six hundred people and had two large ball courts. Families lived in wattle-and-daub structures built around shallow pits. Extended families or small lineages lived in two to four dwellings clustered around a central plaza, with several hundred yards between room clusters. During the Hohokam period, the Gila and Salt rivers ran year-round near modern Phoenix, providing water for the extensive networks of irrigation canals that were a distinguishing trait of Hohokam culture. Dug by hand with stone tools and digging sticks, these canals also had to be cleaned, maintained, and rebuilt after destructive floods. Such an irrigation system indicates considerable social and political complexity because labor had to be organized and directed.

In contrast to the River Hohokam, who lived near present-day Phoenix, the Desert Hohokam of the Tucson area relied more on floodwater farming. *Ak-chin* is an O'odham word that refers to the alluvial fan at the mouth of an arroyo and the cultivation of plants in rock terraces. *Ak-chin* farming is a type of floodwater agriculture in which a brush dam is placed to direct the runoff to certain areas as it flows through the alluvial fan. Locating their fields on these fertile aprons enabled the Desert Hohokam to irrigate with rainfall runoff. They also planted fields where they would be flooded and built some irrigation canals. Both groups supplemented their diet with wild plant foods, including mesquite beans, agave, and cactus. Antelope, deer, bighorn sheep, and rabbits were their preferred sources of protein, but in times of scarcity they also relied on rodents, insects, and reptiles.

By 1150 A.D., the large towns, such as Mesa Verde, had been abandoned, although the total population of the Southwest had not declined. This means that local abandonment of settlements probably reflected movement out of particular areas rather than a sudden increase in mortality. Such mobility, probably an ongoing characteristic of southwestern life, was more dramatic during the twelfth and thirteenth centuries because entire groups of people in single areas moved at the same time.

The "Great Drought" of 1276–1299 A.D., a period of significantly below-average rainfall, has often been cited as the primary reason for the abandonment of settlements. However, most archaeologists agree that that is an oversimplification. Instead of being the calamity that initiated the abandonment process, the drought was probably the final element in a complex sequence of cultural dynamics that unfolded over the course of the twelfth and thirteenth centuries. Archaeologists posit that at the beginning of this period, individual families chose to join other families in large towns because such groups were more effective at protecting access rights to land. At the same time, populations increased, reducing the amount of productive land. As people developed more intensive agriculture to feed larger populations, the protection of access rights became more important, which encouraged greater stability and cohesion among kin units.

After the development of large towns, however, the self-interests of various households threatened to tear the towns apart. Although mechanisms such as public rituals developed, in part, to ensure greater cohesion within communities, only a minority of the communities survived into the late thirteenth century. Adding to the complexity were climate change, agricultural practice, demographic change, and internal and external conflict. During the late thirteenth and fourteenth centuries, although the Hohokam continued to occupy the Phoenix Basin, the Ancestral Pueblo and Mogollon had abandoned their dense settlements in southern Utah and Colorado and much of northeastern Arizona and northwestern New Mexico. New centers had evolved in the Rio Grande Valley of northern New Mexico, what would become the Zuni region of west central New Mexico and the Casas Grandes area of northern Mexico. The present Hopi area became isolated in the northwestern corner of the Pueblo world.

As people and villages were more sparsely distributed across the landscape, differences increased among localities, as demonstrated by more distinctive regional ceramic traditions by the end of the thirteenth century. Economic activity appears to have been concentrated within these localities. After 1150, the most salient characteristic of the Pueblo region was large, multiroom block towns of several hundred masonry rooms with as many as fifty to a hundred kivas. These towns foreshadowed the formation of much larger individual villages in the late twelfth and thirteenth centuries.

In the Phoenix region between 1150 and 1400 A.D., Hohokam villages were scattered about 3 miles apart along the major irrigation canals that distribute water from the Salt and Gila rivers. The larger settlements with 300 to 1,000 people are believed to have served as the primary administrative and ritual centers to coordinate canal use. Other sites had small platform mounds or ball courts and were probably secondary administrative centers. Finally, smaller purely agricultural settlements had only one or two residential compounds. Previously, the Hohokam had cremated their dead, but they now began burying a greater percentage as inhumations; remains that were still being cremated were buried in vessels. As in the Ancestral Pueblo area, the twelfth century saw the abandonment of population centers such as Snaketown and the establishment of new communities elsewhere.

A pattern of relatively short-term occupation in particular locations by large numbers of people, along with rapid growth and decline, characterized the fourteenth and fifteenth centuries in the Rio Grande Valley. In contrast, Awatovi and Oraibi in the Hopi region, which contained as many as 500 to 1,000 people, remained major settlements for several hundred years. Awatovi, a thriving community when the Spanish entered the Southwest in the sixteenth century, lasted until the beginning of the eighteenth century. Today, Oraibi remains the longest continuously occupied settlement in the United States.

Crop failure and intervillage conflict probably caused the failure of some communities. In the late thirteenth and early fourteenth centuries, villagers were designing their towns for defense. They built room blocks at right angles to each other to create open plazas within the pueblo, and narrow passageways to restrict access to these central plazas. Upper-story and even ground-floor rooms could only be entered by climbing ladders placed in openings in the roof; solid masonry walls several feet high confronted anyone standing outside the pueblo. These ladders could be quickly raised from above to provide additional security. The plaza-oriented village plan provided protection from other Ancestral Pueblo and Mogollon groups and, later, Europeans. Evidence of internecine strife can also be seen in the clustering of settlements for defense,[21] in sites that were severely burned,[22] and in skeletal remains that show an increase in trauma and violent deaths, including some evidence of scalping.[23]

However, plazas were not simply designed for defense. Other changes during the late thirteenth and early fourteenth centuries—ceramic decorative styles and the introduction of kiva murals—suggest that modern Pueblo rituals originated during this period and that plazas were used as large public spaces for group dances, as they are today. *Katsinam* play a major role in modern Western Pueblo (Hopi, Zuni, and Acoma) rituals and beliefs. These ancestral spirits, who are believed to bring rain, act as messengers between the gods and the people. Archaeologists posit that this ceremonial system countered increasing conflict that developed within larger and more socially diverse villages. Village survival depended upon social norms, which were reinforced by the public nature of katsinam dances in the open plazas. Everyone in the village had to cooperate so that the elaborate ceremonies could be conducted properly. In the Western Pueblos today, membership in katsinam societies bonds people in the village by cross-cutting potentially disruptive kinship distinctions, such as lineages and clans.

The ties among the peoples of the precontact Southwest through trade relationships are suggested in similarities between ceramic decoration and kiva murals. They exchanged ideas, technologies, and many items, such as obsidian, bison hides, pottery, turquoise mined from Arizona and New Mexico, cotton raised near the modern town of Winslow, Arizona, and prized items from Casas Grandes, located about 150 miles south of the present U.S.–Mexico border.

Arguably the most developed and centralized polity in the precontact Southwest, Casas Grandes (also known as Paquime) reached its zenith between about 1300 and 1400 A.D. Before its growth in this region, people had lived in small agricultural villages, but in the early thirteenth century, they began building a large and spectacular town that became the center of a polity some 40 to 70 miles across in northern and northwestern Chihuahua. The town of Casas Grandes had more than 2,000 rooms in several discrete room blocks and a population in the low thousands, making it easily the largest pueblo that ever existed in the precontact Southwest. Public architecture included at least 18 earthen and stone mounds, such as a circular platform 13 feet high; 3 ball courts more Mexican than Hohokam in design, and a unique and technologically advanced water supply system that included an outflowing sewer system. The most distinguishing features of Casas Grandes, however, are the artifacts and animal remains that demonstrate its role as a trade center. Archaeologists have uncovered tremendous numbers of scarlet macaws (*Ara macao*), a parrot native to the Gulf Coast of Mexico, green military macaws (*Ara militaris*) native to southern Sonora and Chihuahua, and unidentified other species of macaws, as well as their breeding and nesting boxes. These birds played a major role in the rituals of ancient southwesterners, who sacrificed them and used their feathers, believed to be a conduit through which prayer reached the supernatural beings. Thus, macaw feathers were highly prized by nearly all southwestern agriculturalists. Casas Grandes had a privileged social class, unusual in the Southwest, who lived in distinctive residences and were buried in elaborate tombs. These people accumulated and traded macaw, shell, and copper goods for such commodities as turquoise and cotton mined and produced by the Ancestral Pueblo, Mogollon, and Hohokam peoples.

Most scholars argue that the Ancestral Pueblo and Mogollon peoples were highly egalitarian and had minimal differences in political and social status because the considerable variation in annual harvests would have hindered the accumulation of food or luxury items. This is supported by evidence from grave goods. However, others contend that the first groups to arrive in a new location were able to select the most productive land and therefore had better corn harvests and cotton crops, important in trade. Individuals in such families could have then taken on higher-ranking roles in controlling ritual knowledge that was believed to influence the weather and agricultural success.[24] Such societal distinctions based on knowledge rather than wealth would be harder to detect from the archaeological evidence.

Among the Hohokam of the Phoenix Basin the development of elites is much more evident. When the Hohokam were building the largest towns that ever existed in this area, constructing large public buildings, developing far-reaching trade contacts, and producing highly specialized goods, they constructed massive towerlike adobe "big houses" some four stories high. The base of one such structure, which resembles a platform mound, still exists at the site of Casa Grande near Phoenix. It would have taken 15 to 20 families, working full-time, 3 months to erect this building that required nearly 600 roof beams procured from woodland areas at least 60 miles away and more than 1,440 cubic yards of soil to make the adobe walls.[25] Archaeologists posit that this was the home of a high-ranking family that may have controlled ritual knowledge, including the ritual calendar through observations of the sun's movement through holes in the walls of this structure.[26]

Archaeologists know far less about the Patayan, another precontact desert people, because they left behind less tangible evidence than the Hohokam and other groups. The Patayan homeland lay in the area from present-day Gila Bend and Ajo, Arizona westward to California and from Yuma, Arizona northeast to the Grand Canyon. By at least a thousand years ago, the people of the Desert Tradition, of whom the River and Delta Patayan were a part, were living along the Colorado River. The Upland Patayan lived farther east, in the plateau country of present-day northern Arizona that reaches 8,000 feet in elevation. Pinyon and juniper spread across a middle-elevation zone; lower areas have chaparral and grasslands with yucca and cactus; below these, mesquite grows abundantly in desert washes. All of these zones have considerable supplies of game, with mountain sheep, antelope, and deer.

Known for their vast trading networks, the Patayan left an enormous interconnected system of trails across the western desert; their descendants, the Yuman peoples, also traded widely. The River and Upland Yumans traded cultivated foods and manufactured items for raw materials and gathered foodstuffs; archaeological evidence shows that the Patayan and the Hohokam had a similar relationship. Evidence from the site of Las Colinas in present-day Phoenix even suggests that the Patayan and Hohokam may have resided together.

Some of the trails in the western desert, along the Colorado River, are marked by cairns and shrines that indicate pilgrimages to the sacred mountain, Avikwamme, which is also sacred to today's Yuman peoples, who consider it to be their place of emergence. The Patayan created intaglios, gigantic geometric, human, animal, and star figures, by digging into the desert pavement, the layer of pebbles that covers the land. These intaglios are considered to be part of the Patayan pilgrimage to their sacred mountain.

Most archaeologists agree that the descendants of the River and Delta Patayan are the River and Delta Yumans, who farmed the narrow strip on either side of the Colorado River. Before the damming of the river, the snowmelt from the Rocky Mountains brought fertile, silty soil down to their fields in raging spring floods, which the River Patayan depended upon to fertilize their crops. At the modern international border, the Colorado River delta dips to less than a hundred feet above sea level, where it disperses into shallow braided channels. Thick stands of mesquite, ironwood, and cottonwood, as well as cattails and bulrushes, thrive in the marshes. In sharp contrast, the desert rises on either side of the lushly vegetated floodplain.

The Upland Arizona Yumans (Yavapai and Hualapai) continued the primarily hunting and gathering subsistence pattern of the Patayan peoples. Archaeologists have found cultural remains of Havasupai ancestors, an Upland Yuman group, in the plateau region of Arizona that date to 600 A.D.; sometime between 1050 and 1200 A.D., they moved down into Cataract Creek Canyon, probably for defensive reasons; after 1300 A.D., the Havasupai farmed the canyon in summer and augmented their stored agricultural resources by hunting and gathering on the plateau in winter.

The strongest documentation linking a precontact people and their descendants exists between the Mogollon and Ancestral Pueblo and today's Pueblo peoples. Archaeologists have found that some of the Pueblo villages described by early Spanish explorers had been established in the last centuries before contact. Cultural continuity is not as easy to document in the Hohokam region because the people there had abandoned many of their largest settlements sometime between 1350 and 1400 or 1450 A.D. Despite the gap in archaeological evidence between the disappearance of the Hohokam and the Spanish documentation of the O'odham, most scholars today agree that the O'odham are descended from the Hohokam.

When the Spanish entered northern Mexico and southern Arizona, they encountered O'odham-speaking groups ranging from nomadic hunters and gatherers in the driest area to the west, to semisedentary Tohono O'odham farmers in what became the Tucson region, to fully sedentary O'odham groups that were heavily dependent on agriculture and lived in permanent villages along the Gila, Santa Cruz, and San Pedro rivers in what is now the Phoenix area. Many scholars hypothesize that Hohokam society collapsed, especially in the Phoenix Basin, because of civil strife and conflict, unusual fluctuations in river flows that destroyed their network of canals, or disease that flourished in their densely packed towns.

As happened everywhere in the Americas, disease destroyed entire groups of Native peoples in the Southwest. When Fray Marcos de Niza came through this region in 1539, he found a thickly settled area with good-sized settlements and irrigation canals near the confluence of the San Pedro and the Gila rivers.[27] By the time Father Eusebio Kino arrived, about 150 years later, the people were no longer living in large villages but rather in scattered *rancherias*, probably because their populations had been decimated by European diseases. Without any resistance to smallpox, measles, and typhus, thousands of people died within a relatively short period of time. Delayed by low population density in northern Mexico, the earliest epidemics in the Southwest probably occurred sometime between 1593 and 1630 A.D., as documented by a large body of historical data.[28] Census data does not exist for the O'odham area, but in many parts of North and South America, Native population levels fell by 90 percent by the end of the eighteenth century. Such an enormous loss of life caused communities to collapse; not only did massive numbers of people die from disease, but famine also often followed because there were too few individuals healthy enough to tend and harvest the fields. Epidemics also encouraged people to move from towns to less densely settled areas.

The impact of disease on Pueblo peoples is better documented because of the longer and more intensive Spanish presence. In the Rio Grande Valley, disease may have led to the abandonment of as many as half the villages during the first part of the seventeenth century. Pecos, a pueblo that remained inhabited throughout this period, played a major role in Pueblo trade with American Indian groups to the east. The Spanish, beginning with Coronado, used it as a departure point for exploration of the Plains region. Fray Andres Juarez, in charge of the Pecos mission from 1622 to 1635, estimated that Pecos had about 2,000 Native people when he arrived; by 1694, only 736 individuals survived.[29]

The arrival date of Athapaskan speakers—the Navajos and various Apache groups were then one people—in the Southwest is a topic of debate today. Athapaskan-speaking peoples still reside in west central Canada and California, as well as in other regions, and the degree of linguistic similarities and differences among Athapaskan groups indicates that the southwestern Athapaskans separated from their Canadian relatives within the last thousand years. Linguistic differentiation among Southern Athapaskans began about 1300 A.D. when they split into eastern and western groups. The eastern group consists of the Jicarilla Apache, the Lipan Apache, and what were once called the Kiowa-Apache. The western group consists of the Navajo, the Chiricahua Apache, the Mescalero Apache, and the ethnographic "Western Apache"—the San Carlos, White Mountain, Cibicue, and northern and southern Tonto. The divisions that exist today reflect modern reservation organization: the Plains Apache Tribe of Oklahoma (Plains Apaches, previously the Kiowa-Apaches); the Fort Sill Apache Tribe (Chiricahuas); the Mescalero Apache Tribe (Mescaleros, Chiricahuas, and Lipans); the Jicarilla Apache Tribe; the San Carlos Apache Tribe (Western Apaches); the White Mountain Apache Tribe (Western Apaches); the Tonto Apache Tribe (Western Apaches), and the Yavapai Apache Nation (Yavapais and Western Apaches).

According to archaeological and historical evidence, the first half of the sixteenth century was when substantial numbers of Athapaskan speakers entered the Southwest.[30] However, some scholars dispute this date because more recent archaeological discoveries demonstrate the possibility of earlier Athapaskan or Athapaskan-Anasazi (Ancestral Pueblo) communities in the area of Largo Canyon in the San Juan region of northern New Mexico. The evidence consists of early Navajo-type pottery and Navajo-style dwellings dated through dendrochronology.[31] The Navajo-type pottery that has been found is quite unlike Ancestral Pueblo (Anasazi) pottery and resembles artifacts on sites in this area that date to the twelfth and thirteenth centuries, which raises the possibility of much earlier Athapaskan or Athapaskan-Anasazi communities in this region of northern New Mexico.[32]

Although archaeologists do not agree on the route taken, most believe that after small autonomous groups of Athapaskan speakers left Canada, those who would later become the Apache tribes and the Navajos spread southward into the arid plains and mountains from central Texas to central Arizona, and from southern Colorado in the north to the Sierra Madres of the Mexican states of Sonora and Chihuaha, where each group diversified as the people adapted to the local environment and to their neighbors. (Not all Athapaskan speakers took a southward direction; today Athapaskan-speaking peoples live in what is now Canada, Alaska, Oregon, and California.)

Some individual Apache groups adopted a semisedentary way of life through associations with Pueblo peoples, while others remained essentially hunters and gatherers. The Navajo had the most contact with the Puebloans and probably obtained agriculture and agricultural ritual from them; the Western Apaches and Jicarillas also cultivated crops, but less intensively than the Navajos; the Chiricahuas and Mescaleros farmed very little, if at all.[33]

As demonstrated throughout this chapter, our understanding of how present-day Indian groups are connected to their ancestors and to one another comes from a variety of sources. In addition to oral tradition handed down from tribal elders to their descendants, there are historic documents and records. However, the documents are written from the perspective of those who were in power. Archaeology can provide less biased evidence because it is based on material culture remains and offers clues to how precontact cultures have merged, separated, and developed into modern cultures. While oral tradition and written accounts supply important information about the past, archaeology supplements what is known and informs us about what is no longer known by living people. Media coverage today gives the impression of an antagonistic relationship between archaeologists and Native American communities by focusing on the appropriation of the past. It is important not to underestimate the magnitude of this conflict but crucial to be aware of the extent to which archaeologists and American Indian communities are working together. A number of American Indian nations have their own archaeological organizations, most notably the Navajo Nation Historic Preservation Office and the Zuni Archaeological Program.

Linguistics also provides valuable evidence, for it is possible to establish relationships between languages by estimating the length of time it took speakers who separated and lived apart to develop mutually unintelligible languages. In the Southwest, there are at least six major language families, including Uto-Aztecan, Kiowa-Tanoan, Southern Athapascan, Yuman, Keresan, and Zuni.[34] Uto-Aztecan, one of the largest language families in the Americas, is divided into three major groups: Aztecan, Sonoran, and Shoshonean. In the Southwest, O'odham is part of the Sonoran group, while Hopi is part of the Shoshonean group. Kiowa-Tanoan has three major, mutually unintelligible branches among the Eastern Pueblos: Towa, Tewa, and Tiwa. Today, only the people of Jemez Pueblo speak Towa, although the people of Pecos Pueblo were probably also Towa speakers. Tewa is spoken at San Juan, Santa Clara, San Ildefonso, Nambe, Pojoaque, and Tesuque pueblos. Tiwa is spoken at Picuris, Taos, Sandia, and Isleta pueblos, and was the language of Tigua Pueblo near El Paso, Texas. Because Kiowa is spoken by the Plains Kiowa, some linguists consider the Kiowa to be an early Pueblo group that moved onto the Plains, while others think that they are a remnant of a Plains group that adopted Pueblo culture.[35] Furthermore, these hypotheses fail to consider possible Apachean origins of this group. Both Keresan and Zuni are linguistic isolates, which means that they are unrelated to any other known language families. Zuni is spoken only at Zuni, while Keresan is spoken at Cochiti, Santo Domingo, Zia, Santa Ana, San Felipe, Acoma, and Laguna pueblos.

The precontact history of Native peoples in the Southwest is clearly dynamic and characterized by complex social relations through trade, intermarriage, and the exchange of ideas and technologies. The mobility that was an ongoing characteristic of southwestern life reached a peak during the twelfth and thirteenth centuries when entire groups of people in single areas moved at the same time. As we will see, the arrival of the Spanish in the Southwest brought even greater change as they attempted to save souls and to mine for the riches that, according to legend, lay buried in this region.

NOTES

1. Alfonso Ortiz, "Introduction," in *Handbook of North American Indians: The Southwest*, vol. 9 (Washington, D.C.: Smithsonian Institution Press, 1979), 1.
2. Keith Basso, *Wisdom Sits in Places* (Albuquerque: University of New Mexico Press, 1996).
3. Ortiz, "Introduction," 1.
4. Klara Kelley and Harris Francis, *Navajo Sacred Places* (Bloomington: Indiana University Press, 1994), 213.
5. Richard B. Woodbury, "Prehistory of the Southwest," in *Handbook of North American Indians: The Southwest*, vol. 9, ed. Alfonso Ortiz (Washington, D.C.: Smithsonian Institution Press, 1979).
6. Ralph Beals, *Preliminary Report on the Ethnography of the Southwest* (Berkeley, Calif.: National Park Service, 1935).
7. Stephen Plog, *Ancient Peoples of the American Southwest* (London: Thames and Hudson, 1997), 16.
8. Vance Haynes, "Clovis Origin Update," *Kiva* 52 (1987): 83–93.
9. Plog, *Ancient Peoples of the American Southwest*, 37.
10. Elaine Anderson, "Who's Who in the Pleistocene: A Mammalian Bestiary," in *Quaternary Extinction: A Prehistoric Revolution*, ed. P. S. Martin and R. G. Klein (Tucson: University of Arizona Press, 1984), 59, 86; Pat Shipman, "Body Size and Broken Bones: Preliminary Interpretations of Proboscidean Remains," in *Proboscidean and Paleoindian*

Interactions, ed. J. W. Fox, C. B. Smith, and K. T. Wilkens (Waco: Baylor University Press, 1992), 85.

11. Plog, *Ancient Peoples of the American Southwest*, 51.

12. Bruce Huckell, "Late Preceramic Farmer-Foragers in Southeastern Arizona: A Cultural and Ecological Consideration of the Spread of Agriculture Into the Arid Southwestern United States" (Ph.D. diss., University of Arizona; Ann Arbor: University Microfilms, 1990); W. H. Wills, *Early Prehistoric Agriculture in the American Southwest* (Santa Fe: School of American Research Press, 1988); W. H. Wills, "Early Agriculture and Sedentism in the American Southwest: Evidence and Interpretation," *Journal of World Prehistory* (1988); W. H. Wills and Bruce Huckell, "Economic Implications of Changing Land-Use Patterns in the Late Archaic," in *Themes in Southwest Prehistory*, ed. G. J. Gumerman. (Santa Fe: School of American Research Press, 1994).

13. Huckell, "Late Preceramic Farmer-Foragers in Southeastern Arizona"; Wills and Huckell, "Economic Implications of Changing Land-Use Patterns," 40–41.

14. Plog, *Ancient Peoples of the American Southwest*, 55.

15. Plog, *Ancient Peoples of the American Southwest*, 71.

16. Stephen Plog, "Understanding Southwestern Culture Change," in *Spatial Organization and Exchange: Archaeological Survey on Northern Black Mesa*, ed. Stephen Plog (Carbondale: Southern Illinois University Press, 1986).

17. Plog, *Ancient Peoples of the American Southwest*, 113.

18. Debra Martin, Alan Goodman, George Armelagos, and Ann Magennis, *Black Mesa Anasazi Health: Reconstructing Life from Patterns of Death and Disease* (Carbondale: Southern Illinois University Center for Archaeological Investigations Occasional Paper No. 14, 1991), 220, 227.

19. Plog, *Ancient Peoples of the American Southwest*, 116.

20. Peter Whiteley, *Deliberate Acts* (Tucson: University of Arizona Press, 1988), 289.

21. David Wilcox and Jonathan Haas, "The Scream of the Butterfly: Competition and Conflict in the Prehistoric Southwest," in *Themes in Southwest Prehistory*, ed. G. J. Gumerman (Santa Fe: School of American Research Press, 1994).

22. Steven LeBlanc, "Cibola," in *Dynamics of Southwest Prehistory*, ed. L. Cordell and G. Gumerman (Washington, D.C.: Smithsonian Institution Press, 1989).

23. LeBlanc, "Cibola," 357–358; Debra Martin, "Patterns of Health and Disease Stress Profiles for the Prehistoric Southwest," in *Themes in Southwest Prehistory*, ed. G. J. Gumerman (Santa Fe: School of American Research Press, 1994), 106; Wilcox and Haas, "The Scream of the Butterfly," 226–229.

24. Plog, *Ancient Peoples of the American Southwest*, 177–178.

25. David Wilcox and Lynette Shenk, *The Architecture of Casa Grande and Its Interpretation* (Tucson: Arizona State Museum Archaeological Series No. 115, 1977); David Wilcox, David, "Hohokam Social Complexity," in *Chaco and Hohokam*, ed. P. Crown and W. Judge (Santa Fe: School of American Research Press, 1991).

26. J. Molloy, "The Casa Grande Archaeological Zone: Pre-Columbian Astronomical Observation," manuscript, Western Archaeological Center, National Park Service, Tucson.

27. Daniel Reff, *Disease, Depopulation, and Culture Change in Northwestern New Spain 1518–1764* (Salt Lake City: University of Utah Press, 1991), 74.

28. Reff, *Disease, Depopulation*, 113–114, 131–132, 161, 167–168, 233, 276.

29. John Kessell, *Mission of Sorrows* (Tucson: University of Arizona Press, 1970), 170.

30. David Wilcox, "The Entry of Athapaskans Into the American Southwest: The Problem Today," in *The Protohistoric Period in the North American Southwest*, A.D. 1450–1700, ed. D. Wilcox and W. Masse (Phoenix: Arizona State University Archaeological Papers No. 24, 1981).

31. M. A. Stokes and T. L. Smiley, "Tree-Ring Dates from the Navajo Land Claim: II. The Southern Sector," *Tree-Ring Bulletin* 27 (3–4) (1966): 2–11.

32. Linda Cordell, *Prehistory of the Southwest* (Orlando: Academic Press, 1984), 357.

33. Morris Opler, "The Apachean Culture Pattern and Its Origins," in *Handbook of North American Indians: The Southwest*, vol. 10, ed. A. Ortiz (Washington, D.C.: Smithsonian Institution Press, 1983), 368–392.

34. Kenneth and David Harris, "Historical Linguistics and Archaeology," in *Handbook of North American Indians: The Southwest*, vol. 9, ed. Alfonso Ortiz (Washington, D.C.: Smithsonian Institution Press, 1979), 170–177.

35. David Snow, "Prologue to Rio Grande Protohistory," *Papers of the Archaeological Society of New Mexico* 9 (1984): 125–132.

CHAPTER 2

Encounters with Europeans and Mexicans
Trade and Warfare (1529–1853)

When the first Spaniards, shipwrecked Alvar Nuñez Cabeza de Vaca and his three companions, made their way into the Southwest in 1529, the Spanish presence was still relatively new to North America. Driven by the search for slaves to work in agriculture and mining, Christopher Columbus and his followers had traveled from one island to another in the West Indies only a few decades before. The European invasion would lead to the radical transformation of the lives of millions of North American Indians through depopulation, enslavement, and culture change as the Spanish, British, and French competed for dominance. In the Southwest, as elsewhere, horses and guns brought by the Spanish revolutionized the lives of Indian peoples. In the northern sector, the Spanish established control over the compact villages of the Eastern Pueblos for most of the seventeenth century; farther west, the Hopis and Navajos were protected by their isolation and the undesirability of their territory in Spanish eyes. During this period, the Jicarilla and Mescalero Apaches capitalized on their strategic positions by raiding Plains Indian camps for slaves, which they sold to the Spanish. Along with the Navajos, they also raided the weakened Pueblo villages for food. In the southern sector, having defeated Spanish troops, the Yaquis sought Spanish agricultural expertise by inviting Jesuit priests, who came to their villages in 1623. For the most part, O'odham peoples befriended the Spanish against their old enemies, the Apaches, who had intensified their raiding as it became an important means of subsistence. In the western sector, the Colorado River provided a corridor for the entry of European diseases, but the people remained relatively free from European contact during this period. The Upland Yuman groups knew of the Spanish through their friends, the Hopis, but with the Hopis as a buffer, did not come under European control. Because Spain and Mexico played such major roles in the Southwest during this period, this chapter begins with an overview of Spanish and Mexican policies toward indigenous peoples, then traces how the lives of Native Americans in each southwestern region changed between 1529 and 1853, when the land south of the Gila River became part of the United States.

SPANISH AND MEXICAN RELATIONS WITH SOUTHWESTERN INDIANS

The Spanish, driven by economic shortages, sought resources abroad to fill their depleted coffers. Spain had only achieved political unity in 1469, less than a century before its first explorers set sail to secure the legendary riches of the New World. To unite the crowns of Castile and Aragon, Castile had had to distribute conquered land instead of gold to the military nobles who had driven out the Moors. This established a pattern of ownership in which 2 or 3 percent of the population owned 97 percent of the land.[1] The Spanish economy at this time was dominated by sheep-raising nobility who had created an alliance to promote their social and political interests. These two powerful groups—the military and the sheep owners—curtailed the development of commerce and industry. Spain became dependent for its growth upon the seizure of people and resources, most notably silver. As the Spanish began to extract silver from the New World, foreign financiers were eager to lend money against future silver imports. Many second sons who had no hopes of inheriting family land, peasants with dreams of wealth, and impoverished noblemen were lured to the Americas. With little to lose and everything to gain, they were eager to believe magnificent myths of untold riches. Rumors of Puebloan wealth began when a few Spaniards exaggerated what they saw as they traveled through the Rio Grande region: stone houses several stories high became family mansions, the turquoise worn by Native peoples in their ears and draped around their garments became sparkling jewels. Surely, people who lived in such luxury could only finance it with great quantities of precious metals.

Conquest, the major "policy" of Spanish imperialism, can be traced back to medieval Christian wars against Moors in Spain and slave-raiding expeditions in early West Indian history. The Spanish, deeply invested in the centuries-old European distinction between civilized and barbarian peoples, also felt compelled by an obligation to civilize those whom they considered barbaric. Before they even encountered any members of an Indian tribe, they already considered them savages. This prefabricated label meant that culture contact was primarily unidirectional: the Spanish, as Christians and bearers of civilization, were duty-bound to civilize the barbarians, to introduce them and assimilate them to Spanish culture, which was, in their minds, infinitely superior to that of any other people.

The fundamental elements of civilization, from the Spanish perspective, included the acceptance of Spanish regal authority and law, including Christian belief and behavior; the establishment of town life in adobe or stone houses; and the adoption of proper dress, which meant skirts and upper garments for women and trousers and shirts for men. However, instead of transferring the full range and depth of Spanish culture to America, the Spanish administrators and missionaries brought with them a distillation of elements they deemed crucial for the process of civilizing the Indian peoples of the Southwest. Added to this were miscellaneous elements filtered through the personal experiences of individuals, as when a missionary taught Native people a religious festival celebrated only in his home town of Estremadura.

In 1821, Mexico won its war with Spain to become an independent nation. In contrast to the more carefully conceived Spanish program for Indian-European relations, based on many years of experience, the Mexican phase of Indian history was unsettled and fraught with conflict. An enlightened policy, the Plan of Iguala, asserted equal citizenship for Indians, Spaniards, and *mestizos* but was impossible to enforce because of the realities of ethnic life in Mexico.

In 1824, Mexican leaders created a republican constitution to replace the Plan of Iguala. This constitution, as well as the state constitutions that were enacted, declared any differences among the people of Mexico to be nonexistent. Government records were no longer allowed to use the term "Indian" because only the status of "Mexican citizen" was recognized. Instead of leveling ethnic differences, however, this only inflamed them. Ignoring existing cultural differences, the plan was based on the assumption that all peoples were willing to relinquish their traditional beliefs and practices for the Mexican definition of equal citizenship. Furthermore, the Mexican government lacked the centralized power and authority to enforce its policies.

Native Americans refused to give up their way of life to pay taxes, own land individually, and participate in the administration of local government, as prescribed by the Mexican government. Although used on an individual basis, land was held corporately by Indian communities; government surveying efforts meant an invasion of their territory. The Indians met Mexican attempts to impose an alien governmental system with armed resistance. Unwilling to see that their program was ill-conceived and unrealistic, the Mexicans viewed such resistance as a product of subversive activity on the part of Spanish royalists who had influenced the Natives to rebel against the new government. Tribal separatism was seen as a threat to Mexico as a unified, functioning nation.

The intensification of attempts to break up corporate landholdings only strengthened Indian opposition. The Mexican government instituted the Laws of the Reform, which broke up the landed estates of the Church, in 1856; prescribed the survey and distribution of all unused land in 1883; and eliminated all restrictions on large individual holdings in 1894. Its three approaches were military domination, colonization, and deportation. Through the late 1800s, the Mexican government used armed force to suppress Indian resistance, and in cases where it was successful, Indian lands were distributed and their communities destroyed. With some groups, such as the Yaquis, the use of the military only stifled armed resistance temporarily. Early in the nineteenth century, the Mexican government enacted a Law of Colonization that paid non-Indians to take up residence in Indian country and work the land. Based on the assumption that Indians would recognize and choose to emulate the virtues of "civilization" once they had been exposed to them, colonization was tried in all parts of Mexico. Some agricultural colonies of soldiers and their families included forts and an army of occupation. When armed force and colonization did not work, the Mexican government used a policy of deportation from tribal homelands to other parts of Mexico.

However, it was not governmental policy that led to the detribalization and assimilation of most Mexican Indians. Some Indian communities were able to maintain their existence, but most were broken up as hundreds of Indians were slowly forced off their land and into Mexican towns, mining communities, and ranches as laborers. Through intermarriage, kinship relations developed between Mexicans and Indians, and there was as much influence from Indian peoples on those of Spanish descent as the reverse. Even though many Puebloans continued to live in their autonomous towns in New Mexico, there was considerable intermarriage in the Rio Grande area as well.

THE SOUTHERN SECTOR OF THE SOUTHWEST

Throughout present-day southern Arizona and New Mexico and the adjacent Mexican states of Sonora and Chihuahua, the lives of the O'odham, Yaquis, Apaches, and other Indian peoples changed profoundly after the arrival of the Spaniards. In the sixteenth century, the valleys of northwestern Mexico were densely populated with at least several hundred thousand people, while the mountains and deserts in between remained sparsely settled. In 1530, Nuño de Guzmán marched his army into the area in an attempt to claim the region for

Spain. Malaria, typhoid, and dysentery killed 8,000 of his Indian troops and introduced these diseases into the civilian population. A measles epidemic swept northward from central Mexico in 1534, killing 130,000 people in Sinaloa. Slave raiding as well as disease decimated the Native populations.

After a relatively steady advance northward from the Valley of Mexico, Spanish troops finally faltered when faced with Apache resistance south of what would become the U.S. border. Later, travel along what would become El Camino Real, the trail that eventually led to Santa Fe, would become extremely dangerous because of Apache raids in retaliation for the disruption of their territory and as a means of subsistence. The so-called Apache Corridor extended from central Sonora to Santa Fe, and between 1680 and 1775, it was passable only with full military escort. This effectively isolated the Spanish in the Rio Grande Valley, although until the 1680s, trade was possible between these two areas. During the eighteenth and much of the nineteenth centuries, Apache raiding curtailed Spanish and Mexican settlements in southern Arizona and the Arizona-New Mexico-Sonora region.

Before the mid-nineteenth century, the Chiricahua Apaches were seldom differentiated from the Western Apaches because other tribes encountered them in the context of raiding or warfare. When threatened, the Chiricahuas disappeared into their mountain strongholds. Without any kind of sustained contact, outsiders had no understanding of the distinctions among groups of Chiricahuas or Western Apaches, who ranged widely within their home territories to hunt game and gather wild plant foods. To a major extent, raiding for livestock, supplies, manufactures, and captives became a subsistence activity.

Neither Fray Marcos de Niza nor Francisco Vasquez de Coronado mentioned the Chiricahuas after passing through what is now southeastern Arizona on separate expeditions in the mid-sixteenth century. However, most scholars agree that the Chiricahuas were living in the region by that time.[2] Some anthropologists[3] believe that Coronado was describing Chiricahuas when he traveled through the country of a nomadic foraging people who lived in nonagricultural *rancheria* settlements.

The Native American groups of northwestern Mexico spoke Cahitan languages within the great Uto-Aztecan language family. The Sinaloas, Tehuecos, Zuaques, Ahomes, Mayos, Conicaris, Tepahues, and Yaquis, as well as other groups, occupied the rich alluvial floodplains of the Sinaloa, Fuerte, Mayo, and Yaqui river valleys. Except for the Seris, a foraging people who lived on the coast of Sonora, nearly all indigenous peoples in this area lived in rancherias, widely dispersed agricultural settlements with dwellings scattered as far as a half mile apart. The Tarahumaras and Conchos, in the Sierra Madre Occidental of northwestern Mexico, lived in autonomous communities that included shelters ranging from caves to stone masonry houses. The O'odham, whose villages were more compact, lived west of the Tarahumaras in the high Sierras and northward through the valleys of Sonora and into the deserts of what is now southwestern Arizona. In contrast to the rancheria peoples, the Seris practiced no agriculture and relied on the ocean for food, mobility, and refuge more than any other southwestern group. When enemies attacked them on the mainland, they fled to Tiburon or San Esteban islands, and when the Spanish invaded these islands, they escaped to the coast.

Spanish settlements took a range of different forms in the Southwest. The Tarahumaras, Mayos, and Opatas, in whose territory the Spanish settled, experienced the biggest initial impact of Spanish mining camps, agricultural settlements, army garrisons, and towns. However, because Indians were scattered throughout the settlements and isolated from their families in a foreign environment, these communities exerted considerably less intense influence on them than did the mission towns, which are best documented among the Yaquis.

The Yaquis lived along the lower 60 miles of the Rio Yaqui, in a 6,000-square-mile area that included some of the most fertile regions of Mexico. Traveling up the west coast of New Spain on slave raids, Diego de Guzmán fought briefly with Yaquis on the banks of the Rio Yaqui in 1533. Their fighting ability greatly impressed him and led a soldier in his party to write that the Yaquis showed greater bravery on the field of battle than tribes anywhere else in New Spain.[4] Later, Captain Hurdaide, who had defeated the Sinaloas, Tehuecos, Zuaques, and Ahomes, waged a vigorous military campaign against the Yaquis with the largest army assembled in the field in northwestern Mexico, some 4,000 Indian foot soldiers and 50 mounted Spaniards. Seven thousand Yaquis fought with great bravery, and Hurdaide barely escaped with his life. For nearly a year, neither side made any effort to carry the attack further until the Yaquis asked for peace, making it clear that they refused to accept military domination but instead desired contact with Jesuit missionaries, who were regarded highly for their agricultural knowledge.

In 1617, two Jesuit missionaries, Perez de Ribas and Tomas Basilio, traveled to the eastern edge of Yaqui territory, where they were met by thousands of Yaquis. The missionaries baptized two hundred the first day and four thousand within six months; within the next two years, they baptized nearly thirty thousand Yaquis.[5] More missionaries arrived to initiate an intensive program of directed culture change that included agricultural tools and techniques and the consolidation of the Yaqui population from their eighty rancheria villages into eight church-centered towns, in addition to conversion to Christianity.

The Jesuits, who spoke fluent Yaqui, discussed Native ceremonies, suggesting Christian interpretations and explaining Catholicism by encouraging the Yaquis to enact biblical dramas in which Christian elements were blended with traditional beliefs. The Yaqui interaction with Spanish clergy was unusual because it occurred while they were a free people, long before they were subjected to pressure from the Spanish military, civil authorities, or settlers.

With never more than ten missionaries in Yaqui territory, the Jesuits relied on trained Yaqui assistants to administer the new towns, which led the Yaquis to develop their own administrative skills "under the guidance of a benign . . . but rather coercive missionary policy" and "created a psychological environment for the acceptance of change on the part of the Yaquis."[6] Church ritual thus diffused outward from the Jesuits through the recently trained associates to the Yaqui townspeople, a process that facilitated the blending of ritual forms with traditional Yaqui ones, adding meanings the missionaries had not intended.

Yaqui agriculture thrived with the introduction of better tools and new crops, such as wheat, peaches, figs, and pomegranates, and work animals, including sheep, cattle, and horses. The Jesuit-Yaqui economy, with its highly successful agriculture and livestock production, showed the full potential of the Rio Yaqui area, and by the 1730s, Yaqui territory had become famous as the most fertile and productive region in Sonora.

However, there had been deep-seated conflict between Spanish political and economic interests and the Jesuit mission system almost from the time that Jesuits first went to live with the Yaquis. Once the fertility of the Yaqui bottomlands had been demonstrated, this conflict intensified. When silver was discovered about thirty miles from a Yaqui town in 1684, mining increased over the next forty years, along with an influx of Spanish settlers who resented what they perceived to be Jesuit control of valuable agricultural land.

Colonel Huidobro, appointed as governor of the province of Sinaloa in 1734, became increasingly antagonistic to the missionary program and tried to exert greater control over Yaqui land. The Yaquis and Mayos revolted against the Spanish in 1740, and thousands of Indians and Spaniards were killed, resulting in a Spanish victory. Vildosola, the new governor, then instituted severe measures characteristic of typical Spanish frontier relations. On the border of Lower O'odham and Yaqui territories he had a presidio constructed and decreed that Indians would not only need to have missionary permission to leave their villages but would also be impressed for forced labor in mines and on *haciendas*. The Jesuits returned to their missions, intensifying their work during the next quarter century. In 1767, they were expelled from the Americas by edict of the King of Spain.

In 1771, when the Spanish government secularized the Yaqui missions, a new regime took over, designed to serve the civil arm of government and to appease the non-Indian population. Through taxation, government officials could be supported at Indian expense, and through land allotment, Spaniards could obtain Indian lands either through purchase or through assignment after all

Indians had been assigned land. Before this policy could be enforced, however, Mexicans began fighting for their independence from Spain.

Between 1810 and the early 1820s, the war raged to the south, east, and north of Yaqui and Mayo territory. Throughout this time the Indians maintained a disinterested distance, but after independence was won, they were forced to deal with the state of Occidente, which was established in 1824 from what had been the states of Sonora and Sinaloa. In 1825, a state constitution was drafted in keeping with the ideals of the Mexican republic based on equality of citizenship. Though altruistic in theory, in practice it decreed the full participation of Indian people in political affairs through taxation and land allotment. The Yaquis met attempts by Mexican settlers and military to encroach upon their land with fierce resistance. Conflict between Yaquis and settlers escalated into a war that eventually reached genocidal proportions.

In 1825, **Juan Banderas**, a charismatic Yaqui, led a force of two thousand Indians in an attempt to unite the Indians of northwestern Mexico under the flag of King Montezuma and the banner of the Virgin of Guadalupe (a symbol also used by the Mexicans in their fight for independence). Taking his name from these flags, Banderas originally hoped to create an Indian nation in northern Mexico for the Mayos, Opatas, and O'odham people as well as the Yaquis. He replaced this ambitious vision with a more pragmatic attempt at political autonomy for his people within the Mexican republic. Support came from the Opatas and O'odham on the north and the Mayos on the south, and within a year, Banderas's forces had driven out all the white settlers from Yaqui and Mayo territory. By early 1826, they controlled all the settlements of the lower Yaqui and Mayo valleys. When the Mexicans moved the capital of Occidente southward to Cosala, Banderas stopped his attack, for he did not want to expand his control beyond the Yaqui and Mayo homelands.

The new Occidente government raised a smaller but better-armed fighting force that defeated Banderas's troops but lacked the strength to invade Yaqui territory. When Banderas realized that the government would continue its military campaign, he tried to negotiate peace and agreed to submit if Yaqui local government could remain autonomous. However, the Mexican government opposed both goals and executed Banderas in 1833.

Within a year, the Yaquis resumed their fight for independence, but factionalism tore them apart. The Sonoran state government was equally disorganized, with various political leaders competing for control. Attempts to institute the Mexican program were abandoned as a series of Yaqui outbreaks occurred in 1838, 1840, and 1842. From 1857 until 1862, the Yaquis continued to rebel against the state government.

Rebellion against the government's land policies became widespread throughout Mexico during this period. In Guerrero, the Indians continued their resistance against efforts to survey and distribute their land until 1843; in the state of Mexico, the Nahuatl-speaking Indians rose in revolt in 1831 and again in the 1840s; and in Oaxaca, the Zapotecs fought for four years until Governor Benito Juarez put down the rebellion in 1851. **Cajeme**, another Yaqui leader, organized the Yaquis into formal military units and a formidable fighting force, but eventually the Mexican army's superior arms and numbers overwhelmed him and his men. Cajeme was executed in 1887, and although Yaqui resistance continued, ultimately their efforts failed.

In 1903, the Mexican government began to systematically deport the Yaquis. In the eighteenth century, the Spanish government had used deportation against the Seris to quell their resistance, and the Mexican government had continued this policy in the Sierra Gorda by deporting the Huatec Indians to other parts of Mexico. In the 1840s, the state government began to deport Maya from the Yucatan to Cuba, a program that would continue into the late nineteenth century. The deportation of Yaquis continued until 1910, dividing families and selling individuals as slaves to work in brutal conditions on plantations in the Yucatan and Oaxaca. Many Yaquis fled across the border to the United States, where they received political asylum in 1906 and tribal recognition and reservation land in 1978. In 1939, the Mexican government established a reservation near the Yaqui River.

The O'odham in Mexico had their first contact with the Spanish in 1540, when Alvar Nuñez Cabeza de Vaca met some in Sonora, near the border between O'odham and Yaqui territory. Ethnohistorians posit that conflict over sparse resources in northwestern Mexico among the O'odham, Yaquis, and Opatas had resulted in a willingness on the part of some O'odham to join invading Spanish against other groups in the area. When missionaries arrived in 1591, many of the Sonoran O'odham converted to Catholicism.

In 1687, Jesuit Father Eusebio Kino began his work among the Akimel O'odham or River People (once known as Pima) and established extensive contact with the Tohono O'odham or Desert People (once known as Papago) and the Hia C-ed O'odham or Sand People (who lived in the westernmost reaches of Akimel O'odham territory, near the Colorado River). Some thirty thousand Indians lived in an area from the San Miguel River to the Gila River and from the San Pedro River to the Colorado River. His fellow Jesuits continued Father Kino's work after he died in 1711. By the time the Jesuits had been expelled in 1767, they had established over two dozen missions and mission-visiting stations or *visitas*.

Well aware of Apache raiding, the Spanish were eager to enlist the aid of the O'odham Indians as allies because they were also traditional enemies of the Apaches. By the end of the 1760s, however, the Apaches were so powerful that they had forced one group of O'odham, the Sobaipuris, who lived in the

San Pedro Valley beyond the eastern edge of the Sonoran Desert, to relinquish control of their territory. Over time, many O'odham were recruited into the Spanish army to fight against the Apaches.

In 1736, the discovery of a silver deposit near the present Arizona–Mexico border brought Spanish miners to the area. Spanish soldiers had been there since the 1680s; they later constructed two more presidios in response to the 1751 revolt of O'odham Indians against intrusion on their land. Civilian farmers and ranchers moved into the area to provide food for the soldiers. By 1786, the Spaniards had established peace with several Apache bands near Tucson, who were given rations, farmlands near Spanish settlements, and obsolete firearms for hunting.

Spanish contact provided the Tohono O'odham with European animals and crops, as well as skills in mining and cattle ranching that brought them into the cash and barter economy of New Spain. O'odham soldiers were paid in cash and absorbed European ideas of warfare and military organization.[7] The Tohono O'odham response to Catholicism followed its own path: when Catholic priests withdrew from outlying areas because of intensified Apache raiding, the Tohono O'odham continued to carry out Christian rituals. Without pressure to conform to the strictures of Catholicism, they added the veneration of a particular saint, Francis Xavier, to their own religion. They also honored Father Kino by making a pilgrimage to Magdalena, a town in Sonora, where Father Kino died and where his remains are buried, on October 4, the day of Saint Francis of Assisi, founder of the Franciscan Order. Anthropologist Edward Spicer called this process "simple addition" because a powerful saint and the associated ritual—candles, rosaries, and hymns in Spanish—were added to traditional beliefs and practices.[8]

In many ways, it is not surprising that Father Kino elicited such respect and veneration from the Indians. During his quarter century of missionary work, Father Kino is said to have maintained his optimistic approach to life and never departed from his view of the O'odham as friendly, sincere, gentle people who always kept their word. He saw in them consistent good will, and they probably mirrored a similar view of him, for it is said that he never suppressed Indian ceremonies or passed judgment on any of their traditions.

The Akimel O'odham never experienced sustained interaction with Europeans because no Spanish communities were established on the Gila River, near present-day Phoenix. Instead, they visited Hispanic communities, had contact with Spanish expeditions along the Gila River, and were influenced by Sonoran O'odham, who came to live among them and told them what it was like to live with the Spanish in Mexico.[9] The major impact of contact came through the introduction of wheat, which set off a chain reaction that transformed nearly every aspect of Akimel O'odham culture. By adding wheat, planted in the fall and harvested in the spring, to their traditional summer crops, the Akimel O'odham had year-round agriculture and doubled their production. Later, as more settlers moved into Sonora, the market for their wheat grew, leading to a market for other goods, such as basketry, blankets, and captives.[10] The structure of Akimel O'odham society became more formalized and a number of new occupational specialties emerged, along with more sharply defined gender roles. Men took over more of the agricultural work as women manufactured articles for trade. At the same time, the Spaniards withdrew most of their soldiers to fight against Indians farther south. This left the Akimel O'odham even more vulnerable to Apache attacks at the same time that the Apaches were intensifying their raids because of the greater surplus of grain in the towns. The Akimel O'odham responded by marshaling their men—sentinel duty and arms drills were required for all—and by shifting the purpose of their raids on the Apaches from vengeance to planned war campaigns modeled on those of the Spaniards. This led the Akimel O'odham to place a higher value on courage and skill in war and to increase ritual and technological developments related to warfare.

The shift from Spanish to Mexican control of most of the Southwest put the Franciscans living and working among the O'odham in a difficult position. The Mexicans regarded the Franciscans as conservative supporters of Spain, and only their distance from the seat of Mexican government and the government's preoccupation with the unification of the new country kept their missions from being secularized. After about 1810, Apache raiding intensified, isolating but also protecting the order from further Mexican control. The Franciscans managed to continue their work among the O'odham until the 1840s, when their greatly diminished numbers made them relinquish their control to secular clergy in the churches in this region.

In northern Sonora, south of the present international border, relations between O'odham and Mexicans ranged between tolerance and hostility. During the time of year when food was especially scarce, many Tohono O'odham traveled south to work for Mexican farmers and ranchers, returning home with Mexican goods and money. O'odham also served as soldiers for the Mexicans, fighting in campaigns against the Seris. At the same time, Mexican miners, farmers, and ranchers were migrating into Tohono O'odham territory. In the area around Caborca, they encroached on Tohono O'odham lands and water holes until the Indians began what became a state of war lasting from May 1840 until June 1843, when the Indians finally admitted defeat.

The Hispanic frontier never extended north of Tucson, which protected the Akimel O'odham who lived on the Gila River from Spanish and Mexican control. The Spanish belief that agricultural tribes living in permanent villages were more "civilized" than nomadic hunters and gatherers helped to keep the Akimel O'odham free of any Spanish or Mexican settlement on the Gila River.

They were thus able to accept aspects of Hispanic culture that were more compatible with their own beliefs. The major direct contact came from Spanish and Mexican expeditions along the river. Akimel O'odham also visited Hispanic communities, where they interacted with acculturated Sonoran O'odham. As military expeditions diminished in their area, many Sonoran O'odham immigrated to the settlements.

The Mexican period lasted longer for Indians south of the Gila River because this area was not added to the United States until after the **Gadsden Purchase** in 1853. However, the Mexican government had too many pressing problems to try to enforce its plans for taxation and land allotment for Indian peoples within its borders. In addition to the struggle for power between political factions within the Mexican government and ongoing Yaqui resistance, the United States presented a looming threat to Mexico's northernmost territory.

THE NORTHERN SECTOR OF THE SOUTHWEST

The northern sector of the Southwest, which includes the Colorado Plateau and its southern escarpment in New Mexico and Arizona, differs greatly in ecology and elevation from the desert to the south. This region was home to Pueblos, Navajos, and Jicarilla and Mescalero Apaches at the time of Spanish arrival. The Eastern Pueblos were living in autonomous villages with a few hundred to two thousand people at most, on or near the Rio Grande in New Mexico. The Western Pueblos—the Hopis, Zunis, and people of Acoma and Laguna pueblos (capitalized, *Pueblo* refers to the peoples of specific villages; lowercased, *pueblo* means a town community)—were living in a much more arid region that was better protected from intruders by its relative isolation. The Navajos and Apaches had spread into the more or less unoccupied areas between the Pueblo farmlands. Moving in groups of a few families to gather and hunt, the Apacheans lived in small camps in the backcountry, which protected them against Spanish encroachment. They traded meat and hides in Pueblo towns and often wintered beside the town walls; during times of famine, Puebloans had to protect their food stores from raiding Apacheans. Before the Spanish invaded and in the early days of their colonization, pedestrian Apacheans stole Pueblo crops, but after they acquired Spanish horses, they were able not only to raid with a greater element of surprise but also to safely escape with a greater abundance of goods.

Alvar Nuñez Cabeza de Vaca and his companions spread rumors of the famed Seven Cities of Cibola—opulent towns populated by wealthy agriculturalists who owned great quantities of precious metals—when they reached Mexico in 1536.

After their shipwreck on the coast of Texas, they had traveled through Pueblo country, and they greatly exaggerated all they had seen and experienced.

In 1539, when Franciscan friar Marcos de Niza led the first expedition to the Pueblo region, he chose Esteban, a black Moorish slave who had been with Cabeza de Vaca, to be his guide and companion. Esteban, described as a flamboyant, confident individual fond of wearing bright feathers and a crown of plumes on his head, accepted gifts of turquoise, coral, and maidens from the Natives as they traveled northward.[11] When they reached the outskirts of Zuni, Esteban sent a messenger ahead to inform the people that he and his large, well-armed party demanded presents and women. The Zunis decided to kill him so that he would not reveal their location. Fray de Niza held a brief ceremony to claim the land for Spain before he returned to Mexico. Interestingly, Fray de Niza and Esteban live on in Pueblo culture: every year on their feast day, the people of Jemez Pueblo portray a Franciscan priest wearing a long black coat and Esteban, with his black face and a black sheep pelt on his head to indicate his curly hair.[12]

The Pueblos first experienced Spanish brutality in 1540, when Francisco Vasquez de Coronado and several hundred Spanish soldiers and Mexican Indian servants marched into the upper Rio Grande Valley and settled in for the winter near a pueblo. When they requisitioned supplies and women from the villagers—who refused, knowing that they could not possibly support an army nearly as large as their own community—the Spaniards executed two hundred villagers. Pueblos from surrounding villages fought the intruders, leading to the slaughter of hundreds more and the destruction of their villages. Realizing that the famed cities of gold were only a myth, the Spanish withdrew and made no further serious attempts at colonization until 1598.

Father Augustin Rodriguez proposed the next expedition, comprising two other missionaries and nine soldiers. When the soldiers returned to New Spain, the friars chose to remain in the Rio Grande Valley, where they were eventually killed by the Indians.

In 1598, when Juan de Oñate and a colony of several hundred soldiers, Spanish settlers, their Mexican Indian servants, and missionaries arrived, the Eastern Pueblos were living in about 70 villages with a total population of about 50,000. Exacting what he believed to be a pledge of submission to his authority from Pueblo leaders, Oñate proclaimed New Mexico a missionary province of the Franciscan Order. When he failed to find the mineral wealth to support his colony, the Spanish crown briefly considered abandoning the province. Instead, the authorities decided to maintain New Mexico as a royal colony supported almost entirely by the treasury for the sake of the Church. The Spanish justified their empire building with the belief that they were converting souls to Christianity. As previously demonstrated in the southern sector of the Southwest, the Church was also a major agent for the assimilation of Native peoples to Spanish culture.

The Franciscan-Indian relationship in the Pueblo area differed considerably from the Jesuit-Indian relationship farther south. Pueblo communities were as compact as any European village, so further concentration was not possible. Therefore, both the church and the missionaries' living quarters were built at the edge of the pueblo, separated from the rest of the community by a wall. Adding to this sense of physical separation was the fact that missionaries in the Rio Grande area seldom became proficient in Puebloan languages and had soldiers living with them for protection. Either by themselves or with these soldiers, the priests carried out harsh disciplinary actions against Indians who practiced their traditional rituals, including physical punishment and the destruction of Native religious objects. In contrast, missionaries in Sonora lived within Indian communities and were much more accepting of Native rituals. Pueblo villagers were forced to build a church large enough to accommodate all, plus a residence, storage buildings, and stables for the mission, and to attend morning Mass each day. Public flogging was the most common penalty for those who failed to attend. In addition to banning ceremonial dances, the missionaries raided *kivas*, destroyed masks and other religious paraphernalia, and hanged Pueblo priests. In 1661, Franciscan missionaries banned all practices associated with the *katsinam*, including the personification of these spirits by masked dancers.

When Santa Fe was established in 1610 as the capital town, it was inhabited by Spanish settlers employed in governmental administration, trade, or mining. Most Pueblo Indians went there to purchase goods, but Oñate had brought with him several hundred Indians from Tlaxcala in central Mexico, who settled in a barrio. The Spanish also had Apache and Navajo slaves, who worked as household servants or common laborers.

Two kinds of Spanish settlements exerted the strongest influence in the Rio Grande area. First were the *encomienda* land grants to soldiers who had participated in the conquest of Mexico and had accompanied Oñate. Included in the grant was the right of forced labor with compensation. This meant that the *encomendero* had the right to employ Indians who lived on the land grant, and Indians were often forced to work for him with little or no compensation. Furthermore, the encomenderos often disrupted the lives of villagers by interfering in their local affairs. The other kind of settlement was pieces of land granted to Spanish settlers, located beside Indian villages or in uninhabited areas with grazing land and water for irrigation. Although Spanish and Indians clashed over land rights at first, eventually peaceful relations were established and there was considerable intermarriage that led to reciprocal cultural borrowing and influence.

When Oñate established control over individual Pueblo villages, he acknowl-edged their semiautonomous status with certain rights of self-government. Even though a Native political system already existed, headed by *caciques*, Oñate im-posed a new governmental system over which the Spanish had greater control. Each pueblo had a new set of officers: a governor, a lieutenant governor, war cap-tains (present after 1700), a sheriff, irrigation ditch bosses, and church wardens. After their election at the beginning of the year, these officers were confirmed by the Spanish governor, who presented each Pueblo governor with a black cane of office trimmed with silk and silver tassels as a symbol of authority.

The Spanish program deteriorated as conflict escalated among the mission-aries, the civil government, and the military over policies and goals. Competi-tion for the produce and forced labor of the Indians became increasingly bit-ter, tearing apart the new settlement. The Franciscan clergy wanted to build peaceful agricultural communities with Indian laborers who produced tribute in support of the Church. The governors resented this appropriation of natural resources and Indian labor and considered the missionaries to be establishing little kingdoms of their own. These bureaucratic officials wanted to use rev-enue generated by tribute and taxes to pay for administration and development. They also sought to improve their status and increase their personal wealth. As a reward for living in what the Spanish considered an isolated and cultur-ally austere outpost, they had been granted the privilege of engaging in trade and manufacturing, so they felt that Indian labor should further their personal interests as well as those of the civil authority. Finally, the military nobility, whose land grants—following the established Spanish pattern—had been re-wards for their contribution to the conquest, were convinced that the Indians should devote more time to labor on their farms and haciendas. The bitter antagonism between ecclesiastical and government officers, with individuals from each group asserting final authority over Pueblo resources and labor, was incomprehensible to the Indians because the secular and religious realms were so closely integrated in their own culture.

Spanish officials tried to profit from Pueblo trade in salt and hides and the Pueblo production of cloth, along with expanded trade in crops. However, when this failed to produce sufficient financial rewards, the Spaniards added traffic in human beings. The introduction of a lucrative slave trade provided the incentive for Apache bands to increase their raids on Plains Indian camps and villages as well as in eastern New Mexico and adjacent Sonora to acquire women and children, whom they traded at Pecos and at other Eastern Pueblo villages. The Spanish put the slaves to labor in their households and ranches. The Comanches also began raiding for slaves, and then the Apaches escalated their raids, making eastern New Mexico and adjacent Sonora too dangerous for travel.

Oñate's failure to find mineral wealth and general discontent under his policies led to his replacement as governor by Pedro de Peralta in 1607. In 1610, Peralta founded the city of Santa Fe to serve as the new capital of the province and forced Indian workers to build the governor's palace and other municipal buildings. Peralta was one of a number of particularly brutal Spanish governors. Accusing the people of Jemez Pueblo of working with Apaches and Navajos against the Spanish, Governor Fernando de Arguello Caravajal (1644–1647) hanged twenty-nine Jemez leaders.[13] Hernando de Ugarte (1649–1653) killed nine more leaders from Jemez, Alameda, and Sandia.[14]

In 1640 a drought and a destructive Apache raid led to widespread famine and three thousand Indian deaths.[15] The raiding groups—various Apache groups, Navajos, Comanches, sometimes Kiowas or Shoshones—depended for their livelihood on hunting. Those who lived on the Plains relied on immense herds of bison, supplementing game with corn and other vegetables that they seized from the Pueblos. Drought affected these nomadic peoples as much as it did the agricultural Pueblos. When the grass died on the Plains, the bison migrated to places with more abundant resources. Wild plants that Plains and southwestern peoples gathered, such as nuts, berries, and roots, became even scarcer with the lack of rainfall. The Comanches, Navajos, and Apaches, lured by Spanish farms well-stocked with sheep, pigs, and cattle and Pueblo storage bins full of corn, intensified their plundering when their other resources dwindled.

For the Pueblos, a series of extreme droughts led to a crisis. Their agricultural practices were no longer viable, especially after 1665 when drought, famine, pestilence, and raids by nomadic tribes worsened conditions. To fulfill Spanish demands, the Pueblos had to leave their own unfenced plots to be ravaged by Spanish livestock. With their equestrian hunting economy and increased strength and numbers, the Apaches and other nomadic tribes had become increasingly predatory. The Pueblos, whose farm plots lay exposed on the frontier, were forced to bear the brunt of the raids and were afraid to work in their fields. The droughts, famines, and repeated raids of 1663–1669 brought the Pueblos close to starvation and thousands died. Accounts described Pueblo people "lying dead along the roads, in the ravines, and in their huts."[16]

Probably the most dramatic source of change in American Indian societies was the introduction of new pathogens, which could reach groups even before they had direct contact with Europeans. Early explorers did not record accurate population figures, but some anthropologists estimate that within a century the Pueblo population was reduced to a tenth of its former size.[17] Malnourished and living in compact villages clustered along the Rio Grande and its tributaries, the Pueblos were especially susceptible to the spread of diseases to which they had had no previous exposure. The smallpox pandemic of 1520–1524 killed many, and other diseases, such as typhus, measles, cholera, diphtheria, scarlet fever, and bubonic plague, cycled through communities every three to four years.

The Pueblos attributed death and destruction on such a massive scale to disharmony in the universe. From their perspective, these catastrophic events had occurred because they had stopped practicing their ceremonials. Although some Pueblo priests did continue to perform rites in secret in the kivas, the Spanish presence made it difficult to dance the ceremonies that took place in the central plaza of each village. In explaining the Pueblo worldview, **Edward Dozier**, anthropologist and a member of the Santa Clara Pueblo, described the responsibility that humans have to use their thoughts, words, and deeds to perform ceremonies in a spirit of joy and faith that will "keep the seasons moving, allow the sun to rise and set properly, bring rain and snow, quell the winds, and insure a well-ordered physical environment and society."[18] Failure to perform the proper ceremonies, even if caused by an outside agent such as the Spanish that kept them from doing so, brought about imbalance that eventually manifested itself in drought, disaster, illness, and other misfortune. Disharmony in the universe was causing the sky to burn up, plants to cease growing, people to die, enemies to attack, and these arrogant outsiders to make servants of their most respected people.

Conditions continued to worsen as the Spanish persisted in harassing and punishing the Pueblos for failing to provide sufficient tribute as well as for violating other religious or secular rules. For eighty years, the Spanish had enforced their feudal economic system with its religious intolerance and system of punishment. As disasters—the seemingly unending drought, the famine, the epidemics, the repeated raiding by enemy peoples—continued, the Pueblos questioned the new faith that they had adopted and began to return to their traditional beliefs. The Franciscan clergy denounced what they considered to be a retreat into paganism. During his first year as governor, Juan Francisco de Trevino (1675–1677) proclaimed the total prohibition of Native rituals. In 1675, he sent soldiers through the Pueblo villages to arrest the heads of secret societies, the organizers of katsinam dances, and Pueblo priests who performed the rituals. Of the forty-seven Pueblo priests that de Trevino judged as guilty of "sorcery," "witchcraft," and "idolatry," he condemned four to die by hanging and sentenced the rest to prison for many years or to lashings.[19]

Popé, a medicine man from the Tewa-speaking pueblo of San Juan, was one of those forced to endure the shame of a public whipping. He had been urging Puebloans to rebel against the Spaniards for at least ten years, but no one had taken him seriously because the Pueblos had never engaged in large-scale warfare and initiating such a campaign seemed impossible. The various groups of Pueblos—Tanoans, Keresans, Zunis—were so different, and even among the Tanoans, the Tanos and Tiwas were uneasy with each other. But Popé refused to accept any opposition. His hatred and determination gave him patience, and he built a web of alliances between 1675 and 1680. First he explained his plan to those in his own pueblo and then he sought allies in nearby pueblos. Catiti, a religious leader from the Keresan village of Santo Domingo who shared Popé's ideals, convinced others to join. Two Tiwas—Tupatu from Picuris and Jaca from Taos—spread the plan to the leaders of their pueblos. Taos, far from Santa Fe, became Popé's headquarters as he converted more people to his cause.

The Spaniards heard rumors of a revolt, but without definite proof of a conspiracy amid the tension after the public hangings and lashings of Pueblo priests, they were afraid that new arrests might provoke open hostilities. Hoping that the uneasy situation would pass on its own, the Spanish did nothing.

On August 10, 1680 the **Pueblo Revolt** began. All of the missions were destroyed, two thirds of the missionaries and a sixth of the colonists were slaughtered, and warriors from Tano and Tewa villages and Pecos besieged Santa Fe for nine days. Governor Otermin tried to marshal resistance in Santa Fe, but after the water supply was cut off, he decided to join other colonists in their flight to El Paso. Significantly, although the Pueblos killed nearly all the missionaries, they allowed most of the colonists to escape, indicating that their attack was focused on eliminating the mission system and expelling the Spanish from the area.

The Pueblos saw their success as the overthrow of foreign domination and the revival of their own traditional cultures. Historically, the Pueblo Revolt is the most spectacular victory that Native Americans have ever achieved through a combined show of force within what is now the United States. Every pueblo north of Isleta participated by killing Spaniards and providing fighting men to aid in the siege of Santa Fe and the expulsion of the Spanish. Spanish oppression had led Keresans and Tanoans to organize at an intervillage level that had never existed before and would never exist again with such a complete unity of purpose.

Village autonomy, quarrels within each village, and the increase in Apache and Navajo raiding quickly dissolved the spirit of cooperation that had made the revolt so successful. Village leaders were not used to working with leaders of other villages in alliances; each pueblo had its own traditions and its own way of accomplishing things. Within each village, disagreements developed among various religious societies, and personality conflicts or controversial actions of individuals led to the expulsion of some societies from villages. Without the deterrent of Spanish guns and horses, the Pueblos were at the mercy of mounted Apaches and Navajos, who had taken many of the horses left behind by the Spaniards. Raids became increasingly frequent, and food became even scarcer with drought and famine.

When Governor Otermin made the first attempt to reconquer the area in 1681–1682, Pueblo unity was still strong enough to rebuff his efforts, although he did manage to sack and burn most of the pueblos south of Cochiti. Not until 1692 did a new governor, Diego de Vargas, begin a reconquest. By then, Pueblo factionalism and a willingness on the part of some Pueblo villages to consider the Spanish as possible allies against raiding groups made his plan more feasible. A group of men from Jemez, Zia, Santa Ana, San Felipe, and Pecos pueblos, and some Tanos, went to Guadalupe del Paso to speak with the Spanish about the possibility of their return.[20] These men later became instrumental in helping de Vargas succeed in the reconquest. Serving as interpreters, they also kept him informed about the state of factionalism among the various Pueblo villages.

Despite interpueblo dissension, many were not at all willing to accept the return of the Spanish. While de Vargas received token submission and even cooperation from some of the people of Zuni, Hopi, Pecos, and some of the Keresan pueblos, most of the Pueblos resisted. Anticipating punitive expeditions immediately after the revolt, many had abandoned their villages and sought refuge in more defensible areas in the surrounding mountains and mesas.

Many Rio Grande Pueblos sought sanctuary with the Hopis, who had a long tradition of offering asylum to other Indians. Some were absorbed by the Hopis; others eventually returned to their homeland. The Southern Tewas had established settlements near Santa Cruz and refused to surrender at the time of the reconquest. They carried out hit-and-run warfare against de Vargas from a mesa near San Ildefonso and managed to withstand the Spanish attacks for nine months. Finally compelled to sue for peace, they settled in a single village in the vicinity of present-day Chimayo. De Vargas, however, founded a new village, Santa Cruz, that repossessed the Southern Tewa village, so in 1696, the resettled Southern Tewa, along with the people of Taos, Picuris, Santo Domingo, and Cochiti, again rose up, killing twenty-one Spanish colonists and six priests.

Fearing reprisals, the entire group of resettled Southern Tewas fled to Hopi country before de Vargas reached their area. At Hopi, they founded the village of Hano on First Mesa and became known as the Hopi-Tewa, retaining their language and traditions while also being influenced to some extent by Hopi culture. According to their oral tradition, the Hopi-Tewa were invited by the Walpi village chiefs, who knew of their reputation as fearless warriors, to move as a single unit to serve as guards of the mesa trail up to Walpi, protecting the mesa from Utes and Paiutes.[21]

De Vargas, with more than a thousand soldiers, colonists, and Indian servants, stormed Santa Fe to expel the Pueblos who were entrenched there, and he also had to combat considerable Pueblo resistance in other areas. Not until the end of 1696 did he finally secure the submission of all the New Mexico Pueblos, except for the Western Pueblos. The Hopis never again experienced Spanish rule.

Some Pueblos fled from Spanish retribution to the Rio Grande area, to live near the Navajos in Gobernador Canyon. In this region of what is now northwestern New Mexico, both groups experienced a period of intense cultural sharing. By this time, Apacheans had separated into distinct groups. The Eastern Apaches—Lipans, Jicarillas, Plains Apaches (Kiowa-Apaches), Mescaleros, and Chiricahuas—remained more strongly influenced by Plains cultures. Originally bison hunters, they emphasized the solidarity of relationships of the same generation instead of the tie to the mother and her lineage. The Navajos and Western Apaches, especially after the intensified contact around the Pueblo Revolt, incorporated more Puebloan traits into their cultures, such as agriculture and matrilineal descent groups.

Some anthropologists believe that the Navajos adopted agriculture in Colorado during their trek southward in precontact times. Once they were in the Southwest, they used Pueblo crops, agricultural techniques, and agricultural ritual system, which they molded and reinterpreted in terms of Navajo values. When the Spanish introduced livestock into the Pueblo economy, the Navajos incorporated sheep and weaving, probably from the Pueblos with Spanish influence. Sandpaintings, a common feature of Pueblo kiva ceremonies, became a greater focus of ritual among the Navajos, who emphasized individual healing rather than the community goals on which the Pueblos had focused. The Navajos retained their small, scattered camps, never adopting Pueblo forms of settlement in large towns, although in the seventeenth century, some Navajo built rectangular stone homes (*pueblitos*) that resembled small Pueblo houses.

All the Pueblos had experienced great changes from a century of close Spanish contact. The population of their villages dwindled from between 30,000 and 40,000 in 1600 to about 16,000 at the time of the Pueblo Revolt.[22] Many factors led to this decline, especially periodic epidemics of European-introduced diseases. Many converted to Catholicism and chose to live with the colonists. The most tangible changes were economic, beginning with the tools, new crops, and domesticated animals that the Spanish had brought. Pueblo communities were forced into symbiotic relationships with the Spaniards as all groups, from Pueblos to colonists to nomadic bands, became dependent on trade with Mexico.

Spanish-Indian relations changed significantly after the reconquest, as the Pueblos became partners with Spanish colonists in defending New Mexico against nomadic tribes. Both the civil authorities and the Franciscans modified their demands, and what had been oppressive policies became considerably more humane. The encomienda system, a major cause of the revolt, was ended, and the Spanish in New Mexico no longer collected tribute from the Pueblo Indians.

In 1821, the change from Spanish to Mexican government meant a return to greater village autonomy in the management of the pueblo, including ceremonial practices. Twenty missionaries were serving New Mexico in 1822; a decade later their numbers had dwindled to five priests in Pueblo missions. The Franciscan Order did not fill vacancies and closed their missions. By 1830, the Pueblos began to publicly present rituals that they had conducted in secrecy during the period of Spanish oppression, so ceremonies were again held in the plazas and non-Indians were allowed to attend.

The most serious consequence for the Pueblos under Mexican rule was the loss of land to squatters. The doctrine of equal rights proclaimed by the Mexican government was interpreted by many to mean that they had an equal right to all land. As equal citizens, Indians had the right to buy, lease, or use their land as collateral. Many corrupt administrators wrote fraudulent titles to land owned by Indians, then sold them to non-Indians, often without the knowledge of the Pueblos themselves. Although land grants from the Spanish Crown were still recognized, documents could be easily forged. Each of the pueblos still appointed a governor to represent them, but there was no recourse to authority beyond that in Santa Fe, as there had been under Spanish rule, and Pueblo peoples were dependent upon the willingness of government officials there to support Pueblo title. Often, Mexican governors failed to do this, as happened to Taos Pueblo, which lost some of its sacred mountain land when the governor decided in favor of two Mexican citizens. Furthermore, in many cases, as soon as the Indians got a settlement in their favor, more squatters appeared on their land and they were forced to bring another claim to Mexican officials.

An agreement between New Mexico and the allied Comanches, Utes, Navajos, and Jicarilla Apaches also disintegrated under Mexican government. The Spanish administration had nurtured the cooperation of these tribes during the final fifty years of their rule with deference and the distribution of rations and gifts, but the Mexican governors cared little about preserving this alliance. The Mexican administration even summoned Navajo chiefs to Cochiti and permitted irate New Mexicans to massacre them, and it did nothing to stop Mexican slaving raids against the Navajos.

THE WESTERN SECTOR OF THE SOUTHWEST

The sixteenth and seventeenth centuries were a period of great intertribal **warfare** for the Yuman-speaking peoples of the Colorado River Valley, resulting in the migration of groups into new territories and areas previously occupied by others. Highly ritualized and unique within the Southwest, River Yuman warfare probably existed before the intrusion of Europeans and was influenced by Spanish-Mexican incentives.

Of all three regions in the Southwest, the western area was where the lives of Indian peoples remained the least changed initially by Spanish contact. The Quechan (Yuma) nation controlled one of the few Colorado River crossings in east-west routes of commerce, giving them strategic importance in precontact trade and later, trade with Spaniards, Mexicans, and Anglo-Americans. The Quechan (Yuma) and Mojave composed the River Yumans, while farther south, the Cocopah, Kahjwan, and Halyikwamai made up the Delta Yumans. All of the groups enjoyed the annual flooding of the Colorado River and, to some extent, the Gila River, because it created fertile riverine agricultural oases in an area that was essentially desert and semidesert. Contact with Europeans came even later for the the Upland Yuman peoples—the Yavapai, Hualapai, and Havasupai (groups known as the Pai, "the people")—who practiced some agriculture but got most of their subsistence from hunting and gathering on the semiarid plateau of northwestern Arizona. The Havasupai were unusual in their mixed subsistence pattern because they spent summers in Cataract Canyon, part of the Grand Canyon, as rancheria farmers and during the rest of the year lived a more nomadic lifestyle on the rim above the canyon.

There is no way of knowing how many tribes there were or where they lived at the time of first Spanish contact. The Quicama (probably the Quechan) and the Coana were mentioned by Coronado's Lieutenant Alarcon when he sailed up the lower part of the Colorado River in 1540. In 1605, Oñate mentioned the Kohuana (Coana), Halyikwamai, and Cocopa near the mouth of the river, the Halchidoma farther north, and the Amacavas (the Mojaves' name for themselves) farther north in the present-day Parker Valley.

The Jesuit priest Father Kino had the most intensive and warm contact with the Yumans ("Yuma" refers to the Quechan, while all Yuman-speaking peoples are collectively "the Yumans") of the Colorado River in 1698. During his trip in 1690, he had encountered the Opas and Coco-Maricopas among the Pimas on the Gila River, and he saw them again in 1698. In 1700 at least 1,500 Quechans came for an eventful visit of mutual speechmaking. They encouraged him to stay so that other groups—the Halchidomas, who lived upriver, and the Kikimas, Cocopas, and Hoabonomos, from downriver—could hear him speak. Father Kino did not stay, but he did return to the junction of the Colorado and Gila rivers in 1701. With a retinue of 300 Quechan and Pima Indians and no military escort, he traveled south to a Kikima village, where he spent two days talking and listening to the people. Never having seen horses, the Indians were fascinated by demonstrations of horseback racing. Now about 500 Native people joined Father Kino as he crossed the Colorado River and encountered the Cutgan people on the west side of the river and the Cocopa from the south.

Hoping to confirm that California was a peninsula, Father Kino returned the following year and again met the Quechans at the confluence of the Gila and Colorado rivers. They traveled downstream, accompanied by Kikimas, Cutgans, and Cocopas, to see where the Colorado River emptied into the Gulf of California.

In 1706, the Kikimas sent messengers to a Tohono O'odham village in Sonora with a petition for Father Kino to return or to send other missionaries. Not until 1748 did Father Sedelmayr travel to the intersection of the Gila and Colorado rivers, but the Quechan threatened him with hostilities and stole some of his horses.

Seeking a westward land route to California, General de Anza, accompanied by a Franciscan priest, Father Garces, made a series of expeditions through Quechan country in the 1770s. When Father Garces traveled up the Colorado River, he met Mojaves and Havasupais, who treated him cordially. However, when he returned in 1779 to establish a mission downstream from the Gila junction on the west side of the Colorado River, he was forced by a new Spanish policy to be accompanied by a small garrison of soldiers. Father Garces's concerns that the Quechan would interpret a military presence as a threat to their autonomy were justified; in 1781, the Quechan killed all of the Europeans. The Spanish were accompanied by O'odham peoples, Halchidhomas, Cocomaricopas, and Kohuanas on a punitive expedition the following year. The final Spanish contact occurred in 1799, when Cortez encountered an estimated 3,000 Quechan.

The first half of the nineteenth century brought considerable warfare between the powerful Quechans and other Yuman peoples. In the late eighteenth and early nineteenth centuries, the Halchidomas, Kohuanas, and Kavelchadom, who had lived along the Colorado River north of the Quechans, were forced eastward along the Gila River by the Mojaves to their north and the Quechans from the south. By 1857, the three former tribes had merged with the Maricopas.

On August 31, 1857, Quechan, Mojave, Tonto Apache, and Yavapai warriors, having hiked at least 160 miles across the desert from their respective homes along the Colorado River and other areas, made a surprise attack on two Maricopa villages near the confluence of the Gila and Santa Cruz rivers, close to present-day Phoenix. The Quechans could have been seeking revenge for the Maricopa and O'odham presence with the Spaniards on the punitive expedition in 1782. As the people ran out of their burning dome-shaped brush houses, the attackers killed them with clubs and arrows. A few Maricopas who had horses escaped to seek help from the upstream Pima villages. During a lull in the fighting, some of the Mojaves, Yavapais, and Tonto Apaches headed homeward to the north and northwest while about a hundred Mojaves and the Quechans remained, savoring their victory.[23] A force of about 1,200 revenge-seeking Pimas and Maricopas nearly annihilated the Quechans and Mojaves, who were all on foot.[24]

Intertribal warfare was practiced by many, if not all, American Indian peoples, but this event is important because it was the last major battle in the Southwest fought between opposing Indian forces rather than opposing Anglo-American–Indian forces. Even more significantly, although Spanish and Mexican control may not have extended into the western sector of the Southwest, the influence of these two countries had a profound effect on the nature of River Yuman warfare. The lucrative slave trade they introduced affected nearly all Indian peoples in the Southwest.

Hernando de Alarcon was the first to document River Yuman warfare in 1540; as far as is known, only the Quechan and the Cocopas were involved at that time.[25] By the sixteenth century, many small tribes were being forced off the Colorado River by more powerful Indian groups. Anthropologists posit that what began as small-scale intertribal conflict, motivated by a sense of nationalism and revenge and interspersed with periods of peace and trading between enemies, escalated into a desire for the annihilation of their enemies.

In the late seventeenth and eighteenth centuries, O'odham peoples were being pressured by the Apaches to the east, the Spanish to the south, and the Yavapais and Apaches from the north. During the eighteenth century, the O'odham retreated eastward along the Gila River to where it is joined by the Salt River. From the late seventeenth century until the middle of the nineteenth century, Spanish and Mexican settlers encouraged a slave trade that may have pitted previous Indian allies against one another. The O'odham people, Maricopas, and Quechans sold Indians of other tribes in Spanish or Mexican towns.[26] The introduction of horses and European trade goods may have increased the incentive to do this. European-introduced diseases traveled along the Colorado and Gila rivers and led to a serious decline in population.[27] Anthropologists theorize that these new conditions brought major changes in intertribal warfare, increasing intensity and frequency so that entire tribes were now displaced or exterminated.

Horses were unintentionally introduced by the Coronado expedition in 1540 to the Havasupai and other Upland Yumans when some of the Spanish mounts were lost during the first European venture into the Grand Canyon. In 1776, Spanish priest Francisco Garces traveled through Havasupai territory guided by Mojaves and Hualapais. Further European contact was relatively limited, but the Havasupais and Hualapais (essentially one people with different bands), learned more about the Spanish through their allies, the Hopis. The Yavapais did not experience Spanish or Mexican control because their territory was not desirable to Europeans for settlement. Their contact with Spaniards and Mexicans was primarily through trade networks. For nearly all of the Indian peoples in the western sector of the Southwest, the first sustained contact with Euro-Americans came after their land became part of the United States and gold seekers invaded their territory in the 1850s.

NOTES

1. J. H. Elliott, *Imperial Spain 1469–1716* (New York: Mentor Books, New American Library, 1966), 111.
2. Grenville Goodwin, *The Social Organization of the Western Apache* (Chicago: University of Chicago Press, 1942).
3. Ibid., 67; Jack Forbes, *Apache, Navajo and Spaniard* (Norman: University of Oklahoma Press, 1960), 8–9; Jack Forbes, *Warriors of the Colorado: The Yumas of the Quechan Nation and Their Neighbors* (Norman: University of Oklahoma Press, 1965), 345–346.
4. Edward Spicer, *Cycles of Conquest* (1962; reprint, Tucson: University of Arizona Press, 1981), 46.
5. Ibid., 49.
6. Octaviana Valenzuela Trujillo, "The Yaqui of Guidalupe, Arizona: A Century of Cultural Survival Through Trilingualism," *American Indian Culture and Research Journal* 22 (1998): 1–69.
7. Bernard Fontana, "History of the Papago," in *Handbook of North American Indians: The Southwest*, vol. 10, ed. Alfonso Ortiz (Washington, D.C.: Smithsonian Institution Press, 1983), 138.
8. Spicer, *Cycles of Conquest*, 514.
9. Paul Ezell, "History of the Pima," in *Handbook of North American Indians: The Southwest*, vol. 10, ed. Alfonso Ortiz (Washington, D.C.: Smithsonian Institution Press, 1983), 153.
10. D. Jose Agustin de Escudero, *Noticias estadisticas de Sonora y Sinaloa compiladas y amplificadas para la commission de estadistica militar* (Mexico City: Tipografia de R. Rafael, 1849), 142–143.
11. Ross Holland Jr., *Hawikuh and the Seven Cities of Cibola* (Washington, D.C.: U.S. Government Printing Office, 1969).
12. Joe Sando, *Pueblo Nations: Eight Centuries of Pueblo Indian History* (Santa Fe: Clear Light Publishers, 1992), 51–52.
13. Ibid., 62.
14. Charles Hackett, ed., *Revolt of the Pueblo Indians of New Mexico and Otermin's Attempted Reconquest, 1680–1682*. Trans. Charmion C. Shelby. 2 vols. (Albuquerque: University of New Mexico Press, 1942).
15. Marc Simmons, "History of Pueblo-Spanish Relations to 1821," in *Handbook of North American Indians: The Southwest*, vol. 9, ed. Alfonso Ortiz (Washington, D.C.: Smithsonian Institution Press, 1979), 71.
16. R. Gordon Vivian, "Gran Quivara: Excavations in a Seventeenth-Century Jumano Pueblo," in *U.S. National Park Service Archaeological Research Series* 8 (Washington D.C., 1964), 153.
17. Thomas D. Hall, *Social Change in the Southwest, 1350–1880* (Lawrence: University Press of Kansas, 1989), 71.

18. Edward Dozier, *The Pueblo Indians of North America* (New York: Holt, Rinehart and Winston, 1970), 151.

19. John Kessell, *Kiva, Cross and Crown: The Pecos Indians and New Mexico, 1540–1840* (Washington D.C.: U.S. Government Printing Office, 1979), 226.

20. Sando, *Pueblo Nations*, 69.

21. Jesse W. Fewkes, "The Winter Solstice Altars at Hano Pueblo," *American Anthropologist* 1 (2) (1889): 253.

22. Hackett, *Revolt of the Pueblo Indians of New Mexico*, xxxi.

23. Clifton Kroeber and Bernard Fontana, *Massacre on the Gila: An Account of the Last Major Battle Between American Indians, with Reflections on the Origin of War* (1986; reprint, Tucson: University of Arizona Press, 1992), 7.

24. Ibid.

25. Forbes, *Warriors of the Colorado*, 86–88.

26. Kroeber and Fontana, *Massacre on the Gila*, 105.

27. Henry Dobyns, Paul Ezell, Alden Jones, and Greta Ezell, "Thematic Changes in Yuman Warfare," in *Cultural Stability and Cultural Change* (Seattle: American Ethnological Society, 1957), 50–61; Greta Ezell and Paul Ezell, "Background to Battle: Circumstances Relating to Death on the Gila, 1857," in *Trooper West: Military and Indian Affairs on the American Frontier*, ed. Ray Brandes (San Diego: Frontier Heritage Press, 1970), 174–175.

CHAPTER 3

American Expansion

Trade, Treaties, and Reservations

Anglo-American influence permeated the Southwest long before the United States claimed the region. Beginning in the 1820s, the Santa Fe Trail linked New Mexico to the central United States, furnishing an outlet for Navajo weaving and other trade goods, and American traders had well-established ties with Native peoples in this region.

When American settlers poured into New Mexico, they were surprised to find two distinct village cultures living in relatively peaceful coexistence in the upper Rio Grande Valley. First there was an archaic Spanish rural culture, with many borrowed Indian traits. Then there was the Pueblo culture, which had integrated many Hispanic traditions. Americans began to make the same distinction that the Spaniards had between "civilized" Indians—whose cultures were the most similar to their own—and "wild" Indians—nomadic groups who responded with the strongest show of armed resistance to the Anglo invasion of their territory.

Southwestern Indians, in comparison to those in other areas of the United States, had had considerable experience with non-Indian peoples through the colonizing efforts of Spain and then Mexico. Some, such as the Pueblos, had had intense contact during the occupation of their villages by Spanish forces; others, such as the Yavapai, whose country was less desirable to intruders, had had minimal contact. Although traders and explorers, if not settlers, had given all the groups some idea of these strange people, none was prepared for the onslaught of settlers and miners after their region was opened to Anglo-American settlement.

By the time the United States had acquired the Southwest from the Mexicans—most of it through the Treaty of Guadalupe Hidalgo in 1848 and the land south of the Gila River through the Gadsden Purchase in 1853—the government had already developed the concept of the reservation. Derived from English policy, this treatment of tribal groups as separate nations contrasted sharply with the Spanish and Mexican incorporation of Indians as citizens. Despite bitter opposition from the public and press as well as many members of Congress, the Indian Removal Bill of 1830 had been enacted, giving the government authority to allocate western lands to Indians who consented to relinquish their territory in the east. The term "Manifest Destiny" was coined in 1845 to justify the appropriation of Indian as well as Mexican lands. By the mid-nineteenth century, it had become clear that removal would not solve the Anglo-American–Indian conflict, and in 1858, the commissioner of Indian affairs described the basis of the reservation policy: "concentrating the Indians on small reservations of land, and . . . sustaining them there for a limited period of time, until they can be induced to make the necessary exertions to support themselves."[1]

However, a pattern of warfare and raiding nearly half a century old already existed in the Southwest, and it took twenty years for the U.S. government to fulfill the promise of peace that had been made to New Mexicans. With the loss of hunting lands and so many of their people to slavery, the Navajos and Apaches depended upon raiding for their livelihood and the recovery of their loved ones. A brutal campaign against the Navajos led to their incarceration between 1863 and 1868 in New Mexico. By 1863, the survival of groups that lived in the most remote areas of Arizona was threatened. Finding their hunting and gathering territories overrun by miners and settlers, groups such as the Yavapais chose military action as well as negotiation for the sake of their survival. After Naiche's band of Chiricahuas surrendered and were sent into exile in 1886, all of the Native peoples in the Southwest were on reservations.

In 1849, the Bureau of Indian Affairs was transferred from the Department of War to the Department of the Interior, which led to inconsistent policies and conflict with the military about how to subjugate hostile groups and keep them on reservations. Civilian officials known as Indian agents were charged with promoting peaceful relations between Indians and settlers, although they were not given directions or authority to achieve this goal.

The outbreak of the Civil War had little effect on the Indian population except that troops were pulled eastward, depopulating many U.S. Army installations in the western United States. By the summer of 1863, however, so many volunteer regiments had been raised that the United States had more soldiers available for service against the Indians than it had had in 1860.[2] As frontiers-men, most of the new soldiers shared a common hatred of Indians based on stereotypical notions of wandering groups addicted to warfare.

In 1867, President Grant appointed a Board of Indian Commissioners to de-velop a unified and humane policy to guide the Bureau of Indian Affairs. Over strenuous protests from western members of Congress, some of whom favored a war of extermination, Congress and the president established a Peace Com-mission (15 U.S. Stat. 17) that included a new commissioner of Indian affairs, members of Congress, army officers, and civilians. Charged with convincing Indians to locate on reservations, the commission was also empowered to raise detachments of volunteers to force the Indians to comply. President Grant's "Peace Policy" produced a new round of treaties in 1867 and 1868 that pro-vided for reservations isolated from casual white contact, education, annuities of clothing, and land allotment for those who sought it.[3]

THE SOUTHERN SECTOR OF THE SOUTHWEST

By this time, most of the Indian tribes in the Southwest had signed peace trea-ties and were settled on reservations. The Apache tribes and the Upland Yuman tribes had not, and both groups felt the effect of the new Peace Policy. Living primarily in the southern sector of the Southwest, Apache groups, whose hunt-ing territories had been disturbed by Anglo-American settlers and miners, had come to rely on raiding as a subsistence strategy.

Anglo contact with Apaches dated back to the 1820s, when trappers and trad-ers established an informal headquarters at Taos on the upper Rio Grande. In 1826, a hundred Anglo trappers obtained licenses from Santa Fe Mexican of-ficials to trap along the Gila River and twenty of them were killed by Apaches.[4] After the New Mexico Territory came under Anglo-American control, money was set aside for making treaties with Indians who lived along the border be-tween Mexico and the United States. General Kearny and Colonel Kit Carson passed through Apache territory as they followed the Gila Trail between the Rio Grande and the Colorado rivers and, upon informing the Apaches that New Mexico was now under Anglo control, found them to be wary but willing to trade rather than fight. **Mangas Coloradas** and other Apache leaders distin-guished between Anglo-Americans and Mexicans, with whom they considered themselves to be in a continuous state of war. The Mexican states of Chihuahua and Sonora offered bounties on Apache scalps in an effort to control raiding.

Apache leaders, however, found U.S. policy unacceptable even though they were willing to maintain peaceful relations with Anglo-Americans. They refused to sign the treaty because it prohibited Apache raiding in Mexico.

Their wariness of these invaders who claimed control of their territory increased as hostile Anglo prospectors moved in, and clashes between miners and Apaches were common throughout what would become southern Arizona and western New Mexico. Apache-Anglo warfare continued after the Civil War, and the military built eight new forts in Apache country that had little effect on Indian hostilities.

The federal and territorial government could not agree on a unified Indian policy between 1865 and 1871. Representing Arizona settlers who had precipitated the bitter Indian warfare in central and southern Arizona, the Territorial Legislature demanded the extermination or unconditional surrender of all Indians. Many of these settlers decided to take matters into their own hands, resulting in the **Camp Grant Massacre** in 1871. Farsighted leaders like **Eskiminzin** of the Arivaipa band of the Pinalenos had convinced several bands of Apaches to take up a settled life of farming under the protection of soldiers at Camp Grant. Filled with rage at all Apaches and accompanied by a number of Tohono O'odham, who were longtime enemies of the Apaches, a group of Tucson citizens massacred some seventy-seven women and children and seven men, and took twenty-nine children whom they sold as slaves.[5]

In what is now central Arizona, Yavapais and Western Apaches continued fighting miners in the Prescott area. Partly in response to public outcry against the Camp Grant Massacre, in 1871, the federal government realized the importance of quickly implementing the Peace Policy in the Southwest and dispatched Vincent Colyer as secretary of the Board of Indian Commissioners "to collect the Apache Indians of Arizona and New Mexico upon reservations . . . and to promote peace and civilization among them."[6] He quickly established four reservations: one at Camp Apache in east central Arizona, one in southwestern New Mexico, one near Camp Grant, and another in Camp Verde in central Arizona. A temporary reservation was also arranged west of Prescott.

Once the Yavapais found their food-collecting rounds disrupted by miners and ranchers, they began raiding ranches for food. Conflict inevitably followed. The Department of War, still in conflict with the Department of Interior, sent General George Crook to confront the Indians who had refused to settle on reservations. In 1872 and 1873, Crook, guided by Indian scouts and auxiliaries, led a campaign against the Yavapais. The Yavapais call the period between 1863 and 1873 "a ten-year Vietnam War," in the words of Camp Verde Chairman Ted Smith.[7]

This decade-long conflict left central Arizona with a legacy of morbid place names, such as Bloody Basin and Skull Valley. Indian families were the casualties at these places, for unlike the well-armed Apaches, the Yavapais only had their hunting weapons to use in battle. Their weaponry was no match for the guns and ammunition of the U.S. Army; during a single encounter in Skeleton

Cave above the Salt River Canyon, soldiers killed nearly eighty Indians. Defeat finally came when the army systematically destroyed their winter food supply.

When most of the Yavapais surrendered in 1873, they were incarcerated with the Tonto Apaches (a Western Apache subtribe) on a reservation in the Verde Valley, where disease soon reduced their population by a third. After the government promised them an irrigation canal, the Yavapais and Apaches excavated an irrigation ditch with wooden sticks, broken shovels, and rusty spoons. Their successful harvests alarmed government contractors in Tucson, who made huge profits by selling low-quality rations to dependent tribes. In 1874, the contractors forced the government to abolish the Verde Reservation and to relocate the people to the San Carlos Apache Reservation near Globe, Arizona. The Yavapais were forced to walk about 180 miles over rugged terrain in midwinter, sustaining themselves only on the wild foods they could gather and hunt. The forced march not only demoralized their spirit but also brought death to most of them: only 200 out of 1,500 remained alive by the time they were allowed to return to their homeland in the 1880s and 1890s.

When the Prescott Yavapais returned to their home territory, they tried to settle at Fort McDowell, an abandoned military post, but most of the arable land was already occupied by Anglo and Mexican squatters. Living near locations where they could perform wage labor, they worked resolutely to obtain reservation status for their communities. It was not until 1903 that Theodore Roosevelt established the Fort McDowell Reservation by executive order. The Yavapai-Prescott community is contained within the city of Prescott, while the Camp Verde Reservation, not established until 1910, had several noncontiguous parcels added throughout the next sixty years, including Middle Verde, Clarkdale, and Rimrock.

Better armed than the Yavapais, the Chiricahuas led armed resistance against efforts to concentrate all Apaches on the San Carlos Reservation, in the Gila River bottoms. Beginning in 1877, **Victorio**, leader of the Warm Springs "renegades," stirred up the Mescaleros and terrorized Anglo settlements, slipping into Mexico when soldiers tried to pursue his band. In 1880, as Mexican troops surrounded them, a sharpshooter killed Victorio. However, the following year, the Chiricahuas, led by **Naiche** and **Geronimo**, fled the San Carlos Reservation for Mexico. In 1883, with the consent of the Mexican government, General Crook led a military expedition guided by Indian scouts into the Sierra Madre. Although he got Geronimo and Naiche to return to San Carlos, conditions there were so bad that another Chiricahua outbreak occurred in 1885. Crook again sent troops and scouts into Mexico and again they surrendered in March 1886. However, the Chiricahuas ran off before they reached the reservation. Lieutenant Charles B. Gatewood, who knew Geronimo, traveled into the Sierra Madre to talk to the leader, who agreed to surrender. Along with those

Chiricahuas who had served as scouts and those who had not fled the reservation, Naiche and Geronimo's group was sent into exile in Florida prisons. In 1887 and 1888, the Chiricahuas were transferred to Mount Vernon Barracks, near Mobile, Alabama, which was hardly any healthier and led to even more sickness and death. More than 20 percent of the over 500 sent to Florida died before the end of 1889.[8] In 1894, the federal government moved the Chiricahuas to Fort Sill, Oklahoma, where they settled into small communities based on their traditional forms of social organization into local groups and began to raise cattle and crops. However, they were never allowed to return to southern Arizona, in contrast to other southwestern tribes whose reservations were established on a portion of their homeland. In 1912, they were given the option of joining the Mescalero Apache on their reservation in New Mexico, which many accepted. Others chose to remain in the Fort Sill area, where they became known as the Fort Sill Apaches.

When the U.S. government had taken control of the territory south of the Gila River through the Gadsden Purchase in 1853, the Tohono O'odham were split between two countries. About two thirds of their territory was in the United States and the other third remained in Mexico. Mexican nationals were given the choice of staying in the United States or returning to Mexican territory. The O'odham, who lived in more isolated parts of their territory, never received this information about the international boundary and continued to maintain allegiance to Mexico decades later.

Land, for Native people, was not an item of individual possession, and therefore they felt little need to document ownership. The Tohono O'odham continued to follow their seasonal pattern of living in the mountains during the dry season and returning to their fields when it rained. During much of the year, their fields and villages were unoccupied. They also lived in other areas for short periods to harvest desert foods. The Tohono O'odham did not build permanent structures in either of their primary villages. However, the intruding settlers considered any land that the government had not ceded to Indian people to be part of the public domain and open for their settlement. When the Tohono O'odham returned to their villages, they discovered that their lands had been taken. Without any knowledge of the legal system, they had no recourse to recover their territory.

By the 1850s, the Tohono O'odham were feeling the pressure of an ever-increasing flood of Anglo-American settlers, ranchers, and miners into their area. Mining was being done on a larger scale, focusing on Ajo's rich copper deposits and gold and silver in the Baboquivari, Comobabi, and Quijotoa mountains. The newcomers drove the Native people from water sources that they and their ancestors had depended upon for centuries. Some Tohono O'odham took jobs on ranches and in the mines. Wells that were dug for mining communities enabled Native people to establish permanent villages, such as Fresnal and Caba-bi, which they could inhabit year-round instead of dividing their time between summer field villages and winter well villages.[9]

In 1857, the government sent John Walker to be the Indian agent for the Papagos, as the Tohono O'odham were known then. Stationed in Tucson, he dealt with the groups there, distributing agricultural hand tools, knives, cooking implements, flour, and other supplies. The rest of the O'odham were essentially ignored. They first experienced government control when government agents chose Many Skirts as the head chief of the Tohono O'odham in 1865. An important leader at San Xavier, he was not recognized as a leader among other groups who were still small and independent,with their own leaders. Mexicans who continued to live in this area cut down the mesquite trees in order to sell the wood in Tucson, denuding the land of a major resource that was never replaced.

After the Civil War, the U.S. military focused on controlling the Apaches, and by the early 1870s, troops had managed to ensure relatively peaceful conditions that enabled the Tohono O'odham to disperse their villages and to broaden the areas that they used for summer fields. In 1870, when pervasive drought conditions returned, the Tohono O'odham developed a livestock industry that became the keystone of their modern village economy. Abandoned during the Apache wars, much of their homeland was now covered with heavy grass, which made it ideal for cattle. In the beginning, cattle were family property, although families herded them together and kept them in a common village corral.[10] Herding, like hunting, required the cooperation and manpower of the entire village, so the position of hunting chief served as the model for the village official who presided over cattle operations. The industry strengthened the political organization of the village by providing important roles for village chiefs and councils of family heads.[11]

Ironically, the federal government overlooked the protection of land for its Native allies such as the O'odham, who fought against the Apaches with Anglo-Americans. Seldom aggressive toward settlers, the O'odham never experienced army troops in their area; however, this meant that the government ignored them and their rights, even though it recognized O'odham peoples as separate tribes. Anglo-American cattlemen were appropriating Tohono O'odham grazing land and water holes. With no treaty to protect their land, the Tohono O'odham asked for reservations. Three were established by executive order: in 1874, the reservation at San Xavier southwest of Tucson, with more than 71,000 acres; in 1882, the Gila Bend Reservation, with 10,235 acres; and in 1916, the main Tohono O'odham Reservation, with its capital at Sells, west of Tucson, with 2,774,370 acres.

The Tohono O'odham had little opportunity for self-sufficiency based on agricultural development because of a cycle of erosion, arroyo cutting, and extreme drought that began in the 1870s.[12] As early as 1881, wells drilled for mines, ranches, and the expanding city of Tucson began to drain the aquifer under Indian land. During the 1890s, severe erosion damaged the channel of the Santa Cruz River, and after 1912, the Bureau of Indian Affairs began to drill for artesian wells at eleven villages on the large Tohono O'odham Reservation. The lowering of the water table since then has seriously endangered the supply of well water.

In contrast, another O'odham group, the Pimas (Akimel O'odham), in the Phoenix area, experienced great prosperity during the first decade of American rule because they provided supplies for some 60,000 prospectors who passed through their territory between 1848 and 1854 en route to California.[13] The Overland Mail Company, which established a route through their villages in 1858, contracted for the entire Pima wheat crop to ship to California settlements. Before and during the Civil War, the U.S. government relied on the Pimas and Maricopas not only to supplement their military forces against the Apaches but also to supply provisions. The construction of a wagon road linking El Paso and Fort Yuma and the opening of the San Antonio–San Diego stage line in 1857 required food and shelter for men and animals; by 1859, Americans had erected several trading posts and mills.

As the Pimas became more enmeshed in the cash economy, the notion of private property began to supplant ideals of reciprocity and sharing in their culture. Their dependence upon Anglo-Americans for income grew, and the construction of Fort McDowell and Fort Grant in 1865 removed the need for a defense perimeter against the Apaches. Pima men could turn their energies from warfare to farming, and the range of Pima settlements expanded. No longer united against a common enemy, the Pimas did not need the militarism, strict discipline, and united effort that had held their society together. During the period from 1862 to 1869, Pimas moved their villages as far upstream from one another as possible, competing for more advantageous irrigation locations.[14] In 1870, at the peak of their prosperity, they produced three million pounds of wheat.[15]

However, 1870 ushered in the driest conditions in 600 years in the Gila watershed, and the Pimas had to cut back their farmland to less than 20 percent of the area that they had farmed in 1859.[16] Their society, overly dependent upon a cash economy based on wheat, experienced conflict over the allocation of water: in 1879 and 1880, warfare between the villages of Santa and Blackwater erupted over this precious resource; between 1878 and 1898, 24 murders occurred; and between 1860 and 1887, 18 "witches" were killed, according to Pima calendar sticks.[17]

At the same time, Anglo-American settlers in record numbers were invading the land above Pima territory, diverting the water. A brief respite of abundant rainfall between 1881 and 1884 encouraged the Florence Canal Company to construct a diversion dam that would have appropriated the entire flow of the Gila River for non-Indian use by 1887, had the company not gone bankrupt. Nevertheless, settlers and cattle ranchers continued to move into the area, diverting the waters of the river. The Spanish cattle had overgrazed the land, a trend continued by ranchers that triggered erosion and floods, such as the 1868 flood that wiped out three Pima villages.

In 1859, the federal government had created the Gila River Reservation for the Pimas and Maricopas, and in 1879, the Salt River Reservation for those who moved north of Phoenix; their water rights were not protected and their fields remained dry. By 1895, the government had to issue rations to the Pimas, who were forced to shift to wage labor to survive. Many refer to this period as the forty years of famine after the river became an empty bed of sand, replacing the green of their fields spread out alongside for many miles when there had been plenty of water. Alcoholism and violence within families and communities increased at an alarming rate during this time.

THE NORTHERN SECTOR OF THE SOUTHWEST

When General Stephen Watts Kearny and his Army of the West took control of New Mexico from Mexico with barely any resistance in 1846, the Pueblos sent their officers to the capital to have them confirmed by the new administration. Lieutenant W. H. Emory, on the staff of General Kearny, later described the impressive demeanor of the Pueblos, calling them our "fast friends now and forever"[18] because of their willingness to accept the control of the United States. Ironically, less than a year later, a mixed mob of Pueblos and Mexicans massacred and scalped Governor Bent and several other officials in Taos. The outbreak, caused by frustration over land grants rather than rebellion against the United States, was quelled by General Sterling Price, who led troops in from Santa Fe. After heavy fighting, the mixed group of Indians and Mexicans surrendered and the leaders were tried and executed. Such armed hostility from the Pueblos, however, was rare.

When the United States signed the Treaty of Guadalupe Hidalgo with Mexico, it gained control of the territory of New Mexico, which includes present-day Arizona north of the Gila River as well as western Colorado, Utah, and part of Wyoming. The treaty recognized the Rio Grande as the Texas border with Mexico. In 1853, the Gadsden Purchase added the rest of what is now Arizona to the United States.

In 1849, James S. Calhoun was appointed the Indian agent for the New Mexico Territory over some 40,000 Pueblos, Apaches, Navajos, and Utes.[19] Emissaries from the Hopi and other western Pueblos came to learn about policies of the new government and to describe outrages they had experienced on the part of California gold seekers and arrogant settlers who demanded food. Navajo raiding also took a toll, and until most of the nomadic tribes were confined to reservations in the late 1870s, the Pueblos considered raiding to be their major concern. Pueblos supplied auxiliary soldiers to U.S. forces for campaign duty against nomadic tribes. The government's attitude was indicated by proclamations that grouped the Pueblos with other citizens of New Mexico in opposition to the Navajos.

At a time when the dominant government policy was isolating Indians on reservations to ensure peace for Anglo expansion, Calhoun faced a major struggle in making Washington officials grasp the differences between Pueblos and Apaches. He sought to get Congress to confirm Pueblo property rights and to have the voting privilege extended to the Pueblos, whom he described as "the only tribe in perfect amity with the government . . . an industrious, agricultural, and pastoral people."[20]

He developed a plan that formalized U.S.–Pueblo relations and marked the boundaries of Indian lands. However, even though he became governor of the territory the next year and held the position of superintendent of Indian affairs ex officio, Congress failed to act on most of his plans. Such inaction undermined the success of Calhoun's program as well as those of later superintendents. In 1858, Congress did confirm the Spanish land grants of a number of New Mexico Pueblos, but not until 1913 did the federal government recognize its responsibility to actively intervene on behalf of Pueblo land claims.[21] The Pueblos continued to receive little attention because of government involvement in military campaigns against hostile Indians in the Plains and West.

Before the Pueblo Revolt and then beginning with the 1823 Jose Antonio Vizcarra campaign, Navajos had been a major target of the slave trade. The number held captive by New Mexicans continued to grow, and the return of their people became the major Navajo concern at treaty negotiations.[22]

The Navajo had also intensified their raiding for livestock as their economy shifted toward pastoralism, and between 1821 and 1848, had waged almost constant warfare with the Mexicans.[23] By the time their territory became part of the United States, herding and raiding had become inextricably linked, for the Navajos' increased reliance on sheep and goats led them to intensify their raids on herds owned by Anglo-American settlers. This enraged the settlers, who responded by capturing more Navajo women and children for the slave trade. It is estimated that between 1846 and 1850, nearly 20,000 horses and mules and 800,000 sheep and cattle were stolen in northwestern New Mexico, and by 1860, it was reported that as many as 5,000 to 6,000 Navajo slaves were living with families in New Mexican villages.[24]

Treaties proved ineffective because the Navajos did not recognize any centralized authority and Anglos never understood the autonomous nature of Navajo bands. Each band, consisting of ten to forty families, had its own agricultural and grazing territory. As a particular group needed animals, food, or material goods, they organized a raid, which became an established means of livelihood. War leaders organized the raids by getting several groups together and paid little attention to headmen who led local groups in times of peace. This meant that when a headman signed a treaty, it had very little force because he represented so few people. After a series of ineffective treaties and misunderstandings, the Department of War and the Territory of New Mexico decided that organized armed force was necessary. The military established a post that later became known as Fort Defiance, with four companies of cavalry, two of infantry, and one of artillery.

The Navajos saw this as an invasion of their territory, especially when the post commander appropriated a prime pasturage for military horses that Navajos had used for their sheep. Navajo animals found on the grazing land were shot. A Navajo shot a black slave who belonged to the post commander, and the Indians refused to give up the murderer. After three expeditions marched against them, another treaty was signed but with no effect. Throughout 1859, soldiers, accompanied by enemy Navajos, Utes, Zunis, Hopis, and other Pueblos serving as scouts and troops, continued their campaign through Navajo country. A force of over two thousand Navajos attacked Fort Defiance in April 1860, but their bows and arrows were hardly a match for military artillery. Within two hours so many had been killed that they withdrew in defeat.

The following year, when more troops were needed in the east because of the Civil War, Fort Defiance was abandoned, leading the Navajos to believe that they were stronger than the Anglo-Americans. However, as soon as Union troops took over New Mexico Territory, they set about destroying any Indian threat to white settlers. Head of New Mexico territorial affairs General James Carleton developed a plan for the forced relocation of Mescalero Apaches and Navajos—who were traditional enemies—to **Bosque Redondo** (Fort Sumner) in east central New Mexico. Although a military board had recommended another location because of poor water, an inadequate supply of wood, and the threat of floods at Bosque Redondo, Carleton insisted on the location.

He appointed Colonel **Kit Carson** to carry out his plan. Carson led his troops against the Mescalero Apaches in southern New Mexico and brought them to Bosque Redondo before setting out against the Navajos. In 1863, Carson and seven hundred New Mexico volunteers used the scorched-earth strategy later employed by General William T. Sherman in his March to the Sea across Georgia. They slaughtered sheep, tore up cornfields, cut down peach trees, and destroyed any potential means of subsistence. The Utes, Pueblos, and Mexicans, longtime enemies of the Navajo, increased the frequency and ferocity of their raids by seizing Navajo sheep and horses and capturing women and children for slaves. Although the Navajos dispersed to distant areas in search of food and shelter, often with other groups of Indians, by the end of 1864, about eight thousand Navajos surrendered at Fort Defiance, where they began the **Long Walk** to Bosque Redondo. A death march for hundreds, the Long Walk and the succeeding four years of captivity became a focal point for their identity that continues to live in Navajo consciousness today.

By 1865, the Mescalero Apaches had broken away from Bosque Redondo; they eventually accepted another reservation in the Capitan Mountains near Fort Stanton in 1871. Meanwhile, the Navajos were dying in great numbers at Bosque Redondo, which was basically a concentration camp. Carleton had vastly underestimated the number of Navajos and had adequate food, blankets, and shelter for only half of them. Within months, more than two thousand had died of disease brought on by crowded conditions, bad water, and insufficient food resulting from inadequate rations and continued crop failure.

After **Barboncito**, who had been recognized by the U.S. government as "head chief," traveled to Washington in 1868 to plead for his people's return to their country, the government instituted an investigation and decided General Carleton's plan had failed. Recognizing the economic infeasibility and the inhumanity of continued detention, officials decided to make a treaty with Navajo leaders that would allow them to return to a fraction of their former territory. The government provided farming equipment, seeds, cattle, sheep, and goats. The Navajos kept their part of the bargain, ending large-scale raiding. At the same time, they developed a sense of tribal unity for the first time in their history, based on the shared experience of the Long Walk.

Recovery after their return from Bosque Redondo was slow because of drought, corrupt Indian agents, and raiding by other groups, but eventually harvests improved and their herds increased, giving the tribe a degree of economic independence. However, almost as soon as they had been issued sheep and goats, the Navajos, seeking pasturage, expanded beyond the boundaries of their new reservation, creating conflict with white settlers.

In 1876, when the southeastern part of the Navajo Reservation was surveyed for what would become the Santa Fe Railroad, the Navajos were forced to relinquish sections of some of their finest winter pasturage to the railroad and to Anglo settlers. When Navajo leader **Manuelito** went to Washington to protest, he learned that both Navajos and Anglos would be free to homestead the area and that in compensation, lands north of the San Juan River would be given to the Navajos.

A renewal of raiding had become a serious problem by 1879. When these depredations against Zuni and Mexican settlements east and south of the reservation threatened the peace, Manuelito and **Ganado Mucho**, "subchief" of the western part of the reservation, carried out a "purge" of forty "witches"—as the Navajos who were responsible for the raiding were labeled.

Trading posts played a major role in the diffusion of Anglo culture, especially after 1867. Living in the Navajo community where the post was located, the trader and his family encouraged wool production and the development of a market for weaving and jewelry. They also mediated family and tribal problems, sold goods, buried Navajo dead, and helped Navajos in communicating with the world of Anglo-American bureaucracy.[25] By 1873, Navajo blankets had become an important source of income, and in 1874, Lorenzo Hubbell opened a trading post in what became the town of Ganado, Arizona, so named because it was the home of the Navajo leader. Anglo-American influences increased when the first train arrived in 1881 and a coal mine opened in Gallup, New Mexico, south of Fort Defiance.

As the Navajo population and livestock outgrew their original land base, the government added land to the west in 1878, to the south and east in 1880, and to the north in 1884. The Hopi reservation was created in 1882, but the Navajos were encouraged to expand into the area by the local Indian agent, later called a superintendent, who administered government programs. More homesteaders moved into New Mexico Territory after the early 1880s, and clashes between Navajos and Anglo-Americans became common, especially in the southeast area where railroad land checkerboarded Navajo land.

In compliance with the treaty of 1868, schools were established that Native children were compelled to attend. The Navajos, however, considered education to be a threat to their way of life and to the Navajo family, and parents resisted sending their children to boarding schools that were often so far away that the children were not able to return home even in the summer.

THE WESTERN SECTOR OF THE SOUTHWEST

For the Hualapais, conflict with Anglo-American intruders followed a pattern similar to that experienced by their relatives, the Yavapais. After a wagon road was constructed through the center of their country in 1857, the Hualapais had continuous contact with immigrants. Known then as the "35th Parallel Route," this trail from the Rio Grande to California would eventually become Route 66. In 1859, in response to Mojave raiding, the U.S. military built Fort Mojave on the western edge of Pai country. After a brief respite during the Civil War, the Pai were inundated with Anglo-Americans who began to settle in the central mountains. Prospectors flooded the area when gold was discovered in 1863 and mines opened near Prescott. In 1863, when Arizona Territory was created from New Mexico Territory, business began booming to supply the new capital cities, first Fort Whipple and then Prescott. Men blazed hundreds of miles of mule trails and wagon roads to bring goods from steamboat ports at La Paz, Fort Mojave, and Hardyville on the Colorado River.

Ranchers followed prospectors and soldiers, their herds trampling, devouring, and displacing the wild plants and game that had sustained Upland Yuman peoples. When Pais killed horses, mules, and oxen for food, settlers demanded their removal. In 1865 the Hualapai Wars erupted when drunken Anglos murdered a Hualapai leader. The Hualapais retaliated by killing miners, and the U.S. Army retaliated by setting fire to their villages. Tenacious fighters led by brilliant leaders, the Hualapais fought so fiercely that "officers from Prescott say they would prefer fighting five Apaches to one Hualapai."[26]

However, the army burned camp after camp, killing nearly a quarter of the Hualapai population by the end of 1868. Further weakened by an epidemic of whooping cough, the Hualapais surrendered and were forced to walk to La Paz, near present-day Ehrenburg on the Colorado River. Disease, spoiled rations, and starvation took their toll, and many died, weakened from the heat and humidity to which they, as lifelong mountain dwellers, were not accustomed. In the spring of 1875, the Hualapais left for home, trudging for days over plains of sagebrush until they reached the pine-covered hills of their homeland ("Hualapai" means "people of the pine trees"). When they neared their old homesites, the people "began to run, laughing and shouting."[27]

Their leader promised the territorial governor that they would remain at peace, and the Hualapais were allowed to stay in their homeland. By then, most of the land was held by Anglo settlers and miners and their traditional means of subsistence was gone, so the Hualapais were forced to become laborers in the mines and on ranches. In 1881 railroad crews diverted the spring water that had made farming possible for the Peach Springs band, forcing them to give up their fields; the Peach Springs depot site eventually grew into the central Hualapai village.[28]

The Hualapais managed to survive through wage work and as army scouts who tracked the Chiricahua Apaches. Concerned for the welfare of their scouts, the army recommended a Hualapai Reservation, which was established in 1883, south of the Grand Canyon on about a tenth of their original territory.

The Hualapais were one of the few groups in the Southwest to send people to become disciples of the Ghost Dance prophet, Wovoka. Wovoka's message was based on the promise that the performance of the Ghost Dance—a movement that by 1889 was sweeping Indian country—would bring their dead loved ones back to life, ensure the peaceful disappearance of Anglo-Americans, and restore the earth to its natural balance. The Hualapais held their first Ghost Dance in 1889.[29] But when the performance failed to revive a man who had just died, they lost faith in this practice and held their last Ghost Dance in 1895.[30]

Unlike other Upland Yumans, the Havasupais were not forced to flee or to fight for their land. Protected in their isolated area deep in the Grand Canyon, they were not defeated but did lose most of their land, including their fields at Moenkopi near Tuba City, to Mormons and Navajos. In the early 1880s, government officials who did not understand the importance of their winter hunting-and-gathering territory on the rim of the Grand Canyon restricted the Havasupais to a 518-acre parcel of land in Cataract Canyon, a side branch of the Grand Canyon where they farmed during the summer.

Having heard Hualapai accounts of their forced removal to La Paz, the Havasupais agreed to this small area. Many families, however, continued to winter in their old homes on the plateau, although hunting became increasingly difficult because of an influx of tourists, prospectors, and ranchers with herds of cattle and flocks of sheep. Once sections of railroad land were released for homestead and mineral rights in the late 1880s, even more Anglo settlers flooded into the area.

In the 1880s the Havasupais, suffering from malnutrition caused by a shortage of game and foods that they had hunted and gathered on the plateau, became even more susceptible to diseases and began dying from smallpox, measles, and influenza. In desperation, they joined the Hualapais in the performance of the Ghost Dance. In 1891, the Havasupais held a four-day Ghost Dance in Cataract Canyon, which was witnessed by several Hopis.[31] The Havasupais continued the practice until the early years of the twentieth century.

The Native peoples along the Colorado River were the last to feel the onslaught of Anglo-American settlers. Intertribal warfare, so interwoven into the fabric of River Yuman cultures that its origin was included in their stories of creation, had brought about considerable change in tribal territories. By the nineteenth century, only the Mojaves, Quechans, and Cocopahs lived on the Colorado River. First identified by the Spanish as the Cocomaricopa, the Maricopas, as they are known today, had moved eastward to settle along the middle Gila River near the Pimas. By 1840, the remnants of other River and Delta Yuman tribes—the Halyikwamais, Kahwans, Halchidhomas, and Kavelchadom—had joined the Maricopas. After they had expelled the Halchidhomas, the Mojaves invited, or at least tolerated, the arrival of the Chemehuevis, a group that had broken away from the Las Vegas Southern Paiutes. By the early 1850s, the Chemehuevis had claimed the rich Chemehuevi and Colorado River valleys. These groups continued to live in the lush, linear oasis of the Colorado River Valley until Anglo-Americans realized the strategic importance of the river. From the mid-1800s until construction of the railroad in 1877, they relied on it as a major transportation route, using a fleet of steamboats to supply troops stationed at Fort Yuma and Fort Mojave and miners in the gold fields of California and Arizona.

The Mojave (Ahamakav, "the people who live along the river") homeland encompassed a vast area that straddled the Colorado River and extended some 15 miles north of present-day Davis Dam almost to present-day Blythe, California, and south for nearly 170 miles. Encountering Anglo-American trappers and fur traders in the 1820s, the Mojaves served as guides through rough mountain terrain and across the desert along the Mojave Trail to the Pacific coast. They were known as great travelers and sometimes covered 100 miles a day in a loping run. Encounters with Anglo-Americans increased by the late 1840s as explorers sought a route for a transcontinental railroad, steamboat captains attempted to determine the navigability of the Colorado River, and prospectors came through their country en route to California gold fields.

Distracted by intertribal warfare, the Mojaves were still reeling from their unprecedented defeat by the Pimas and Maricopas in 1857 when they attacked a wagon train the following year. The U.S. military responded by building Fort Mojave in the Mojave Valley and used rifles to mow down Mojave warriors in 1859, ending any resistance. Mojave leader Irrateba (also spelled Irataba, Arateba, and Yara Tav) and his followers decided to move to the Colorado River Valley, where the Colorado River Indian Tribes' Reservation (CRIT) was established in 1865. The CRIT Reservation runs north to south along 90 miles of shoreline, stretching from just north of Parker, Arizona nearly to Blythe, California, with acreage in both Arizona and California. Nearly three quarters of the tribe chose to remain behind with Chief Homose Kohote in the Mojave Valley, where the Fort Mojave Reservation was established in 1911.

When the Southern Paiute Chemehuevis moved into the Colorado River area in the early 1850s, they numbered a few hundred people. Although they continued to speak their language in the Uto-Aztecan language family, they adopted many Mojave traits, such as floodplain farming and a sense of tribal unity based on warfare. By 1904, the Chemehuevis were considered to be the most successful farmers on the river.[32] That year, the government established the Chemehuevi Reservation to protect their land in the Chemehuevi Valley. About 200 Chemehuevis decided to join the Mojaves on the CRIT Reservation; the Mojaves had settled on the north end near Parker, and the Chemehuevis took up residence farther south.

The Quechans (Yumans), another River Yuman people, lived along the Colorado River at its confluence with the Gila River, one of the few river crossings in east-west routes. Their control over such a strategic position made them important in precontact trade and later in Spanish, Mexican, and Anglo-American trade and travel. The U.S. Army built Fort Yuma in 1852 to protect American interests by assuring the growth of steamship and railroad travel in the area, and the town of Yuma, Arizona grew around this army post. During the California gold rush, the Quechans ferried prospectors across the river, but when Anglo competitors put them out of business, they became pilots and woodcutters. After the completion of the railroad in 1877 ended the steamship industry, men found employment as laborers while women worked as domestic help. In 1844, the government established a reservation for the Quechans on the west side of the Colorado River. Over the next ten years, Anglo settlers became so envious of these farmlands that they coerced tribe members and in some cases forged their signatures on a fraudulent "agreement" with the federal government. This document promised the Indians irrigation water in return for the cession of land that remained after individual allotments were issued in a local application of the Dawes Severalty Act of 1887. This resulted in the loss of the Quechans' most fertile land along the river.[33]

Farthest south on the Colorado River, some Cocopah families were divided by the international border when they came under Anglo-American control, experiencing a situation similar to that of the Tohono O'odham. Until U.S. immigration officials stopped their seasonal movement across the border in the 1930s, they remained in close contact. Cocopah leader Frank Tehanna pressured the government to establish a reservation for the Cocopahs in the United States in Somerton, Arizona in 1917.

NOTES

1. Commissioner of Indian Affairs, *Annual Reports to the Secretary of the Interior* (1858; reprint, New York: AMS Press, 1976–1977), 9.

2. Robert M. Utley, *Frontiersmen in Blue: The United States Army and the Indian, 1848–1865* (New York: Macmillan, 1967), 216.

3. William T. Hagan, "United States Indian Policies, 1860–1900," in *Handbook of North American Indians: History of Indian-White Relations*, vol. 4, ed. Wilcomb E. Washburn (Washington, D.C.: Smithsonian Institution Press, 1988), 53.

4. Edward H. Spicer, *Cycles of Conquest* (Tucson: University of Arizona Press, 1962), 245.

5. Spicer, *Cycles of Conquest*, 250.

6. Spicer, *Cycles of Conquest*, 250.

7. Stephen Trimble, *The People: Indians of the American Southwest* (Santa Fe: School of American Research Press, 1993), 233.

8. Morris E. Opler, "Chiricahua Apache," in *Handbook of North American Indians: The Southwest*, vol. 10, ed. Alfonso Ortiz (Washington, D.C.: Smithsonian Institution Press, 1983), 408.

9. Paul Ezell, "History of the Pima," in *Handbook of North American Indians: The Southwest*, vol. 10, ed. Alfonso Ortiz (Washington, D.C.: Smithsonian Institution Press, 1983), 167.

10. Robert A. Hackenberg, "Pima and Papago Ecological Adaptations," in *Handbook of North American Indians: The Southwest*, vol. 10, ed. Alfonso Ortiz (Washington, D.C.: Smithsonian Institution Press, 1983), 167.

11. Hackenberg, "Pima and Papago Ecological Adaptations," 167.

12. Hackenberg, "Pima and Papago Ecological Adaptations," 167.

13. Hackenberg, "Pima and Papago Ecological Adaptations," 170.

14. Hackenberg, "Pima and Papago Ecological Adaptations," 170.

15. Silas St. John, Letter, Pima Villages, New Mexico, to A. B. Greenwood, Commissioner of Indian Affairs, Washington, D.C., 16 September 1859, in Letters Received—Pima Agency, 1859–61, Record Group 75, National Archives, Washington, D.C. Bernard L. Fontana, "The Faces and Forces of Pimería Alta," in *Voices from the Southwest*, ed. D. C. Dickinson, D. Laird, and M. Maxwell (Flagstaff, Ariz.: Northland Press, 1976), 51.

16. Annual Reports to the Secretary of the Interior (1870; reprint, New York: AMS Press, 1976–67), 338.

17. Frank Russell,"The Pima Indians," in *26th Annual Report of the Bureau of American Ethnology for the Years 1904–1905* (1908; reprint, Tucson: University of Arizona Press, 1975), 3–389.

18. U.S. Army Corps of Topographical Engineers, *Lieutenant Emory Reports: A Reprint of Lieutenant W. H. Emory's Notes of a Military Reconnaissance*, ed. Ross Calvin (Albuquerque: University of New Mexico Press, 1951), 58.

19. Marc Simmons, "History of the Pueblos Since 1821," in *Handbook of North American Indians: The Southwest*, vol. 9 (Washington, D.C.: Smithsonian Institution Press, 1979), 209.

20. William A. Keleher, *Turmoil in New Mexico, 1846–1868* (Santa Fe: Rydal Press, 1952), 44–45.

21. Simmons, "History of the Pueblos Since 1821," 210.

22. David M. Brugge, "Navajos in the Catholic Church Records of New Mexico, 1694–1875," *Research Report* 1 (Window Rock, Ariz.: The Navajo Tribe, Parks and Recreation Research Section, 1973), 61–66.

23. Frank McNitt, *Navajo Wars, Military Campaigns, Slave Raids and Reprisals* (Albuquerque: University of New Mexico Press, 1972), 59–91.

24. Spicer, *Cycles of Conquest*, 216–217.

25. Frank McNitt, *The Indian Traders* (Norman: University of Oklahoma Press, 1962).

26. Henry Dobyns and Robert Euler, *The Navajo Indians* (Phoenix: Indian Tribal Series, 1972), 46.

27. Stephen Hirst, *Havsuw 'Baaja: People of the Blue Green Water* (Supai, Ariz.: Havasupai Tribe, 1985), 46.

28. Trimble, *The People*, 205.

29. Hirst, *Havsuw 'Baaja*, 56.

30. Henry Dobyns and Robert Euler, "The Ghost Dance of 1889 Among the Pai Indians of Northwestern Arizona," *Prescott College Studies in Anthropology* 1 (1967).

31. Hirst, *Havsuw 'Baaja*, 56.

32. Trimble, *The People*, 407.

33. Robert L. Bee, "Quechan," in *Native America in the Twentieth Century: An Encyclopedia*, ed. Mary Davis (New York: Garland, 1994), 524.

CHAPTER 4

Surrender, Self-Determination, and Sovereignty

The ordeal of the Chiricahua Apache people was, in many ways, a barometer of anti-Indian racism in the Southwest and in the United States as a whole. When Naiche and his band of about 20 Chiricahua Apaches surrendered in 1886, despite government promises to the contrary, they were not allowed to join their families; instead they were imprisoned in Florida, Alabama, and Oklahoma for 27 years. The federal government then designated every Chiricahua man, woman, and child a prisoner of war, whether or not they had participated in warfare against the United States, and also exiled them from their homeland. This included those who had served as scouts for the U.S. Army and those who had been living peacefully on the reservation, more than 400 people.

After the Civil War, the United States needed a new beginning. Many Anglo-Americans had lost families and homes in the war; some had even lost an entire way of life, and the promise of the American West beckoned to them. Ranchers, farmers, and speculators pressed westward as four new trunk railways linked the Pacific to the rest of the country; Americans settled more land in the last three decades of the nineteenth century than they had during the previous 300 years.[1] In order to build an empire, a rigid division with a strict social and cultural hierarchy must be constructed and upheld between members of the dominant society and members of the subaltern societies that they overcome. This distinction is based on the fear that acknowledging the authenticity of previously excluded historical narratives of minority groups threatens the social coherence of the nation. In the nineteenth century, the United States was constructing not only its national boundaries but also its national identity based on the principle of Manifest Destiny. The country could not afford to acknowledge that the cost of this enterprise was being paid by the indigenous peoples of the continent, for that would have brought into question the morality of the entire project.

How Anglo-Americans reacted to tribal peoples in North America depended in large part upon the degree of difference they perceived from themselves. The Spanish considered the Pueblos to be "civilized" because they lived in agricultural communities that were not totally dissimilar from their own. Anglo-Americans applauded the Akimel O'odham for their industriousness and contribution to the market economy by raising and selling wheat to the army and to prospectors and settlers traveling to destinations farther west.

However, Anglo-Americans had a far different response to nomadic groups because their way of life and their appearance were so utterly alien. Furthermore, these groups showed no intention of acknowledging the benefits of "civilization" by relinquishing their traditional ways of life. Those whose populations had been decimated by European-introduced diseases posed little threat, and it was not until after the Civil War that the Apaches experienced the full brunt of U.S. military force. However, military confrontation was inevitable, especially when the destruction of their traditional subsistence patterns led them to rely on raiding as a way of life. The Apaches, and the Chiricahuas in particular, came to embody resistance to civilization; ironically, by the time they were transported to Florida, the Seminole wars were so long in the past that Floridians considered the Apaches a tourist attraction. Geronimo, Naiche's strategist, and the unfettered and dangerous life that he embodied became exotic commodities that would bring income to Florida cities, and Pensacola and Saint Augustine vied for the prestige that his celebrity would bring.

Why did the Chiricahuas surrender? They made a choice not only so that families could be reunited but also so that their people would not die off completely. Eugene Chihuahua explained that his father, Chihuahua, was the first of the chiefs to surrender so that his men could rejoin their families, who were already in custody, and so that his people could live on: "My father, like Cochise, did not want to see his band exterminated; and he well understood what was in store for them if they continued to fight the losing fight."[2]

Although the Chiricahuas' internment as prisoners of war in prisons and on military bases was unique, their experience illustrates many of the trends of the reservation era and the extreme pressure that was exerted upon Indian peoples to assimilate. Federal Indian policy at the beginning of the twentieth century was intended to gradually reduce Indian land holdings to make way for settler expansion and to educate and assimilate Indian children into Anglo-American culture. Reservation life was meant to be transitional in nature, despite the language of the treaties that stipulated the federal government's continuing commitment as a trustee for Indian nations. State officials, federal policy makers, and the non-Indian residents of the Southwest anticipated the day when reservation land would be opened to settlement and exploitation of natural resources by non-Indians. Nevertheless, Native communities managed to hold onto some of their land, withstanding the enormous pressures of forced assimilation. Although the Chiricahuas were forced to relinquish their territory, they maintained their underlying cultural values by practicing their ceremonies, reciting oral histories, and producing hide paintings that recorded the core of their identity, the girl's puberty ceremony.[3]

FORCED ASSIMILATION AND LAND LOSS

The surrender of the Chiricahua Apaches in 1886 marked the end of significant military resistance to the westward expansion of the United States. In 1887, the federal government passed the **Dawes Severalty Act**, which was driven by the goal of forced assimilation to "civilize" Indians. The knowledge of how to handle individually owned, or allotted, property was considered to be a major condition of civilization. A sense of responsibility that came from the experience of private land ownership would help to prepare Indians for citizenship. Individual land ownership was also believed to stimulate economic improvement and industriousness and, above all, a desire to be like Anglo-Americans. Tribal ties would then disappear.

In the Southwest, only small portions of the Navajo, Akimel O'odham, Tohono O'odham, and Colorado River Indian Tribes Reservations were allotted, and the program was not followed through, except on a small part of the Navajo reservation that was opened to Anglo settlement. One reason southwestern lands were not allotted in the period between 1913 and 1921 was the opposition of Commissioner **Cato Sells**, a Texas banker who argued that these semi-arid lands would not support Indians and that the Indians had not been sufficiently educated to protect themselves.[4]

Reformers and expansionists shared a paternalistic perspective that considered the Anglo-American lifestyle to be superior and Indian peoples in need of protection and guidance from representatives of this superior society.[5] Both groups considered schools to be a crucial vehicle for "civilizing" American Indian children. In 1879, Lieutenant Richard Pratt established Carlisle Industrial Training School in Pennsylvania. Pratt argued that removing the child from the tribal environment increased the efficacy of assimilation into Anglo-American values, appropriate behavior, and useful skills for a self-sufficient future. Probably the most famous off-reservation boarding school, Carlisle was based on a military regime that was thought to instill a sense of discipline crucial to the assimilation process. This meant that children were forced to relinquish their languages and clothing when they arrived. Officials cut the boys' hair and pinned the girls' hair neatly onto their heads in a reflection of Anglo-American styles. Boys were forced to put on trousers and military uniforms, while girls had to wear long, modest dresses with petticoats and undergarments that cinched in their waists. In addition to studying academic subjects as well as various trades and vocations, students were expected to work part time to help defray the administrative costs of their education.

The loss of their children to boarding schools was devastating to American Indian families. It was even worse for the Chiricahua Apache imprisoned at Fort Marion in Saint Augustine, Florida, far from the Southwest. Their greatest fear at the time of imprisonment was the breaking up of their families, and it was soon justified when Richard Henry Pratt took 44 of their children in December 1886 and the following April, another 62. The Chiricahua had been able to avoid much of the contagion experienced by other groups because of their limited contact with Europeans. Their dispersed population had helped them escape the devastating death rates experienced by such sedentary groups as the Pueblos. However, boarding schools were ideal places for the spread of disease, and students were particularly susceptible to tuberculosis. At least a hundred Chiricahua children died from tuberculosis at Carlisle Institute.[6]

After Carlisle was closed in 1918, a national school system for Indians was organized, with day schools and government boarding schools on reservations. Catholic and Protestant missionaries also operated schools on the reservations. Off-reservation boarding schools included Haskell in Kansas, Genoa in Nebraska, and Chilocco in Indian Territory. In the 1890s, conditions in Indian schools worsened due to congressional budget cuts that led to shortages in food, clothing, and shelter. Crowded conditions provided an ideal environment for the spread of highly contagious tuberculosis.

Although not directly linked to the Dawes Act, the Religious Crimes Codes of 1883 were also driven by the government's assimilationist goals. This legislation suppressed Native ceremonies, especially those that seemed most offensive to missionary groups. In an effort to replace Native beliefs and practices with Christianity, the government funded missionary-managed reservation schools and assigned different reservations to different denominations.

The Religious Crimes Codes were impossible to enforce, and any attempts to do so only meant that certain ceremonies were practiced in secret. Although missionary schools replaced some aspects of Native religion, their primary effect was the addition of diversity to existing religious beliefs and practices. The boarding school program, however, had a major impact on southwestern Indians, and from the 1890s to the 1930s roughly a quarter of the children experienced boarding school life.[7]

Throughout the history of the United States, the federal government and the military have had conflicting viewpoints and have worked at cross-purposes, vacillating from one administration to another. Nowhere was this more evident than in the treatment of American Indians, and the situation endured by the Chiricahua Apache prisoners of war illustrates many of the trends of the reservation era. Representatives in Congress tried to satisfy the demands of their constituents; officers favored military action; and Indian rights organizations sought to protect the well-being of Native peoples. Torn between benevolence and severity, the federal government struggled to satisfy the demands of the Department of War and the Department of the Interior and to respond to President Grant's Peace Policy that had created a Board of Indian Commissioners to evaluate and direct the administration of Indian affairs. Seldom did those in Washington understand or experience actual conditions in the local area, which were characterized by complex relationships among several groups.

The Department of the Interior, which was repeatedly entreated by the Department of War to take custody of the Chiricahuas, failed to foster the means to economic self-reliance for the tribe.[8] When the Chiricahuas were moved to Fort Sill, Oklahoma, in 1894, they were told that this would be their permanent home. But by 1910, the military decided to take over Fort Sill for artillery training and displaced the Indians who lived there. Allowing the Chiricahuas to return to their homeland was out of the question because of the undiminished hatred toward them in the Southwest. In 1913, most of the Chiricahuas moved to the Mescalero Apache Reservation in New Mexico, and the following year, those who had chosen to remain in Oklahoma were placed on allotments. Both groups were finally freed from their status as prisoners of war.

For most of the Indians in the Southwest, who were allowed to remain on a portion of their homelands, administration was handled by Indian agents who lived on the reservation and used funds provided by the Bureau of Indian Affairs (BIA). Agents gave orders to their employees, who consisted of government farmers and teachers; maintained technical assistance to the Indians; secured pupils for schools; and protected the Indians from the encroachment of Anglo-American settlers near the reservation. State governments had no control over reservation affairs, and state populations soon became antagonistic to reservation communities. Even though the Indians did not directly control their own affairs, many understaffed, poorly funded local agencies depended upon people in the Native community for the implementation of programs, which made it possible for Native peoples to subvert the assimilationist agenda and to adapt new conditions to their own terms.

Nevertheless, southwestern Indian communities felt the influence of the superintendent and his staff on the development of their reservations. Without allotment, superintendents concentrated on developing existing resources, such as farming and stock raising. Although little was accomplished in comparison with off-reservation improvements, some advances were made: increased acreage of irrigated land, crop improvement, and increased grazing land. The appropriation of water resources by the expanding white population presented an escalating problem.

By the late 1920s, conditions on reservations had become so severe that the federal government launched an investigation. Native leaders in the Southwest had been claiming that poverty was rampant, boarding schools had damaged their children, and Indian people should be allowed to practice their traditions openly. Indian rights groups also called for reforms to federal Indian policy. In 1928, the federal government responded with *The Problem of Indian Administration*, a document popularly known as the **Meriam Report.** Through on-site interviews with Indians and non-Indians on reservations and at off-reservation boarding schools, specialists confirmed that living conditions were deplorable and that Native Americans lived in poverty, were in poor health, and received substandard education. Highly critical of federal policy, the congressional committee reviewing the report recommended improvement in the administration of these areas through the BIA.

CULTURAL PLURALISM AND PATERNALISTIC POLICIES

In the aftermath of the Meriam Report and the election of Franklin Roosevelt in 1932, federal Indian policy changed abruptly. Cultural pluralism and the rebuilding of self-sufficient Indian communities replaced the goal of forced assimilation. However, without any Indian representation, a paternalistic system of government led to economic development on the reservations that lagged far behind off-reservation development. For example, while the government plan for the Pimas along the Gila River encouraged them to become small farmers on ten-acre irrigated plots, off-reservation economic development entailed much larger farm units with more highly mechanized agriculture.[9]

Albert B. Fall, a senator from New Mexico who later became Secretary of the Interior, advocated the termination of federal responsibility to Indians. Fall was convinced that the large nontaxable reservations in the Southwest were impeding the economic development of the entire region. Between 1922 and 1923, he introduced or supported four bills that applied mainly to the nonallotted reservation Indians of the region and their land rights. One bill supported Anglo settlers along the Rio Grande and would have resulted in a loss of Pueblo land and water rights and threatened their culture, while another bill provided for the allotment of the Mescalero Apache reservation and the creation of a national park from part of the reservation. The third bill gave the Secretary of the Interior power to enforce the termination of most federally recognized tribes by appraising the value of their properties, distributing the tribal wealth among competent Indians, and ending any future federal responsibility to them. Finally, the last bill opened all Indian reservations to oil development by permitting the state and the Department of the Interior Bureau of Reclamation to share oil royalties equally with the Indians.[10]

In 1924, these bills were defeated with the help of public outcry generated by Indian defense groups. The **American Indian Defense Association** was the most outspoken of the Indian rights societies that were active in the 1920s. **John Collier**, its executive director, led this small group of wealthy, liberal individuals primarily from California. Convinced that individualism and materialism were destroying Western civilization, Collier believed that the values inherent in Pueblo society could save it.[11] In 1922, he stated the goals of what would become the American Indian Defense Association the following year: Indians' rights to basic civil liberties must be recognized; remaining Indian reservations should be conserved through communal and corporate enterprises; Indian cultures and societies must be preserved; federal assistance must be extended to Indian communities through Department of Agriculture advice and assistance programs, public health services, and Farm Loan Bank credits.[12]

Collier helped create the **All-Pueblo Council** to show that Indians could organize effectively as a political entity to defend their rights and had the potential for self-government. This lobbying organization lacked formal powers but provided a means of inter-Pueblo communication regarding federal legislation that threatened its members' rights. The Bureau of Indian Affairs tried to dissolve the council and eventually formed an organization of its own, the U.S. Pueblo Indian Council, which Collier encouraged the All-Pueblo Council not to join.

Between 1922 and 1924, Collier clashed repeatedly with Commissioner Burke on the issue of Indian religious freedom. Misled by Protestant church groups opposed to Indian practices, Burke held that certain Native religious ceremonials should be abolished. In response to criticism that the government had not upheld its responsibilities in the area of Indian education, Burke favored sending Pueblo children to distant boarding schools. Collier led opposition to both practices, especially restraint of Native religious practices.

The **Indian Citizenship Act of 1924** (43 U.S. Stat. 253) decreed that all Indians were citizens of the United States, with all the rights and obligations of citizens, if they lived away from a reservation. Even if they resided on a reservation, they could still vote for state and national officials, unless they lived in

Arizona or New Mexico; Indians in those two states were not allowed to vote until 1949.

The year after John Collier became Commissioner of Indian Affairs in 1933, he introduced into Congress the **Indian Reorganization Act (IRA)**, also known as the Wheeler-Howard Act. Its provisions included the promotion of local Indian self-government through tribal constitutional governments. This act also completely stopped land allotments. Emphasis shifted from off-reservation boarding schools to on-reservation day schools, which meant that children could attend school and stay close to their families. Future congressional policy was also supposed to promote the study of Indian cultures.

Even though he was forced to compromise on important aspects of the Indian Reorganization Act, Collier still found ways to work toward his original goals, such as persuading Congress to establish the Indian Arts and Crafts Board (49 U.S. Stat. 891) to promote economic development through arts and crafts. He also obtained funds to purchase and rehabilitate Indian lands, especially in the Southwest, through contracts with the Public Works Administration, the Resettlement Administration, and its successor, the Farm Security Administration.[13]

Although it was never organized under the regulations of the IRA, what came to be known as the Navajo Tribal Council functioned almost identically to the tribal councils instituted under the act. The first stage in the development of an intercommunity organization to represent the Navajo Tribe (today, the Navajo Nation) began when government agents appointed former war chiefs to control raiding. When **Manuelito** died, the system of overall organization broke down except for non-Indian BIA superintendents. In the next stage, a group of Navajos were selected by Anglos to advise government agents; in the final stage, power was given to an elected representative group that functioned under a constitution and assumed some responsibility for internal affairs within reservation boundaries.[14]

The Navajo Tribal Council had met for the first time in 1923. As early as 1901, the federal government had begun to subdivide the administrative structure of the Navajo area, when Tuba City was designated as the headquarters of the western Navajo (Diné); in 1902, a separate agency was established at Keams Canyon for the lands occupied by the Hopis and the surrounding territory occupied by the Navajos. The government established the San Juan or northern agency in 1903, while continuing to administer the southern half from Fort Defiance. In 1907, Crownpoint became the agency headquarters for Pueblo Bonito (Eastern Navajo), and in 1908, the Leupp agency was created to supervise the 1901 executive order supplement.[15]

Although assimilationist rhetoric persisted through the first decade of the twentieth century, American popular thought about Indians was "pushed aside by racism, nostalgia, and disinterest," as Frederick Hoxie has pointed out.[16] The

BIA's primary motivation was the establishment of a body that could represent tribally held resources, thus facilitating transactions with mineral companies that wanted to drill on Navajo land, administer timber resources, and develop the underground water supply for stock purposes. At the same time, non-Indian farmers and ranchers wanted to restrict the expansion of Navajo lands. Complicating the situation was the location of the Navajo Reservation in three territories (later three states). Earlier, the railroad had been granted land south and east of the reservation through a checkerboard arrangement that granted alternative sections of the executive-order reservation to one or more of three companies. Thus, instead of owning a continuous area, the Navajos only owned the sections not owned by the companies.[17]

Due to the size of the Navajo Reservation, the tribal council was ill equipped to deal with local issues, and by 1927, the reservation was divided into smaller units, known as chapters. The people in each chapter elected officers who met to discuss specific issues, and in many ways, the chapter organization formalized the existing tradition of local groups. Eventually, 110 chapters were established within the Navajo Nation; they not only dealt with local issues but also helped to keep the tribal council informed about concerns around the reservation. However, the 1923 *Regulations Related to the Navajo Tribe of Indians*, the document that provided for the Navajo Tribal Council, had no plan for the establishment of a governing body as an instrument for tribal self-determination; the federal government intended to maintain tight control over reservation affairs.[18]

Despite his good intentions, Commissioner Collier came to be greatly disliked by the Navajos because his programs threatened their relative economic independence and isolation from Anglo society. One of the few tribes in the United States that had experienced such independence, the Navajos remained prosperous through their herding economy and rug-weaving industry until the Great Depression of the 1930s. Most other tribes had to endure heavy-handed paternalism, but the Navajos did not need as much government support, which meant that the government lacked the economic leverage with them that it had with other tribes.[19]

Coming out of the Indian Reorganization Act, the **Johnson-O'Malley Act** broke down some of the social isolation of reservation populations by enabling the Bureau of Indian Affairs or the tribal councils to contract with state governments or private corporations. Although they were still separate from the local governments of their areas, Native peoples were no longer limited to contact with federal bureau officials. Instead, they began to participate more in the societies that surrounded their reservations. Conceived of as a transitional vehicle, "the medium of the tribe as an organized entity set up to deal with the outside influences" was considered to be the best way to encourage assimilation to Anglo culture.[20] Accepting the culturally destructive and isolating nature of boarding schools, the federal government instituted day schools so that children stayed in touch with their parents and communities. This also meant that Indian children were often in closer contact with non-Indian children in state and county schools in their own localities.

Some tribes outside the Southwest benefited greatly from the IRA, especially those that had lost nearly their entire reservations through allotment. However, for others, such as the Hopi of Arizona, who already had a successful form of traditional government, the new system increased tribal factionalism. Traditionally, each Hopi village was organized along the lines of a Greek city-state, capable of making its own decisions and governing independently as a theocracy in which clans played a major role. When the federal government tried to impose a centralized form of government like that of the United States, with a tribal council based in one village, factions inevitably developed.

During the Great Depression of the 1930s, wool and lamb prices plunged as opportunities for off-reservation labor declined. Believing that he needed to remedy the problems facing the Navajos within President Roosevelt's first term, before another administration might reverse his actions, Commissioner Collier used the available money and backing to implement too many changes simultaneously. He saw a **Livestock Reduction** program and a soil erosion-control program as absolutely necessary, with public works programs to minimize the economic impact of stock reduction. He also sought the expansion of reservation boundaries and the consolidation of off-reservation landholdings as well as the restructuring of Navajo tribal government.

Collier maintained that, by the time of the depression, the Navajo population had outgrown its resource base and severe overgrazing had destroyed ground cover, leading to wind and water erosion. In 1933, Collier asked the Navajo Tribal Council to sanction and implement stock reduction. Until this time, most Navajos had been able to ignore the existence of the council because it had little effect on their everyday lives. Suddenly, this was no longer possible, and people began to view the tribal council with apprehension and alarm because it endorsed something as unacceptable as the killing of their livestock. The more traditional among them felt they had an obligation to look after these beings that were gifts from the Holy People. The more pragmatic factored both market and subsistence value into their economics, in contrast to Anglo ranchers. As Garrick Bailey and Roberta Bailey point out, horses were used for transportation and food; sheep were used to feed people at ceremonies, to pay healers for conducting ceremonies, and for food and wool; goats and cattle provided milk and food.[21]

Officials tried to implement the stock reduction program as quickly as possible, but the initial reduction in sheep fell considerably short of the projected number. The government managed the program poorly as Navajo resistance intensified, and Navajo police forced owners to sell their animals at low prices. Their methods created great bitterness, for many goats and sheep were shot and their carcasses were left to rot while others were captured and left to starve in their holding pens.

To cushion the economic impact of stock reduction, Collier got the federal government to extend national public work projects, primarily construction projects, to the reservation. Navajos built and improved roads, drilled water wells, installed windmills, and constructed water reservoirs through the Soil Conservation Service, the Civilian Conservation Corps, and the Indian Service. Nevertheless, they never forgot the massive trauma of livestock reduction. The program influenced Navajo attitudes toward not only land use but also tribal government, health care, education, and religious observance.[22]

SELF-DETERMINATION AND SOVEREIGNTY

In December 1941, when the United States entered World War II, American Indians enlisted in the military in record numbers. Many were leaving the reservation for the first time. World War II marked a turning point for Indian people because it brought them into greater contact with Anglo culture and the wider world. Military service had a profound effect because this war marked the largest single exodus of Indian males from the reservation. Serving in the armed forces provided an opportunity for Indians to compete in an arena where their skills as warriors inspired respect. Since they were not forced into segregated units as were African American soldiers, Indians had considerable contact with Anglo-Americans.

The Colorado River Indian Tribes experienced a tightening of government control during World War II, despite their objections, when their reservation was used as an internment camp for people of Japanese ancestry. Established in 1865, this reservation was originally intended for the Mojave Indians alone. Later the Mojave, who settled on the north end of the reservation near Parker, Arizona, were joined by about 200 Chemehuevis, who took up residence farther south. Under the provisions of the **Indian Reorganization Act**, in 1937 the members of the Colorado River Indian Tribes adopted a constitution and elected a tribal chairman. In 1942, after the beginning of World War II, President Franklin Roosevelt signed Executive Order 9066 establishing the War Relocation Authority, which created internment camps for Japanese Americans. The Poston Relocation Center (divided into camps I, II, and III), one of 10 wartime camps established in the United States to house 20,000 internees, was located on Colorado River Indian lands between 1942 and 1945. By not opposing the plan, the tribal council avoided losing this land permanently to the Department of War; in compensation, they received improvements to the land and the development of irrigation facilities.[23]

Part of federal Indian policy after World War II was the theory of surplus Indian populations, which held that "where the land base was insufficient to support the total number of tribal members, a 'surplus' of people must be moved off the reservation base onto other lands."[24] In 1945, the Bureau of Indian Affairs opened farming lands and farming opportunities on the Colorado River Reservation to Navajo and Hopi immigrants suffering the impact of the depression and federal stock-reduction programs. Some of the lands they settled on were those previously developed under the War Relocation Authority, including empty barracks once occupied by the Japanese Americans. Concerned that they would be overwhelmed, the Mojave and Chemehuevi stopped the flood of newcomers in 1952 by rescinding Ordinance No. 5, which reserved a portion of the CRIT Reservation for colonization by other Indians. The Department of the Interior ignored this action and did not repeal Ordinance No. 5 until April 30, 1964.[25]

The U.S. victory in the Pacific Theater was due in large part to an elite group of marines known as the **Navajo Code Talkers,** who developed a code based on the Navajo language. Japanese cryptographers were never able to decipher messages sent in this code, and even Navajo speakers were unable to understand the new meanings of Navajo phrases that the Code Talkers had created to designate specific military terminology. This special communication unit worked behind enemy lines to report on Japanese troop movements and was credited with providing crucial information that helped the Allies take control of the South Pacific. An Akimel O'odham (Pima) Indian, **Ira Hayes,** became one of the most famous soldiers of World War II when he was photographed along with five other marines as they raised a replacement flag on the summit of Mount Suribachi on Iwo Jima under heavy fire. This iconic photo helped to reignite popular support in a war-weary nation.

Native American men and women in the military earned a decent living for the first time in their lives; this enabled them to buy consumer goods, such as refrigerators, radios, and heaters, that they brought back to the reservation. Military life provided a taste of the Anglo world that they had not previously known, along with a steady job, money, and status. They urged their siblings and children to pursue education, and many of them used the postwar G.I. Bill (Servicemen's Readjustment Act of 1944) to obtain higher education.

Despite the experience of the Colorado River Indian tribes, government policy in the years immediately following the end of World War II indicated that certain rights previously denied to Indians would be recognized. In 1947, Felix Cohen, the chief counsel of the Association on American Indian Affairs, brought suits against the states of New Mexico and Arizona for failing to extend welfare benefits to Indians under the Social Security Act; these states "grudgingly complied with the law" and the suits were dropped.[26] Congress responded to the severe economic problems on the Navajo reservation due to the return of thousands of war veterans and defense plant workers as well as a severe drought during the summers of 1946 and 1947. First the government appropriated two million dollars in emergency relief funds; then it instituted a long-range study of their economic situation that resulted in the Navajo-Hopi Rehabilitation Act in 1950.[27]

However, government policy soon began to shift in response to congressional criticism of the **Indian Reorganization Act**. Economic programs similar to the Navajo-Hopi Rehabilitation Act failed to get government support, and Dillon S. Myer was appointed as the new commissioner of Indian affairs. Shortly after he took office, Myer announced that because the economics of the postwar period made the subsistence farming program of the New Deal years less viable, he would institute a **relocation** program. Convinced that the unemployment crisis on reservations was caused by the return of some 113,000 Indians who had left during the war, Myer believed that the solution was persuading large numbers of Indians to relocate away from the reservations, in urban, industrial areas such as Los Angeles. Some 61,600 Indians moved to major metropolitan areas between 1950 and 1967.[28] The program was eventually discontinued when the government realized that over half the Indians enrolled returned to their reservations when they experienced culture shock from living in urban environments away from their families and friends. At the same time, economic programs were being developed to bring industry to the reservations. Instead of relocation, government policy began to focus on vocational training programs and general educational programs in public schools and reservation boarding schools.

Ethnic identity and political activism became important themes of the 1960s. The **American Indian Movement** was founded, and fish-ins, the Alcatraz Island occupation, the Trail of Broken Treaties, and Wounded Knee brought national attention to Native American issues. At the same time, a number of national task forces, commissions, and congressional committees investigated living conditions on reservations and discovered severe problems in the government administration of Indian affairs as well as low levels of health, education, and family income. The Kennedy and Johnson administrations also encouraged a shift from the termination policy toward self-determination for Indian communities.

In response to this, federal Indian policy was marked by huge increases in expenditures, and pan-Indian organizations demanded control over programs that affected their welfare. The Office of Economic Opportunity began a series of community action programs in 1965 that augmented federal appropriations for education, health, and welfare. The Area Redevelopment Act of 1961 and the Economic Opportunity Act of 1964 brought financial aid to chronically depressed areas, helping to improve economic conditions for many Indians on reservations. Encouraged by the valuable experience they had gained, Indians demanded greater control over the planning and administering of programs previously controlled by the Bureau of Indian Affairs. In 1970, Commissioner Louis R. Bruce signed contracts that turned over the administration of all formerly BIA-run programs on their reservations to the Zuni, whose major reservation is in New Mexico, and to the Salt River Pima and Maricopa of Arizona; he also gave all-Indian school boards in Arizona and New Mexico full authority over the expenditure of school funds, the hiring of teachers, and curriculum.[29]

Congress showed its commitment to Native education by passing three education acts. The Indian Education Act of 1972 provided financial assistance to local educational agencies for elementary and secondary school programs. The Indian Education Assistance Act of 1975 and the Education Amendments Act of 1978 supplemented the funding for Indian schools and students. Indians responded with a high level of community participation, and by 1984, more than 3,000 Indian students were enrolled in 19 tribally controlled community colleges.[30]

Although tremendous strides were made toward self-determination in the 1970s and 1980s, many Native Americans criticized Congress, the Bureau of Indian Affairs, the Indian Health Service, and the Office of Indian Education for thwarting grassroots Indian control of programs through excessive regulation and self-perpetuating bureaucracy. The 1980s began a period of federal budget cuts that have severely hurt Indian programs.

Two of the most important recent developments in federal Indian policy have been the 1990 **Native American Graves Protection and Repatriation Act (NAGPRA)** and Indian gaming legislation. Through NAGPRA, Congress established a policy and process for the return of aboriginal human remains, associated funerary objects, and other items of cultural importance to the tribal owners.

As federal funding diminished in the 1980s, tribal governments sought other means of generating the revenue necessary to finance their programs. Gaming enterprises have been especially important for tribes that lack considerable natural resources or a sizable tax base, but gaming remains controversial. Fearing a loss of income, off-reservation gaming enterprises and state lotteries raise fears about competition and the possibility of organized crime infiltration. The federal government enacted the **Indian Gaming Regulatory Act of 1988 (IGRA)**, which separates gaming into three classes and allocates regulatory jurisdiction over each class among tribal, federal, and state sovereigns.

In the Southwest, Indian gaming enterprises continue to provide much-needed income not only for Native Americans but also for local businesses, such as automobile sales when tribal governments purchase vehicles for the expansion of tribal police departments. In Arizona, voters passed legislation that supported Indian gaming with the provision that some of the earnings go to finance non-Indian programs. The Tohono O'odham Nation has used gaming income in ways similar to other Indian nations in the Southwest: to build and staff their own college and to construct a new nursing home so that tribal elders can be cared for in more familiar surroundings. In 1995, tribal lawmakers created a scholarship fund with casino profits, and the scholarships now enable many students to pursue higher education. To ensure that they not only educate themselves but also use the skills and knowledge they gain to benefit the Tohono O'odham Nation, scholarship recipients are required to sign a contract agreeing that, upon completion of their schooling, they will return to work on the reservation for a period equal to half the time they have spent in school.

In June 2007, after six years of planning and construction, the Tohono O'odham Nation Cultural Center and Museum, a state-of-the-art complex with a library, collections facilities, exhibit galleries, a radio station, meeting areas, and a kitchen, opened its doors. Scheduled to coincide with the beginning of the traditional Tohono O'odham year, the Saguaro Harvest Moon, when the saguaro fruit was harvested, the opening ceremonies lasted two days. Tribal officials and respected elders related stories about the planning and construction of the museum and all that it embodied in terms of cultural pride and ongoing traditions. Museum staff estimated that nearly 3,000 people attended the first day alone to tour the facilities and take part in many activities, such as a film festival, traditional singing and dancing, orations by youth, demonstrations by Native artists, and traditional games, and to enjoy Tohono O'odham foods.

In addition to their tribal governments, southwestern peoples today have developed grassroots organizations that provide additional social services. One of the organizations that contributed to the opening of this museum and cultural center was Tohono O'odham Community Action (TOCA). With a focus on indigenous solutions rather than "solutions" from the outside, TOCA strives to maintain the material basis from which cultural practices developed and to encourage community self-sufficiency. TOCA was founded on the principles that many tribal communities are using to strengthen their cultures today. By drawing upon cultural traditions, such organizations seek to create lasting solutions. Instead of focusing on problems, they focus on assets and resources that are necessary to create a healthy and sustainable community. They go beyond the preservation of cultural activities, such as songs, stories, and ceremonies, to maintain the material basis out of which these practices began, thus keeping the culture alive and vital. Most significantly, these community-based organizations educator and scholar Emory Sekaquatewa, whose tribe has repeatedly voted down any efforts to establish casinos on its land, feels that the most serious problem for Indians today is the taste for the trappings of American materialism faced by young people.[33]

The media constantly bombard children and adults, inculcating in them a powerful desire to acquire the material objects of modern Anglo-American culture in order to reach any level of personal fulfillment. The fact that these messages are transmitted through the printed word, television, and other media gives them additional power, especially over children whose values are still forming. Acquisition becomes an immediate priority, leading to the abandonment of traditional culture. As the whole community slowly takes on these values, cultural institutions become less important and meaningful.

In nonliterate societies, the practice of customs and ceremonies are what impart values. When children see those around them investing their time and energy in traditional activities they consider significant and from which they gain wisdom to deal with everyday problems, the children come to understand what a vital source of strength these practices and values can be. But if the messages they receive, either from their elders' actions or from the media, convey the desirability of a modern Anglo-American lifestyle, including instant gratification as a value, they begin to believe that this is the way to satisfaction of spirit.

Complicating this process is the commitment of time that it takes to actively practice customs instead of passively watching television. In order to fulfill her ceremonial responsibilities in preparation for her pueblo's feast day, Ada Melton drives up to Jemez Pueblo every night during the week after working a full day. She does this because "My father is a *fiscale*: we're obligated to show our support by dancing. By night I'm up at Jemez practicing in the kiva."[34] Yet the rewards are more than worth the effort: "It's really comforting, that kiva. . . . It is a very familiar place, a place where all of us belong."[35] Hualapai Sylvia Querta agrees that ties to family and tradition are what make life meaningful. When she was first married, she moved to the Bay Area in California, where she and her husband spent two years. "I was young and I . . . got caught up in the excitement of shopping, of having a car, going to the movies and concerts and games." It was a life totally unlike the one she had known at Peach Springs, in a community where everyone knew and depended upon one another. In the city, "We lived in an apartment. We didn't even know who lived next door or under us or on top of us."[36] Eventually they moved home, back to familiar canyons and familiar faces.

Another threat comes from the marketing of Native American cultures because it increases outside interest in Indian arts and public performances. Although this generates income, it also distorts the perception of Indian cultures.

Emory Sekaquaptewa explains that cultural forms, such as dance, become substitutes for the substance and meaning they were developed to convey, a process that is not apparent to outside observers who believe that they are seeing "true Indian culture."[37] Young Indian people, especially those who have not been raised with a strong traditional foundation, may come to believe that they are participating in their own traditions when in reality, these forms are not supported by any depth of underlying belief and meaning.

Intimately related to the loss of culture is the loss of language, another major problem facing southwestern Indians today. Throughout the world, indigenous languages continue to disappear at an alarming rate. Although Indian children are no longer punished for speaking their own languages, teachers and school administrators still often urge parents to encourage them to speak English. Schools are heavily dominated by English, implying that Native languages are inferior. Another linguistically destructive force has been evangelical missionary efforts, which oppose indigenous languages as "reservoirs of paganism and satanic influence."[38] On the San Carlos Apache Reservation in Arizona and the Alamo Navajo Reservation in New Mexico, some fundamentalist churches forbid members to speak their native languages or even to attend any event at which the languages are spoken.[39] Even evangelical groups that do not forbid the use of Native languages discourage members from attending traditional religious events, including healing ceremonies, which are the context for some of the most complex and creative language use.

The mass media not only reinforces the desirability of modern Anglo-American culture but also plays a major role in emphasizing the dominance and prestige of English to susceptible young people. Many parents, forced to work two jobs to support their families, have no choice but to spend less time with their children, who may then be exposed to a greater amount of English-language television. Furthermore, to increase their children's chances of academic success, parents may decide not to raise them bilingually.

As people mature, their ideas about what constitutes a good life change. Just as Sylvia Querta related earlier, the decision to relocate off the reservation is seldom a permanent one. During their time away, most Native Americans stay in close touch with their families and with what is happening on the reservation, often visiting frequently, depending upon the distance involved. Aunts, uncles, cousins, or parents may visit their relative's home in the city for short or prolonged periods, as situations allow. A person who grew up on the reservation may even leave for as long as twenty to thirty years for military service or a college degree and career, then retire and return home to serve in tribal government, start a small business, or devote their time to silversmithing, painting, or pottery-making. The support base remains strong, both on the reservation and in town. When a young adult reaches the age of employment, he or she often goes to stay with a relative who is already established in an urban setting. This is especially true of cities in the Southwest but also of places as far away as Los Angeles and Seattle. This flexible system adapts to the shifting job market and various stages of life that family members experience.

Creating jobs on reservations is not easy. How can a Native community that may be located far from an urban center expand its economic base without a significant loss of culture? This is the situation faced by the Zuni in New Mexico. Even though the proposed Zuni-Cibola National Historical Park, a community-based institution to be run by the Zuni, was ecologically sound, the Zuni people voted it down, fearing that tourism would disrupt their spiritual life.[40]

In terms of natural resources, one of the most fortunate southwestern tribes is the White Mountain Apache Tribe, which carefully developed their timber and tourist industries. At full capacity, the Fort Apache Timber Company employs 450 people in a sawmill and in the harvesting of ponderosa pine, spruce, and fir within 800,000 acres of tribal forest land. Tourists generate income as they escape the summer heat of lower elevations for the 5,300-foot altitude of the White Mountains and camp or lease summer cabins, purchasing camping, fishing, and hunting permits from the tribe. Many people from Tucson and Phoenix go to Sunrise Park Resort, one of the best ski resorts in the Southwest. However, in the summer of 2002, the Rodeo-Chediski fire consumed most of the forests on the White Mountain Apache Indian Reservation, a devastating loss from which the tribe has struggled to recover.

Southwestern Indian peoples are facing incredible challenges. The overwhelming and inescapable presence of the modern world through the mass media, education, Christianity, economic pressure to relocate off the reservation, and competition in the job market force them to continually reinvent themselves without losing their core identities as Indians. Yet despite the pressures to assimilate, Native American societies continue not only to survive but also to flourish. Their resilience is evident in their continued presence despite Spanish, Mexican, and Anglo-American attempts to destroy their cultures.

Many resources provide strength, including oral tradition, which not only reinforces the continued existence of the past in stories and song but also offers the wisdom to deal with contemporary problems. The strength and flexibility of family ties can provide a solid foundation. And finally, Native American cultures have never been static; Indian societies had been responding to changing conditions for centuries before Europeans ever set foot on the North American continent. Southwestern Indian peoples remain rooted in their continuous relationship with the land on which they continue to live and in the practice of their traditions, which provide a strong sense of identity that enables them to face the challenges of today's world.

NOTES

1. Walter LaFeber, *The New Empire: An Interpretation of American Expansion 1860–1898* (1963; reprint, Ithaca: Cornell University Press, 1998), 12.

2. Eve Ball, *An Apache Odyssey: Indeh* (1980; reprint, Norman: University of Oklahoma Press, 1988), 100.

3. Trudy Griffin-Pierce, *Chiricahua Apache Enduring Power: Naiche's Puberty Ceremony Paintings* (Tuscaloosa: University of Alabama Press, 2006).

4. Lawrence C. Kelly, "United States Indian Policies, 1900–1980," in *Handbook of North American Indians: History of Indian-White Relations*, vol. 4, ed. Wilcomb E. Washburn (Washington, D.C.: Smithsonian Institution Press, 1988), 70.

5. Frederick E. Hoxie, *A Final Promise: The Campaign to Assimilate the Indians, 1880–1920* (Lincoln: University of Nebraska Press, 1984), 2, 3, 5, 10, 15, 39, 41, 43; Arrell M. Gibson, *The American Indian: Prehistory to the Present* (Lexington, Mass.: D. C. Heath, 1980), 491–495; Francis Paul Prucha, *The Great Father: The United States Government and the American Indians*, 2 vols. (Lincoln: University of Nebraska Press, 1984), 609–610, 621–622, 631.

6. Henrietta Stockel, *Survival of the Spirit* (Reno: University of Nevada Press, 1993), 111–112.

7. Edward Spicer, *Cycles of Conquest* (Tucson: University of Arizona Press, 1962), 349.

8. John Anthony Turcheneske Jr., *The Chiricahua Apache Prisoners of War: Fort Sill 1894–1914* (Niwot: University of Colorado Press, 1997), 3–4.

9. Spicer, *Cycles of Conquest*, 350.

10. Kelly, "United States Indian Policies, 1900–1980."

11. John Collier, *From Every Zenith: A Memoir* (Denver: Swallow Publishing, 1963), 93, 123.

12. John Collier, "The Red Atlantis," *Survey* 49 (October 1922): 15–20, 63, 66.

13. Kelly, "United States Indian Policies, 1900–1980," 73.

14. Spicer, *Cycles of Conquest*, 352.

15. Peter Iverson, *Diné: A History of the Navajos* (Albuquerque: University of New Mexico Press, 2002), 98.

16. Hoxie, *A Final Promise*, 113.

17. Lawrence C. Kelly, *The Navajo Indians and Federal Policy, 1900–1935* (Tucson: University of Arizona Press, 1968), 20–21.

18. Spicer, *Cycles of Conquest*, 350–352.

19. Richard White, *The Roots of Dependency: Subsistence, Environment, and Social Change Among the Choctaws, Pawnees, and Navajos* (Lincoln: University of Nebraska Press, 1983), 212–314.

20. Spicer, *Cycles of Conquest*, 352.

21. Garrick Bailey and Roberta Bailey, *A History of the Navajos: The Reservation Years* (Santa Fe, N.M.: School of American Research Press, 1986), 101.

22. Iverson, *Diné*, 137.

23. Amelia Flores, "Colorado River Indian Tribes," in *Native America in the Twentieth Century*, ed. Mary B. Davis (New York: Garland, 1994), 125.

24. Ibid.

25. Flores, "Colorado River Indian Tribes," 125.

26. Kelly, "United States Indian Policies, 1900–1980," 74.

27. Kelly, "United States Indian Policies, 1900–1980," 75.

28. Alan L. Sorkin, *American Indians and Federal Aid* (Washington, D.C.: Brookings Institution, 1971), 121.

29. Kelly, "United States Indian Policies, 1900–1980," 78.

30. Edmund J. Danziger Jr., "Self-Determination," in *Native America in the Twentieth Century,* ed. Mary B. Davis (New York: Garland, 1994), 224.

31. Stephen Trimble, *The People: Indians of the American Southwest* (Santa Fe, N.M.: School of American Research, 1993), 438.

32. Trimble, *The People,* 438.

33. Emory Sekaquaptewa, interview by author, August 20, 2003.

34. Trimble, *The People,* 438.

35. Trimble, *The People,* 438.

36. Trimble, *The People,* 436–437.

37. Emory Sekaquaptewa, interview by author, August 20, 2003.

38. Ofelia Zepeda and Jane Hill, "The Condition of Native Languages in the United States," in *Endangered Languages,* ed. R. H. Robbins and E. M. Uhlenbeck (Oxford, England: Berg, 1991), 139.

39. Elizabeth Brandt, "Applied Linguistic Anthropology and American Indian Language Renewal," *Human Organization* 47, no. 4 (1988): 324.

40. Trimble, *The People,* 441.

Main street, Chinle, Arizona. Horses and cattle range freely throughout the small town near Canyon de Chelly, about a half-hour drive from Diné College in Tsaile, Arizona. The town has a shopping center and supermarket, a high school, elementary school, numerous churches, and many fast-food restaurants.

Hogan with Ned Hatathli Cultural Center, Diné College, Tsaile, Arizona. Diné College, once known as Navajo Community College, was founded in 1968 and was the first of many tribal colleges throughout the United States. The college now offers a four-year degree program.

The Navajo Code Talker Memorial in Window Rock, Arizona, designed and executed by Navajo/Ute sculptor Oreland Joe. More than 400 Navajos, with 29 being the original Navajo Code Talkers, stepped forward to develop and use the most successful and significant military code during World War II in the Pacific. This code was used to win battles at Guadalcanal, Tarawa, Saipan, Okinawa, and Iwo Jima. The Navajo Code was not declassified until 1968, which meant that the Code Talkers did not receive public recognition until long after World War II.

Navajo Nation Council Chamber, Window Rock, Arizona. This is the building where the governing body for the Navajo Nation meets to discuss issues and policies. Each chapter, roughly equivalent to a township, has a representative who brings the concerns of his or her local area to the legislative meetings held here. He or she then brings back policy decisions and other information to local chapter meetings, held on a monthly basis.

The registration table at the annual meeting of the Diné Long-Term Elder Care Conference, July 21–23, 2008. The Navajo Nation has created an Elder Task Force at the Fort Defiance Indian Hospital to be proactive about the needs of their elders. This conference was held inside the Navajo Nation Museum and Library, Window Rock, Arizona.

Representatives from the Native Resource Development Company, Inc., one of the private Navajo-run companies created to care for Navajo elders who live on the reservation. Taken at the Diné Long-Term Elder Care Conference, Window Rock, Arizona, 2008.

The Navajo Nation Museum, Library, and Visitor's Center, Window Rock, Arizona.

Avery Denny prepares for a class that he teaches at Diné College. Mr. Denny is also a
Nightway chanter and a respected elder and spokesperson for the Navajo Nation. Taken at
his home in Pinon, Arizona.

The framework for a tipi used for Native American Church ceremonies at a Navajo homestead in Many Farms, Arizona. The hogan next to the house is used for traditional ceremonies.

Revivals and Pentecostal churches are common throughout the Navajo Nation. A variety of churches are represented, including but not limited to Catholic, Mormon, and Jehovah's Witnesses. Ganado, Arizona.

A bas-relief of stylized Apache Mountain Spirit masks decorates the bridge over the Salt River, which divides the White Mountain Apache and San Carlos Apache reservations. All Apache groups recognize these powerful supernatural beings. The presence of the Mountain Spirit dancers summons great power that ensures the continuation of the Apache peoples.

A statue of Richard "Rick" Glenn Lupe (1960–2003), respected White Mountain Apache wildland firefighter. He led a team that worked 36 continuous hours to create the 14-mile-long barrier that stopped the Rodeo-Chediski Fire's advance toward the towns of Show Low, Pinetop-Lakeside, and Hon-dah in 2002, when 6,600 firefighters fought this most devastating wildfire in Arizona history. After Lupe died in the line of duty, all state flags in Arizona flew at half staff in his honor. STATUE BY TANDY WHITE, OUTSIDE THE LARSON PUBLIC LIBRARY, PINETOP-LAKESIDE, ARIZONA.

The Cochise Stronghold, southeastern Arizona. This place provided a secure home for Cochise, the Chiricahua Apache leader, and his people. Lookouts could easily spot strangers approaching at a great distance. The Chiricahuas were the only southwestern group to be exiled from their homeland forever.

In the early morning, a White Mountain Apache woman sets up her wares at the bottom of the Salt River Canyon, Arizona. This rest stop has become a favorite tourist site because of its access to the river and magnificent scenery.

Stairs to the terreplain, Fort Marion, Saint Augustine, Florida. Most of the nearly 500 Chiricahua Apache prisoners lived in 130 Sibley tents on the terreplain. After Naiche and his small band decided to surrender in Mexico in 1886, federal troops forced the remaining Chiricahuas, who had been living peacefully on the reservation at San Carlos, onto trains to be shipped to the Florida prison, where they began a 27-year period as prisoners of war.

Chiricahua Apache children upon their arrival at Carlisle Indian Industrial School, Carlisle, Pennsylvania, 1886–1887. Upon arrival, the child's physical self was systematically mortified as all previous bases of self-identification were ignored or destroyed. Admission procedures included undressing, bathing, disinfecting, haircutting, and the issuing of institutional clothing. Perhaps the most dehumanizing aspect was the alphabetical assignment of names after the children were lined up in order of height. Photo courtesy of National Park Service.

The Inn of the Mountain Gods Resort and Casino, an enterprise of the Mescalero Apache Tribe. Nearly everyone at Mescalero today has a mixture of Mescalero, Lipan, and Chiricahua Apache heritage. When the federal government removed the Chiricahuas from prisoner-of-war status, only 87 of about 260 chose to remain in Oklahoma, where they were allotted 80-acre tracts of land. Most of the Chiricahuas chose to go to New Mexico, where politically they became part of the Mescalero Apache Tribe, even though they settled on their own part of the reservation known as Whitetail.

Chiricahua Apache children after being inducted into Carlisle Indian Industrial School, Carlisle, Pennslvania, 1886–1887. The transformation of their appearances as well as their demeanors showed the power that the federal government held over these children and by extension, over the Chiricahuas. Put another way, the extended struggle for domination over American Indians was played out through the bodies of the students at Carlisle and other Indian boarding schools.
PHOTO COURTESY OF NATIONAL PARK SERVICE.

The spacious golf course, framed by tall pines, at the Inn of the Mountain Gods Resort and Casino near Ruidoso, New Mexico. This elegant and popular resort is a major source of income for all three tribes that comprise what is now the Mescalero Apache Tribe.

Arriving in Supai, Havasupai Reservation. The only means of travel into the remote town of Supai is by foot, by horse or mule, or by helicopter. After initial switchbacks, the trail reaches a red-rock inner gorge, where it follows a sandy wash for most of the remaining 6.75 miles. Guests must make advance reservations with the Havasupai Tourist Office or lodge before embarking from Hualapai Hilltop. Tourism only provides seasonal employment; once the season ends, most households are forced to rely on one salary from a job at the school or in federal or tribal administration.

Havasu Falls, Havasupai Reservation. Navajo Falls, Havasu Falls, and Mooney Falls are strung out along Havasu Creek beyond the village of Supai. The tribe takes its name from this water: *ha* (water), *vasu* (blue-green), and *pai* (people). Its color comes from a high concentration of lime, which creates the travertine terraces in pools below the falls. The mist and spray from the plummeting water also deposit lime on the cliff walls in flaring aprons of travertine. Nearly everyone lives in the canyon year-round.

Arizona's Grand Canyon, which is sacred to many tribes. Only the Havasupai live in part of the Grand Canyon today; their reservation is located in a narrow side canyon called Cataract Canyon.

Main Street, Supai, Arizona. Supai has no paved streets or parking lots, nor does it need any, for the only motorized vehicles are the tribe's tractor, backhoe, and fire truck, along with a few three-wheelers used by community health workers. Horses are the lifeblood of the Havasupai, for they bring tourists and their gear, haul supplies, and transport the U.S. mail, which leaves the village postmarked, "The Mule Train Mail Havasupai Indian Reservation."

Spirit Mountain (right). The Emergence Place of Yuman peoples, Spirit Mountain is located in the Newberry Mountains of southern Nevada and is visible in three states. To the south, the land slopes sharply, like a huge plate tilted toward the great Colorado River, which divides California from Arizona. Throughout history, this river has been a conduit for vast, sweeping change and the almost constant movement of peoples.

The Fort Mojave Tribe's Avi Casino and Hotel, whose shape was inspired by their sacred mountain, Spirit Mountain. Near Needles, California, the Fort Mojave Reservation is located on both sides of the Colorado River. The Avi Casino and Hotel is on the California side.

The central plaza of the Indian Pueblo Cultural Center, Albuquerque, New Mexico. Constructed in the late 1970s, the center was built in the D shape of Pueblo Bonito in Chaco Canyon. Each of the New Mexico Pueblos has its own exhibit space and chooses how it will be represented. Dances are held for the public in the central plaza.

The portal in front of the Palace of the Governors on the Santa Fe plaza. In 1998, the Portal Program included more than 850 artists from some 400 households from all federally recognized tribes in New Mexico, as well as Hopis and Navajos from Arizona and representatives from other Native American groups that have ties to New Mexico. Program participants spend time with their friends and fellow artists and interact directly with customers, something they could not do as easily if they sold their work from their homes or through shops.

Corn Mountain, Zuni Pueblo. Situated about 40 miles southwest of present-day Gallup, New Mexico, Zuni lies in a fertile valley rimmed by flat-topped mesas, just west of the Zuni Mountains. Three miles southeast of the pueblo, sacred Corn Mountain towers 1,000 feet above the plain; in the past, this mountain served as a refuge for all the people of Zuni during times of conflict with outsiders. One of the sharp, clear bands of sandstone that compose this mesa is said to be the high-water line of a flood that occurred at the time of Creation.

The beehive ovens of a mother and her daughters, Zuni Pueblo. As in all the Western Pueblos, descent is matrilineal. Residence was traditionally matrilocal, which meant that the house was owned by the women of the matrilineage, with husbands residing in their wives' households. Thus, daughters would remain near their mother and each would have her own oven near her mother's.

Wave clouds over Baboquivari, Tohono O'odham Reservation, southern Arizona. Baboquivari is home to I'itoi, also known as Elder Brother, the supernatural who is said to have created the O'odham after a flood swept away all the people who had forgotten their spirituality and their relationship to the animals and plants. The Tohono O'odham have the main reservation west of Tucson, and noncontiguous reservations at San Xavier and Gila Bend. PHOTO BY KEITH PIERCE, 1966.

Baboquivari High School, Sells, Arizona. The film *Pride and the Power to Win* tells the inspiring story of how students, administrators, educators, and the community worked together to revive their school, which had fallen to the lowest academic standard in Arizona. The tradition of consensus building became the basis for their approach. Tribal elders shared their knowledge, and students took field trips around the reservation to see how technology affected their local environment.

Part II

People, Places, and Events

agriculture   Nearly all southwestern Native peoples (except for some Apache groups) practiced some degree of agriculture. Evidence exists of cultigens in the Southwest by 1000 B.C., and archaeologists are reasonably sure that in some areas people were practicing agriculture by about 1500 B.C. By roughly 300 B.C., the River **Hohokam** had developed such an extensive network of irrigation canals to water their fields that they regularly produced enough corn, beans, and squash to support settled villages along the Gila and Salt rivers. The **Patayan**, another precontact people, established summer camps along the Colorado and Gila rivers where they planted, tended, and harvested crops. The **Mogollon**, who lived in the mountains of central Arizona and New Mexico, continued to rely on hunting and gathering much longer than other precontact groups because their land had only limited area suitable for agriculture; by the end of the A.D. 1300s, however, they had become farmers who lived in pueblos. The **Ancestral Pueblo (Anasazi)**, whose earliest period is known as Basketmaker II (500 B.C. to A.D. 600), cultivated corn and squash, collected wild seeds and nuts, and hunted game.

Agricultural products may have accounted for as much as 85 or 90 percent of the Pueblo diet. Known as the most skilled dry farmers in the world, the Hopi of northern Arizona live in an area of sporadic and unpredictable rainfall that only receives an annual average of 8 to 10 inches of precipitation. To maximize the moisture content of the soil, they have developed specially adapted strains of plants and planting methods.

Allen, Paula Gunn (Laguna Pueblo and Sioux, 1939–)   Paula Gunn Allen's multicultural, multilingual background provides the major theme of her novels and poetry. Her mother was Laguna Pueblo, Scots, and Sioux-Metis, while her father was Lebanese American. Known for her efforts to introduce the public to the new literature of contemporary Native American writers, Allen has published books such as *The Sacred Hoop: Recovering the Feminine in American Indian Traditions* (1986), in which she analyzes the work of several Native writers. Her anthology, *Spider Woman's Granddaughters: Traditional Tales and Contemporary Writing by Native American Women* (1989), reflects her commitment to the strong role of women in Pueblo society and to American feminist movements. She has won numerous awards, including a National Endowment for the Arts fellowship in 1978 and the 1990 Native American Prize for Literature.

American Indian Defense Association   The most vigorous of the Indian rights societies that were active in the 1920s, the American Indian Defense Association criticized federal policy that sought to assimilate Native Americans into the dominant culture and to terminate federal responsibility toward them. **John Collier** led this small group of individuals from California, whose goals were the recognition of Indian rights to basic civil liberties and the survival of remaining Indian reservations through corporate and communal enterprise. The organization also sought to preserve Indian cultures and societies and to extend federal assistance to Indian communities in the form of Department of Agriculture assistance programs, public health services, and Farm Loan Bank credits.

American Indian Language Development Institute (AILDI)   A major force for the continuing vitality of Native American languages, AILDI was created in 1979 by academic linguists and Native American parents and educators interested in learning to read and write in their own languages. They held workshops in various tribal communities and campuses throughout the Southwest until 1990, when AILDI became based at the University of Arizona (UA) in Tucson. At the institute's annual summer workshops, educators learn how to combine Native American traditions with modern teaching methods to help their students succeed. All of the courses lead toward regular UA degrees, as well as bilingual and English as a second language (ESL) endorsements; thus, the institute helps Native Americans obtain degree certification as teachers (see **Ofelia Zepeda**).

American Indian Religious Freedom Act (AIRFA) (1978) Traditional Indian religions have been outlawed or actively discouraged for most of the history of the United States. The government provided financial support to missionaries in their efforts to "convert and civilize" the Indians. The 1883 Religious Crimes Code prohibited Native American religious practices. In 1934, under the administration of **John Collier** as commissioner of Indian Affairs, the federal government finally recognized the right of free worship on Indian reservations. However, obstacles still remained, such as the prohibition of peyote, a sacrament in **Native American Church** ceremonies. In 1978, Congress enacted the American Indian Religious Freedom Act (42 U.S.C. 1996) to protect and preserve the rights of indigenous people to practice the traditional American Indian, Eskimo, Aleut, and Native Hawaiian religions, including access to sites, use and possession of sacred objects, and the freedom to worship through ceremonials and traditional rites. However, this act has been challenged by non-Indian groups regarding such aspects as the use of peyote, access to sacred sites, and the religious rights of American Indians incarcerated in prisons. Native American organizations and civil rights groups are working to strengthen legislation regarding religious freedom.

Ancestral Pueblo (Anasazi) (500 B.C.–A.D. 1550) "Ancestral Pueblo" is a more recent term of reference for the people formerly known as the Anasazi, which is the English approximation of a Navajo word that means "ancient enemies" and is used to refer to all the precontact peoples who lived throughout the Colorado Plateau. They left behind dramatic cliff dwellings and multistoried pueblos. Ancestral Pueblo culture was complex, with its broadest division between the Eastern and Western Anasazi. The first Ancestral Pueblo period is Basketmaker II (500 B.C.–A.D. 600), when people lived primarily in rock shelters and cultivated corn and squash, collected wild seeds and nuts, and hunted game. The people of Basketmaker III (A.D. 600–800) lived in pit houses and made pottery. The Pueblo I (A.D. 800–1000) and Pueblo II (A.D. 1000–1150) periods saw the construction of above-ground masonry pueblos and the widespread distribution of decorated black-on-white pottery; it was during this time that the Chaco culture developed. Pueblo III (A.D. 1150–1300) was also known as the Great Pueblo period, during which a return to dry weather forced the Ancestral Pueblo to adjust to twenty-five years of harsher farming conditions. In the west, they did this by contracting the area of occupation and building smaller settlements; in the east, they aggregated into large communities. The final period, Pueblo IV (A.D. 1300–1550), began with a massive population movement as the people of the Four Corners area abandoned this region for new villages in the central mountains. Some of their new communities were separate from those of the

Mogollon; others joined previously existing Mogollon villages. Today, many Navajos consider the Anasazi to have been their ancestors.

"Apaches"   Apachean-speaking peoples moved into the Southwest before the sixteenth century and separated into seven groups. All but the Lipan and Kiowa-Apache (also known as the Plains Apache) remained in the Southwest. The **Navajos** developed their own culture, while the other Apache groups separated into the Mescalero, Chiricahua, Jicarilla, and Western Apache tribes. Today, the official divisions (as decided upon by their tribal governments) of the Apaches in the Southwest are Mescalero Apache (comprising those descended from Mescalero, Chiricahua, and Lipan Apaches); Jicarilla Apache; Camp Verde (Yavapais and Apaches); Fort McDowell (Apaches, Yavapais, and Mojaves); San Carlos Apache (Western Apaches); Tonto Apache (Western Apaches); and White Mountain Apache (Western Apaches).

Apache Wars   Some Apaches, such as the White Mountain and Cibecue Apaches (part of a larger entity known as the Western Apache) agreed to keep peace with the United States and even to serve as U.S. Army scouts to help defeat the Tonto and Chiricahua Apaches. Others, most notably the Chiricahua (see **Chiricahua Apache Prisoners of War Descendants; Naiche**), continued to resist reservation status. The Apache Wars lasted from 1881 to 1886.

Apodaca, Paul (Navajo, 1951–)   Born in Los Angeles of Navajo, Mexican, and Spanish ancestry, Paul Apodaca is an artist actively involved in the Native American, Hispanic, and arts communities on the national and local levels. He began working with the Bowers Museum in Orange County, California in the early 1970s as an artist-in-residence, exhibiting artist, and curator of Native American art as well as overseeing the museum's California history and folk art collections. In addition to his extensive involvement with many arts funding agencies, has has also worked for the state of California to design state arts programs and to develop a new administrative plan for the California State Indian Museum. He has been a professor at Chapman University; has taught at the University of California, Irvine and California State University, Fullerton; and has been honored with numerous grants and awards, including the Smithsonian Institution Museum Professional Award, the Orange County Human Rights Award, and the Academy of Motion Pictures Arts and Sciences Award for his documentary film *Broken Rainbow* (1986).

Archaic tradition (c. 6000 B.C.–200 A.D.)   In the Southwest, the Archaic period, which refers to both an interval of time and a way of life, began sometime after 6000 B.C. Archaeologists divide the period into the Early Archaic and the

Late Archaic. Humans were becoming much more specialized in their subsistence patterns and developing the tools they needed to make a living from the plants and animals found in their area. The global warming trend that began about 10,000 years ago meant that the Southwest became much drier and many large game animals disappeared. Archaic period societies within each area of the Southwest developed their own adaptations to local resources, although all shared an emphasis on plant foods and a highly mobile lifestyle. The people were forced to develop new techniques to hunt the small, fast game—deer, antelope, squirrels, rodents, and rabbits—available after the horses, camels, and elephants of the previous Paleo-Indian period became extinct. Because they had to follow a seasonal round of movement across the landscape to harvest wild plants as they ripened and to hunt animals, their tools, equipment, and shelters were lightweight, and they left fewer material remains than did the sedentary people who followed them in time. Most Late Archaic sites that date between 1000 B.C. and A.D. 200 have yielded evidence of corn. Corn, beans, and squash were introduced from what is known today as Mexico, and, sometime in the closing centuries B.C., the idea of making and firing pottery containers also made its way north. The earliest ceramic vessels appeared in the Southwest about A.D. 200 and had become widespread by A.D. 500.

Armijo (Navajo, fl. mid-1800s)   Headman in the Navajo War of 1863–1864, Armijo took the name of the governor of New Mexico before 1846, when the territory was still part of Mexico. He was a prominent farmer who advocated peaceful relations between Indians and whites until violence erupted; then he became a supporter of **Manuelito.** He surrendered at Fort Canby and was relocated with his followers to Bosque Redondo, where he signed the treaty that established the original Navajo Reservation.

art   Southwestern Indian peoples have a long tradition of creating jewelry, pottery, baskets, textiles, and stone and wood carvings. In precontact times, the **Hohokam** carved palettes from stone and used clay to made ceramic effigy vessels, figures, and pottery bowls. The **Mogollon** also made distinctive pottery; especially noteworthy are the pieces painted with geometric and life forms produced by one particular group, named for the Mimbres Valley in New Mexico. The Basketmakers, the earliest **Ancestral Pueblo (Anasazi)**, are named for the finely crafted baskets, textiles, netting, and other fiber objects that they made for tools, clothing, and ornaments; during the Basketmaker III period (A.D. 600–800), they made pottery. The **Patayan** excavated the desert pavement as the background for their gigantic geometric patterns and figures of humans, animals, and stars, many of which remain today.

The modern painting tradition gained strength (after the off-reservation boarding school system encouraged some artistic expression) at the Santa Fe Indian School (now the Institute of American Indian Arts), where students were taught to paint on canvas. With the construction of railroads in the Southwest, this region became accessible to tourists, who could then buy craft items directly from Native artists. Traders encouraged Navajo weavers to adapt their blankets into rugs for the commercial market. In the early twentieth century, museums began exhibiting American Indian art. Southwestern Native peoples have continued to develop their techniques and to introduce new styles and methods that have become part of the body of tribal tradition, such as Hopi silver jewelry made with the overlay technique and Maria and Julian Martinez's elegant black-on-black pottery. Today, many southwestern Native artists continue to use traditional tribal images and themes in their work, while others reach out in many new directions by creating distinctly "nontraditional" forms.

assimilation   A guiding philosophy behind many U.S. government Indian policies, assimilation holds that Native Americans should be incorporated into the dominant culture to the extent that tribal cultures no longer exist separately. This is different from acculturation, the exchange of cultural features through continuous firsthand contact, a process that, although it alters the original cultural patterns of a group, still allows them to remain distinct. In 1879, the off-reservation boarding school system was initiated in an effort to instill Anglo values in Indian children and thus into future generations of Indian people. The **Dawes Severalty Act** of 1887 stressed individual land ownership, which was considered to be a hallmark of "civilization." Even though the government policy of land allotment was ended by the **Indian Reorganization Act** of 1934, efforts at assimilation did not stop. In the early 1950s, the philosophy of assimilation still drove government policy and resulted in efforts to **terminate** Indian tribes, removing their official status and all government benefits to which they were entitled.

Athapaskan languages   The Athapaskan language family is found in three geographic areas—northern Athapaskan, Pacific Coast Athapaskan, and Southern Athapaskan—that includes Canada, Oregon, California, Alaska, and the American Southwest. Southern Athapaskan languages are Navajo, Western Apache, Mescalero, Chiricahua, Jicarilla, and Lipan. It is generally agreed that Athapaskan originated in interior Alaska and parts of northwestern Canada. An Athapaskan language, Navajo, served as the basis for a code that remained unbroken throughout World War II (see **Navajo Code Talkers**).

Atsidi Sani (Old Smith, Navajo, c. 1830–c.1870)   An artist and medicine man who is given credit for the introduction of silversmithing among the Navajo, Atsidi Sani fashioned his first silver pieces in 1853 after learning the basic techniques from Nakai Tsosi and a blacksmith, George Carter. He took his knowledge with him to Bosque Redondo, where he had contact with Mexican ironworkers, and passed on his craft to his sons. Atsidi Sani was also a minor headman who became a prominent chief and after 1858, a major force in Navajo political affairs.

Banderas, Juan (Yaqui, d. 1833)   Juan Banderas was a **Yaqui** resistance leader who commanded a force of two thousand fighting men against Mexican soldiers when they came to enforce the new tax laws in 1825. Banderas envisioned an independent Indian state in northern Mexico and adopted the **Virgin of Guadalupe** as his symbol, as had the Mexicans when they fought for independence from Spain. Enlisting the aid of other Indians in addition to Yaquis, Banderas's forces drove out all the settlers who had taken land in Yaqui and Mayo territory over the previous fifty years. After he assumed control over all the settlements of the lower Yaqui and Mayo valleys in 1826, he ceased to attack. Mexican troops attacked and continued fighting until Banderas agreed to peace in 1827, believing that the Yaqui towns would remain autonomous. He received a pardon from the Mexican government and was recognized as captain-general of the Yaqui towns and paid by the state. Banderas again organized armed resistance when the Mexican government made plans to tax the Yaquis, divide their lands for individual ownership, and extend the municipality-state system of organization into Yaqui towns. In 1832, Banderas and his men established control of the towns, but the following year his force of a thousand Indians was defeated and he was captured and executed by the Mexican government.

Banyacya, Thomas, Sr. (Hopi, 1910–1999)   Hopi elder Thomas Banyacya Sr. was a controversial figure who considered himself the spokesperson for Hopi traditionalists. His mission, he believed, was to tell the outside world of dire warnings contained in the ancient Hopi prophecies. Adamantly against the Hopi Tribal Council, he felt that it was not truly representative of the Hopi people but had been imposed by the federal government in the 1930s after the passage of the **Indian Reorganization Act.** He claimed that the **Navajo-Hopi Land Dispute** came about because major corporations had persuaded the tribal council to sell out their rights to the land. Banyacya spoke out against the relocation of the Navajo from Hopi land because he held that clearing this area would allow mining companies to gain access to its deposits of coal, uranium, and oil shale.

Barboncito (Navajo, c. 1820–1871)   Between 1863 and 1866, Navajo military and spiritual leader Barboncito, along with Delgadito (his brother) and **Manuelito**, headed Navajo resistance to U.S. government attempts to exile or exterminate the tribe. After the United States took control of the region in 1848, they waged a campaign to stop Navajo and Apache raiding that was a response to settler encroachment and the taking of Navajo women and children as slaves. Open warfare erupted when the military instituted a scorched-earth policy in an attempt to exile the Navajo to Bosque Redondo in New Mexico. Kit Carson took Barboncito prisoner in 1864, forcing him to go to the relocation camp, where supplies were grossly inadequate and the land was completely unsuited to farming. In 1865, Barboncito and about 500 followers escaped and rejoined Manuelito. In 1868, they signed a treaty that established the Navajo Reservation.

Begay, Harrison (Navajo, 1917–)   One of the best known and most prolific Navajo artists, Harrison Begay was born in White Cone, Arizona. He studied art under Dorothy Dunn at what later became the Institute of American Indian Arts in Santa Fe; Dunn was known for a style of teaching that encouraged Native artists to draw from their traditional visual expressions instead of basing their work on European styles.

Beginning in 1942, Begay served in the U.S. Army, a period of duty that included the Normandy campaign. Discharged in 1945, he began to focus on his painting. He divided his time between Clay Lockett's shop in Tucson and Parkhurst's in Santa Fe, with occasional freelancing. He returned to the Navajo Reservation, where he spent most of the 1960s and 1970s, except for a short period during which he painted at Woodard's shop in Gallup, New Mexico. Begay is one of the few Southwest Indian artists who has been able to support himself by painting.

Working with Tewa Enterprises, Santa Fe, Begay ventured into the silkscreen reproduction of his paintings. Although Tewa Enterprises has reproduced the work of other Native artists, none has been as popular as the Begay prints, in large part because his fine-lined and flat-color work is especially suitable for this kind of duplication. Furthermore, his watercolor images of horses and colts, deer and fawns, and sheepherding children in stylized landscapes appeal to a wide audience, and the far lower-priced serigraphs (fine art silkscreen prints) are more affordable for many people than his original paintings (Clara Lee Tanner, *Southwest Indian Painting: A Changing Art*, 2nd ed. [Tucson: University of Arizona Press, 1980], 301–312).

Blessingway   Considered to be the backbone of Navajo religion, Blessingway is a ceremony used for many reasons to invoke positive blessings needed for a long and healthy life or for the protection and increase of possessions. A Blessingway ceremony may be done to bless a new home or public building, to install a tribal officer, to protect a departing soldier, to protect livestock, to consecrate a marriage or ceremonial paraphernalia, or to bless a new singer. The Navajo **Girl's Puberty Ceremony** is a form of Blessingway, meant to secure blessings for a long, healthy, and prosperous life (Leland Wyman, *Blessingway* [Tucson: University of Arizona Press, 1970]).

Bosque Redondo (Fort Sumner)   After fighting a brutal war against the U.S. Army, many Navajos surrendered at Fort Defiance and were forced to endure the **Long Walk** to Bosque Redondo, also known as Fort Sumner, in east central New Mexico in 1863 (see part IV of this book: Correll 1979, under "Published Primary Sources"). Brigadier General Carleton, who had selected this location with the idea of developing a self-sufficient agricultural community of Navajos and Mescalero Apaches, had overlooked the poor conditions there and seriously underestimated the number of Navajos. He had estimated the total at about 5,000, but by March 1865, there were nearly twice that number. Lack of food, water, shelter, firewood, blankets, and other necessities led to malnutrition, starvation, and the spread of various diseases. In addition, other tribes raided the captured Navajos. Public opposition grew against the Fort Sumner program, and in 1866, General Carleton was relieved of his duties as commander of the Department of New Mexico. In 1868, a peace treaty was signed with the Navajo and they were allowed to return to what was now their reservation, a portion of their homeland.

Cajeme (José Maria Leyva, Yaqui, d. 1887) Cajeme was a Yaqui leader (whose name means "he who does not drink") who was appointed *alcalde* mayor of the Yaqui and Mayo towns in 1874. With Mayo lieutenants, Cajeme led an uprising against the Mexican government. He attempted to institute a more centralized government than the Yaqui towns were accustomed to and to concentrate power in his own hands. He appointed himself captain-general, a title recognized by the Yaqui but one that had been abolished by the Mexican government. Setting himself up as judge over all the Yaqui towns, he regarded himself as the highest authority, even higher than the eight Yaqui governors of the towns. Yaquis were willing to accept his authority as a tribal military chief but opposed his usurpation of judicial power. After a lengthy period of armed resistance against the Mexican army, Cajeme was captured and executed in April 1887, effectively ending all but guerrilla fighting against the Mexicans.

Camp Grant Massacre (1871)   **Eskiminzin** of the Aravaipa band of the Pinaleno Apaches had convinced several bands of Apaches to take up a settled life of farming under the encouragement of the post commander and the protection of soldiers at Camp Grant in the San Pedro Valley, Arizona. Other Pinalenos and Chiricahuas had been raiding Tohono O'odham villages and settlements along the Santa Cruz. Driven by hatred of all Apaches, a group of citizens from Tucson enlisted some Tohono O'odham to help them take revenge. At dawn on April 30, 7 Anglos, 48 Mexican Americans, and 92 Tohono O'odham surprised the sleeping Aravaipas when most of the men were away and murdered about 125 people—all but 8 were women and children—and captured 27 children, whom they turned over to the Tohono O'odham to sell as slaves in Sonora (Angie Debo, A *History of the Indians of the United States* [Norman and London: University of Oklahoma Press, 1970], 268–269).

Carson, Christopher (Kit) (1809–1868)   Born in Kentucky, Kit Carson ran away to Santa Fe when he was sixteen. He worked as a trapper from 1829 until 1842, when he began guiding John C. Fremont's first three explorations. He served as a scout and courier in the Mexican War and from 1854 to 1861 was Ute Indian agent at Taos. He fought against the Confederates and Indians between 1861 and 1865 as a colonel (brevetted brigadier general, 1865) in the New Mexico Volunteers, leading military campaigns against the Mescalero Apaches in 1863 and against the Navajos in 1863. The Navajos were forced to go on the **Long Walk** to **Bosque Redondo** in New Mexico, where they were incarcerated for four years. Carson had two children by his first wife, who was Arapaho; none by his second, who was Cheyenne; and eight by his third wife, who was Mexican.

Chaco culture (c. A.D. 920–1320)   The complexity of Chaco, the pinnacle of Eastern **Ancestral Pueblo** culture, was evident in the settlement's physical layout, with planned, formal pueblos with great *kivas* that were linked by a system of roads. Developed during the Pueblo I period (A.D. 800–1000), Chaco Canyon in northwestern New Mexico featured Pueblo Bonito, a 900-room, 4-story masonry pueblo. Its back wall was an almost unbroken vertical wall of masonry probably for defense and its inner side was a terraced crescent with many windows and roof entryways that faced a great plaza. Two great subterranean kivas that could accommodate hundreds of people were built in the central plaza for ceremonies. Major construction at Chaco peaked between A.D. 1050 and 1100, then declined sharply; road construction was concentrated between A.D. 1030 and 1100. Although Chaco Canyon was not abandoned at this time, archaeological evidence indicates that political leadership shifted to the San Juan region after A.D. 1130.

Chato (Alfred Chato, Chiricahua Apache, c. 1860–1934)   A leader in the Apache Wars of 1881–1886, Chato accompanied **Geronimo** when he left the

San Carlos Reservation in 1881 and headed for Mexico. In 1884, Chato and about sixty other Apaches were forced to surrender. When Geronimo, who also had surrendered, wanted to leave the reservation again, Chato tried to persuade him to stay and later helped General George Crook pursue him. As a leader of the Apache delegation to Washington, Chato pleaded for the right of the Chiricahua Apaches to stay in their homeland. In spite of his assistance in securing the surrender of Geronimo, Chato was imprisoned in Florida, Alabama, and Oklahoma, along with the Chiricahua he had pursued. Later he resided on the Mescalero Apache Reservation in New Mexico.

Chiago, Michael (Tohono O'odham, 1946–)   Born in the village of Kohatk on the Tohono O'odham Reservation, Michael Chiago began drawing and dancing when he was a boy. After attending St. John's Academy High School in Laveen, Arizona, he joined the marines and served in Vietnam and Okinawa. He later studied commercial art at Maricopa Technical School and developed his own technique and style. Chiago draws on his years of experience as an outstanding powwow dancer who has toured throughout Arizona, California, Nevada, and the East Coast, and his paintings often depict dramatically costumed Native dancers. His body of work, which spans more than thirty years, is characterized by his pride in his Tohono O'odham heritage as well as his ability to depict the details of the Sonoran Desert. The vibrant colors of his watercolor paintings have unusual depth and brilliance that bring alive the land and the culture of his people. His work is included in the permanent collection of the Heard Museum in Phoenix, Arizona as well as in collections throughout the Southwest.

Chiricahua Apache Prisoners of War Descendants   It was inevitable that the nomadic tribes of the Southwest, dependent on extensive hunting and gathering territories, would clash with Anglo-Americans who sought to establish settlements, exploit the mineral wealth of the area, and establish safe military and commercial roads that linked the Southwest with other regions of the country. The federal government built forts and military posts as the army launched military campaigns against various Apache bands. In 1874, the Department of the Interior began a program to consolidate many Western Apaches, Chiricahuas, and Yavapais onto the San Carlos Reservation. The Chiricahuas especially resented being confined there, and in 1882, a group fled for Mexico. After pursuit by General George Crook, 335 Chiricahuas returned to San Carlos; others returned later that year and the following year. Hostilities and rivalries made life difficult in the confinement of the reservation, and the government decided to arrest **Geronimo**. In 1885, 42 Chiricahua men and their families, including **Naiche**, the son of Cochise, and Geronimo, headed for Mexico.

Pursued by the army and tracked by Apache scouts, in 1886 the Chiricahuas decided to surrender for the sake of their future survival. For the next 27 years, nearly 500 Chiricahuas—including noncombatants—were designated prisoners of war and sent to prison sites in Florida, Alabama, and eventually Fort Sill, Oklahoma. In 1913, when the military decided to use Fort Sill as an artillery training base, the federal government gave the Chiricahuas a choice of settling on allotted land in the Fort Sill area or on the Mescalero Apache Reservation in New Mexico. The Chiricahua Apache Prisoners of War Descendants is a contemporary organization whose members are descended from the last band of Chiricahuas that surrendered in 1886 in Mexico; they include the descendants of Naiche Geronimo, and the people who were with them (Trudy Griffin-Pierce, *Chiricahua Apache Enduring Power: Naiche's Puberty Ceremony Paintings* [Tuscaloosa: University of Alabama Press, 2006]).

Clovis (c. 9000 B.C.)   Named for a find made at Clovis, New Mexico, the Clovis people lived along the shorelines of ancient lakes, where mammoths and other big game grazed in a lush grassland. They killed these enormous animals with what is called a Clovis point, a chipped stone point some four or five inches long that they lashed to a wooden shaft with a sinew thong. Clovis points have been found as far north as Alaska and as far south as Chile and were used from Arizona to Nova Scotia.

clowning   Religious clowning is common throughout the Southwest as a means of social commentary and control. Clowns take the form of helmeted Chapyekam in the **Yaqui Easter ceremony**, clowns who wear sack masks in the Tohono O'odham *wigida* ceremony, Navajo and Apache clowns, and many kinds of Pueblo clowns, who appear both in *katsinam* dances and in social dances. Many anthropologists feel that clowning originated with Pueblo katsinam. Clown associations play a prominent role in Pueblo society and prescribe conformance to Pueblo mores by ridiculing individuals who have been reported for deviant behavior and publicly burlesquing them during ceremonies. Clowns often engage in sexual humor and imitate various outsiders with whom the community members have had contact.

Cochise (Chiricahua Apache, c. 1812–1874)   A leader who commanded allegiance from every local group in the Chokenen (Central Chiricahua) band of Chiricahua Apaches, Cochise was known for his military genius, wisdom, and deep sensitivity to the needs of his people. Chiricahua bands usually had several local group leaders, but Cochise was such a remarkable person that the members of all the groups recognized him as their overall leader. In 1863, soldiers tortured and shot **Mangas Coloradas**, Cochise's father-in-law, under a flag of truce, proving to Cochise that they could not be trusted. Most of Mangas Coloradas's band chose to follow Cochise, and until 1872, he led his people in the Apache Wars. His friendship with Thomas Jeffords, romanticized in Elliot Arnold's *Blood Brothers* and in the motion picture and television show *Broken Arrow*, actually began either when Jeffords was captured or when he was a trader. Nevertheless, Jeffords did become one of the few men Cochise trusted, and he, Cochise, and General O. O. Howard worked together to establish a Chiricahua reservation in southeastern Arizona in 1872. The region was peaceful until Cochise's death in 1874.

Collier, John (1884–1968) Best known for his attempts to reform federal Indian policy between 1923 and 1945, Collier organized the **American Indian Defense Association** in 1923. He devoted his entire life to a series of reform causes with the underlying theme of the denunciation of individualism and materialism in favor of community enterprise. He believed that Pueblo ideals that emphasized cooperation for the common good could help save Western society, which he felt was being destroyed by individualism. Between 1923 and 1933, Collier fought against the **assimilationist** philosophy as manifest in the **Dawes Severalty Act** by successfully defending Indian title to their land. He also forced the government to remove restrictions to the practice of Indian religious ceremonials and helped win public opinion in favor of further reforms that formed the basis of the **Indian Reorganization Act** in 1934. From 1933 to 1945, during his term as Commissioner of Indian Affairs, Collier advocated the enlargement of Indian reservations, the revival of Indian tribal governments, and the revitalization of Indian cultures. He was most successful in easing assimilationist pressure upon southwestern Indians but was unable to convince Congress that assimilation of Indians into Anglo society should be abandoned as national policy. Despite his good intentions, Collier became greatly disliked by the Navajos, primarily because the **Livestock Reduction Program** not only challenged their economic autonomy but also threatened their sense of identity. Under pressure to push through his plans before President Roosevelt left office, Collier and his staff tried to implement too many changes simultaneously. In addition to the reduction of livestock on the reservation and a program to control soil erosion, Collier introduced public works programs to minimize the economic impact of stock reduction. He further sought to expand reservation boundaries through congressional legislation and to restructure tribal government by consolidating Navajo administration into a single agency.

cultural pluralism The opposite of **assimilation**, cultural pluralism, or multiculturalism, holds that cultural diversity is desirable. This philosophy encourages the practice of Native American cultural traditions. The underlying assumption is that each group has something to offer and to learn from other groups. A person who believed in cultural pluralism was Commissioner of Indian Affairs **John Collier,** who dedicated his life to ensuring equal rights for Native American societies, including the right to practice their own cultural traditions. He also felt that Anglo-American society could benefit from learning about Native American, specifically Pueblo, beliefs.

The Dawes Severalty Act (The General Allotment Act) (1887)   Named after Massachusetts Senator Henry L. Dawes, this act provided for the allotment of Indian reservations into 160-acre farms, with the land held in trust for 25 years. Unallotted lands were opened for sale to non-Indians. The stated goal of this policy was to make Indians self-sufficient through the adoption of Euro-American style agriculture and to assimilate them into white culture via the responsibilities of individual ownership of land, which included taxation. Only a few small tribally owned areas in the Southwest were allotted.

Delgadito (Navajo, c. 1830–c.1870)   See under **Atsidi Sani**.

Delshay (Tonto Apache, c. 1835–1874)   Facing the starvation of his people while General George Crook and his troops pursued him after the Apache Wars, Delshay agreed to surrender and to settle near Camp McDowell on the Verde River in Arizona. But when unscrupulous government contractors sent shoddy goods to corrupt Indian agents, Delshay and his people were forced to steal or starve. They took matters into their own hands and left Camp McDowell, and did not surrender until 1873 when they were forced to do so. Feeling trapped, they again fled the area until a bitter winter forced them to sue for peace in 1874. Crook offered a reward for Delshay's head, and two separate groups of Apaches—from the Camp Verde Reservation and from the San Carlos Reservation—each brought in a head and tried to claim the reward.

disease   Europeans transmitted numerous communicable diseases to Native peoples, causing such a major demographic transformation that epidemic disease is considered by many to be the reason Native Americans lost the continent. Europeans had developed immunity or partial immunity, but Native peoples had not been exposed to these diseases previously. According to some estimates, between 3 and 12 million Native people were living in the present-day United States around 1500 (Duane Champagne, *Social Change and Cultural Continuity Among Native Nations* [Lanham, Md.: AltaMira Press, 2007], 117). Each wave of European immigrants, beginning with the Spaniards in the sixteenth century, carried its own set of Old World pathogens—typhus, bubonic plague, diphtheria, cholera, scarlet fever, measles, and others—that decimated

Native southwestern populations. The smallpox pandemic of 1520–1524 killed many Pueblo people. Other diseases cycled through communities every three to four years, in what must have seemed like an endless cycle of illness and death. While direct contact with Spaniards caused these infectious diseases to spread, many pathogens were transmitted by Native traders and trade goods. Mormon migration brought another wave of diseases between 1847 and 1856 that devastated populations in the Great Basin area, echoing the extent of the earlier Spanish transmission. There is no way of knowing the total Native population in the Southwest before European-introduced diseases; some estimates place the death rate in some societies as high as 95 percent. Furthermore, these populations had been so reduced by the time ethnographers recorded accounts of their cultures in the nineteenth century that it was impossible to determine accurately how complex their social organization and cultures had been before contact (Henry Dobyns, *Their Number Become Thinned: Native American Population Dynamics in Eastern North America* [Knoxville: University of Tennessee Press, 1983]; John Duffy, *Epidemics in Colonial America* [Baton Rouge: Louisiana State University Press, 1953]; Russell Thornton, *American Indian Holocaust and Survival: A Population History Since 1492* [Norman: University of Oklahoma Press, 1987]).

Dodge, Henry Chee (Navajo, 1860–1947)   The first tribal chairman of the Navajo Nation, he was renamed after his father's death for Captain Henry Linn Dodge, the Indian agent to the Navajos. He experienced the Navajo exile and incarceration at **Bosque Redondo** and was later adopted by an agency worker, who taught him English. In 1884, Dodge succeeded the great chief **Manuelito** and traveled to Washington, D.C. to meet President Chester Arthur. He became wealthy through his sheep ranch and trading post, and in 1922, he was one of three members of the Navajo Business Council that negotiated corporate agreements with business interests in the area. After the Navajo Tribal Council was created in 1923, he became its first chairman. Although he stepped down in 1928, he remained influential and in 1933 helped introduce the **Livestock Reduction Program.** In 1942, he was again elected tribal chairman.

Dozier, Edward P. (Awa Tside, Santa Clara Pueblo, 1916–1971)   Raised traditionally on the Santa Clara Reservation, Dozier went on to become a renowned anthropologist and Indian rights activist. After serving as an officer during World War II, he attended the University of New Mexico and then the University of California in Los Angeles. He is known for his work on the Tewa people who moved to Hopi in the late seventeenth century, where they developed the distinctive community of Hano at First Mesa. He authored more than twenty scholarly articles and two books and held academic positions at the University of Oregon, the University of Arizona, the University of the Philippines, and the University of Minnesota.

Enemyway Ceremony   The Enemyway Ceremony is a complex nine-day ceremony frequently performed in the summer and autumn months to cure Navajos of inappropriate contact with a non-Navajo's death. Illness may result from a variety of circumstances including, but not limited to, combat situations, automobile accidents, hospital work, or contact with human remains in archaeological ruins. This is the only Navajo chant to use a specially decorated staff known as the rattle stick. The rattle stick design represents the symbol for the bow associated with Monster Slayer, a major Navajo deity, who is one of Changing Woman's twin sons; this bow symbol represents the weapons Monster Slayer obtained from his father, the Sun. Monster Slayer used these weapons to kill great monsters that inhabited the earth during ancient times. On its east side, this rattle stick bears the bow (Monster Slayer's symbol); on its west side, it bears the wide hair queue (symbolic of his twin brother, Born-for-Water). Through the process of the ceremony, the illness-causing enemy is slain (see part IV: Franciscan Fathers 1910 and Haile 1938 and 1947 under "Navajo").

Eskiminzin (Aravaipa-Pinal Apache, c. 1825–1890)   Eskiminzin, a leader of the Arivaipa band of the Pinaleno Apaches (both later subsumed under the San Carlos subtribe of the Western Apache), persuaded his people and several other bands of Apaches to settle at Camp Grant, where they adopted a peaceful, agricultural lifestyle. Eskiminzin realized that settled life under the protection of soldiers was the only course for survival. However, while he and most of the fighting men were away, his people were attacked and killed by a group of Tucson citizens, Mexican Americans, and Tohono O'odham Indians in 1871 during the **Camp Grant Massacre.**

Gadsden Purchase   The 1853 Gadsden Purchase added what is now southern Arizona and New Mexico to the United States. After the Southwest and California were acquired from Mexico, a transcontinental railroad linking them to the rest of the country became a necessity. The most suitable route was south of the Gila River, which was under Mexican control at that time. In 1853, President Franklin Pierce sent South Carolinian James Gadsden to buy the 30,000-square-mile wedge of territory between western Texas and southern California for $10 million. His treasury depleted by the recent war with the United States, Mexican President Santa Anna signed the treaty on December 30.

Ganado Mucho (Navajo-Hopi, c. 1809–1893)   Son of a Navajo mother and a Hopi father, Ganado Mucho was a Navajo headman, rancher, and peacemaker. In the 1850s, his large herds made him suspected of cattle theft, but, denying these charges, he signed an agreement with other peaceful Navajo ranchers to report and return any stolen livestock. He did not participate in the raiding or warfare that was so widespread between the Navajo and the army with its Ute Indian allies. Ute and Mexican raiders killed two of his daughters and a son, but he still encouraged peace during the Navajo War of 1863–1866. Facing starvation, Ganado Mucho's band surrendered, and he led them on the **Long Walk** to **Bosque Redondo,** where they were held as prisoners. In 1868, Ganado Mucho and other leaders signed the peace treaty that resulted in the Navajo Reservation. He returned there with his people, continuing his efforts for peace until his death.

gathering   Even in southwestern societies that depended upon agriculture, collecting wild plants still contributed considerably to the economy. Before the introduction of agriculture, wild plants provided an even greater part of the Native diet than did game. Women were nearly always responsible for gathering them. Among the Tohono O'odham, wild plants probably provided more food year round than did agriculture and hunting combined, so women contributed more to the economy than did men. Some peoples, such as the Yavapai of central Arizona, depended on an annual round of gathering that they supplemented with hunting. With intimate knowledge of the terrain, they knew exactly where to find specific plant foods as they ripened, and they returned to these places each year. In autumn, women harvested and processed berries, seeds, and the fruit of the banana yucca, while men stood guard in areas where they were vulnerable to attack. They used grinding stones to pulverize seeds and nuts on bedrock mortars before storing them in pots and baskets sealed with plant gum. These containers were then cached in caves and other protected places. Entire bands congregated at large stands of agave, a staple of the Yavapai diet because of its year-round availability, to spend as long as three or four months harvesting, roasting, and drying the hearts of these plants that would see them through the winter.

Geronimo (Chiricahua Apache, c. 1825–1909)   Famed Apache war leader Geronimo was born into the Bedonkohe band of the Chiricahua Apache. When their leader, **Mangas Coloradas**, was killed, most of the Bedonkohes, including Geronimo, joined **Cochise's** band of Chokenen Chiricahuas. Hunger for land led Anglo-Americans to abolish the Chiricahua Reservation in 1876 and to uproot the Chiricahua from their homeland. The government planned to consolidate the disparate groups of Apaches from Arizona and southwestern New Mexico on the San Carlos Reservation, where they suffered from insufficient rations and conflict among Anglo administrators as well as among themselves. Geronimo and others, however, refused to submit, and broke out. He was captured several times but always managed to escape until his final surrender in 1886, which led to twenty-seven years of captivity. Along with those Chiricahua who had served as scouts for the army and those who had not fled the reservation, the tribe were sent into exile in Florida, then Alabama, and finally Fort Sill, Oklahoma, where Geronimo died.

Girl's Puberty Ceremony   An Athapaskan tradition that the Apaches and Navajo brought with them to the Southwest, the Girl's Puberty Ceremony celebrates the passage of a young girl into womanhood. Held at or near the time of her first menses, the ceremony takes different forms for the Navajo, who call it the *Kinaaldá*, and for the various Apache tribes, who have their own versions. The ritual reaffirms traditional values and infuses the girl with White Painted Woman's powers of renewal and rebirth. Emphasizing four crucial life objectives, the ceremony stresses the attainment of a healthy old age, having a good disposition and maintaining friendly relationships with others, developing the endurance and strength necessary to carry out adult responsibilities as an Apache woman, and ensuring that the girl will always have an abundance of all that she needs in life, including shelter and food for herself and her family (see part IV: Frisbie 1967 under "Navajo"; Basso 1966 and 1970a, Farrer 1980 and 1991 under "Apache"; and *The Sunrise Dance* under "Films").

Gorman, Carl Nelson (Navajo, 1907–1998)   **Navajo Code Talker** and well-known artist Carl Gorman was among the first to use traditional Navajo motifs in contemporary art. His distinguished family included traditionalists, tribal leaders, and silversmiths. His father was a cattleman and Indian trader; his mother was a traditional weaver who translated many hymns from English into Navajo. Together, they founded the first Presbyterian mission at Chinle. During World War II, Gorman joined the marines and served as one of the Navajo Code Talkers. After the war, he studied at the Otis Art Institute in Los Angeles under the G.I. Bill and later worked as an illustrator for Douglas Aircraft. He also taught Indian art at the University of California, Davis and established his own silkscreen business. Represented in many public and private collections, Gorman's innovative works include a wide range of styles and media.

Gorman, R. C. (Navajo, 1932–2005)   A leading contemporary artist and son of Carl Gorman, R. C. Gorman was born in Chinle, Arizona on the Navajo reservation. His artistic ability was encouraged at an early age, and he was drawing by the time he was three years old. As a child, he herded sheep and lived in a hogan with his grandmother. After graduating from Ganado Presbyterian High School, he studied art at Northern Arizona University in Flagstaff and at

San Francisco State University. When he was the first artist awarded a grant by the Navajo Tribal Council for study outside the United States, Gorman went to Mexico City College to study art. Already well known for his drawing and painting, in 1966 he turned to lithography under the tutelage of master printer José Sanchez in Mexico City. Lithography is the art of producing a picture on a flat, specially prepared stone, using greasy pencils and/or washes from an oily liquid; this image is then etched into the stone with acid in a solution of gum arabic, inked, and printed. A separate image must be prepared for each color of the picture and each color is printed separately; great care must be taken to register the separate color images so that they fit together correctly in the completed picture. In the 1970s, Gorman began to work with the master printers of the world-famous Tamarind Institute in Albuquerque to produce a large body of lithographs. He was the only living artist to be included in the 1973 Metropolitan Museum show "Masterworks of the Museum of the American Indian," and in 1975, he was the first artist chosen for a series of solo exhibitions of contemporary Indian art at the Museum of the American Indian.

government   The first Native peoples in the Southwest probably governed themselves by consensus under family leadership. Over time, as some groups developed agricultural societies that lived in permanent villages, more structured forms of government became necessary. Among the Puebloan peoples, several different patterns emerged. Among the Western Pueblos, clans dominate government, religious, subsistence, and community affairs, and government is essentially theocratic. Social control is maintained through gossip and "enforcement" by special *katsinam* as well as through avoidance of an offender. The Keresan Pueblos have the most centralized authority in the form of powerful medicine societies, while the Eastern Tanoan Pueblos alternate leadership in the form of a dual chieftainship according to moiety, the dual division of a village. For six months one moiety governs and for the other six months, the other moiety rules. More nomadic peoples tended to be governed by a headman, who attained his position through his generosity and the respect in which others held him; however, he exercised little control or actual authority. The O'odham make decisions by consensus, which means that agreement has to be reached no matter how long the process takes; the headman can only voice his opinion.

Contemporary tribes, nations, and Native communities in the Southwest (as elsewhere) elect the members of their tribal councils, a form of government that was established after the Indian Reorganization Act. The tribal government of each group selects their official designation. Some groups continue to be known as tribes, such as the White Mountain Apache Tribe and the Hopi Tribe, while others use "nation," such as the Navajo Nation and the Tohono

O'odham Nation. Still others call themselves "Indian communities," such as the Gila River Indian Community.

Hatathli, Ned (Navajo, 1923–1972)   After a traditional childhood, Ned Hatathli attended boarding school and then the Haskell Institute in Lawrence, Kansas but left to join the navy when World War II broke out. After the war, he completed his Ph.D. in education at Northern Arizona University and returned to the reservation to become a leader in the movement toward greater economic opportunity. He helped found the Navajo Arts and Crafts Guild, and in 1955 he was elected to the Navajo Tribal Council and appointed director of tribal resources. When the tribal council decided to create Navajo Community College (now known as Diné College), he became the school's first president.

Hayes, Ira Hamilton (Pima, 1923–1955)   Born into a Pima farming family, Ira Hayes grew up traditionally until World War II broke out and he joined the marines, becoming part of the invasion force that attacked the Japanese stronghold of Iwo Jima. To signal the end of Japanese control, Hayes and five others raised a replacement flag on the summit of Mount Surabachi under heavy Japanese fire, an act that was commemorated in the famous photograph. He developed a drinking problem while on the War Bonds Tour across the United States and was never able to regain a sense of balance in his life. He was buried in Arlington Cemetery as a hero.

Hisatsinom (c. 500 B.C.–A.D. 1540)   Both archaeologists and the Hopis trace Hopi ancestry to the Hisatsinom (Hopi for "people from long ago"), who lived in northeastern Arizona. The first substantial presence in the Hopi mesa area dates to about 700 A.D. at Antelope Mesa, east of present-day Keams Canyon. Numerous small villages flourished between 900 and 1100 A.D. when aboveground dwellings replaced pit houses. A subsequent period of extended drought resulted in the clustering of the area's population into larger villages such as Oraibi, Betatakin, and those found in Canyon de Chelly. By the 1500s, Hopi society was highly developed with an elaborate ceremonial cycle, complex social organization, and advanced agricultural system. *Katsinam* are linked to all aspects of Hopi existence, including each of the above-mentioned social complexes (see part IV: Colwell-Chanthaphonh and Ferguson 2007, Whiteley 2002 under "Archaeological Studies").

Hohokam culture (A.D. 700–1350)   The Sonoran Desert was home to the Hohokam culture, and these people farmed the fertile valleys of the Salt, Gila, and Santa Cruz rivers in southern Arizona. Based on riverine farming and canal irrigation, their culture produced elaborate pottery, stone carvings, and textiles. They also traded widely and practiced a rich ceremonial tradition. What most distinguishes the Hohokam from other precontact peoples is the fact that they cremated their dead and that they constructed an extensive network of irrigation canals to water their fields. They dug these canals by hand, using digging sticks and stone tools. They also had to periodically clean and maintain the canals and gates and to rebuild them after floods. Hohokam society had to develop a considerable degree of social and political complexity in order to direct the labor to build and maintain such irrigation networks and to make decisions about who received water, how much, and when. The Hohokam culture developed through expanding trade networks, the elaboration of household structures, greater complexity in material culture, and a ritual system based on a sacred public ball game, played on ball courts similar to those found throughout Mesoamerica. The people also had elaborate mortuary rituals that included offerings of ceramic and stone vessels, stone axes, arrow points, and stone palettes, indicating a belief in an afterlife. Hohokam artifacts include human and animal figures made of clay and stone, shell jewelry, and pottery. The Hohokam began to abandon their villages in the mid-1300s, long before the arrival of the Spaniards, but most archaeologists believe that contemporary O'odham peoples are their descendants. The O'odham consider the Hohokam to be their ancestors.

Homol'ovi (c. A.D. 1250–1425)   Located 60 miles south of present-day Hopi villages, Homol'ovi (Hopi for "the place of little hills") is ancestral to the villages of the modern Hopi. Four separate pueblo ruins run along a 20-mile stretch of the Little Colorado River near Winslow, Arizona. Occupied between A.D. 1250 and 1425, Homol'ovi is considered by the Hopi to be the home of specific clans. The people of these pueblos raised corn, beans, squash, and cotton. Cotton was a valuable commodity that enabled them to **trade** for goods from as far away as Mexico. Around 1400, the inhabitants of Homol'ovi began to move to the steep-sided Hopi mesas, which provided protection and a constant supply of water. The site of Homol'ovi is a key link between precontact Hopi people and the contemporary Hopi villages because it is where the change in style to katsinalike figures occurred in *kiva* murals. Archaeologists consider this relatively sudden change to mark the beginning of a major shift in worldview.

Hopis   The Hopi people live on and near the southern escarpment of Black Mesa in northeastern Arizona on a reservation that is surrounded by the Navajos. The Hopi language is a member of the Uto-Aztecan family. These westernmost Puebloan people live in thirteen villages of three fingerlike projections south from Black Mesa and to the west along Moenkopi Wash. Despite the fact that each village was traditionally a separate political entity, the federal government imposed a form of tribal government as a single governing body. Regardless of village origin, all Hopis are part of the Hopi Tribe.

Houser, Allan (Haozous) (Chiricahua Apache, 1914–1994)   An internationally recognized sculptor and painter, Allan Houser used his art to bridge the spirit of Apache culture and contemporary American life. His father, a grandson of **Mangas Coloradas** and a nephew of **Geronimo,** was among those imprisoned by U.S. troops when the Chiricahua Apaches were deported from Arizona. Allan Houser was one of the first children born at Fort Sill, Oklahoma after the Chiricahua were released from captivity. He grew up hearing his father's stories about the days when their people wandered freely across their Arizona homeland, and throughout his life, he drew inspiration for his art from these tales, songs, and myths. In 1936 he began to study painting at the Santa Fe Indian School, and he later painted two murals for the Department of the Interior in Washington, D.C. During World War II, he worked as a pipefitter's assistant in Los Angeles while taking art classes at night. By 1949, Houser had created his first monumental work in stone, a seven-and-a-half-foot figure honoring Native American servicemen who had died in World War II. Guggenheim fellowships followed, and in 1962, he joined the art faculty of the Institute of American Indian Arts in Santa Fe. During his lifetime, his work was acquired by the U.S. mission to the United Nations, the British Royal Collection, the National Portrait Gallery of the Smithsonian, and the Pompidou Museum in Paris. He left a lasting legacy of human dignity in his monumental bronze, steel, and stone sculptures of Plains warriors, Navajo and Pueblo shepherds, and Apache mothers and children.

housing   Although contemporary Native peoples live in the same wide range of housing as Anglo-Americans, precontact southwestern peoples lived under rock overhangs or in caves. Later they developed pit houses, and Ancestral Pueblo peoples built masonry pueblos and cliff dwellings. Their descendants, the Pueblo peoples, lived in apartmentlike houses with rectangular, flat-roofed rooms built flush against each other. In the Rio Grande area, they used adobe (clay); farther west, they built these houses primarily of stone on which they spread plaster. Over a frame of logs and poles, River Yuman peoples of the lower Colorado River used a thatch of arrow weed that they covered with sand. Placing the door in the middle of the southern wall, they constructed a nearly flat roof and used sand to cover it and three sides, so that the house was only visible from the front. A number of related families lived in each house. Upland Yuman houses were less permanent dome-shaped huts constructed of poles and branches on a four-pole foundation covered with juniper bark or thatch and occasionally mud; their winter homes were more substantial and were plastered with mud to keep out the cold. The Navajo hogan was originally an east-facing conical structure with a forked-pole foundation covered with earth; this evolved into a polysided structure with walls of horizontal logs or slabs of stone, depending upon the available materials, and a cribwork roof. Mud was plastered over the outside and on the roof. (Today, many Navajo homesteads have a hogan that is kept for ceremonial use.) The Apache wickiup also had a pole foundation but was a less permanent structure covered with thatch instead of earth. The O'odham people built sprawling settlements with a round house and ramada (an open-sided shade with a brush roof supported by posts) for the men's nightly council meeting. Each family had a compound that consisted of a ramada, a cooking enclosure, food storage houses, a corral, and a house made of brush.

hunting   All Native southwestern peoples once depended upon hunting for part of their subsistence. The **Paleo-Indians** hunted mammoths and other large game animals with spears, while the people of the **Archaic period** that followed had to depend on smaller game because climatic shifts led to the extinction of large mammals. Game was often scarce for the Pueblos, whose hunting land was either controlled by the entire pueblo or shared with outsiders. The rabbit was the most common single species of game, captured in a communal drive by all the men in the pueblo. Most Apache groups relied heavily on hunting and wild plant gathering, as did the Upland Yumans except for the Havasupai, who farmed in the summer. Among the Chiricahua Apache, bands controlled hunting tracts, while patrilocality among the Tohono O'odham and River Yumans kept together lines of men who had hunted over the same territory for many generations. Hunting rituals preceded the pursuit of game, and many groups had a hunt shaman (see **religion**).

Indian Gaming Regulatory Act (IGRA) (1988)   When federal funding diminished significantly during the 1980s, Indian governments pursued alternative means of generating the revenue needed to finance important tribal programs. Tribes that lacked a sizable tax base or considerable natural resources often turned to gaming to provide the needed revenue. Although there were initial concerns about the possibility of organized crime infiltration, competition with non-Indian gaming enterprises, and state lotteries, Indian gaming has become recognized as a highly successful means of economic development. Federal, state, and tribal governments have addressed these concerns through federal statute and tribal-state agreements.

In 1988 the federal government enacted the Indian Gaming Regulatory Act (IGRA), which separates gaming into three classes and allocates regulatory jurisdiction over each class among tribal, state, and federal sovereigns. Class I consists of social games of minimal value, as well as traditional Indian games played in connection with ceremonies. Class I gaming is under exclusive tribal regulation. Class II includes bingo, pull tabs, lotto, and similar games, and is subject to tribal regulatory jurisdiction with oversight by the National Indian Gaming Commission. Class III includes all other forms of gaming, including casino-style gaming. Class III activities must be authorized by a tribal ordinance and approval by the chairperson of the gaming commission. The state must allow Class III gaming for any purpose by any person, but the tribe must conduct the activity to conform with a state-tribal compact that sets forth the parameters of permissible gaming. This contract also establishes the extent of state regulation; it is designed to balance the economic needs of the tribe and the protective goals of the state. (See the discussion at the end of chapter 4 regarding the Tohono O'odham Nation for an example of how one southwestern Indian tribe is using its gaming revenues.)

Indian New Deal   The focal point of the reforms known as the Indian New Deal was the **Indian Reorganization Act**. While Commissioner of Indian Affairs **John Collier** was preparing this legislation, he launched the Indian New Deal through a series of administrative orders. The Indians were guaranteed full expression of their religious and cultural traditions, and compulsory attendance by Indian students at Christian religious services while attending government schools was prohibited. The debt charged against tribal funds as a result of earlier federal loan programs was canceled. Collier also got President Roosevelt to abolish the pro-**assimilationist** Board of Indian Commissioners. He worked closely with the Secretary of Agriculture to obtain agriculture and reclamation relief funds for Indians. Other aspects of Collier's Indian New Deal included a bill that repealed twelve objectionable nineteenth-century statutes limiting Indians' basic civil liberties and the Pueblo Relief Act, which increased monetary awards to the Pueblo Indians of New Mexico for losses of their land and water determined under a 1924 statute. The **Johnson-O'Malley Act** gave the Secretary of the Interior authority to contract with states to provide for educational, medical, and social welfare needs of Indians.

Indian Reorganization Act (1934)   For most tribes, the most important result of the Indian Reorganization Act (IRA) or Wheeler-Howard Act, which was signed into law June 18, 1934, was the abandonment of the federal government's allotment policy. The IRA heralded a major change in federal Indian policy: during 50 years of allotment, Indians had lost nearly 90 million acres of land guaranteed them by treaties and the executive orders that had established their reservations; the IRA returned some of it. However, in contrast to most of the rest of the country, the Southwest had not been subject to the division of tribal domains into separate individual farms primarily because land in the region was less desirable to settlers. Thus, southwestern Native peoples were able to continue practicing their communal systems of land tenure. Based on the idea of self-determination for Indian people through self-government, the IRA promoted communal enterprises as a means to economic improvement and the formation of tribal constitutional governments. Although the IRA was intended to reorganize the Bureau of Indian Affairs (BIA) so that it fostered true self-government among tribes, it actually increased the power of the Secretary of the Interior, who supervised the BIA, and failed to correct the abuses of authority among BIA reservation superintendents.

Irateba (Irataba, Arateva, or Yaratev, Mojave, c. 1814–1878) Irateba, the chief of the Huttoh-pah band of Mojaves, responded peacefully to the first Anglo-American expedition into his country, by army Lieutenant Ives in 1849. He later traveled with other expeditions to San Diego and Los Angeles and served as a guide on Ives's overland explorations that went up the Colorado River from 1856 through 1857. He gained a reputation for his knowledge of animal life, food resources, geography, and topography of the region. As whites encroached in greater numbers, the Mojaves were alarmed and attacked settlers in 1858. Soldiers then built Fort Mojave and called a meeting with Irateba and other chiefs, some of whom they held hostage. Irateba was not among the hostages; when he later became chief of his people, he traveled to Los Angeles in 1861 to negotiate better conditions for them. However, the discovery of gold in California and Mormon pressure had stirred up Indian–white relations. The government asked Irateba to tour eastern cities so that he could see the power of the government. He did so and also received a silver-headed cane from President Lincoln. He advocated peace when he returned, but a rival faction of Mojaves captured him and held him captive, causing him to lose prestige and power among his people.

Johnson-O'Malley Act (1934) Based on the premise that social services to Indians would be best supplied by state governments, this act authorized the Secretary of the Interior to enter into contracts with state and local governments for the funding of educational and welfare programs in order to offset federal costs. An amendment added two years later enabled parties other than the state to contract with the Department of the Interior. In 1975, the Indian Self-Determination and Education Assistance Act reformed the Johnson-O'Malley Act by authorizing tribes to make contracts for education with businesses in the public sector. As the program evolved, enrichment aspects and Indian parental control were strengthened, which won support from Indian communities. When the Bureau of Indian Affairs tried to take away funding for the program in 1986, Congress represented the overwhelming support of Indian people by restoring funding.

katsinam   Spirit beings who serve as intermediaries to the Hopi deities, katsinam embody the spirits of nature in tangible form. As such, they are not worshiped but rather are respected as powerful forces that help bring much-needed rain and other blessings. The word *katsina* refers to both the incorporeal katsina spirit and the dancer who brings this spirit to life.

Young girls are given a *tihu*—a small, carved wooden representation of a katsina—that they treat as their child, and the tihu bestows upon them the power of reproduction. As girls grow older, each tihu that they receive will be more elaborate, with a fully carved head and body.

Children are taught that the katsina spirit is a real being, a symbol of abundance, goodness, and generosity associated with reproduction, and that they must pray for the abundance of what they receive. Katsinam also admonish: the Soya Katsina comes at a certain time of year to try to take the children. When their parents protect them, the children learn both the value of good behavior and that they can count on their relatives. Upon initiation into the Katsina Society at puberty, young men enter the adult world of their fathers, uncles, and brothers, learning that katsinam are danced by humans. When he is finally allowed to participate as an adult, a young man achieves great spiritual fulfillment as he puts aside his personal identity to become the katsina he represents.

Keresan languages   A language isolate, Keresan is spoken only by certain Pueblo tribes in the southwestern United States. Its two closely related divisions are Western Keresan, spoken by the people of Laguna and Acoma pueblos, and Rio Grande or Eastern Keresan, spoken in the pueblos of Zia, Santa Ana, San Felipe, Santo Domingo, and Cochiti.

kinship   A range of descent reckoning is found among southwestern Native peoples. The Western Pueblos, as well as the Navajo and Western Apache and the Southeastern Yavapai, take their clan identity from their mother; this means that women own the houses, make important decisions, and care for the ritual possessions of the family. The clan, composed of lineages that are believed to be related through a common ancestor, is a corporate group that holds ritual knowledge and economic goods in common for future generations. The Eastern Keresan Pueblos have a more equal relationship between maternal and paternal relatives, with more importance placed on the nuclear rather than the extended matrilineal family. Although the Keresans have clans, they appear to govern only exogamy, marriage outside one's clan. The Tanoan Pueblos of the Rio Grande area are bilateral, which means that descent is reckoned through both parents.

Kiowa-Tanoan languages   Kiowa-Tanoan languages include Kiowa, spoken on the Great Plains, and its southwestern divisions of Tiwa, Tewa, and Towa as well as Piro. Tiwa is spoken in Taos, Picuris, Sandia, and Isleta pueblos, and, although only a few words remain today, was the language of the Tiguas, a small federally recognized tribe that lives in the community of Ysleta del Sur near El Paso. Tewa is spoken in the Rio Grande pueblos of San Juan, Santa Clara, San Ildefonso, Pojoaque, Nambé, and Tesuque. Tewa speakers continue to live in Hano on First Mesa with the Hopi in Arizona; they established this village after leaving the Rio Grande area between the Pueblo Revolt of 1680 and the Spanish reconquest in 1692 so that they did not have to face Spanish reprisals. The people of Jemez (and the extinct pueblo of Pecos) speak Towa. Piro was spoken by the people of Piro Pueblo, who once lived from just below Isleta to the present location of Socorro, New Mexico.

kiva   A kiva is a ceremonial structure built by the Pueblo peoples or their ancestors. In some pueblos it is partly or wholly underground, and it may be either circular or rectangular. Though used for ceremonies, a kiva is also a men's workshop and, among the Western Pueblos, a men's dormitory.

Klah, Hosteen (Navajo, c. 1867–1937)   When Hosteen Klah was a young boy, he fell off a pony and had to use crutches, and an uncle who was a medicine man performed the Wind Chant over him. After this five-day ritual, the Fire Ceremony was also sung over him, which inspired Klah to learn the ceremonies. It was discovered that he was a hermaphrodite, an honorable state in Navajo culture because it combines both sexes. Klah was chosen to become a weaver at the World's Columbian Exposition in Chicago in the early 1890s and later became an outstanding artisan, although traditionally most Navajo weavers were women. (Today, more men are weaving than in the past.) He continued his studies as a medicine man and became a respected practitioner of the Night Chant, and worked with Dr. Washington Matthews to record this ceremony. Realizing that sandpainting is an important component in many ceremonies, Klah decided to preserve these images in his rugs and wove more than two dozen ceremonial-inspired textiles. He became friends with Mary Cabot Wheelwright, who founded the Wheelwright Museum of the American Indian in Santa Fe to memorialize Klah's work.

Livestock Reduction Program (Navajo)   During the 1930s, a critical element of **John Collier**'s policy was the reduction of Navajo herds to combat overgrazing that had resulted in erosion and permanent deterioration of the range. The initial reduction in the fall of 1933 showed that a voluntary program would not work because the Navajos were unwilling to surrender what was to them a way of life and a gift from the Holy People. Stock reduction the following year was hindered by growing suspicion and resistance from the Navajos as well as poor management on the part of the government. In some cases, the animals were allowed to starve in their holding pens; in other cases, they were shot and the carcasses were burned. Many Navajos call Livestock Reduction "the Second Long Walk" because it was as much a violation as the **Long Walk** of 1863–1868, when they were exiled from their homeland and forced to walk to Bosque Redondo.

Loloma, Charles (Hopi, 1921–1991)   Charles Loloma, whose art is known internationally, created distinctive jewelry by using traditional forms, the stylistic attributes of contemporary art and industrial design, and unusual combinations of materials, such as gold and diamonds with wood and turquoise. His work was so innovative that his early jewelry was rejected by judges at the Gallup Indian Art Show as non-Indian, despite the fact that he was full-blooded Hopi and was born and raised on the Hopi Reservation. In 1939 he painted murals for the Golden Gate International Exposition in San Francisco, and in 1940 the Indian Arts and Crafts Board commissioned him to paint murals for the Museum of Modern Art in New York. Drafted into the army, he worked as a camouflage expert in the Aleutian Islands. Four years later, after his discharge, he chose to follow an unusual course by studying ceramics, which is traditionally a woman's art among the Hopi, at the well-known School for American Craftsmen at Alfred University in New York. After he received a Whitney Foundation fellowship to study the clays of the Hopi area, he and his wife opened a shop in Scottsdale, Arizona. Loloma also taught ceramics at Arizona State University before he became head of the Plastic Arts and Sales departments at the Institute of American Indian Arts in Santa Fe. Loloma will always be remembered for his talent in bringing out the intrinsic visual qualities of such varied materials as silver, gold, turquoise, coral, shell, and wood in his dramatic designs.

Lomahaftewa, Linda (Hopi-Choctaw, 1947–)   A painter whose work focuses on Plains Indian culture, Linda Lòmahaftewa studied at the Institute of American Indian Arts in Santa Fe and at the San Francisco Art Institute before becoming an art educator in the 1970s. She taught at the San Francisco Art Institute, California State College in Sonoma, and the University of California at Berkeley. Her work has been shown in more than forty exhibitions, including shows in New York City and California. She is listed among other prominent contemporary Native American artists in two editions of *Who's Who in American Indian Arts.*

The Long Walk (1863–1868) Brigadier General Carleton, U.S. military commander for New Mexico, decided that the Mescalero Apaches and the Navajo should be removed to **Bosque Redondo** (Fort Sumner). Despite the fact that a board of officers recommended that another location be selected because of lack of wood, poor water, and threat of floods, Carleton continued with his plans for establishing this military post on the Pecos River in east central New Mexico. In 1863 he instructed Colonel **Christopher (Kit) Carson** to inform the Navajo that if they did not go to Bosque Redondo, they would be killed. Carson was told to practice a scorched-earth policy, with troops destroying cornfields, fruit trees, water holes, hogans, animals, and people. Starving, many Navajos surrendered near the end of 1863 and the beginning of 1864 at Fort Defiance (then known as Fort Canby). They were forced to walk over 300 miles to Bosque Redondo in what was essentially a death march; stragglers, including pregnant women who went into labor, were shot. After a long period of imprisonment during which many died, a peace treaty was signed and the Navajos were allowed to return to a portion of their homeland.

Lovato, Charles (Santo Domingo Pueblo, 1937–) In Santo Domingo, one of the most conservative Rio Grande pueblos, it is not considered appropriate to leave permanent records of ceremonial dances and other village activities. In keeping with this tradition, Charles Lovato, while using themes and symbols from his Santo Domingo heritage, has become known for abstract rather than representational painting. He studied art at what was then known as the Santa Fe Indian School, where he developed his own style, with images that tell a story that is reflected in the title of the painting. *In Search of Food* depicts deer tracks followed by mountain lion tracks. His titles are usually poetic, such as *With the Sunrise Comes the Sounds of Life*, which shows yellow flames emanating from one of three pots, along with geometric designs, tracks of humans, animals, and birds; this casein painting won the Bialac Purchase Award at the Heard Museum Fair in 1968. Lovato's work also won awards at the Gallup Ceremonials in 1969 in the abstract field. In 1970, at the Philbrook show, his abstract acrylic painting won the top award in the Southwest Artists category. He has won many more awards since then and become a world-famous artist (Clara Lee Tanner, *Southwest Indian Painting: A Changing Art*, 2nd ed. [Tucson: University of Arizona Press, 1980], 194–197).

MacDonald, Peter (Navajo, 1928–) Known for his defense of Navajo land and energy resource rights, Peter MacDonald was tribal chairman for three terms, beginning in 1965. During World War II, he joined the marines as one of the **Navajo Code Talkers**. When MacDonald returned from the war, he earned a bachelor's degree from Bacone College in Muskogee, Oklahoma and then a degree in electrical engineering from the University of Oklahoma. In 1963 he served on the New Mexico Economic Development Advisory Board and later became director of the Office of Navajo Economic Opportunity (ONEO). Between 1965 and 1968 he helped bring in over $20 million in federal grants. During his terms as Navajo Tribal Chairman, he fought to renegotiate mineral leases and the control of Colorado River water rights as well as to keep industrial development under tribal control; he was also an outspoken critic of the Bureau of Indian Affairs. Despite charges of fraud and favoritism during his administration, he contributed greatly toward Navajo self-determination and energy use management.

Mangas Coloradas (Chiricahua Apache, c. 1791–1863)   Mangas Coloradas was a statesman and leader of the Chihennes (Eastern Chiricahua) band of Chiricahua Apache. In 1837, Mexican trappers, motivated by the Mexican government's bounty on Indian scalps, massacred a number of important Chihennes leaders, and Coloradas united his people in retaliation. After the United States took control of the region in 1848, miners poured into his homeland. Some of them captured and whipped Coloradas, who survived and increased his attacks against U.S. and Mexican miners. In 1863, he was invited to a peace parley and was killed under a flag of truce.

Manuelito (Navajo, c. 1818–1894)   Navajo leader Manuelito was a powerful warrior against the Mexicans, Hopi, and Zuni, leading many raids and thus rising to prominence. In 1860, the year after troops had destroyed his home, crops, and livestock, Manuelito and another headman led warriors who nearly captured Fort Defiance. Despite a brief period of peace, open warfare erupted when the government sent **Kit Carson** to kill or relocate all Navajos to **Bosque Redondo** near Fort Sumner, New Mexico. Manuelito's band maintained resistance against Carson's troops, holding out the longest among Navajo bands, but starvation led them to surrender in 1866. With other headmen, Manuelito traveled to Washington, D.C. to petition for a Navajo reservation that was established in 1868. He served as principal Navajo chief and chief of the tribal police. He later returned to Washington to meet President Ulysses S. Grant.

Masayesva, Victor, Jr. (Hopi, 1951–)   Victor Masayesva, from the Hopi village of Hotevilla on Third Mesa, is one of the most original artists working today. Known for his intellectually and visually complex layering of video and audio effects as well as his still photography, he has produced a large body of award-winning work that integrates his personal vision as an artist with the inspiration he draws from his tribal heritage. His photographs of fellow Hopis and community activities reflect a level of intimacy and trust that is seldom captured by outside photographers. Although many of his images depict contemporary Hopi life, many of his video pieces focus on the Anglo-American world's devaluation of Indian people's experiences and encompass American Indians in more general terms. In 1992, for example, he envisioned the history of Hollywood film through Indian eyes in communities where local people were hired to as actors, entitling his piece *Imagining Indians*. Anglo-American control is shown in a fictional scene set in a dentist's office, intercut with interviews and selections from Hollywood movies. The Corporation for Public Broadcasting (CPB) has funded much of Masayesva's cutting-edge work (Elizabeth Weatherford, "Film and Video," and Natasha Bonilla Martinez, "Photography," in *Native America in the Twentieth Century*, ed. Mary B. Davis [New York and London: Garland, 1994], 201, 451).

The Meriam Report *(The Problem of Indian Administration)* **(1928)** Lewis M. Meriam, appointed as technical director of a survey of Indian affairs commissioned by the Rockefeller Foundation and conducted by the Institute for Government Research, edited the 872-page report *The Problem of Indian Administration*. The staff of law professors, historians, sociologists, and educators traveled widely, inspecting locations and conducting interviews with agency workers, Indian leaders, and local whites. The major recommendations of their report focused on improving services and administration by the Bureau of Indian Affairs to deal with the extreme poverty, lack of dependable health care, inadequate education, and poor living conditions found on every reservation and at every off-reservation boarding school they visited. The report condemned the existing federal Indian educational system as well as the land allotment provisions of the **Dawes Severalty Act** and urged the federal government to replace its policy of **assimilation** with one of **cultural pluralism**, although it cautioned that Indians had lost their past means of subsistence and would have to adjust to Anglo-American culture.

Mimbres culture (A.D. 900–1200) The Mimbres, named for the river near their homeland in present-day southeastern New Mexico, were a **Mogollon** people known for making some of the most imaginative and elegant pottery ever produced in North America. Around A.D. 700 they began to decorate their pottery with designs, probably as a result of influence from the **Hohokam**. However, it was not until A.D. 900 that Mimbres potters began to create their distinctive black-on-white pottery, possibly inspired by the pottery of the **Ancestral Pueblo**. Each piece was different and featured geometric patterns that were both bold and delicate, with stylized naturalistic designs that included such images as turkeys, fish, bears, humans, mountain lions, flowers, and bats. The Mimbres created pottery that featured both ceremonies and daily life in graphic style. They framed each design with a precisely rendered

¾-inch border near the rim of the bowl comprising as many as 15 parallel lines. So prized were these bowls that they were buried with the dead.

Mogollon culture (A.D. 700–1130)   While the **Ancestral Pueblos (Anasazi)** lived on the Colorado Plateau and the **Hohokam** lived in the river valleys of southern Arizona, the Mogollon lived in the central mountains of Arizona and New Mexico, where limited farmland led them to rely primarily on game such as deer and turkey and wild plants. Their culture got its name from the Mogollon Mountains of southwestern New Mexico, named for Juan Ignacio Flores Mogollon, who governed New Mexico from 1712 to 1715. They began making pottery around A.D. 200 but continued to rely on baskets, which were more practical for their hunting-and-gathering lifestyle. As their culture developed, with influence from the **Ancestral Pueblo** people, they built ceremonial rooms, plazas, and great kivas that show they placed considerable importance on religion in their community life. After the Great Drought in the 1200s, the Ancestral Pueblo migrated south into the mountains and lived in large pueblo communities with the Mogollon for almost a century. Around A.D. 1300, the Mogollon's lifestyle became much more like that of the Ancestral Pueblo, including the emphasis on farming, social patterns, and religion. By A.D. 1400, they had abandoned their last mountain pueblo. The Zuni are the only present-day group in the American Southwest who are descended from the Mogollon.

Montezuma, Carlos (Yavapai, 1867–1923)   A full-blooded Yavapai who was captured as a child by the Akimel O'odham, Carlos Montezuma was raised by a white photographer who gave him his name. In 1884, Montezuma graduated from the University of Illinois; five years later he earned a degree in medicine from the Chicago Medical College. He then worked as a doctor on a series of reservations; in later years, his frustration with the health system led him to advocate the abolition of the Bureau of Indian Affairs and the reservation system itself. Montezuma worked at Carlisle Indian School in Pennsylvania and then opened a private practice in gastroenterology in Chicago. Once established, Montezuma devoted his life to activism for Indian rights, especially the abolition of the BIA. He spent his last thirteen years working against the relocation of the Fort McDowell Yavapai. As the people on this reservation fought for land with water rights, Montezuma assisted them with time and resources. With his understanding of both tribal and Anglo worlds, he wrote essays and gave speeches that were acknowledged by government officials, such as Theodore Roosevelt and Woodrow Wilson.

music and dance   Indispensable to all rituals and ceremonies, most types of music are valued primarily for their power rather than for their aesthetic aspects. Some music is produced for the pleasure of music making, both by individuals and by groups. In the Southwest, three principal styles exist: Puebloan, O'odham, and Navajo. Pueblo musical style, considered to be one of the most complex in North America in post–Columbian times, is characterized by rhythmic accompaniments that range from steady beats to rhythmic designs coordinated with the melody and terraced or cascading contours. O'odham music features a smooth, relaxed singing technique with relatively simple rhythms and melodic patterns. The basic style of Navajo and Apache music is related to northern **Athapaskan** music, although Navajo ritual music demonstrates Pueblo influences. Instruments used in the Southwest include musical rasps and a wide variety of drums, including water drums. Rattles are made from domesticated gourds, turtle shells, pottery, and animal hooves. Flutes are used in sacred ceremonies as well as in courtship. While southwestern music is primarily ceremonial, there are also work songs, such as the corn-grinding songs of the Pueblos. Navajo gambling songs seek to contact spiritual power. To fit the needs of complex religious ceremonials, ritual songs are organized into set series, from short suites of a few songs to elaborate song cycles for ceremonies that last several days. Navajo ceremonies such as the **Enemyway** and the **Nightway** require great concentration, for each song series must be performed correctly or else it may invalidate the entire ceremony. The most highly respected Navajo religious practitioners are called singers or chanters because most of each ceremony that they perform involves singing. These lengthy rituals are so complicated and involve such extensive memorization that a chanter only specializes in one or two major ceremonials. The **Nightway** brings in teams of Yeibechai dancers who dance in strict formation. The **Enemyway,** although no less sacred in nature, also includes a popular social dance in which women choose their partners. Today, Apache ceremonial dances center on the **Girl's Puberty Ceremony.** Pueblo dances are especially elaborate, particularly the **katsina** dances of the Hopi, and may involve as many as 200 dancers, who bring the various katsinam spirits to life by dancing them. Other Pueblo dances are social dances.

Naiche (Chiricahua Apache, c. 1857–1921)   Younger son of the great Chiricahua Apache leader **Cochise,** Naiche assumed leadership after the death of his elder brother. He guided his people through their transition to the San Carlos Reservation but escaped to freedom with others in 1881. Naiche and his key strategist, **Geronimo,** led their people on raids along both sides of the U.S.–Mexico border. Ultimately he and his group surrendered, returned to the reservation, and were then moved to a more favorable area known as Turkey Creek. However, the government imposed so many restrictions upon them, including that they become farmers, that in 1885 they fled to Mexico, where they resumed their raids on both sides of the border. In 1886, Naiche, Geronimo, and their followers were exiled to Florida, then Alabama, then Fort Sill, Oklahoma. During this period, Naiche produced a series of notable hide paintings of the Apache **Girls' Puberty Ceremony** (Cecile R. Ganteaume, "Naiche's Deer Hide Paintings," *American Indian Art Magazine* 28, no. 1 [winter 2002]: 44–55, 86; Trudy Griffin-Pierce, *Chiricahua Apache Enduring Power: Naiche's Puberty Ceremony Paintings* [Tuscaloosa: University of Alabama Press, 2006]). In 1913, when the federal government decided to take back Fort Sill, some Chiricahuas decided to remain in the area and were given allotments of land. Others, including Naiche, decided to move to the Mescalero Reservation in New Mexico; he lived there the rest of his life.

Nailor, Gerald (Navajo, 1917–1952)　Gerald Nailor, born near Crownpoint, New Mexico, was an outstanding painter and muralist. He studied with Dorothy Dunn at what later became the Institute of American Indian Arts in Santa Fe; later, he continued his studies under O. Nordmark in Oklahoma. He had a facility with many media, working in tempera, watercolor, oils, and, for his murals, fresco. His figures of stylized Navajo women, dancers, and animals appear to flow with the movement intrinsic to Navajo poetry; he suggests the context with a few symbolic touches that enhance but never overpower the subject. Rhythmic motion is always present in his paintings of horses and people: a flowing line is conveyed through horses' prancing gait and flying manes while women's necklaces and earrings are flung with their dancing gestures. Nailor's paintings are remarkable for their subtle use of line to convey fluid movement, satisfying composition, and rich color, which he often grades from light to dark to give dimension to an otherwise flat plane. His murals are on display in many federal buildings, such as the Department of the Interior Building in Washington, D.C. Some of his paintings were reproduced by Tewa Enterprises; like the work of Harrison Begay, Nailor's graphic style lends itself to reproduction through serigraphy (Clara Lee Tanner, *Southwest Indian Painting: A Changing Art*, 2nd ed. [Tucson: University of Arizona Press, 1980], 329–334).

Nakai, R. Carlos, Jr. (Navajo-Ute, 1946–)　Composer and musician R. Carlos Nakai Jr. is one of the most prominent figures in Native American music today. In 1998 he was chosen as both the Best Male Artist and Best Flutist at the Native American Music Awards. He is the first traditional player to earn a gold record for sales of over 500,000 copies for his 1989 *Canyon Trilogy*. His repertoire covers everything from Native American songs to classical, jazz, and New Age genres, and choreographer Martha Graham used Nakai's music for her last work. He has written and performed scores for film and television and tours the United States, Europe, and Asia most of the year. He also holds workshops on performance practice. He wrote *The Art of the Native American Flute* with composer James DeMars.

Nampeyo (Hopi-Tewa, c. 1860–1942)   Born in the village of Hano, on First Mesa, Nampeyo became the most famous Hopi potter by developing the Sikyatki revival style. Some anthropologists believe she was inspired by the pottery shards that her husband brought home when he helped archaeologist Jesse Walter Fewkes excavate the remains of a Hopi village called Sikyatki in 1895. (Other specialists contest this interpretation.) Among the ruins were elegantly proportioned pots decorated with striking, symbolically rich designs in red, brown, and black on a background of light yellow-brown clay. Fascinated by their beauty, Nampeyo is believed by some to have added her own creative interpretation to the prehistoric pottery style. Her descendants and other First Mesa women continue the tradition of fine pottery making, using lines, bands, scrolls, and other geometric elements with stylized bird imagery, such as feathers, beaks, and wings; or *katsinam*, clouds, lightning, and rain.

Native American Church (NAC); Peyote Religion   Archaeological evidence shows that peyote was used 10,000 years ago in Mexico, but it did not become popular among Indians of the western United States until the nineteenth century. At that time, horses enabled Plains Indians to travel into the southern United States and Mexico, where they found the cactus peyote (*Lophophora williamsii*). Peyotism was described by James Mooney in 1890 after he attended meetings with the Kiowa Indians of Oklahoma. The tops, or buttons, are eaten and produce vomiting as well as a pleasant euphoria and visual distortions that are conducive to the all-night ceremony of the Native American Church, a pan-Indian religious movement that uses peyote as a religious sacrament. Although peyotism is practiced today throughout the western United States, members face opposition from federal, state, and even tribal governments. In 1944, the Native American Church of Oklahoma became the Native American Church of the United States; in 1955, when several Canadian churches joined the organization, it became the Native American Church of North America. Navajo members of the Native American Church carry cards that verify their membership and grant permission for them to use peyote (see part IV: Aberle 1966 under "Navajo"; Deloria 1992 and Peregoy, Echo-Hawk, and Botsford 1995 under "Politics").

Native American Graves Protection and Repatriation Act (NAGPRA)
Passed in 1990 and in effect the following year, NAGPRA established a congressional policy for the return to tribes of aboriginal human remains, associated funerary objects, and other objects of cultural significance. Federal agencies,

museums, universities, and any institution that receives federal funds in any form are subject to this law that requires a review committee to oversee the process of implementation and identification. Each institution must conduct an inventory of its holdings that includes determining the cultural affiliation of each item, including human skeletal remains. The staff must then notify the appropriate tribes or organizations, and the items must be transferred if the Native American group wants them.

Scholarly consensus is divided on the specifics of repatriation, especially in such well-known cases as Kennewick Man, which created considerable controversy. Tribal groups could not present a clear linkage of these precontact remains to any existing cultural affiliation, and the courts eventually ruled that the remains of Kennewick Man should be retained for further scientific study. The ruling supported the perspective that the scientific and public value of remains and artifacts outweighs any claim that Native Americans may have on them. This argument holds that the scientific value is important not only to the public at large but also to Native peoples themselves as scholars attempt to reconstruct the histories of Native Americans. Furthermore, scientists say that recent technological advances require further study, such as the detection of immunoglobulins that can indicate past disease experiences and DNA sequencing from bone that can establish genetic relationships among populations. As science progresses, as yet unforeseen advances will enable scholars to learn even more from the remains, about both Native Americans and peoples of the world at large.

However, other scholars believe that allowing the remains of Kennewick Man to be studied further rather than returning them to the closest appropriate Native group destroyed a sense of trust that will take many years to rebuild. This position, taken by many Native Americans, holds that repatriation must occur despite any scholarly or public good that may be derived from the remains or objects. Many American Indians were appalled at the decision regarding Kennewick Man because they consider the human remains of their ancestors to be sacred. Their reaction is based on the lengthy history of exploitation of Indian remains and sacred objects that have been treated as exotic curiosities by non-Indians; American Indians hold that Anglo-Americans would never excavate the graves of their own ancestors or study their remains. Furthermore, throughout history, many of these collections were obtained illegally, from burial scaffolds, graves, and battlefields as well as by "pot hunters."

With increased political sophistication, American Indian groups have pressured the federal government to enact legislation that protects their ancestral remains and sacred objects. In many cases, especially in the Southwest, American Indians are actively working with non-Native scholars in the fields of archaeology and biological anthropology. Such collaboration increases understanding on both sides, so that scientists better comprehend their findings in connection to living cultures and Native southwesterners are better able to document the specifics of their peoples' past (see part IV: Colwell-Chanthaphonh and Ferguson 2007, Whiteley 2002 under "Archaeological Studies").

Navajo   An Athapaskan-speaking people, the Navajos occupy the largest reservation in the United States today. Situated on the Colorado Plateau, the Navajo Reservation encompasses the northeastern portion of Arizona, the northwest corner of New Mexico, and a strip of Utah south of the Colorado River. In the late 1960s, the Navajos declared nationhood and officially became the Navajo Nation (see **housing; music; Navajo Code Talkers; Navajo-Hopi Land Dispute; Navajo Peacemaker Court; religion**).

Navajo Code Talkers   During World War II, Navajos were recruited into the marines to create and use a code based on the Navajo language. A pilot project in 1942 with 29 Navajo volunteers grew to a force of more than 400 by the end of the war. Used in nearly every South Pacific campaign in which the marines participated, the Navajo code eventually developed into a vocabulary of more than 619 terms. Japanese military cryptographers were never able to decode messages sent in this code, which was invaluable in such critical battles as Iwo Jima and Okinawa.

The concept of using Native American languages as a code was not new. During World War I, one regiment of U.S. troops had a company of Native Americans who spoke 26 different languages or dialects, most of which had never been transcribed at that time, and in 1918, Choctaws transmitted combat information in their own language. In 1940, based on the success with Choctaw, the Army Signal Corps experimented with the use of the Comanche language. However, the idea was discarded because many words, such as "tank" and "aircraft carrier," could not be translated precisely. After Pearl Harbor, the marines took another look at this idea, turning to the Navajo people and the Navajo language, which came to play such a vital role in defeating the Japanese in the Pacific.

Navajo-Hopi Land Dispute   The 1882 executive order that created the Hopi Reservation inside the much larger Navajo Reservation failed to specify that the land was for exclusive Hopi use or to acknowledge the hundreds of Navajos already living on the designated 2.6 million acres. Conflict between the two tribes was inevitable because of land shortage, opposing lifestyles (agricultural versus herding), and differing worldviews. The more agricultural Hopi lived in villages, farmed outlying fields, and kept shrines in distant areas; their population increased slowly. In contrast, the Navajo population skyrocketed, soon outgrowing the land base, as uncontrolled grazing by their stock led to extreme deterioration and desertification. From the Navajo perspective, any temporarily unoccupied land was unused and thus available.

In 1958, Public Law 85–547 was passed, enabling tribes to commence legal cases against each other before a three-judge panel of the U.S. District Court of Arizona, to determine the rights and interests of each. The Hopi filed a case in 1960 claiming that the entire 2.5 million acres of the 1882 executive order area should be set aside for their exclusive use. The Navajo contended that they were the "other Indians" referred to in the order. In 1962, the court ruled that the Hopi Tribe had exclusive rights over District 6, and that the Navajos and Hopis had joint, undivided, and equal right and interest, both as to the surface and subsurface, including all resources of the land of the area outside of District 6. This shared land is known as the Joint Use Area (JUA). Congress passed legislation for appropriations for the Navajo Nation to purchase public land to replace the land they gave up as well as compensation for those who were willing to move. Most Navajos complied by leaving Hopi land, except for a small group in the Big Mountain area. According to the terms of a 75-year lease that has been established in an effort to resolve this issue, the federal government is paying the Hopi rent for those Navajos still living on Hopi land. However, not all resisters have signed leases, and some remain on the land without them.

Navajo Peacemaker Court   Instituted in 1990, the Navajo Peacemaker Court handles cases involving land, property, vehicle, and marriage disputes, saving thousands of dollars in legal fees and years of lengthy court battles. By incorporating traditional values into the modern legal process, Peacemaker Court is less confrontational than the U.S. district court and allows everyone to speak, even those who do not usually have a voice in the courtroom, such as the children of alcoholics who describe how deeply their parents' behavior frightens and hurts them. The peacemaker guides, advises, and mediates from a traditional perspective based on two basic principles, *hózho*—harmonious relations with the human, holy, and natural worlds—and *nitséskees*—right thinking, based on the creative power of thought and intention. Based on fair compensation rather than punishment, Peacemaker Court does not polarize those involved but rather unites them in finding a mutually acceptable agreement so that they can move on with their lives. By allowing them to see and hear the impact their behavior has on their loved ones, giving people a voice, and empowering everyone to reach their own solution, Peacemaker Court is a powerful tool for the restoration of hózho (Marianne O. Nielsen and James W. Zion, eds., *Navajo Nation Peacemaking: Living Traditional Justice* [Tucson: University of Arizona Press, 2005]).

O'odham The Akimel O'odham (river people) and the Tohono O'odham (desert people) are the probable descendants of the precontact **Hohokam**, who practiced irrigation agriculture using an extensive system of canals stemming from rivers throughout the Gila River and Salt River valleys in Arizona. The O'odham language belongs to the Uto-Aztecan language family. The present-day Akimel O'odham reside along the dry Gila and Salt rivers in central Arizona. The Gila River Indian Community was formally established by Congress in 1895 and the Salt River Pima-Maricopa Indian Community was established in 1879. Laveen, a town in the Gila River Indian Community, is the home of the Maricopas (Pee-Posh, "the people"), a River Yuman people who moved from the Colorado River in the mid-eighteenth century to live with their allies, the Akimel O'odham.

The Tohono O'odham Nation (formerly known as Papago) has a reservation composed of three areas: the San Xavier Reservation, created in 1874 near Tucson; the Gila Bend Reservation, established in 1882 near the city of the same name; and the main reservation established in 1917 in Sells, Arizona.

Ortiz, Alfonso (San Juan Pueblo, 1939–1997) Born in San Juan Pueblo, Alfonso Ortiz was best known for his book *The Tewa World: Space, Time, Being, and Becoming in a Pueblo Society* (1969). As both an anthropologist (he earned his Ph.D. from the University of Chicago) and a member of San Juan Pueblo, Ortiz had a unique insider perspective. His book was inspired through the realization that many of the extant texts about the Pueblo people were incorrect. However, by divulging privileged information, Ortiz offended some of the tribal elders.

Ortiz taught at Pitzer College and Princeton University before returning to New Mexico in 1974 to become a professor at the University of New Mexico. He also served as the editor of *New Perspectives on the Pueblos* (School of American Research, Albuquerque: University of New Mexico Press, 1972) and the *Handbook of North American Indians* (vols. 9 and 10 [Washington, D.C.: Smithsonian Institution Press, 1979 and 1983, respectively]). Ortiz received the John Guggenheim Fellowship, a fellowship at Stanford University's Center for Advanced Study in the Behavioral Sciences, and a MacArthur Foundation "genius" grant. Active in American Indian affairs, he belonged to the National Advisory Council of the National Indian Youth Council. From 1973 through 1983, he was president of the Association on American Indian Affairs.

Ortiz, Simon (Acoma Pueblo, 1941–) One of the best known Native American poets, Simon Ortiz was born in Albuquerque, New Mexico and raised at Acoma Pueblo. He began publishing his poetry while attending the University of New Mexico. After earning an M.F.A. from the University of Iowa, he taught creative writing and Native American literature at San Diego State University, the University of New Mexico, and Sinte Gleska College in Rosebud, South Dakota. The National Endowment for the Arts gave him a Discovery Award in 1969 for his poetry. Ortiz considers the political movements of the 1960s as major influences because he was one of the first authors of that time to write about his heritage and culture. Reflecting the oral tradition, his work is characterized by a strong storytelling voice.

Paladin, David Chethale (Navajo, 1926–1984)   A famous abstract painter, David Paladin led a remarkable life, using his art to explore and express his spiritual roots both as a Navajo person (from his mother) and as a person of Euro-American, Christian ancestry (from his father). During World War II, he endured starvation and torture as a prisoner in a Nazi concentration camp. Afterward, he not only created powerful abstract art but also became a Unitarian minister who worked in prisons and as a police chaplain. Paladin lived with great passion and spirituality, expressing his creativity as he reached out to others through his actions as well as through his remarkable paintings.

Paleo-Indian tradition (9500–6000 B.C.)   The long period before sedentary life developed is known as the Post-Pleistocene period, which is divided into the Paleo-Indian and Archaic periods. Archaeologists call the first Americans the Paleo-Indians, and they were known for their skill in hunting mammoth and other huge animals that inhabited the land in the final centuries of the ice age. Humans had spread out across the continent and were adapting to various regions by developing the specific tools they needed to make a living. Before 10,000 B.C., the southwestern climate provided so much more moisture than today that lakes and savannas covered areas that are now desert and grass plains. The people who lived there **hunted** the mammoth, extinct bison, tapir, sloth, and ancestral forms of the horse, camel, and antelope. As the climate shifted, lakes dried up and meadows gave way to deserts; the large game animals also began to dwindle, and the people had to rely on smaller game and wild plants. In the Southwest, about 6000 B.C., the Paleo-Indian tradition gave way to the **Archaic tradition**.

Patayan culture (A.D. 700–1350)   The Patayan people left remains from Ajo and Gila Bend in Arizona westward to California and from the Grand Canyon southward to Yuma, Arizona. The Colorado River provided an oasis where they could raise crops in territory that was primarily a desert, but the annual flooding that brought fertile alluvial soil to their farmlands also destroyed their riverine sites, making them the least known of all the prehistoric peoples of the Southwest. The ephemeral nature of Patayan sites as well as the difficulty of excavation in such harsh desert terrain has made archaeology extremely difficult. Much of their material culture was also very perishable; moving around vast areas annually, they built brush shelters and used nets and baskets. The contemporary Yuman peoples, who live along the lower Colorado River to its delta and in the canyons and plateaus of the upper Colorado River, are considered to be the descendants of the Patayan. The Patayan created an enormous interconnected system of trails that they used in searching for food, during war, and for trade that linked them to the people of coastal California and the **Hohokam** of southern Arizona. Some trails probably also reflect religious pilgrimages since they link the intaglios, enormous earth figures that depict geometric, human, animal, and star forms.

Piestewa, Lori Ann (Hopi, 1980–2003)   The first woman in the American armed services to be killed in action during the war in Iraq, Lori Ann Piestewa was one of a group of eleven U.S. Army mechanics in the 507th Maintenance Company who became lost near Nasiriya in southern Iraq on March 23 and were ambushed by Iraqi soldiers. Her family in Tuba City, Arizona, includes two other veterans, her father and grandfather, and two young children. The city of Phoenix has renamed a major freeway and a landmark mountain, formerly known as Squaw Peak, after her.

Plan of Iguala (1821)   Named for the location of the revolutionary army headquarters where Mexico declared its independence from Spain, the Plan of Iguala declared equality of citizenship for all inhabitants of Mexico, whether Europeans, Africans, or Indians. However, the implementation of this plan ignored cultural differences and the fact that Indians might not want to assume the Mexican concept of citizenship, which included taxation, individual land ownership, and participation in the municipality-state system of political organization.

Popé (Tewa, San Juan Pueblo, c. 1633–1690)   An important spiritual and military leader, Popé united the Pueblos and led the 1680 **Pueblo Revolt** against the Spanish in the upper Rio Grande area of New Mexico. In 1598, Spaniards established a feudal society over the Pueblo Indians in the Santa Fe region. They forced the Native people to provide labor and to pay taxes in the form of crops, cloth, and pottery; forbid them to practice their traditional religion; and tried to convert them to Catholicism. The Pueblo people, however, compartmentalized the two religions by continuing to practice their own rituals in the *kivas*. Popé, a medicine man from San Juan Pueblo, was repeatedly captured and flogged by Spanish authorities; these beatings became a symbol of resistance for his people that enhanced his efforts to recruit men and women for a rebellion against the Spanish. Preaching that their ancestral spirits had instructed him to restore traditional practices, he found many followers for what became the Pueblo Revolt. Pueblos recaptured Santa Fe, forcing the Spanish to retreat to El Paso. The Pueblo alliance dissolved over the course of the next twelve years under pressures from Ute and Apache raiders as well as drought; the Spanish eventually reestablished control but tempered their policies.

Pueblos   The Spaniards referred to Native peoples who lived in stone or adobe houses in towns in the Southwest as "Pueblo" Indians because the word *pueblo* means "town." Most Pueblo communities are located along the Rio Grande and its tributaries in New Mexico. Pueblo cultures, which appear to outsiders to be homogeneous, are distinctive with linguistic, regional, and social variations. Pueblos have existed for centuries and were thriving communities when Francisco Vasquez de Coronado came to the region in 1540–1542. Each pueblo is its own tribal entity and has its own government. In addition to the Pueblo communities described below, there are also Hopis and Zunis (described under their own entries). Ysleta del Sur (Tigua Indian Tribe) is located within the city of El Paso, Texas, and Tortugas (also known as Tigua; Los Indigenes de Guadalupe; Los Inditos de Las Cruces, Piro, Manso, Tiwa Tribe; San Juan de Guadalupe Tiwa Tribe) is located immediately south of Las Cruces, New Mexico. Acoma, a Keresan-speaking pueblo, is located about sixty miles west of Albuquerque on Acoma Mesa and the surrounding area. Cochiti, another Keresan-speaking pueblo, lies on the west bank of the Rio Grande in north central New Mexico, about twenty-five miles southwest of Santa Fe. Isleta stretches across the fertile bottomland of the Rio Grande about twelve miles south of Albuquerque; the language spoken there belongs to the Southern Tiwa group in the Kiowa-Tanoan language family. Jemez, a Towa language in the same family, is spoken in the pueblo of that name, located about fifty-five miles northwest of Albuquerque. Laguna, whose residents speak a Keresan language, is forty-five miles west of Albuquerque. Nambé, one of the Tewa pueblos, is about fifteen miles north of Santa Fe. Picuris is the second smallest of the Rio Grande pueblos; its residents speak a Northern Tiwa language in the Kiowa-Tanoan family. Pojoaque, one of the eight northern Tewa pueblos, is located about sixteen miles north of Santa Fe. San Felipe, a Keresan-speaking pueblo, is on the west bank of the Rio Grande near Albuquerque. San Ildefonso, a Tewa pueblo, is about twenty-five miles northwest of Santa Fe along the northern Rio Grande. The northernmost Tewa-speaking community in north central New Mexico, San Juan is on the east side of the Rio Grande just north of its confluence with the Rio Chama. Thirteen miles north of Albuquerque, Sandia Pueblo residents speak Southern Tiwa, in the Kiowa-Tanoan language family. Santa Ana, a Keresan-speaking pueblo, is located near Bernalillo, New Mexico along the Rio Grande. Santa Clara is a Tewa-speaking pueblo on the west bank of the Rio Grande, just south of the junction with the Rio Chama. A Keresan-speaking pueblo, Santo Domingo lies on the east bank of the Rio Grande in north central New Mexico, about thirty-five miles southwest of Santa Fe. Taos, a large multistoried pueblo, is seventy miles up the Rio Grande from Santa Fe and is populated by speakers of the Northern Tiwa language in the Kiowa-Tanoan family. Tesuque, a Tewa-speaking pueblo, is about nine miles north of Santa Fe. Zia, seventeen miles from Bernalillo, New Mexico, is one of the five Keresan-speaking pueblos.

religion   Elaborate displays of mortuary goods buried with the dead suggest that the precontact Native peoples of the Southwest prepared their loved ones for an afterlife. The **Hohokam** cremated their dead along with their personal belongings and ceremonial items in areas devoted solely to this purpose. Items connected to Mexican cultures—stone palettes, ceramic figurines, and stone censers—were also associated with this elaborate Hohokam death ritual. The **Mimbres** people buried their dead under the floors of their homes and covered the head of each corpse with a pottery vessel that had been ceremonially "killed" by punching a hole through the bottom of the bowl.

The present-day peoples of the Southwest—the Yumans, O'odham, Puebloans, Yaqui, and Athapaskans—come from many different cultural traditions, so many diverse belief systems are reflected in their practices. However, one underlying belief that they share is the religious significance of the land and the natural environment. Native religions are rooted in a sense of place, and their notions of identity are closely tied to specific local environments. Crucial for economic survival, animals, plants, and natural phenomena are intimately related to the conceptualization of supernatural power and ritual. Instead of separating the sacred and the profane as did the Europeans, Native southwesterners regard every part of the natural and supernatural worlds as fundamentally spiritual. Ceremonials have focused on the maintenance of the animals and plants that sustain human life and on restoration of individual and community health. This means that rituals center around hunting, gathering, and cultivation as well as curing and warfare. Usually performed by a practitioner who communicates with the supernatural in order to influence events such as plentiful wild game, abundant harvests, or restoration to health, rituals generally include music in the form of chanting and dancing that brings the presence of supernatural power into the human realm. In the Southwest, practitioners tend to be of two types: either a shaman, who acquires supernatural power through a vision or dream journey, or a priest, who undergoes an apprenticeship during which he or she learns a codified body of ritual that must be performed properly to be effective. Some southwestern Native peoples, such as the Navajo, have both kinds of practitioners—handtremblers are more shamanistic and diagnose illness, while chanters are more priestlike and perform healing ceremonies that stress the precise execution of the ritual.

When Catholicism was introduced, Native peoples responded in several different ways. Edward Spicer characterized these responses by contrasting three types. Dozier said that the Pueblos, who had had Catholicism forced upon them as part of Spanish oppression, compartmentalized the two religions as they practiced Catholicism in public but their own rituals in the secrecy of the *kivas*. The Yaqui, however, who defeated Spanish troops and then invited the Jesuits to come, fused or synthesized traditional beliefs and practices with Catholicism (see **Yaqui Easter Ceremony**). The Tohono O'odham, said Dozier, simply added aspects of Catholicism, such as the veneration of Saint Francis Xavier, to their traditional beliefs and practices. The Navajos are known for their ability to incorporate sacred and secular traditions into their own culture, remaking what they have borrowed into something that is distinctly Navajo. Many aspects of Pueblo ritual, including masked dancers, prayer sticks, and sandpaintings (as they are known by the Navajos; many scholars call them drypaintings because they use other materials in addition to sand) have been remade into Navajo forms to become a fundamental part of ceremonial practices.

Another important distinction in the Southwest is between crisis rituals and calendrical rituals. Crisis rituals are performed according to need and are not dependent upon an annual schedule—healing ceremonies of the Navajo are held when they are needed to cure a patient. The *katsinam* ceremonies of the Pueblos are calendrical because nearly all of them are held at the same time every year.

repatriation See **NAGPRA**.

resources   Tribal economies shrank at the beginning of the twentieth century as the federal government, through the General Allotment Act, moved the best land on reservations out of tribal control. The **Indian Reorganization Act** stopped this massive loss, but the paternalism of federal government policies kept re-created tribal governments from pursuing economic development. Considerable barriers to developing their resources and economies exist, including regulation of property by the Bureau of Indian Affairs, conflict with state governments over economic activities, and restricted access to Indian-owned property. Internally, they face political difficulties among factions, cultural difficulties in dealing with the modern economy, and the need for additional skills among the Indian population. The self-determination movement of the 1970s and 1980s aided economic development by expanding the power of tribal governments and enabling them to select and implement appropriate strategies.

The struggle for Indian people today is to take control of resources that are technically theirs. In the Pacific Northwest, the salmon-fishing tribes went to court to obtain a clear right to take half of the fish. Only after they had accomplished this could they earn substantial incomes from a traditional activity, upgraded by modern technology. However, even after they had obtained rights to half the fish, tribes had to settle among themselves which runs belonged to which reservations and set up commissions to negotiate with states in order to enforce the division of the harvest with non-Indians.

Water rights are a major issue in the arid Southwest. Oil and gas leasing is another area where the struggle for control is crucial. Only recently have tribal governments been able to drive hard bargains for their oil, gas, and mineral resources. Once agreements are written, enforcement depends upon the BIA; tribes have learned that they must watch their resources themselves in order to ensure adequate enforcement.

In recent years, Indian tribes and nations have taken advantage of the unique status of reservations as federally protected enclaves within states to engage in business enterprises that would otherwise be heavily taxed or regulated by the state, such as the sale of tobacco. The development of casino gaming can generate considerable income, and there is an ongoing struggle with the states to preserve tribal jurisdiction. The **Indian Gaming Regulatory Act** set guidelines for various types of gaming enterprises run by Indian tribes, nations, and communities.

Because tribal **governments** were imposed by the federal government, they usually did not fit the traditional tribal structure. However, in some cases, these imposed systems do work, especially when coordinated by a strong and honest tribal chairman, such as on the White Mountain and Mescalero reservations. Once a tribe has obtained effective rights to a tribal enterprise, it needs institutions for economic development, professional record-keeping, personnel systems, and a judicial system that is independent of the electoral political system. It is important that the tribal courts enforce agreements impartially. The day-to-day management of enterprise activities must be insulated from interference by elected officials; independent boards can serve as effective buffers. Businesses need to retain a certain degree of autonomy, as does the White Mountain Apache lumber mill, which prospered when its manager was able to make day-to-day decisions without interference. The exact form of internal political systems can vary substantially. For example, a pueblo can continue its traditional methods of selecting political leaders as long as they retain the ability to run day-to-day operations without continuous interference. A political leader can even work as a laborer in one of the tribal enterprises if he is willing to abide by the limitation of his powers in that position. For example, at Cochiti Pueblo, a leader has the power of appointment and dismissal, but no ability to control other details.

The development of tribal resources and economies has many challenges, especially because Indian tribes and nations struggle with a tremendous need for jobs and income and internal and external obstacles that must be overcome. Lawyers must often be hired to pursue tribal rights in court. Political leadership must let go of a certain amount of control in order to allow business managers to oversee business affairs, either in individual enterprises that use tribally owned resources or in tribal enterprises. A legal and policy framework must be in place that assists entrepreneurs while also protecting the Indian tribe or nation from the negative aspects of economic development.

Romero, Juan de Jesus (Deer Bird, Taos, 1874–1978)   Leader of Taos Pueblo, Juan de Jesus Romero devoted his life to the return of the sacred Blue Lake in eastern New Mexico to the pueblo. In 1906 he began working for the return of the lake and the ancestral lands that surround it. Blue Lake is a place of great spiritual significance to the people of Taos Pueblo, who believe that the world was created there. They return to celebrate annual ceremonies acknowledging the creation of the world and of humanity. The tribe filed a lawsuit against the federal government for the lake and the land, and in 1965, the government awarded them cash compensation that they refused to accept because they wanted the lake itself. In 1970 Romero went to Washington, D.C. to speak to President Richard Nixon about this issue. A motion was passed by Congress to return Blue Lake and the 48,000 acres that surround it to the Taos, and in 1971, President Nixon signed this bill into law. In 1974, Romero was awarded the prestigious Indian Council Fire Award for his lifelong efforts for the return of Taos Blue Lake.

Sells, Cato (1859–1948)   Commissioner of Indian Affairs from 1913 to 1921, Cato Sells, a rancher-banker from Cleburne, Texas, is best remembered for his policy of forced patenting of Indian trust lands. He sought to hasten the assimilation of Indians by launching what he called the New Policy, a program that eased requirements for competency in handling one's own affairs. In 1906 an amendment to the **Dawes Severalty Act** empowered the Secretary of the Interior to remove restrictions on allotted Indian lands before the end of the 25-year trust period if the allottee was competent to handle his own affairs. Under the Sells administration, all adult Indians of one half or less Indian blood, as well as those who had received diplomas from government schools upon reaching the age of twenty-one, no longer received government benefits. Between 1917 and 1920, more than 21,000 Indians lost federal protection, had their lands fee-patented (property taxes applied to their allotments), and were made to pay local taxes. Many lost their land through tax foreclosure. Sells did, however, oppose allotment for southwestern Indians because he believed that the semi-arid lands of the region could not support Indians if they were allotted. In 1924, Sells's interpretation of the 1906 amendment was ruled illegal and during the 1920s, legislation was enacted to restore lost lands. The capital of the Tohono O'odham Nation, Sells, Arizona, is named for him.

Silko, Leslie Marmon (Laguna Pueblo, 1948–) Acclaimed novelist Leslie Marmon Silko was born in Albuquerque, New Mexico and spent her childhood at Laguna Pueblo, where her grandmother and aunt taught her the traditions of Laguna storytelling. Silko earned a bachelor's degree from the University of New Mexico. Her first short story, "The Man to Send Rain Clouds," based on an incident that had occurred at Laguna, won a National Endowment for the Humanities Discovery Grant. Silko's national reputation was established by the novel *Ceremony* (1977), which portrays the struggles of its part-Laguna protagonist as he tries to find healing after World War II; he must come to terms with the colonization of his people. She was awarded a prestigious MacArthur Foundation fellowship with a five-year annual stipend of $33,600 to pursue her writing. Silko's 700-page novel, *Almanac of the Dead* (1991), brings together stories and traditions of her people with a depiction of the decline of Western society.

Southern Paiutes The Southern Paiutes are a linguistic and cultural group in the northern Southwest and the southeastern Great Basin area, today represented by ten contemporary groups. Five of these have united to form the Paiute Tribe of Utah. The three Southern Nevada tribes are Moapa, Las Vegas, and Pahrump, with Pahrump being the only modern Southern Paiute political group not recognized by the federal government. The Kaibab Paiute Tribe has a reservation on the "Arizona Strip," the area north of the Grand Canyon. The San Juan Paiute Tribe's communities are located in both Arizona and Utah, within the Navajo Reservation. The Chemehuevi are historically Southern Paiute and speak Paiute. They live on a reservation along the Colorado River and also on the Colorado River Indian Tribes Reservation.

syncretism See under **Yaqui Easter Ceremony**.

Taos Blue Lake See under **Romero, Juan de Jesus**.

Tapahonso, Luci (Navajo, 1953–) Luci Tapahonso, internationally known Navajo poet and short-story writer, is from Shiprock, New Mexico, where she grew up in a family of eleven children. Her first language was Navajo, but she learned to speak English at home before starting school. She began to write poetry at the age of eight or nine. Majoring in English, she earned a graduate degree at the University of New Mexico, where she also became an assistant professor of English, women's studies, and American Indian studies. She went on to become an associate professor of English at the University of Kansas, and now teaches poetry writing and American Indian literature as a professor of English at the University of Arizona in Tucson.

Tapahonso writes for popular magazines as well as for a wide range of academic and poetry journals. She has written numerous books of poetry and stories and one children's book, and her poems and prose have appeared in many anthologies. She has served on a number of editorial boards and has been a juror for the Poetry Society of America, the Associated Writing Program Awards, and the Stan Steiner Writing Awards. She is on the advisory board of the Telluride Institute Writers' Forum, has been a member of the Kansas Arts Commission and the New Mexico Arts Commission, and serves on the Board of Trustees for the National Museum of the American Indian. She is a sought-after speaker and appears frequently on public broadcasting shows.

termination   Termination was a government policy that attempted to end the special federal-tribal relationship and thus end tribal government and sovereignty, treaty rights, federally supplied services, and the nontaxable status of Indian lands. Termination entailed not only the loss of a land base—and the cultural identity that went with it—but also the loss of educational programs, government employment, and job training. It contributed to even greater poverty, a still lower standard of living, and an increased rate of disease, along with the loss of access to the Indian Health Service, among Native peoples. Popular in the 1940s after World War II, termination came from the belief that the communal aspects of Indian culture were too similar to the communist systems that the United States had fought against in foreign policy. The sense of nationalism that pervaded the country at this time also meant that Native American sovereignty was perceived as a threat to American patriotism and sovereignty. Intended as a prelude to termination, the Indian Claims Commission Act (1946) allowed tribes to sue the government for compensation in past land transactions. In 1947, the Indian Affairs Subcommittee of the House Committee on Public Lands held hearings on bills to "free" Indians from the Bureau of Indian Affairs, and the Senate Civil Service Committee directed the acting Commissioner of Indian Affairs to classify tribes according to their readiness for termination. The biggest boost to the policy came in 1952, when Dwight Eisenhower and Republican congressional majorities brought more conservatives into positions of influence. Public Law 280 was pushed through Congress the following year. This law directed several states to assume law-and-order jurisdiction on most reservations and authorized any other state to take similar action without Indian consent. Congress made plans to phase out the Bureau of Indian Affairs and to end separate Indian nation status. After heavy criticism from various groups and effective opposition from the National Congress of American Indians, termination was rejected by the early 1960s. Church groups had also protested the social injustice it embodied, while state and local governments had feared the financial burden of taking over social services on reservations. Congress later restored many tribes affected by termination legislation. In the Southwest, Utah Southern Paiute groups, "terminated" in 1954, established a legal corporation in the 1970s to reverse the process and restore their trust lands. Their federally recognized status was restored in 1980 after long legal battles, and five Utah-based groups went on to form a larger tribal entity, the Paiute Indian Tribe of Utah.

trade Far from any coastline, the **Hohokam** obtained shells through a trade network that extended eastward to the Gulf Coast and westward to the Pacific. Evidence of such far-reaching networks exists in many prehistoric southwestern sites. Trade probably provided the impetus for the spread of Hohokam culture during the late 700s, and even earlier, the Hohokam had ceramic figurines, stone palettes, and stone censers that reflect a strong connection to Mesoamerican cultures. Probably inspired by Mesoamerican concepts of a sacred ball game, they built huge ball courts. To the north, the **Mogollon** made jewelry from trade items such as copper bells from Mesoamerica and shells from the Hohokam. At **Chaco Canyon,** traders gathered from many distant regions to exchange valued goods: macaws and metal items from what is now western and northern Mexico, turquoise from present-day New Mexico, salt from Zuni lakes, and seashells from the Pacific Ocean and the Gulf of California in exchange for pottery, cornmeal, and turquoise jewelry produced in and near Chaco. Using cotton as a commodity, the **Hisatsinom** traded for shells from the Gulf of California, pottery from **Awatovi**, obsidian from present-day Flagstaff, and copper bells and macaws from Mesoamerica. Farther west, along the Colorado River, the **Patayan** and their Yuman descendants created an enormous network of trails, physical evidence of their wide-ranging travels across the desert. The Mojave journeyed to the coast of California to trade with the Chumash for shells and acorns as well as to the Hopi for cotton cloth and blankets. When Spaniards established a community in the Rio Grande Valley in 1598, they introduced many European goods that were also traded widely. Over time, mission communities and small mining towns became trading sites, and in the 1880s, the railroad supplied goods to newly created trading posts. Traders encouraged Navajo women to produce rugs instead of the blankets that had long been traded throughout the West. Fascinated by a romanticized conception of Indians, tourists traveled west and bought pottery, silverwork, basketry, and rugs made by southwestern Native peoples. Today, the arts and crafts of this region are sold not only throughout the country but also throughout the world.

Treaty of Guadalupe Hidalgo   On February 2, 1848, in the town of Guadalupe Hidalgo, near Mexico City, a peace accord was finally signed that ended the conflict between the United States and Mexico. Mexico had broken off diplomatic relations in March 1845 in protest over the annexation of Texas. U.S.–Mexican relations were strained over two issues. Mexico refused to agree with the treaty that General Santa Ana was forced to sign after his defeat at San Jacinto because it set the boundary between the two nations at the Rio Grande. Previously, Texas had been part of the Mexican state of Texas-Coahuila, whose southern boundary only extended to the Nueces River, 150 miles farther north. Mexico had had a number of political upheavals since winning independence from Spain in 1821, and an international commission had ruled that it pay more than $2 million for harm to citizens of the United States and their property. President James Polk sent special envoy John Slidell to Mexico City to resolve the Texas border dispute, giving him the power to propose that if Mexico accepted the Rio Grande as the southern and western borders of Texas, the United States would pay $5 million for New Mexico and $25 million for California and assume responsibility for the remaining amount of the damage claims. When the newly established Mexican government refused to discuss this offer, President Polk sent troops and the Mexican War of 1846–1848 began. The war culminated in General Winfield Scott's invasion of Mexico and the surrender of Mexico City on September 17, 1847. The Treaty of Guadalupe Hidalgo established the Rio Grande as the boundary of Texas and placed California and New Mexico under U.S. control in return for a payment of $15 million. The U.S. government also assumed payment to citizens for the remaining claims against the Mexican government.

Tsabetsye, Roger (Zuni, 1941–)   Educated at the Institute of American Indian Arts in Santa Fe, New Mexico, where he later taught, Zuni Roger Tsabetsye is known for his painting, ceramics, and silverwork. He has shown his work at the Museum of Santa Fe, the Heard Museum, the Scottsdale Indian National Art Show, the New York American Indian Art Center, and many other exhibitions. Known for his abstracts, Tsabetsye uses tribal design elements to portray religious subject matter. *Yei Masks* features four masks that sweep diagonally across the canvas as they emerge from a cornstalk toward the sun; his dynamic presentation suggests they have power that extends far beyond the limits of the painting. Tsabetsye is the founder and owner of Tsabetsye Enterprises, a company that merchandises Zuni jewelry at the retail and wholesale levels.

Uto-Aztecan languages The Uto-Aztecan language stock comprises more than thirty languages that spread throughout the western United States and western Mexico. Some linguists place the origin of this language family in the American Southwest. The Northern branch includes the Numic languages of the Great Basin, several languages of California, and Hopi, in its own sub-branch. O'odham belongs to the Tepiman branch, while Yaqui is Cahitan. There is an Aztecan branch—the language of the Aztecs—from which the name of this language family is derived; the southernmost Aztecan languages are spoken in Nicaragua and El Salvador.

Velarde, Pablita (Santa Clara Pueblo, 1915–2006) Pablita Velarde studied under Dorothy Dunn, who taught many Indian artists at what was once the Santa Fe Indian School. In 1938 Velarde built her own studio in her home pueblo, Santa Clara, and began her long and productive career as a painter. She started by creating murals of the daily life and culture of the Rio Grande Pueblos. To create a textured painting material, she developed a technique that uses pulverized colored rocks and is especially suited to traditional designs and pictographs. Velarde's paintings feature vivid imagery that depicts Pueblo stories. She wrote and illustrated a book based on tribal stories, *Old Father the Story Teller*, and her painting of the same name shows an elder sitting in the plaza telling stories to the many children who surround him. Migrating ancestors follow the Milky Way in the night sky above their heads and Pueblo designs and animals, including a village, are woven into the background. The rapt expression on the faces of the children testifies to the storyteller's ability to make the tales come alive in the minds of his audience.

Virgin of Guadalupe A religious and folk symbol as well as an emblem of statewide culture and history, the Virgin Mary of Guadalupe is said to have appeared in 1531 in Mexico City to the Christianized Aztec Juan Diego. The Indian peasant was on his way to Mass when a beautiful woman surrounded by a body halo appeared to him and announced her presence. She is usually portrayed standing on a half-moon that rests on the shoulders of a cherub and surrounded by a spectacular sunburst or body halo. She is depicted and prayed to throughout the Southwest and Mexico.

warfare Before warfare with Spaniards, Mexicans, and Anglo-Americans to defend their homelands, various tribal peoples fought with each other, often as a matter of revenge expeditions. Originally directed at conquest and the seizure of territory, intertribal wars took on a new character after 1830, when several communities had been forced to relinquish their land. As early as the sixteenth century, many small tribes, such as the Halyikwamai and Halchidhoma, were losing their struggles for independence and being forced off the Colorado River because their farmlands were under attack from River Yuman tribes both up-river and downriver. Some anthropologists theorize that the River Yumans resorted to warfare for economic reasons, instead of intensifying their agricultural production, but others point out that the Mojaves, Quechans, and Halchidhomas cultivated wheat in historic times, which would have given them an additional crop. Other motives included vengeance for the loss of kinsmen, a strong sense of tribal nationalism (unusual in the Southwest), and the conviction held by each tribe that they were the creator's chosen people.

water rights   Scholarly consensus recognizes the severity of this issue and that historically, the federal government has failed to ensure that American Indian communities have adequate water rights for economic self-development through agriculture. Conflicts over this vital resource between Indians and non-Indians have occurred throughout the history of the arid Southwest. The Akimel O'odham experienced one of the most dramatic and sudden shifts in well-being of any Native group when Anglo-Americans upstream from them reduced the water supply that reached their reservation. The tribe's economy had prospered greatly after they acquired wheat from the Spaniards because its cultivation complemented their indigenous staple, maize, thus doubling their production. For the first fifteen years of Anglo-American rule, their economy continued to expand as they supplied the army and traders with wheat. However, after the Civil War ended, an influx of land-hungry settlers claimed land upstream from them and opened large canals, plunging the Akimel O'odham from the status of prosperous, independent farmers to that of wage laborers and welfare recipients.

The landmark Indian water rights case occurred in 1908. *Winters v. United States* assured Indians of rights to water sufficient to irrigate the lands set aside for them by the creation of their reservation. However, the United States pursued a policy of building dams for irrigation in the western regions of the country, demonstrating that even when the Indian water rights had been established in law, they might not be upheld in the face of economic change. As the non-Indian population in the desert Southwest continues to grow, the interpretation of the *Winters* doctrine will yield greater litigation in the years to come (see part IV: McCool 2003 under "Politics").

Wauneka, Annie Dodge (Navajo, 1910–1997)   Known for her tireless work to improve the health, education, and legal services of her people, Annie Dodge Wauneka was awarded the Presidential Medal of Freedom in 1963 by Lyndon B. Johnson. At the time when tuberculosis was rampant on the Navajo reservation, many Navajos were still reluctant to go to hospitals because they associated them with dying and death. Wauneka traveled from hogan to hogan explaining how tuberculosis was communicated and that there were doctors who could administer medicines to help them regain their health. Because the people trusted her, she was able to help stop the spread of this disease. As the leading advocate for better health care for the Navajos, she also labored for many years to obtain better medical facilities for the Navajo Nation. When the federal government failed to live up to its promises, she spoke out forcefully. This November 2, 1953 statement is characteristic: "We were promised health centers, field clinics, traveling doctors, nurses, dentists and a large number of public health nurses. Instead of giving us more and better medical service, we see the Fort Defiance hospital almost closed. Every day, sick Navajos are turned away because the hospital cannot take care of them" (Peter Iverson, ed., *"For Our Navajo People": Diné Letters, Speeches and Petitions 1900–1960* [Albuquerque: University of New Mexico Press, 2002], 152).

Yaqui   The homeland of the Yaqui (known as Yoeme in their own language) is along the Rio Yaqui in southern Sonora, Mexico, but they became political refugees who sought protection in the United States after a failed effort to win independence from Mexico and subsequent persecution. The Yaquis have a number of villages in southern Arizona; the major villages are Guadalupe (near Scottsdale), Old Pascua (northwest of Tucson), and New Pascua, which is on the Yaqui Reservation.

Yaqui Easter Ceremony   Still practiced today, the Yaqui Easter Ceremony marks the culmination of the Yaqui ceremonial year. When the Yaqui invited the Jesuits to come to them, the priests tried to make the last days of Jesus real to the people by having them dramatize Jesus's persecution and crucifixion. The Spanish priests never envisioned that the Yaqui would fuse Native beliefs and practices with Catholic doctrine and liturgy into a unique tradition that would eventually become a vital marker of their cultural identity. (This process is an example of syncretism.) While some Native concepts have been integrated into Catholic traditions, others have been completely reconceptualized. Still other components of the Easter Ceremony, such as the Deer Dancer, have remained untouched by Christianity.

This elaborate morality play dramatizes the triumph of Yaqui institutions over evil. On the first Friday of Lent, a few timid *Chapayekas* wearing helmet masks with long, thin noses—*chapa* means "sharp" and *yeka* means "nose" in Yaqui—begin the search for Jesus, but by Holy Week, their numbers grow and they become more aggressive, marching around the village and mocking the religious devotions of the faithful. They battle with the forces of good, represented by the *Matachinis*, who are soldiers of the Virgin Mary, and little children dressed as angels. On Holy Saturday, the Chapayekas are finally defeated with flowers, music, and prayer. They strip off their coats, blankets, and masks, flinging them at the foot of an effigy of Judas, which is set on fire, scourging the evil forces. The Chapayekas are then hurried to the church to be rebaptized.

Yavapai Wars   The Yavapais had little contact with whites until gold was discovered in central Arizona in the early 1860s. When ranchers and miners began to disrupt their food-collecting rounds, the Yavapai bands began to raid for food. Between roughly 1863 and 1873, when most surrendered, the poorly armed Yavapai fought with their hunting weapons and struggled to survive after their winter food supplies were destroyed by the army. Unlike the well-armed Apaches, they had few guns and were no match for the sophisticated arms and ammunition of the U.S. Army. Today central Arizona bears a legacy of morbid place names, such as Bloody Basin and Skull Valley, named for the many Yavapai families who were massacred there.

Yuman   Yuman is both a cultural and a language group with several divisions. The two major divisions are the Upland Yumans and the River Yumans. The Upland Yumans live in the uplands of northern and central Arizona and include the Havasupai, Hualapai, and Yavapai. The political divisions of the Yavapais include the Fort McDowell Yavapai Nation, Camp Verde, and the Yavapai Prescott Indian Tribe. The River and Delta Yumans are the Mojave, Quechan, Cocopah, and Maricopa, whose homeland is the area on the Arizona and California sides of the Colorado River; the Maricopa today live near the Akimel O'odham in southern Arizona. The modern political divisions of the River Yumans include the Fort Mojave Tribe, the Quechan Tribe, the Cocopah Tribe, and the Colorado River Indian Tribes (whose heritage is Mojave, Chemehuevi, Hopi, and Navajo).

Zah, Peterson (Navajo, 1928–)   A past chairman of the Navajo Nation, Peterson Zah earned a degree from Arizona State University and trained VISTA (Volunteers in Service to America) workers for their service on Indian reservations throughout the United States. Working with this domestic Peace Corps program helped him develop skills that later served him well at DNA-People's Legal Services, Inc., a nonprofit organization, with offices on several reservations, sponsored by the state of Arizona for economically disadvantaged Indian people. During his ten years as executive director of DNA, Zah supervised tribal court advocates, attorneys, and 120 employees; under his leadership, several landmark cases that established the rights of Native American individuals and nations were won in the Supreme Court. Zah was the only Navajo leader to be elected both Navajo Tribal Chairman (in 1982) and Navajo Nation President (in 1990; he was defeated by Albert Hale in 1995). He has worked tirelessly for Navajo education by raising funds for scholarships, educational services, and new schools, and by developing curriculum materials on Navajo culture and history.

Zepeda, Ofelia (Tohono O'odham, 1952–)   Born in Stanfield, Arizona, Ofelia Zepeda is a respected poet, scholar, and linguist. Well known for her leadership in the revitalization of American Indian languages, she spoke only Tohono O'odham until she was seven years old. Even before she earned her bachelor's degree, she taught O'odham linguistics at the University of Arizona. In those early years, course material was virtually nonexistent, and Zepeda worked with noted MIT linguist Kenneth Hale, who helped the university create its linguistics program. As she began to study O'odham, she worked with Hale on lesson plans that eventually became part of her dissertation and first book, *A Papago Grammar* (1983). Her calm bearing belies the vast amount of work that she continues to undertake: in addition to writing, editing, and classroom teaching, she codirects the annual **American Indian Language Development Institute**, which teaches American Indian educators how to work with Native-speaking students. In 1999, she was awarded a MacArthur "genius" grant. More recently, she was named a Regents' Professor in recognition of the contribution that she has made to scholarship, teaching, and research. She continues to teach in the linguistics department at the University of Arizona.

Zuni   The Pueblo of Zuni, a federally recognized Indian tribe, has a reservation with four tracts of land in Arizona and New Mexico. The main body of the reservation, which is in western New Mexico, was established in 1877 by executive order. The Zunis are the only present-day group in the American Southwest who are descended from the **Mogollon**.

Zuni language   The people of Zuni Pueblo in western New Mexico speak what is considered to be a language isolate. This means that it is unrelated to any other known languages. Although some linguists have posited a link between Zuni and California Penutian, if it existed, it was so long ago that no evidence remains to support this claim.

Part III

Chronology

75,000–45,000 B.C.
Human migration from Asia becomes possible with the first exposure of the
Bering land bridge.

23,000–12,000 B.C.
The opportunity for an extended period of migration becomes possible with the
second exposure of the Bering land bridge.

9500–6000 B.C.
Paleo-Indian culture, the culture of early Native people in the Americas characterized by big-game hunting, exists in the Southwest.

6000 B.C.–200 A.D.
With the disappearance of large game due to climatic change, the people of
the Archaic period are forced to live in small groups that follow a seasonal
round in order to exploit available environmental resources, including
wild plants and animals.

1500 B.C.
In some areas of the Southwest, people are practicing agriculture based on the
cultivation of corn, beans, and squash.

500 B.C.–1550 A.D.

Ancestral Pueblo (Anasazi) culture, characterized by multistoried pueblos with great *kivas*, cliff dwellings, and black-on-white and glazed pottery, is widespread in the Four Corners area of the Colorado Plateau.

300 B.C.

The River Hohokam are producing enough corn, beans, and squash, using their extensive network of irrigation canals, to support settled villages along the Gila and Salt rivers.

300 B.C.–1400 A.D.

Hohokam culture, characterized by red-on-buff decorated pottery, a ball-court ritual complex, large-scale irrigation systems, cremation burial, and artifacts that include etched and painted shell jewelry, carved stone bowls, stone palettes, and figurines, is widespread in the Sonoran Desert.

200 B.C.–50 A.D.

The first making and firing of pottery containers in the Southwest occurs at the Coffee Camp site in southern Arizona.

700–1130

Mogollon culture, characterized by masonry-walled pueblos, kivas, and unpainted brown corrugated pottery, extends from eastern Arizona into central New Mexico in an area of deep valleys and high mountains.

700–1350

Patayan culture, characterized by a highly developed system of trails, brown plainware pottery containing mica in its tempering material, and intaglios—immense geometric figures and figures of humans, animals, and stars excavated in the desert pavement—extends on either side of the Colorado River, southward from the Grand Canyon to the Gulf of California.

900–1200

The Mimbres, a Mogollon people living in the Mimbres Valley in New Mexico, create their black-on-white pottery with animal and bird figures and geometric patterns.

950–1000

Migration begins to the Rio Grande Valley. The Tiwas migrate to the Rio Grande, splitting the tribe into northern and southern Tiwas.

1150–1250

Keresans move from Chaco Canyon. Some go to the Rio Puerco area while others go east and then south to the Rio Grande.

1200s–1850s

An amalgam of Yuman subgroups, drawn from the Halchidhoma, Kavelcha-dom, Kahwan, and Halyikwamai, begin to migrate from the Colorado River to the Gila River area. Probably decimated by River Yuman warfare, these tribal remnants coalesce into a body that eventually becomes known as the Maricopa.

1275–1300

The Four Corners area is deserted. By this time, the Acoma, the Santa Ana, and the Zia are in their present locations.

1350–1400

Athapaskans (Navajos and Apaches) arrive in the Southwest.

1400–1525

According to oral history, the organization that later becomes known as the All-Indian Pueblo Council is created to counteract raiding from nomadic tribes.

1492

Columbus arrives in the Caribbean.

1493

The papal demarcation decree recognizes the obligation of the Spanish monarch to convert Indians to Christianity as well as Spain's claim to America.

1500

Linguistic evidence shows that at this time, one group of Apaches moves eastward to the southern Plains (to become the Kiowa-Apaches) while the Western Apaches and Navajos move westward and southward.

1512

The most extensive statement of early Spanish policy, the Laws of Burgos, focuses on the institution of *encomienda*, land grants to soldiers who participated in the conquest of Mexico, as a means to convert the Indians by congregating them near the *encomenderos*, who are charged with instructing them in the Catholic faith.

1519–1521

The Spanish conquer the Aztecs in Mexico.

1528

Spaniards are shipwrecked off the Texas coast, and four survivors make their way toward Mexico.

1529

First European contact with southwestern Indians when shipwreck survivors Alvar Nuñez Cabeza de Vaca and three companions reach the Southwest.

1533

Pizarro and his army conquer the Inca empire in Peru.

The Yaqui Indians successfully resist the first European intrusion into their territory by slave raider Diego de Guzmán.

1537

Pope Paul III issues a papal bull proclaiming that American Indians are entitled to liberty and the possession of their property.

1539

Franciscan friar Marcos de Niza leads an expedition into Zuni and Acoma country and is the first to report the existence of the pueblo of Acoma. He is guided by Esteban, the Moorish slave who had been with Cabeza de Vaca. The Zunis kill Esteban for his brazen behavior and threats. Friar Marcos observes Hawikuh from a distance and returns to report that there are Seven Cities of Cibola.

Francisco de Vitoria lectures at the University of Salamanca, stating that the Indians of the New World are free men and thus exempt from slavery.

1540

Francisco Vasquez de Coronado explores Pueblo country, and members of his party travel on to the Grand Canyon and as far east as Kansas. Pedro de Tovar, part of this expedition, travels to an eastern Hopi settlement where he encounters hostility and attacks the village. He then peacefully visits the six other Hopi communities. Lopez de Cardenas arrives later and tries to establish permanent headquarters in present-day Bernalillo. When a Spaniard tries to attack an Indian's wife, the Indians respond with outrage. A battle is fought and many Indians are killed. When Coronado's thorough explorations find no evidence of precious metals, his expedition is considered to be a failure, and southwestern Indians are left undisturbed for the next forty years.

Hernando de Alarcon makes the earliest recorded contact with the Cocopa at the mouth of the Colorado River.

1542

The Catholic Church is required by the New Laws of the Indies to expand its activities in order to prepare Native people for integration into Spanish-American society. An attempt to legislate against *encomienda*, these laws are openly disobeyed or provoke an armed *encomendero* response.

1550

The principal critic of the age of conquest, Dominican Bishop Bartolome de las Casas, writes an eyewitness account of Spanish atrocities against Indian peoples and asserts that Spaniards are obligated to restore to Indian ownership the lands and goods that they have taken. In response, the king summons a formal hearing to consider questions of morality in Spanish imperialism.

1573

The military conquest of Native people is forbidden by the Pacification Ordinance.

1581

Lay Brother Augustin Rodriguez and military leader Francisco Sanchez Chamuscado bring a party of thirty-one missionaries to Pueblo country.

1583

Antonio de Espejo outfits and leads a relief party to locate two friars who had remained behind during the Rodriguez-Chamuscado expedition. This party enters Hopi country to search for gold and is welcomed by the people of five villages. They also encounter some Yavapais as they travel through the southern portions of Yavapai territory. The Spanish Crown decides to plan permanent settlements in New Mexico.

1590–1591

Gaspar Castaño de Sosa undertakes an independent colonizing expedition without permission from Spain. He plants crosses and appoints officials at all Pueblo villages and locates Picuris Pueblo, which has been missed by previous Spanish explorers because of its secluded location. The viceroy appoints Captain Juan Morlete to find and return de Sosa to Mexico under guard.

1593

Francisco Leyba de Bonilla and Antonio Gutierrez de Humana settle at San
Ildefonso Pueblo without permission. Humana kills Bonilla, and Plains
Indians kill the rest of the party while they are exploring that area.

1595

Don Juan de Oñate is awarded a contract from the Spanish Crown to colonize
New Mexico at his own expense.

1598

Don Juan de Oñate, accompanied by settlers and soldiers, leads his first expedition to the Rio Grande area, taking formal "possession" of New Mexico just
below El Paso del Norte and ignoring Pueblo ownership of the land. The
first recorded assembly of thirty-eight Pueblo leaders with the Spanish occurs at Santo Domingo Pueblo. (Thus the date of 1598 appears on the logo
of the All-Indian Pueblo Council even though they existed as a pan-Pueblo
organization much earlier.) They give Oñate the right to settle and swear
allegiance to the king of Spain. The Spanish divide Pueblo country into
districts and assign Franciscan missionaries to seven pueblos. The Spanish
establish their first settlement near present-day San Juan Pueblo.

1598–1680

This is the most intensive period of Spanish missionary activities among the
Pueblos. By 1617, eleven mission churches have been built. Fray Alonzo
de Lugo is at Jemez Pueblo from 1598 to 1601, while Fray Geronimo Za-
rate de Salmeron is at San Juan Pueblo from 1618 to 1626. From 1628 to
1630, Fray Martin de Arvide is at Jemez Pueblo. Fray Juan de Salas is at
Isleta Pueblo in 1621, and the church there is completed by 1629.

1599

In response to treatment by the Spanish, the Acomas kill Juan de Zaldiver,
Oñate's nephew. As hostilities intensify, the Acomas lead a punitive effort. When the Spaniards defeat them, they take Acoma children under
age twelve and condemn the rest to slavery. They punish men over twenty
years of age by cutting off one foot and one hand.

1600

The Lipan and Jicarilla no longer have contact with the Western Apache and
Navajo. During the next century, the Lipan move into central and southern Texas and the Jicarilla establish themselves in northern New Mexico
and southern Colorado.

1604

Juan de Oñate's expedition meets the Mojave near the junction of the Colorado and Bill Williams rivers and farther south; this is the first Spanish-
Mojave contact.

1609–1614

Muslims are expelled from southern Spain.

1610

The Spanish abandon their settlement near San Juan Pueblo. Pedro de Peralta
replaces Oñate and founds the city of Santa Fe. Over the next four years,
he forces Indian workers to build the Palace of the Governors, ushering
in a seventy-year period of Indian servitude.

1617

In response to a request from the still-undefeated Yaqui Indians, the Jesuits send
missionaries, beginning an intensive program of directed culture change
that includes the introduction of Christianity, the addition of new agricultural items and techniques, and the consolidation of the Yaqui population into seven church-centered towns.

1620

The King of Spain issues a royal decree requiring that each pueblo choose a
governor, lieutenant governor, and other officials by popular vote at the
end of each year to carry on its affairs. As a symbol of authority, each governor receives a silver-crowned cane with a cross on the silver mount that
symbolizes the Church's support to his pueblo.

1629

Franciscan missionaries settle among the Hopi, building churches at three
settlements.

1630s

Jesuits begin ministry to the Opata Indians in Mexico.

1632

Angered that they are being forced to replace their traditional religion with
Catholicism, the Indians at Taos Pueblo kill Padre Pedro de Miranda,
his guard, and two soldiers. They also resent the feudal system, including
taxation, that has been forced upon them.

1633

An agent and custodian of the Inquisition, Fray Estevan de Perea, arrives to conduct witchcraft and bigamy investigations among the Pueblos.

1634–1647

The Pueblos respond to continued religious persecution from the Spanish with conspiracies and sporadic outbreaks. At this time, Pueblo resistance still takes the form of isolated incidents.

1640

The Franciscans threaten to abandon their New Mexico missions in response to severe conflict between Spanish civil and religious authorities over mistreatment of the Indians and the collection of taxes and goods.

In fear of Governor Luis de Rosas, the people of Taos Pueblo flee to Apache country.

1650

The Pueblos of Jemez, Isleta, San Felipe, Cochiti, Taos, and the now-extinct Tiwa village of Alameda unite with Apaches to expel the Spanish, but their plans are discovered and nine leaders are hanged; others are sold into slavery.

1655

A missionary catches a Hopi in an "act of idolatry" and beats him severely in public, then applies turpentine to his body and ignites it, killing the man.

1661–1664

Governor Diego de Peñalosa forbids the exploitation by friars of Pueblo Indians in the manufacture of cotton robes. When he returns to Mexico City, the Inquisition tries him for offenses against the Spanish clergy. Later, Peñalosa's stories help inspire the La Salle expedition (1684–1687), which seeks to limit the expansion of Spanish holdings in the New World.

1676

Apache Indians destroy several pueblos and churches, killing Spaniards and Christianized Indians. Some Apaches are captured and hanged or sold into slavery.

1680

The Rio Grande Pueblos revolt against the Spanish, successfully driving them out of the area. The Hopi fully support the revolt by killing the four missionaries stationed among them. The Rio Grande Pueblos remain free and independent of the Spanish from 1680 to 1692, while the Hopi, protected by their distance from Santa Fe, are never again under Spanish control.

1681

Governor Otermin returns with troops to sack Isleta and burn Sandia Pueblo. The people seek asylum among the Hopis.

1687

Jesuit Father Eusebio Kino begins ministry among the Upper Pimas, now known as the O'odham.

1689

Governor Domingo Jironza de Cruzate burns Zia Pueblo and the people flee to an area west of Jemez Pueblo.

1692

Governor Diego de Vargas enters Pueblo country.

Some Tewas seek asylum among the Hopi and found the village of Hano on First Mesa, where their descendants remain today and are known as the Hopi-Tewa.

1693–1696

De Vargas completes the reconquest of New Mexico with the aid of Pueblo leaders and the assistance of a growing number of Pueblo allies.

1699

The Spanish recognize the existence of Old Laguna, a pueblo said to have been formed by refugees from the Pueblo Revolt of 1680.

1700–1706

Many present-day pueblos are reestablished after the return of Pueblo people from their flight to Hopi and Navajo country.

1701

Hopi and Tewa warriors destroy the easternmost of the Hopi villages, Awatovi, because the village has again received Franciscan missionaries. The survivors disperse among the Hopi villages.

1736

The discovery of a silver deposit near the present Arizona–Mexico border brings Spanish miners into Tohono O'odham territory.

1740

Yaquis join Mayo Indians in revolt against Spanish settlers who seek to overrun their territory. Sparing only the Jesuits, they kill or drive out all Spaniards.

1767

By edict of the King of Spain, the Jesuits are expelled from New Spain and replaced by the Franciscans.

1771

Missions in Yaqui territory are secularized because settlers want Indian land.

1776

Franciscan missionary Francisco Garces makes the first direct Spanish contact with the Hualapais. He continues to travel through their region and along the Colorado River until Yuman Indians kill him in 1781. The Hualapais remain isolated from Anglo and Spanish incursions for the next seventy years.

1776–1783

The American Revolution is fought.

1778

The first major U.S. treaty with Indians—the Delaware tribe—is signed.

1780–1781

A smallpox epidemic kills 5,000 Pueblos, especially the Hopis.

1790

The Trade and Intercourse Act of 1790 is the first of several such laws (1793, 1796, 1802, 1834) passed to control trade between Native Americans and Anglo-Americans. These laws establish the precedent that title to land can only be transferred by contract between the federal government and a Native nation. The Trade and Intercourse Act becomes important legal precedent for Native American land claims across the United States.

1803

Congress ratifies the Louisiana Purchase, adding over 800,000 square miles to the United States, which virtually doubles the size of the nation. The western boundary is extended to the Rocky Mountains and the United States has control of the entire Mississippi River.

1821

The Plan of Iguala does away with all legal distinctions regarding Indians for the inhabitants of New Spain. Spain and Mexico sign the Treaty of Cordoba, which embodies the same principle.

Mexico becomes an independent country, and the Southwest becomes a part of Mexico. Mexico's Declaration of Independence reaffirms the equality of Indians with non-Indians.

William Becknell pioneers the Santa Fe Trail as a trade route between the Missouri frontier and Santa Fe.

1822

Trade is opened between Mexico and the United States along the Santa Fe Trail. William Becknell leads his second trade expedition to Santa Fe, introducing the use of wagons to carry goods westward across the southern Plains. Anglo access into Pueblo country becomes much easier.

1824

The Bureau of Indian Affairs is established in the U.S. Department of War.

Mexican leaders create a republican constitution to replace the Plan of Iguala that maintains the same principle of equality of citizenship and requires Indians to pay taxes, own land individually, and allow the participation of non-Indians in the administration of their local government.

1825

The Mexican government and the Sonoran state government try to impose political and economic control on the Yaqui Indians, who respond by initiating a movement for the founding of an independent indigenous state. Juan Banderas leads a force of 2,000 Yaquis that drives all non-Indians from their territory.

1826

Trapper and fur trader Jedediah Smith travels through Mojave country.

1830

The Indian Removal Act authorizes the president to set up districts west of the Mississippi to which Indian title has been removed and exchange these districts for Indian-held lands in the East.

1833

Mexicans execute Yaqui leader Juan Banderas.

1838

Towa-speaking people from Pecos Pueblo resettle at Jemez Pueblo.

1839

Most of the remaining Five Civilized Tribes (Cherokee, Chickasaw, Choctaw, Creek, and Seminole) are relocated to lands in present-day eastern Oklahoma and Arkansas.

1840s

The Franciscans relinquish their hold on the churches in O'odham territory.

1840–1843

The Tohono O'odham resist Mexican settlers in armed conflict to protect their land and water holes but are finally forced to capitulate.

1844–1845

A cholera epidemic decimates the Indians of the Gila Valley in Arizona.

1845

Manifest Destiny becomes the ideological justification for aggressive territorial expansion.

1846

The United States proclaims war against Mexico and annexes the Territory of New Mexico.
Colonel Doniphan negotiates the first treaty with the Navajo Indians.

1848

Under the terms of the Treaty of Guadalupe Hidalgo, Mexico consents to the Rio Grande as the boundary of Texas and agrees to cede all of California and most of New Mexico (which includes present-day Arizona) to the United States in return for a payment of $15 million and the assumption of $3.25 million in damage claims against the Mexican government.

1849

The Bureau of Indian Affairs is transferred from the Department of War to the newly established Department of the Interior.
A treaty with the Navajos permits the federal government, for the first time, to influence the internal affairs of a tribe.
James S. Calhoun is appointed Indian agent in Santa Fe but is not able to carry through his plans because of congressional inaction. Although treaties

are signed with the Apaches and other tribes, warfare is widespread in the Southwest throughout the 1850s.

1850

James S. Calhoun acts as agent for a treaty between the United States and the Pueblos, but the Senate never ratifies it.

Congress passes the Organic Act, which creates the Territory of New Mexico and settles the controversy with Texas over the region east of the Rio Grande.

1853

The Gadsden Purchase adds what is now southern Arizona and southwestern New Mexico to the United States in return for $10 million to Mexico. However, it establishes an international boundary through what was Cocopah territory, leaving some Cocopah on the Mexican side. The same situation occurs for the Tohono O'odham of southern Arizona.

1856

The Laws of the Reform break up the landed estates of the Catholic Church in Mexico.

1857

Maricopa and Akimel O'odham Indians defeat Quechan-Mojave allies in a major battle next to Pima Butte on the Gila River in southern Arizona; this disastrous defeat leads to the demoralization and decline of the Mojave.

1858

Congress passes an act confirming the original Spanish land grants for Acoma, Jemez, Cochiti, Picuris, San Felipe, San Juan, Santo Domingo, Zia, Isleta, Nambé, Pojoque, Sandia, San Ildefonso, Santa Clara, Taos, and Tesuque pueblos.

1859

Mojave warriors are mowed down by rifle fire at Fort Mojave, ending the tribe's resistance.

Congress creates the Gila River Reservation for the Pimas (Akimel O'odham) and Maricopas.

1861–1865

Civil War in the United States causes the withdrawal of most troops from western outposts. But by mid-1863, volunteer regiments replace army troops in frontier installations.

1862

Brigadier General James H. Carleton develops a plan for the forced relocation of traditional enemies, the Mescalero Apaches and the Navajos, at
Bosque Redondo on the Pecos River in east central New Mexico.

1863

To carry out General Carleton's plans, Colonel Kit Carson leads troops against
the Mescalero Apaches in southern New Mexico, taking them to Bosque
Redondo before setting out against the Navajos.

Gold is discovered near Prescott, Arizona, bringing an influx of prospectors.

"The Long Walk" begins when Kit Carson and his troops bring more than
8,000 Navajos to Bosque Redondo, a location without potable water and
unsuited for farming.

President Abraham Lincoln signs land patents for Nambé, Cochiti, Isleta,
Jemez, Picuris, Zia, Sandia, San Felipe, San Ildefonso, Pojoaque, San
Juan, Santa Clara, Taos, Tesuque, and Santo Domingo pueblos. Pueblo
governors receive the land patents and each governor is given a silver-
headed cane that symbolizes the political recognition of their tribe.

1865

The Mescalero Apaches break away from Bosque Redondo. Their numbers
vastly underestimated, the Navajos starve without adequate food, blankets, and shelter. Epidemics, droughts, poor agricultural land, and raids
by other tribes lead to the death of thousands.

The Colorado River Indian Tribes Reservation is established for the Mojave
Indians. Later, about two hundred Chemehuevis join them, settling on
the south end of the reservation.

1866–1869

The Hualapai War begins when Anglos kill a respected Hualapai leader, Wauba
Yuma, and about 250 Hualapai warriors engage U.S. troops in battle the
following year. Anglo soldiers burn Hualapai rancherias, destroying crops
and food caches and forcing the Hualapai to surrender.

A malaria epidemic sweeps through the Indians of the Gila Valley in Arizona.

1867

Congress establishes a Peace Commission that includes a new commissioner of
Indian affairs, members of Congress, army officers, and civilians charged
with convincing the Indians to locate on reservations or, with help from
detachments of volunteers, forcing the Indians into compliance.

1868

After Navajo leader Barboncito travels to Washington to plead for the return of his people to their territory, the government investigates conditions at Bosque Redondo and determines that General Carleton's plan is a failure. Navajo leaders sign a treaty with the federal government establishing their reservation.

The federal government licenses Anglo traders on the Navajo reservation.

Mexican troops massacre 120 Yaquis in the church at Bacum, which becomes a symbol of Mexican cruelty to Yaquis.

1869

The nation's first transcontinental railroad is completed through Utah.

John Wesley Powell explores the Grand Canyon.

The government tries to force the Hualapais onto a one-square-mile reservation at Camp Beale Spring.

1870

Stretching along the Colorado River in the states of Arizona, California, and Nevada, the Fort Mojave Reservation is established by Department of War General Order No. 19 and by executive order in 1911.

The federal government recognizes the Hopi by establishing the Moqui Pueblo Agency.

1871

Congress ends the practice of negotiating treaties with tribes as though they are independent powers. The last treaties are signed with tribes.

An Apache uprising begins in New Mexico and Arizona.

Driven by hatred of all Apaches, 7 Anglos, 48 Mexican Americans, and 92 Tohono O'odham slaughter about 125 Western Apaches (primarily women and children) peacefully settled at Camp Grant in southern Arizona. This becomes known as the Camp Grant Massacre.

An executive order establishes the Rio Verde Reservation in the middle Verde Valley, and the Yavapais are given three months to settle there.

1871–1872

The federal government establishes four Apache reservations: Fort Apache for the Cibicue people and northern bands of the White Mountain division; Camp Verde in central Arizona for the Northern and Southern Tontos along with some Yavapai bands; Camp Grant for the San Carlos and the southern White Mountain bands; and Ojo Caliente, New Mexico for the

Chiricahuas. When unrest develops, Camp Grant is abandoned and an area is set aside at San Carlos on the Gila River.

1872

Congress authorizes the extension of federal services to the Pueblos.

The massacre at Skeleton Cave occurs when the U.S. Army wipes out a large band of Yavapais in the Salt River Canyon of Arizona.

General Crook forces the Tonto Apaches to surrender, and their families are taken captive at Camp Verde.

1873

Troops have brought most Yavapais onto the Rio Verde Reservation, where the they produce several successful harvests. Fearing a loss of profits, Tucson contractors who supply Indian reservations press for a government order to relocate the Yavapais onto the Apache Reservation at San Carlos.

1874

The Department of the Interior begins a "removal program" directed at concentrating all Western Apaches, Chiricahuas, and Yavapais on the San Carlos Reservation in Arizona.

The Hualapais are removed from Camp Beale Springs to La Paz, on the Colorado River Indian Tribes Reservation. They suffer greatly on their forced march to La Paz, where they are treated as prisoners of war. Disease and hunger kill almost half. The following year many return to their homeland but discover that Anglo-Americans have appropriated their land.

The Tohono O'odham receive their first reservation at San Xavier through executive order.

1875

Yavapais and Tonto Apaches are relocated to San Carlos in a forced march over 180 miles of rough terrain with insufficient supplies in midwinter, which kills many. White Mountain and Cibecue people are also brought in from Fort Apache and 235 Chiricahuas come, although the most "hostile" groups remain free.

1876

An overwhelming force of Sioux, Cheyenne, and Blackfoot warriors wipe out the 220 men under General George Armstrong Custer at the Little Bighorn River.

The U.S. Supreme Court upholds the decision of the New Mexico Supreme Court that the Intercourse Act of 1834 is not applicable to the Pueblo Indians, depriving them of protection for their territory and allowing about 12,000 non-Indians to settle on Pueblo land.

1877

The federal government issues a land patent to Acoma Pueblo.

Chiricahua chief Victorio and his followers bring the number of Indians at San Carlos to over 5,000. Many of the different groups have never been in contact before, and tension is high. Six months after Victorio's arrival, he escapes with over 300 men, women, and children.

1878

The southern Plains tribes conduct their last successful bison hunt, and starvation becomes commonplace on many reservations.

The Ute Indians are removed from New Mexico to a reservation in Colorado.

The first addition is made to the Navajo Reservation by executive order. Subsequent additions come in 1880, 1884, 1901, 1905, 1907, 1908, 1911, 1917, 1930, 1933, and 1934.

1879

The Carlisle Industrial Training School in Pennsylvania, the most famous off-reservation Indian boarding school, is founded. Designed after a military model by Richard Henry Pratt, the school is intended to acculturate Indian children rapidly. They are taken away for three and later, five years; during summer vacations the children are placed with white families rather than being allowed to return home.

The Salt River-Maricopa Indian Community is established.

The railroad links New Mexico to the East.

Victorio surrenders at Ojo Caliente but escapes again.

1880

The Havasupais receive a reservation of 518 acres at the bottom of Havasu Canyon, which drains northward into the Grand Canyon.

1880s and 1890s

Indian agents at San Carlos allow many Yavapais to return to their homelands so that their land at San Carlos will be free for leasing to Anglo-American mineral interests. Some remain and intermarry with Apaches.

1881

The nation's second transcontinental railroad is completed by way of southern California and Deming, New Mexico, providing an economical way to ship raw wool east to be processed. The wool trade soon expands and trading posts become numerous both on and near the Navajo reservation.

The Albuquerque Indian School is established. In 1886, the federal government takes over its management from the Presbyterian Church, which had been running the school under contract with the United States.

More Apaches flee from San Carlos when Anglo troops are killed at Cibecue while attempting to arrest the leader of a nativistic cult. It takes two years to capture the nearly 1,000 Indians who escape.

1882

An executive order creates the Hopi Indian Reservation, but the land set aside is for "Indian," not exclusively Hopi, use.

The Gila Bend Reservation is established for the Tohono O'odham.

1883

President Chester Arthur establishes the Hualapai Reservation on roughly a tenth of their original territory.

The federal government issues a land patent to Santa Ana Pueblo.

The Religious Crimes Codes make it a federal crime to practice Native ceremonies.

1884

The government establishes a reservation for the Quechans on the west side of the Colorado River.

Peace with the Apaches is finally restored, and several groups, including Naiche and Geronimo's band of Chiricahuas, are taken to Fort Apache.

1885

The Major Crimes Act makes it a federal crime for Indians to commit murder, manslaughter, rape, assault, larceny, burglary, and arson against other Indians in their own nations.

Naiche's Chiricahua Apache group breaks out of Fort Apache.

1885–1886

Yaqui leader Cajeme unites Yaquis and Mayos in a campaign against the Mexicans.

1886

The U.S. Supreme Court upholds the Major Crimes Act of 1885 in *United States v. Kagama*, originally a California case.

Naiche's group of Chiricahua Apaches surrenders in Mexico; the warriors are sent to Fort Pickens in Pensacola Bay, Florida. Their families are sent to Fort Marion, St. Augustine, Florida, along with more than 500 other noncombatants. All Chiricahuas are designated "prisoners of war" and remain so for twenty-seven years.

1887
The General Allotment (Dawes) Act provides for the allotment of tribal lands to individuals. "Surplus" land (left over from allotment) is opened to Anglo-American settlers. Southwestern tribes are not subject to allotment, except for small portions of the Navajo, Akimel O'odham, Tohono O'odham, and Colorado River Indian Tribes Reservations.

The imprisoned Chiricahuas are transferred from Florida to Mount Vernon Barracks, near Mobile, Alabama.

The Jicarilla Apache Reservation is established by executive order in northern New Mexico.

The Mexican government executes Yaqui leader Cajeme. Mexican troops begin military occupation of Yaqui towns, and many Yaquis flee across the border to the United States.

1890
The last major conflict between U.S. troops and American Indians occurs when troops kill more than half of the unarmed 350 Sioux assembled for a Ghost Dance at Wounded Knee, South Dakota.

1891
Congress establishes the Court of Private Land Claims to conduct investigations and hearings, and to render opinions in the form of decrees. In time, the court confirms most of the Pueblo tribally owned lands outside the boundaries of the original Spanish land grants.

1894
The federal government moves the Chiricahuas to Fort Sill, Oklahoma.

1895
The Gila River Indian Community (separate from the Gila River Indian Reservation) is established for the Akimel O'odham by Congress on 374,361 acres of land.

1900
The Mexican government institutes a program for large-scale deportation of Yaqui Indians to the Yucatan.

Pojoaque Pueblo is abandoned, and most of the survivors go to Nambé Pueblo.

1903

The Fort McDowell Reservation is established by executive order near Phoenix, Arizona, and the Yavapais must fight to maintain their land and water rights. Yavapai Dr. Carlos Montezuma leads a continual battle to avoid relocation and for the development of irrigation at Fort McDowell.

1906

The split at Oraibi occurs between the "friendlies," those open to Anglo cultural influences, and the "hostiles" who oppose them. Tribal leaders engage in a bloodless competition that results in the expulsion of the hostiles. The new Hopi village of Hotevilla is founded about seven miles north of Oraibi.

The U.S. government gives political asylum to the Yaquis.

1909

Congress issues a land patent to Laguna Pueblo.

1910

The Camp Verde Reservation is established for the Yavapais and Western Apaches.

1911

The Society of American Indians is established to work for the reform of Indian policy.

The Southern Pueblos Agency of the Bureau of Indian Affairs is established in Albuquerque. Offices in Santa Fe administer the northern pueblos.

1913

The Chiricahua Apaches are finally freed from prisoner-of-war status. Some of them move to the Mescalero Apache Reservation in New Mexico, where their political status is subsumed under that of the Mescalero Apache Tribe. Others remain in the Fort Sill area, where they are eventually given parcels of land instead of communally owned land.

New Mexico is admitted as the forty-seventh state and Arizona is admitted as the forty-eighth state.

The government establishes the Ak-Chin Reservation for the O'odham.

The Supreme Court reverses its decision of 1876, and the 12,000 non-Indians who settled on Pueblo land are now considered to be trespassers.

1916

The main Tohono O'odham Reservation is established at Sells, west of Tucson.

1917

The Cocopah Indians receive their first 446 acres of reservation lands.

1922–1923

Four bills are introduced into Congress that apply mainly to the nonallotted reservation Indians of Arizona and New Mexico. The first deals with a property dispute between Pueblo Indians and white settlers along the Rio Grande; passage would mean considerable Pueblo loss of land and water rights without compensation (the Bursum Bill). The second would allot the Mescalero Apache reservation and create a new national park from part of the land. The third would give the Secretary of the Interior the power to terminate federal status of Indian tribes. The fourth would open all Indian reservations created by executive order to oil development.

1922

The Pueblos hold a reorganization meeting of the All-Indian Pueblo Council when John Collier assembles the people to explain the Bursum Bill.

The Mescalero Apaches receive clear title to their land.

1923

The American Indian Defense Association is formed, partly in response to the four bills brought before Congress beginning in 1922; this organization is the most outspoken of the Indian rights societies in its criticism of federal Indian policy. John Collier, the executive secretary, supports the All-Indian Pueblo Council as a way to help Indians organize effectively in the defense of their rights and to serve as a symbol for Indian self-government.

1924

Congress grants citizenship to all Indians, including the right to vote. However, Indians in New Mexico and Arizona are not given the vote because these states do not pass the legislation.

Congress passes the Pueblo Lands Act to determine the status of Indian land claims using the exterior boundaries of the Spanish land grants.

1928

The Meriam Report criticizes allotment and federal Indian policy by describing conditions of extreme poverty, poor health, and substandard education that exist in Native communities and federally run schools for Indian children.

1931

The federal government confirms the original land grant to Zuni Pueblo.

1933

Commissioner John Collier asks the Navajo Tribal Council to sanction and implement stock reduction. Until 1937, this program is primarily voluntary.

Pojoaque Pueblo is restored to the Pueblos by order of the Pueblo Lands Board and federal court. Some Pojoaque people return home to live there.

The United States issues a land patent to Zuni Pueblo.

1933–1942

President Franklin D. Roosevelt institutes the Civilian Conservation Corps with an Indian Division that lays the groundwork for the eventual organization of American Indian wildland firefighters.

1934

Congress passes the Indian Reorganization (Wheeler-Howard) Act that ends allotment and reaffirms the right of Indians to govern themselves, but under an organizational structure determined by the U.S. government. Some land is restored to reservations.

The Johnson-O'Malley Act enables the states, instead of individual school districts, to contract directly with the Education Division of the BIA.

1935

The Bureau of Indian Affairs establishes the United Pueblos Agency in Albuquerque.

The Yavapai-Prescott Tribe receives a reservation near Prescott, Arizona.

1936

Congress passes an act to legally merge the people of Pecos Pueblo, who have been living at Jemez Pueblo, with the people of Jemez Pueblo.

1937

Members of the Colorado River Indian Tribes adopt a constitution and elect a tribal chairman under the provisions of the Indian Reorganization Act.

The Livestock Reduction Program becomes coercive and far-reaching among the Navajo. Many animals are shot and left to rot. This program continues until 1945. The negative psychological impact is overwhelming, and many Navajo turn to the Native American Church.

1941–1945

Native Americans participate in World War II.

1942

President Franklin D. Roosevelt signs an executive order establishing the War Relocation Authority to create internment camps for Japanese Americans. The Poston Relocation Center on the Colorado River Indian Tribes Reservation is one of ten wartime camps. By not opposing the plan, the tribal council avoids the permanent loss of this land to the Department of War.

1943

The federal government founds Los Alamos National Laboratory as an atomic research center. Indians from nearby pueblos continue to be employed there today.

1944

The National Congress of American Indians (NCAI) is founded and becomes the most important pan-Indian rights movement in the United States.

1945

The Bureau of Indian Affairs opens farming lands on the Colorado River Indian Tribes Reservation to Navajo and Hopi immigrants suffering the effects of the depression and federal stock-reduction programs. Although the Mojaves and Chemehuevis rescind this ordinance, concerned that their reservation will be overrun, the Department of the Interior does not rescind the original order until 1964.

1946

The Indian Claims Commission Act is created to settle outstanding Indian claims as a step toward ending federal responsibilities toward tribes.

1947

Counsel for the Association on American Indian Affairs brings suits against the states of New Mexico and Arizona for their failure to extend welfare benefits to Indians under the Social Security Act. When the states grudgingly comply with the law, the suits are dropped.

1948

The first official Native American firefighting unit, the Mescalero Red Hats, is organized on the Mescalero Apache Reservation.

A federal court decision gives Indians in Arizona and New Mexico the right to vote.

1949

The Secretary of the Interior approves the Laguna Pueblo constitution under the terms of the IRA.

1950

Congress passes the Navajo-Hopi Rehabilitation Act, a relief package to help ease economic problems caused by returning war veterans and defense-plant workers and a severe two-year drought.

1952

Anaconda Company and Laguna Pueblo sign the first lease providing for the development of uranium deposits discovered on the Pueblo land grant.

The Bureau of Indian Affairs establishes the relocation program through an employment opportunities act. When Indians move to cities, jobs, adult education, vocational training, and some financial aid are provided. Relocation offices are established in major cities. However, the effort does not succeed for a variety of reasons, including the lack of employment when unions will not accept Indians as members even though they have training in carpentry, bricklaying, and mechanics. Urban poverty, disruption of family and tribal relationships, and inadequate educational and support services contribute to the failure of this program.

1953

Congress calls for the termination of federal recognition and services for Indian tribes with the adoption of House Concurrent Resolution 108, which includes a timetable for ending federal obligations to Indians. Public Law 280 transfers civil and criminal jurisdiction to select states as a major step in ending federal responsibilities.

1955

Health programs for Indians are transferred from the Bureau of Indian Affairs to the Public Health Service of the Department of Health, Education, and Welfare.

1962

The Santa Fe Indian School is replaced by a new art school, the Institute of American Indian Arts.

1965

The All-Indian Pueblo Council adopts bylaws and a constitution to infuse the existing traditional group with an Anglo-American organizational structure in order to create more effective economic and educational programs. This structural reorganization is also intended to give the Pueblos a more unified voice on issues such as water and land rights and the preservation of Indian cultural values.

1968

The American Indian Movement (AIM), which demands justice for Indian people through militancy, is founded in Minneapolis.

The first tribally run college in the United States, Navajo Community College (now known as Diné College), is founded in Tsaile, Arizona.

1970

Commissioner Louis R. Bruce signs contracts that turn over the administration of all formerly BIA-run programs to the Zuni Indians, whose major reservation is in New Mexico, and to the Salt River Pima and Maricopa Indians of Arizona.

Congress votes to return Taos Blue Lake to Pueblo ownership, ending sixty-four years of struggle by the tribe to regain this sacred site.

1971

The Native American Rights Fund, which challenges injustice in the court system, is founded.

1972

The Indian Education Act mandates community and parental participation in school programs and encourages programs that stress culturally relevant and bilingual curriculum materials. This act also establishes the Office of Indian Education in the Department of Education.

1973

The siege at Wounded Knee, South Dakota, lasts for seventy days and brings AIM and Native militancy into public awareness.

1975

The Indian Self-Determination and Educational Assistance Act is passed, with the goals of fostering tribal self-government and transferring many of the functions of the Bureau of Indian Affairs to individual tribes.

1976

The All-Indian Pueblo Council takes administrative control of the Albuquerque Indian School.

1978

The Indian Child Welfare Act takes the responsibility for Indian children from external agencies and gives it to the tribes.

Congress passes the American Indian Religious Freedom Act (AIRFA), designed to review and update federal policies so that Native Americans have a legal right to practice their traditional religions, possess sacred objects, and gain access to sacred sites.

The federal government passes the Tribally Controlled Community College Assistance Act.

The Yaquis receive tribal recognition and reservation land from the U.S. government in southern Arizona.

1979

The Seminoles begin operating high-stakes bingo games on their reservation in Florida. Three years later, the U.S. Supreme Court rules that the "retained sovereignty" of Indian tribes exempts the Seminoles from state regulation.

1980

The Pueblos observe the 300th anniversary of the 1680 Pueblo Revolt.

The White Mountain Apaches join with a timber company to sue the state of Arizona, maintaining that state motor carrier and fuel taxes do not apply on the reservation. The U.S. Supreme Court agrees, based on the fact that the federal government controls taxes on reservations.

1983

President Ronald Reagan declares that the termination of federal responsibilities to Indians is no longer a goal and proposes greater funding for tribal self-government and resource development.

1984

A federal study demonstrates that two thirds of the BIA budget is consumed by the bureau itself.

1986

Additional land is added to the Cocopah Reservation, bringing their holdings to 6,000 acres.

The Navajo Nation establishes a Human Research Review Board (HRRB) to protect the Navajo community, its people, and the Navajo Nation's heritage.

1988

Congress passes the Indian Gaming Regulatory Act, which separates gaming into three classes and allocates regulatory jurisdiction over each class among tribal, federal, and state governments.

The U.S. Supreme Court rules that the American Indian Religious Freedom Act is a policy statement and not law, and therefore does not afford rights to the protection of sacred sites or the religious use of peyote in the Native American Church.

1990

Congress passes the Native American Graves Protection and Repatriation Act (NAGPRA), which covers the return of sacred materials, materials of cultural patrimony, and associated and unassociated funerary objects to the tribes to whom they belong.

The Smithsonian Institution returns 3,500 photographs taken in the nineteenth and twentieth centuries to Zuni Pueblo.

Zuni Pueblo celebrates the passage of the Zuni Land Conservation Act, which authorizes the appropriation of $25 million to repair Zuni land destroyed by erosion.

1992

The U.S. Congress amends the National Historic Preservation Act so that federally recognized Indian tribes can take on formal responsibility for the preservation of significant historic properties on tribal lands.

1997

The Navajo Nation opens the Navajo Museum, Library, and Visitor's Center.

Senator Slade Gorton (R-Washington) proposes that economically successful tribes be indirectly taxed and that tribes waive their sovereign immunity in order to receive Bureau of Indian Affairs funding. This proposal is rejected.

2001

Using income from their gaming enterprises, the Tohono O'odham open their own college on the reservation.

2003

Controversy flares when the Havasupais discover that tribal genetic material was not destroyed after being used in a tribally approved diabetes study but was instead used as data for more than twenty scholarly papers, nearly all unrelated to diabetes research. Most significantly, this event destroys a sense of trust that will take many years to rebuild. Tribal communities in Arizona tighten control over all types of research and declare a moratorium on medical research, especially that which involves genetic material.

2007

The Tohono O'odham celebrate the opening of the Tohono O'odham Museum and Cultural Center, financed by their gaming enterprises, which has taken six years to plan and construct. Throughout their history, the O'odham learned patience by enduring months of intense heat and drought each summer as they waited for the rains to come. During the opening ceremonies, tribal leaders describe the museum as the embodiment of tribal traits that have enabled them to endure and thrive in the desert: patience, perseverance, and resourcefulness.

Part IV

Resources

1. RESEARCH: METHODS AND HISTORY

Most of the research on southwestern cultures has been done by archaeologists, sociocultural anthropologists, and historians. Early American travelers and explorers speculated about the precontact structural remains and the living communities that they encountered. Often their reports drew from Indian oral tradition as well as Spanish legends, such as those that linked the Casa Grande ruins of southern Arizona and the Rio Grande Pueblos to the Aztecs of Mexico.[1] The following paragraphs sketch researchers' efforts to improve their theories and methods over time using data from the Southwest. Before tracing the development of these fields in the Southwest, an understanding of the methods used by each discipline is helpful.

The essence of scholarly research is the critical use of sources, whether historical documents, interview data, field notes, or other primary source material. Primary source material is written by participants in the events that are being studied and may take the form of reports, field notes, maps, transcripts, journals, and letters. It is the job of anthropologists to identify Anglo-American bias and to explore previously overlooked source material such as oral histories and museum collection data. Archaeologists and sociocultural anthropologists study various kinds of data, which is often used to inform both kinds of research.

"Ethnography" refers to fieldwork in a particular culture, while "ethnology" is cross-cultural comparison and the comparative study of ethnographic data, of society, and of culture. "Society" refers to organized life in groups, while "culture" refers to the traditions and customs that govern the behavior and beliefs of a group. With the permission of the community, sociocultural anthropologists undertake ethnographic fieldwork by conducting participant observation, living in the society about which they want to learn. By learning the appropriate ways of behaving and communicating and understanding relationships among the people in the community, anthropologists try to develop a "theory" of how a given society is organized and how its members understand the world. With the permission of community members, the anthropologist conducts and records interviews with individuals; this material is considered to be data, as are the field notes taken by the researcher. The finished product is considered to be an ethnography of a particular group of people.

Archaeologists study human behavior and cultural patterns and processes through the culture's material remains. Data come from the careful digging and methodological recording of successive layers of deposits that make up an archaeological site. The aridity of the Southwest has been a gift to archaeologists, preserving an abundance of sites and extensive prehistoric remains that have resulted in the most nearly absolute chronology for any area in the United States. The dry environment has facilitated an exceptionally accurate dating method known as dendrochronology—dating through the use of tree rings.[2] Furthermore, there was a clear connection between the Native peoples of precontact times and those of postcontact times, which allows archaeologists to trace the evolution of cultures for thousands of years.[3]

Because of the quality of the archaeological remains, scholars working in this region were able to make significant contributions to their developing discipline. By identifying diagnostic features for each prehistoric cultural sequence, they were able to place each sequence in time and to divide sequences into periods. They were also able to establish the coexistence of people and extinct animals at such sites as Folsom, New Mexico, where spear points were found in the ribs of an extinct bison.[4]

American travelers and explorers in the Southwest in the mid-1800s speculated on the connections between prehistoric structural remains and the living tribes that they encountered. Often motivated by the desire to collect artifacts for their wealthy sponsors, the early explorers wanted to bring back pots and other objects that would justify their claims of treasure waiting to be excavated. To their credit, they did see the great need to protect these prehistoric ruins through legislation and were able to get the federal **Act for the Preservation of American Antiquities** passed in 1906. This was the foundation for later acts that extended the scope of protection.

As interest grew, anthropological societies became popular, and the Bureau of Ethnology was founded in the 1870s. Trained observers accompanied expeditions and began to build a base for comparative studies by collecting specimens, writing reconnaissance reports, making sketches, and accumulating other data. In 1880, the Archaeological Institute of America sent pioneer archaeologist-historian Adolph F. Bandelier to gather information on Pueblo peoples and to investigate the ruins. After a brief attempt to work at Santo Domingo, where his questions and photography aroused considerable resentment, Bandelier moved to Cochiti pueblo and also surveyed prehistoric ruins on the Pajarito Plateau. His novel *The Delight Makers* (1890) represents the first attempt to base the reconstruction of the life pattern of a precontact Pueblo community on historical and ethnological data.[5]

Frank Hamilton Cushing's 1886–1889 expedition to the middle Gila River Valley in southern Arizona was the first major scientific field expedition in southwestern ruins, but final reports were not produced until 1945 by Emil W. Haury. The groundbreaking aspect of Cushing's work came from the use of archaeological data rather than existing ethnological situations to derive specific sociological conclusions from precontact material culture.[6] Cushing theorized that the association of different forms of burial and architectural characteristics indicated a class system among the precontact people who had inhabited the area. Another precedent set by his expedition was its multidisciplinary nature. Some members of the group focused on skeletal studies[7] while others produced documentary research,[8] surveys of prehistoric irrigation,[9] and observations of the Pima (Akimel O'odham) Indians,[10] who lived nearby.

Jesse Walter Fewkes excavated sites in Arizona and southwestern Colorado, drawing from information he had previously collected about the Western Pueblos of Zuni and Hopi. He excavated the ruins of Awat'ovi and Sityatki at Hopi, Homol'ovi and Chevelon outside of present-day Winslow, and the Chavez Pass ruin south of Meteor Crater. He worked at Casa Grande in southern Arizona between 1906 and 1908, applying the name **Hohokam** to the precontact peoples in that area to distinguish them from precontact peoples of the Colorado Plateau. First given prominence by Father Eusebio Kino in 1694, Casa Grande Ruins attracted so much popular attention that in 1877 a movement began for its preservation and for the establishment of an archaeological society in Arizona. Mary Hemenway, who had sponsored Cushing and Fewkes, along with Captain John G. Bourke and a group of Bostonians, obtained congressional support for the preservation of Casa Grande in 1889, with funds for its stabilization in 1891. The following year, Casa Grande became the first federal reservation for a precontact site in the United States.[11]

However, Casa Grande was not fully protected because the definition of defacing the ruins, which was punishable by fines, did not include unauthorized excavations and the removal of specimens. In 1906, this was remedied with the passage of the act for the preservation of antiquities on federal lands. The Bureau of American Ethnology stepped up its compilation of an archaeological cata- logue of sites on federal lands in the Southwest shortly after the act was passed. Their surveys provided inventories on new monuments established under the antiquities act as well as information on previously understudied areas.[12]

Until the early 1900s, archaeologists attributed all precontact ruins in the Southwest to the Pueblo culture and attributed any regional variation to dif- ferences in environmental factors or migration. To correct this misconception, many people with intense interest as well as great physical endurance conduct- ed fieldwork to thoroughly document the various precontact cultures of the Southwest in a manner acceptable to the highly critical scientific community. Many individuals have investigated the **Ancestral Pueblo (Anasazi)** culture, beginning with Richard Wetherill, the rancher who discovered Cliff Palace, the largest cliff dwelling in the Southwest. Some of the major figures include Alfred Kidder at Pecos, A. E. Douglass at Show Low, and Jeffrey Dean at Kiet Siel and Betatakin. Other researchers into the Anasazi past are Jesse Walter Fewkes, Victor and Cosmos Mindeleff, Byron Cummings, Harold and Mary Russell Ferrell Colton, J. O. Brew, Al Lancaster, Earl Morris and his daughter Elizabeth, Watson Smith, Robert Euler, George Gumerman, Alexander Lind- say, and Douglas Schwartz.

The first breakthrough on relative chronology in southwestern sites occurred when George Pepper[13] suggested that Basketmaker material represented an earlier development than that of the Pueblo. This led archaeologists to begin to distinguish between early and late ceramic design and form and between culture areas.[14]

Interest in such groundbreaking work on southwestern precontact sites led universities in the region to begin offering courses in archaeology. Byron C. Cummings and Edgar L. Hewett established departments of archaeology and archaeological societies, developing the first generation of southwestern-trained archaeologists. University field schools began in the 1930s to train students by excavating a single site over a period of years. These included the University of Arizona Field School at Kinishba and at Point of Pines and the University of New Mexico Chaco Canyon Field School. Between 1928 and 1937, a number of privately endowed southwestern institutions became prime leaders in the archaeology of the region by investigating a range of different sites instead of focusing on a single site.

At Pecos Pueblo, Alfred Kidder was able to prove cultural continuity from precontact into postcontact times. He began work at Pecos in 1915 and contin- ued until 1929. Based on further studies analyzing potsherds in the Rio Grande area that led to a sequence of pottery types, Kidder synthesized the precontact period of the Colorado Plateau. Through this work, he developed methods of precontact archaeology that would influence generations of archaeologists in the Southwest.[15] In 1924 he published *An Introduction to the Study of Southwestern Archaeology*, in which he proposed several precontact culture areas that replaced what had previously been considered to be regional variations of the same culture. In 1927 Kidder convened archaeologists and anthropologists interested in the Southwest at the first Pecos Conference, which has since become an annual gathering. The first conference created a formal classification system with the following units: Basketmaker II, Basketmaker III, Pueblo I, Pueblo II, Pueblo III, Pueblo IV, and Pueblo V. Artifacts and other material culture traits, such as pottery and architecture, characterized each of these cultural units.[16] The perfection of dendrochronology by A. E. Douglass in 1929 made absolute dating possible, much "to the envy of prehistoric archaeologists elsewhere in the world."[17]

In 1928, Harold S. and Mary Russell Ferrell Colton established the Museum of Northern Arizona in Flagstaff. Encompassing geology, zoology, meteorology, and ethnology as well as archaeology, the museum sponsored surveys and excavations. Colton and Lyndon L. Hargrave, hired as the assistant director of the museum, led numerous excavations, and from their work came the first keyed handbooks of pottery types based on taxonomic relationships. This eventually led to the system for identifying pottery types that is still used today.

Two years later, personal funds from John D. Rockefeller Jr. established the Laboratory of Anthropology Incorporated in Santa Fe, New Mexico. Although specializing in a different geographical area, this institution sponsored similar projects, including surveys and excavations of the surrounding region and a focus on Rio Grande Pueblo crafts.

William S. Fulton founded the Amerind Foundation Incorporated in 1937. Like other privately endowed southwestern organizations, it focused on the archaeology of southeastern Arizona and, later, northern Mexico at Casas Grandes under Charles C. Di Peso.

Gila Pueblo Archaeological Foundation was another privately endowed southwestern institution. An expedition to Casa Grande National Monument in 1927 sparked Harold S. Gladwin's interest in the Hohokam, and he undertook stratigraphic excavations. The following year, he and his wife, Winifred, founded this institution that then initiated the largest archaeological survey in the Southwest. In 1930, Emil W. Haury joined Gila Pueblo as assistant director. The staff conducted archaeological surveys throughout the region to trace the "red-on-buff" culture, as the Hohokam were first known (in reference to their distinctive pottery), but no evidence could be found beyond the Gila River Valley. In 1931, Haury's excavations of a site on the south shore of Roosevelt Lake in the Tonto Basin led him to conclude that the "red-on-buff" culture was definitely distinct from the Anasazi (Ancestral Pueblo) culture. Harold and Winifred Gladwin presented the Hohokam in a publication in 1933, with a tentative chronology, pottery description, and comparisons of other precontact southwestern cultures.[18]

Emil Haury and Russell Hastings, both under the auspices of the Gila Pueblo Archaeological Foundation, conducted a 1931 survey into eastern Arizona and western New Mexico, yielding the first clues of the existence of the **Mogollon** culture. Haury excavated Mogollon Village (1933) and Harris Village (1934), and in 1936, he reported his findings in *The Mogollon Culture of Southwestern New Mexico*. Edwin Sayles and Ernst Antevs defined the preceramic Cochise culture, publishing their results in 1941.

Convinced that the only way to learn more about the Hohokam was through excavation, Gladwin began a major dig on a site that he had recorded along the Gila River near the Akimel O'odham village of Sacaton. Snaketown got its name from a translation of an O'odham term meaning "the place of the snakes." This landmark in the archaeology of the Southwest provided such a wealth of data that the resulting scientific paper became the standard by which the Hohokam were known for the next thirty years, proving once and for all that this was indeed a distinct culture. Under Haury's direction excavation began at Snaketown in 1934 and revealed two ball courts, an irrigation canal, some forty houses, mounds, and more than five hundred cremations, along with the pottery, stonework, and ornate shell jewelry that were hallmarks of the Hohokam culture. In 1937, the scientific paper on Snaketown came out and Haury left Gila Pueblo to become the head of the Department of Anthropology at the University of Arizona. The break between Haury and Gladwin probably occurred over disagreement on the interpretation of Snaketown data.[19] Gladwin published papers in 1942 and 1948 that considerably collapsed Haury's chronology, casting doubt on his stratigraphic studies.

In 1941 and 1942, Haury went on to lead a team from the University of Arizona in the excavation of Ventana Cave, a rock shelter in the Castle Mountains west of Tucson on the Tohono O'odham Indian Reservation. Another landmark in southwestern archaeology, Ventana Cave provided evidence for continuous human habitation from pre-**Clovis** times to the present. The stratified deposits there also became the model for the interpretation of the **Archaic** tradition of southern Arizona.

The documentation of the final major precontact culture in the Southwest, the **Patayan**, was done without the financial backing and resources of private archaeological foundations. Two independent scholars, Malcolm Rogers and Julian Hayden, had the intense interest and physical endurance to conduct archaeological fieldwork completely on their own. Rogers, schooled in geology and mining chemistry, returned to work on his father's avocado ranch near

San Diego during World War I. Curious about the scattered stone tools that he found on nearby mesas, he expanded his explorations and identified what he called a "scraper-maker culture" because scraping tools were most abundant among these artifacts. Rogers was so fascinated that he roamed hundreds of miles, documenting hundreds of sites in his field notebook in the Patayan country of southwestern Arizona and the Coastal Range of southern California, where he came across rock shelters, shrines, and trails. Without the vertical stratigraphy of other sites, Rogers relied on what he called "trail stratigraphy," a method that took into account geological changes, such as arroyo cutting, to determine the relative age of pottery types. With this method and a few rare caves and sites that did have vertical stratigraphy, he accurately developed a cultural sequence according to a series of pottery types based on changes in vessel design, temper, and shape. In the late 1920s, Rogers published his first papers, continuing his investigations and proposing the first Patayan chronology in 1945.

Julian Hayden, the other great explorer into the Patayan culture, learned archaeology by excavating sites in Arizona, including the Hohokam Grewe site near Casa Grande, Ventana Cave, Pueblo Grande, Snaketown, and Kiet Siel on the Navajo Reservation. In 1930 he met Malcolm Rogers, and eight years later, they joined forces to excavate a site north of San Diego. Hayden's 1958 explorations in the Sierra Pinacate of northern Mexico convinced him of the accuracy of Rogers's framework for desert archaeology. For the group originally called "Yuman" by the Gladwins, Lyndon Hargrave and Harold S. Colton decided that "Patayan" ("old people" in the Yuman language) was a better label because it would differentiate between present and prehistoric cultures.[20]

During World War II, little field research was conducted, and researchers used the time to review and synthesize the findings of previous efforts. Haury considered the ramifications of contact between the Southwest and Mexico, while Brew focused on archaeological systematics. Walter W. Taylor tried to resolve theoretical conflicts by suggesting a comprehensive approach that investigated relationships within cultures. By the late 1940s, new dating techniques helped archaeologists sort out the dating of finds much more accurately than through dendrochronology. Carbon-14 dating, fluorine, archaeomagnetism, and palynology (the study of pollen) helped researchers to reconstruct change in ancient environments.

After the war, the Southwest experienced a population boom that brought increased development and urban sprawl. Beginning in the 1950s, archaeologists were able to get key legislation passed, as well as stricter enforcement of existing acts, to protect archaeological sites. Laws included stipulations that protected the salvage of archaeological remains in the construction of highways, reservoirs, and pipelines. Many individuals and institutions completed earlier studies and continued existing research programs. Paul S. Martin continued his lengthy investigation on Mogollon sites in western New Mexico from the late 1930s into the 1950s. During the 1950s and '60s, archaeologists explored the connections between Mesoamerican cultures and those of the American Southwest. Two projects that demonstrated the effectiveness of a multidisciplinary approach were the National Park Service study on Wetherill Mesa at Mesa Verde and the Navajo Reservoir salvage project in northern New Mexico. The latter inspired a renewed interest in Native rock art, as well as in the benefits of using vertebrate remains and palynological and alluvial data to aid in the reconstruction of past environments.

Scientists created specialized compilations from the wealth of data produced in these wide-ranging studies on such topics as ceremonial wall paintings, pottery types, and cotton weaving. Investigators also synthesized enormous amounts of data to create studies on cross-cultural linkages, correlations between culture areas and chronology, and precontact groups and linguistics.[21] The Historic Preservation Act of 1966 extended the federal program into the states. As new techniques developed and more studies were conducted, archaeologists and other specialists were better able to reconstruct past environments that yielded such information as the dispersal of domestic plants in the Southwest, precontact disease patterns, and climatic changes.

Other studies focused on the precontact architectural and geographic influences on modern Pueblo Indian social relations. Historical and ethnological studies helped fill in the gaps between late precontact peoples and living peoples. Random sampling, statistics, and computer analysis made it feasible to test hypotheses related to processes of cultural change, and today, all large-scale archaeological research projects include interdisciplinary approaches.

The major change in archaeological and ethnological research is the active role taken by Indian nations in establishing their own review boards to approve research proposals. Most tribal nations in the Southwest, such as the Navajo, have developed their own archaeological and historic preservation departments. Nearly all proposed development requires archaeological surveys beforehand, conducted by trained archaeologists employed by the Navajo Nation.

With such rich, continuously practiced cultural traditions, the Southwest has drawn sociocultural anthropologists in considerable numbers. The founding of the Bureau of American Ethnology in 1879 reflected the awareness that westernization was rapidly changing indigenous societies. Shortly after its founding, the bureau sent Frank Hamilton Cushing, under the direction of James and Matilda Coxe Stevenson, to conduct firsthand research into the beliefs and customs of the Zuni Indians. For the next four and a half years, Cushing lived with the Zuni, mastering their language and participating in many of their activities. Scholars disagree over how deeply he penetrated Zuni culture. Edmund Ladd, a Zuni who is also an anthropologist, believes that, contrary to some accounts, he was never a full member of the Bow Priest Society. Cushing did produce carefully detailed studies of Zuni origin stories that proved to others the wealth of research opportunities in southwestern Indian cultures.

The Southwest is unique not only because of the magnitude of material written about its peoples but also because the ethnologists who created this body of literature have played such a prominent role in shaping the direction of anthropological thought.[22] The region was especially appealing because of the amazing degree of cultural and linguistic diversity among Native societies, archaeological evidence of their rich precontact traditions, and the fact that these societies had not been previously studied in a systematic manner. Indigenous societies were also relatively intact in comparison to those in other regions, which made it easier to trace culture history as well.

Ethnologists such as Adolph F.A. Bandelier, Jesse Walter Fewkes, and Cosmos Mindeleff began investigating the development of forms of social organization among the Puebloan groups, using the details of oral traditions, especially creation stories and migration legends, to hypothesize. Although their ideas were eventually discarded as conjectural, they demonstrated the need for verifiable data. Yet as anthropologist Keith Basso[23] points out, other studies — Washington Matthews on the Navajo and John Peabody Harrington on the Tewa — combined some speculation with detailed descriptions of continuing cultural practices. Before 1925, critics had claimed that southwestern studies were simply "mere collection of facts," but Mathews and Harrington went far beyond this to show that Indian customs and beliefs deserved to be analyzed in their own right for their extensive cultural details and rich symbolic content.[24]

Southwestern ethnology was also shaped by Franz Boas, often called the father of American anthropology. Just before 1900, he argued that the first task of anthropology was to fully describe the customs in individual societies in a region and their historical sources. Only after systematic and detailed collection of facts could anthropologists develop theories about the origin and evolution of cultural traditions. Boas's emphasis on induction led southwestern anthropologists to a more conservative approach in interpretation of factual data and stimulated closer study of Native cultures. Ethnologists focused on compiling thorough inventories of cultural traits or components, with attention to details and efforts to trace them to their historical relations.

Understandably, this approach did not lead to theoretical breakthroughs, but it did preserve large amounts of irreplaceable data. Elsie Clews Parsons's monograph on Isleta Pueblo (1932) became part of her classic study, *Pueblo Indian Religion*, published in 1939. The two encyclopedic volumes were the culmination of two decades of research. Less exhaustive but equally valuable is the research on Yuman cultures collected by Alfred L. Kroeber (the Hualapai,

1935), Leslie Spier (the Havasupai, 1928 and the Yumans, 1933), C. Daryll Forde (the Quechan, 1931), and Edward W. Gifford (the Cocopah, 1933).

Furthermore, this research raised the question of how environmental factors influence the development of social organization. Esther S. Goldfrank's (1945) study of how irrigation among the Navajo affected leadership foreshadowed Edward Dozier's hypothesis that intensive irrigation practices resulted in the centralized leadership of the Rio Grande Pueblos, put forth in *The Pueblo Indians of North America* (1970). The Western Pueblos, Dozier felt, did not need to develop the governmental controls found farther east because they relied primarily on floodwater and dry farming techniques, and their smaller population density meant that kin groups were able to provide a sufficient labor force to work the land effectively. Although most anthropologists agree that multiple factors led to differences in social and political systems between the Eastern Tanoan Pueblos and the Western Pueblos, Dozier laid the groundwork for later studies.

Between 1900 and 1925, the prevailing position among southwestern ethnologists was that a culture was equal to the number of traits that comprised it, so they compiled exhaustive inventories of cultural elements; this emphasis led anthropologists to neglect consideration of the function of these traits as well as the role of culture in guiding human behavior.[25] Then in the 1930s, two groundbreaking developments in anthropological thought changed their approach and led them to focus on understanding how the elements of a culture contributed to the system as a whole.

A. R. Radcliffe-Brown and his students applied British functionalist theory to studies of kinship and social organization. Based on the assumption that a culture is not simply an accumulation of unrelated traits, functionalist theory holds that a set of underlying principles provides the basis for these parts to relate to other parts, thus contributing to the structure of the overall system. The second development, from the work of Edward Sapir and Ruth Benedict, explored the psychological basis of how cultures are patterned and treated culture as a psychological phenomenon.

By refusing to relinquish their emphasis on culture history, which they combined with a functionalist approach, southwestern ethnologists were able to make a significant contribution to anthropological theory.[26] One of the first results was Morris Opler's reconstruction of Apachean kinship systems in 1936. The depth of this theoretical contribution is especially evident in Fred Eggan's comparison of Western Pueblo social organization, published in 1950. A major criticism of functionalism is that it "freezes" cultures in time by using a synchronic rather than a diachronic approach that takes into account changes over longer periods. Eggan argued for the importance of including historical explanation because change is such a fundamental aspect of cultures. By combining the strength of a functionalist approach—documenting how elements contribute to the whole social system—with an analysis of historical relations, it is possible to gain a much more complete understanding of the complex development of social organizations.

The scope of ethnography broadened significantly with the perspective on southwestern Indian societies as dynamic, interrelated wholes, turning interest to the range of cultural mechanisms that had provided the means of adaptation to three centuries of Spanish, Mexican, and Anglo-American cultures. Some of the key studies include Ruth Underhill on the Tohono O'odham (then known as Papago) (1939), Edward Spicer on the Yaqui (1940), Morris Opler on the Apache (1941), and Clyde Kluckhohn and Dorothea Leighton (1946) on the Navajo.

Based on her fieldwork at Zuni (1930, 1932, 1934), Ruth Benedict developed the theory that every culture has its own distinctive pattern based on ideological premises that guide behavior. Cultural patterning occurs when children internalize these basic premises that shape their personalities. A culture contributes not only language and a kinship system but also conceptions of the universe and the place of humans within it. These conceptions shape and determine the personality of everyone within the culture. Instead of focusing on the components of social systems, Benedict's work centered on culture and the individual and initiated a new field of research known as "culture and personality" studies. Between 1935 and 1950, such studies took many forms in the Southwest, including the use of psychoanalytic and psychobiological theories in the interpretation of life-history materials (e.g., Leighton and Leighton 1949) and the effect of child-rearing practices on personality formation (e.g., Goldfrank 1945). According to anthropologist Keith Basso,[27] this body of research contributed several major findings. First, it demonstrated that individuals in southwestern Indian societies experienced psychological conflict and that these societies have a range of cultural practices that relieve such tensions (e.g., Kluckhohn 1944). This research also revealed that the range of variation in personality—the number of people who have "typical" personality characteristics versus the number who do not—is just as great in Indian populations as in Anglo-American populations of the same size. Most importantly, it revealed the inadequacy of existing theories and the need for a more sophisticated theory that related the development of personality to cultural variables as well as to the unique biological and idiosyncratic histories of individuals.

Another major area of southwestern research has been Indian religion, beginning with descriptions of myths and religious beliefs before 1900. As the concept of diffusion became popular, anthropologists concentrated on the spatial distribution of traits, such as masked dancers and the use of prayer sticks. Functionalism led researchers to focus on how religious institutions integrated communities and how the purposes of the institutions changed over time. Ruth

Underhill showed that certain types of ceremonial patterns were functionally interdependent with particular forms of economic subsistence.

Two massive studies of religious symbolism were the previously mentioned *Pueblo Indian Religion* by Elsie Clews Parsons (1939) and Gladys Reichard's *Navaho Religion: A Study of Symbolism* (1950). Parsons was fascinated by the fact that, in contrast to their Anglo and Indian neighbors, "the Pueblos have appeared homogeneous; yet . . . within the population [exist] wide variations."[28] She collected extensive data for her comprehensive survey of Pueblo social organization and religious beliefs and practice. Comparing Pueblo cultural traits, their diffusion, and change over time, she related the historical development of ceremonial complexes to features of social and political systems. Instead of focusing on variation and borrowing or other processes of change, Gladys Reichard examined the details of Navajo ceremonies and the cosmology, symbolism, and belief system that they reflected by indexing supernatural beings, ritualistic ideas, and rites in their ritual contexts.

One of the best examples of the creative use of psychological theories, Clyde Kluckhohn's (1944) research with the Navajo showed how ritual, myth, and belief in witchcraft helped individuals adjust and society survive. For the individual, said Kluckhohn, a belief in witchcraft allayed anxiety, giving the person a sense of control over the unpredictable demands of life. From the societal perspective, witchcraft beliefs kept ceremonial practitioners and the wealthy from attaining too much power, lest they be accused of achieving material success through undesirable practices. Such beliefs also prevented actions that might be socially disruptive and affirmed social solidarity by defining morally reprehensible behavior.

The 1930s and the 1940s were a time of increased ethnographic research in the Southwest. Morris Opler wrote extensively on the Jicarilla (1936, 1946) and Chiricahua Apaches (1941, 1942), while Grenville Goodwin produced material about the Western Apaches (1939, 1942). W. W. Hill (1936, 1938), Clyde Kluckhohn and Leland Wyman (1940), and J. Ladd (1957) published work on the Navajo. Ruth Underhill continued her work on Tohono O'odham (Papago) culture (1939, 1946) and Edward Spicer published research about the Yaqui (1940, 1954).

Acculturation studies became popular just before 1950 as ethnologists focused on processes of cultural and social change. While some located analysis at the level of the individual, others chose the level of cultural systems; still others chose to analyze change through the spread of nativistic movements. Evon Vogt (1951) and John Adair and Vogt (1949) focused on the mechanisms that individual Navajo and Zuni veterans used to adapt to living in Anglo-American culture during World War II, and then those that helped them to reenter their own societies. Interested in the impact of European cultures on Indian cultures, Edward Spicer (1961, 1962) interpreted historical events in terms of cultural processes, showing how cultural traits or complexes were accepted, modified, and spread. Spicer identified several processes—fusion, addition, substitution, and compartmentalization—that produced adjustments to other cultures. The third type of approach analyzed the spread of a nativistic movement as an example of adjustment to conditions produced by the stress of contact between different cultures. David Aberle's (1966) examination of Navajo peyotism demonstrated that although Navajos had been previously exposed to this religion, it did not take hold until their economic and cultural autonomy had been weakened by the stock reduction program of the 1930s.

Since the early 1960s, new approaches have led to increased specialization and compartmentalization, so that no single theme predominates and a spectrum exists, with "behaviorists"—who use statistical models to explain structure in patterns of social action—at one end and "mentalists"—who find structure in the symbolic codes that underlie behavior—at the other end.[29] Studies that are concerned with change and tend to use behaviorist methods include Jerrold Levy and Stephen Kunitz's work on social pathologies (1971) and Indian drinking (1974), Richard Ford's analysis of Tewa intertribal exchange (1972), Robert Hackenberg's edited volume on modernization among the Tohono O'odham (1972), and two studies of urban migration, Theodore Graves's on personal adjustment of Navajo migrants to Denver (1970) and William Hodge's on the Albuquerque Navajos (1969). In contrast, research on folk classification tends not to focus on change and employs a mentalist methodology; several outstanding examples include Charlotte Frisbie's book on the Navajo Girl's Puberty Ceremony (1967), Keith Basso's work on Western Apache witchcraft (1969), and Gary Witherspoon's study of Navajo categories (1970).

A major shift in southwestern ethnology has come from Native American contribution to scholarship. More Indian people are becoming anthropologists and are working independently or collaborating with Anglo scholars to study their own cultures and languages. Alfonso Ortiz's groundbreaking study of the Tewa worldview (1969) exemplifies this trend. Other studies include Vernon Mayes and Barbara Bayless Lacy's Navajo ethnobotanical book (1989), Oswald Werner and Kenneth Begishe's work on Navajo anatomical terms (1970), and Klara Kelley and Harris Francis's study of Navajo sacred places (1994).

Recent research covers an increasingly broad range of subjects as scholars integrate current anthropological theory with southwestern ethnology. Biomedical concerns, such as cultural constructions of the body, health, illness, and personhood—the relations among human beings and other entities—provide the basis for Maureen Schwarz's work (1997) with the Navajo. Thomas Csordas (1999) demonstrates how ritual healing and identity politics interact on several levels in contemporary Navajo society. Studying the hanta virus epidemic (stigmatized as "the Navajo mystery illness"), a serious drought on the reservation, Native American Church healing, and Navajo Christian faith healing, he distinguishes between the struggle that individual actors undergo to assert a shared identity and the struggles of group members with ambiguous commitments to attain individual identity.

Concepts of hegemony and globalization play a major role in Thomas Hall's examination of processes of social change in the Southwest (1989). Deborah House (2002) explores language shift in the light of hegemony—internalized judgments about the social value of Navajo versus English language usage—and identity politics—Navajo self-identification is based on the language, the divine origin of the clan system, and the spiritual connection with the land. Bernadette Adley-Santamaria, a White Mountain Apache doctoral student, is documenting language loss among her people as a result of present-day missionary proscriptions against Native language. Cultural imperialism—the attitude that traditional religion and language use are "evil" and exemplify "devil worship"—also plays a role in the public destruction of Navajo medicine bundles at religious meetings, a trend well documented in the work of Charlotte Frisbie (1987). Frisbie also traces the transaction chains of Navajo medicine bundles to show that while religious conversion influences the disposal of many of these sacred objects, they may be ultimately sold at high prices to wealthy Anglo collectors through esoteric art dealers. Frisbie's work, as well as that of many other scholars, has played a major role in the passage of **NAGPRA** and the return of cultural patrimony to Native American societies.

Early ethnographic research often amounted to exploitation: Native people were not consulted about their willingness to participate, nor were they allowed to see the results of the finished studies. In the late 1800s at Zuni, Frank H. Cushing established an all-too-familiar pattern that was repeated by many anthropologists, slowly winning acceptance but eventually betraying the trust of the Zuni people.[30] The anthropological report written by Elsie Clews Parsons about Taos Pueblo infuriated the people and led to reprisals against those who had worked with her.

American Indians became aware of the power wielded by anthropologists after World War II, when they served as expert witnesses for the federal government and for the tribes in Indian Claims Commission cases.[31] Many Indians never forgave the failure of most anthropologists to combat federal policies of forced assimilation, including the termination legislation of the 1950s.[32] In the 1930s, during the administration of Commissioner of Indian Affairs John Collier, President Franklin Delano Roosevelt, and Secretary of the Interior Harold Ickes, anthropologists were consulted about meeting the contemporary needs of Native Americans. Based on a position of advocacy, the Society for Applied Anthropology was founded in 1940 to encourage the use of anthropological data and theory to solve contemporary social problems. By the 1960s, applied anthropology had become a recognized part of the discipline.

However, by this time, Native American scholars had developed a growing intellectual resistance. This stance has been exemplified in the work of Sherman Alexie and the late Vine Deloria Jr., who objected to the perceived elitist perspective of many anthropologists and the idea that Native Americans were disappearing.

Today, American Indians have taken control of the research that is conducted regarding their cultures, and collaborative work between Native and non-Native researchers is much more common. Indian communities in the Southwest, as well as tribal communities throughout the United States, have developed their own preservation and archaeology departments or other tribal entities to evaluate and oversee archaeological and ethnological research. Anthropologists must now submit formal proposals to gain clearance for their work, and must demonstrate that their research will be of significant benefit to the tribal nation. (See the end of chapter 4 for a discussion of the stand that tribal governments are taking toward genetic research.)

NOTES

1. Albert H. Schroeder, "History of Archaeological Research," in *Handbook of North American Indians: The Southwest*, vol. 9, ed. Alfonso Ortiz (Washington, D.C.: Smithsonian Institution Press, 1979), 5.
2. Stephen Plog, *Ancient Peoples of the American Southwest* (London: Thames and Hudson, 1997).
3. Ibid.
4. Jefferson Reid and Stephanie Whittlesey, *The Archaeology of Ancient Arizona* (Tucson: University of Arizona Press, 1997), 15.
5. Schroeder, "History of Archaeological Research," 6.
6. William A. Longacre, ed., *Reconstructing Prehistoric Pueblo Societies* (Albuquerque: University of New Mexico Press, 1970).
7. Washington Matthews, J. L. Wortman, and J. S. Billings, "Human Bones of the Hemenway Collection in the United States Army Medical Museum," *Memoirs of the National Academy of Sciences* 7, no. 6 (1893): 141–286.
8. Adolph F.A. Bandelier, "Hemenway Southwestern Archaeological Expedition: Contributions to the History of the Southwestern Portion of the United States," *Papers of the Archaeological Institute of America, American Series* 5 (Cambridge, 1890).
9. Frederick W. Hodge, "Prehistoric Irrigation in Arizona," *American Anthropologist* 6, no. 3 (1893): 323–330.
10. Schroeder, "History of Archaeological Research."
11. Schroeder, "History of Archaeological Research," 7.
12. J. Walter Fewkes, "Preliminary Report on a Visit to the Navajo National Monument, Arizona," *Bureau of American Ethnology Bulletin* 50 (1911); Walter Hough, "Antiquities of the

Upper Gila and Salt River Valleys in Arizona and New Mexico," *Bureau of American Ethnology Bulletin* 35 (1907); Jean A. Jeancon, "Explorations in Chama Basin," *Records of the Past* 10 (1911): 92–108; Edgar L. Hewett, "Antiquities of the Jemez Plateau, New Mexico," *Bureau of American Ethnology Bulletin* 32 (1906).

13. George H. Pepper, "The Ancient Basket Makers of Southeastern Utah," *Journal of the American Museum of Natural History* 2, no. 4 (Supplement, 1902).

14. Hough, "Antiquities of the Upper Gila and Salt River Valleys."

15. Alfred V. Kidder, "Pottery of the Pajarito Plateau and of Some Adjacent Regions of New Mexico," *Memoirs of the American Anthropological Association* 2, no. 6 (1915): 407–462.

16. Reid and Whittlesey, *The Archaeology of Ancient Arizona,* 179.

17. Reid and Whittlesey, *The Archaeology of Ancient Arizona,* 180.

18. Reid and Whittlesey, *The Archaeology of Ancient Arizona,* 81.

19. Reid and Whittlesey, *The Archaeology of Ancient Arizona,* 84.

20. The material on the documentation of the Patayan is based on Reid and Whittlesey, *The Archaeology of Ancient Arizona,* 116–119.

21. See T. J. Ferguson and Chip Colwell-Chanthaphonh, *History Is in the Land: Multivocal Tribal Traditions in Arizona's San Pedro Valley* (Tucson: University of Arizona Press, 2006) for an excellent example of cross-cultural linkages and multitribal accounts of an area in southern Arizona.

22. Keith H. Basso, "History of Ethnological Research" in *Handbook of North American Indians: The Southwest,* vol. 9, ed. Alfonso Ortiz (Washington, D.C.: Smithsonian Institution Press, 1979), 14.

23. Basso, "History of Ethnological Research," 15.

24. Basso, "History of Ethnological Research," 15.

25. Basso, "History of Ethnological Research," 17.

26. Basso, "History of Ethnological Research," 17.

27. Basso, "History of Ethnological Research," 19.

28. Elsie Clews Parsons, "The Religion of the Pueblo Indians," *XXI Congres International des Americanistes* (1924):140.

29. Basso, "History of Ethnological Research," 20.

30. Marc Simmons, "History of the Pueblos Since 1821," in *Handbook of North American Indians: The Southwest,* vol. 9, ed. Alfonso Ortiz (Washington, D.C.: Smithsonian Institution Press, 1979), 219.

31. Deward E. Walker Jr., "Anthropologists and Native Americans," in *Native America in the Twentieth Century,* ed. Mary B. Davis (New York: Garland, 1994), 31–43.

32. Ibid.

2. BIBLIOGRAPHIES AND RESEARCH AIDS

Calloway, Colin G., ed. *New Directions in American Indian History.* Norman: University of Oklahoma Press, 1988.

Correll, J. Lee, Editha L. Watson, and David M. Brugge. "Navajo Bibliography with Subject Index." Rev. ed. 2 vols. (*Research Report* 2.) Window Rock, Ariz.: The Navajo Tribe, Parks and Recreation Research Section, 1969.

——. "Navajo Bibliography with Subject Index." (*Research Report* 2, *Suppl.* 1.) Window Rock, Ariz.: The Navajo Tribe, Parks and Recreation Research Section, 1973.

Danky, James P. and Maureen E. Hady, eds. *Native American Periodicals and Newspapers, 1828–1982: Bibliography, Publishing Record, and Holdings.* Westport, Conn: Greenwood, 1984.

DeWitt, Donald L. *American Indian Resource Materials in the Western History Collections, University of Oklahoma.* Norman: University of Oklahoma Press, 1990.

Hill, Edward E., comp. *Guide to Records in the National Archives of the United States Relating to American Indians.* Washington, D.C.: National Archives and Records Service, 1981.

Iverson, Peter. *The Navajos: A Critical Bibliography.* Bloomington: Indiana University Press, 1976.

Johnson, Steven L. *Guide to American Indian Documents in the Congressional Serial Set: 1817–1899.* New York: Clearwater, 1977.

Kluckhohn, Clyde, and Katherine Spencer. *A Bibliography of the Navaho Indians.* New York: J. J. Augustin, 1940.

Laird, David. *Hopi Bibliography.* Tucson: University of Arizona Press, 1977.

Miller, Jay, Colin G. Calloway, and Richard A. Sattler, comps. *Writings in Indian History, 1985–1990.* Norman: University of Oklahoma Press, 1995.

Murdock, George P. and Timothy J. O'Leary. *Ethnographic Bibliography of North America.* 4th ed. 5 vols. New Haven: Human Relations Area Files, 1975.

Powell, Donald M. "A Preliminary Bibliography of the Published Writings of Berard Haile, O.F.M." *The Kiva* 26, no. 4 (1961): 44–47.

Prucha, Francis Paul. *A Bibliographical Guide to the History of Indian–White Relations in the United States.* Chicago: University of Chicago Press, 1977.

——. *Indian–White Relations in the United States: A Bibliography of Works Published, 1975–1980.* Lincoln: University of Nebraska Press, 1982.

Swagerty, William R., ed. *Scholars and the Indian Experience: Critical Reviews of Recent Writing in the Social Sciences.* Bloomington: Indiana University Press for the Newberry Library, 1984.

3. PUBLISHED PRIMARY SOURCES

Abel, Annie H., ed. *The Official Correspondence of James S. Calhoun While Indian Agent at Santa Fe and Superintendent of Indian Affairs in New Mexico.* Washington, D.C.: U.S. Government Printing Office, 1915.

Correspondence of the first U.S. Indian agent in Santa Fe after the Southwest became part of the United States. He proved to be an honest and capable administrator, as this correspondence demonstrates. Includes a biography.

Alvord, Lori Arviso, M.D. and Elizabeth Cohen Van Pelt. *The Scalpel and the Silver Bear.* New York: Bantam, 1999.
A moving account by the first Navajo female surgeon, who details her struggle to blend biomedical practice and the principles of balance and harmony inherent in Navajo philosophy.

Arny, William F.M. *Indian Agent in New Mexico: The Journal of Special Agent W.F.M.*
Arny. Ed. Lawrence Murphy. 1870; reprint, Santa Fe: Stagecoach Press, 1967.
Journal of an Indian agent in the Territory of New Mexico from the 1850s to the 1870s. Known for his thoroughness and concern for Indian people, Arny visited every Pueblo and prepared reports that delineated specific problems with suggestions for their alleviation.

Ball, Eve. *In the Days of Victorio: Recollections of a Warm Springs Apache.* Tucson: University of Arizona Press, 1970.
Eve Ball's writings, well received by the Apaches, were motivated by her desire to make history understandable to everyone. Long before oral tradition was accepted as a source, Ball worked to preserve accounts of Apache elders who had survived the army's campaigns against them by recording their life histories.

——. *Indeh: An Apache Odyssey.* Norman: University of Oklahoma Press, 1988.
This remarkable book tells the story of Chiricahua warriors from those who were part of Naiche and Geronimo's group and their descendants through the words of Daklugie and Eugene Chihuahua.

Bandelier, Adolph F.A. *The Southwestern Journals of Adolph F. Bandelier.* Ed. Charles Lange and Carroll Riley, with Elizabeth Lange. 4 vols. Albuquerque: University of New Mexico Press; Santa Fe: The School of American Research Museum of New Mexico Press, 1966–1976.
Sent by the Archaeological Institute of America in 1880 to gather information on southwestern Indians, Adolph Bandelier lived with the people of Cochiti Pueblo after he had offended those at Santo Domingo. An archaeologist and historian, he took many photographs and collected a considerable body of information.

Barrett, S. M., ed. *Geronimo's Story of His Life*. New York: Duffield, 1906. (Reprinted as *Geronimo, His Own Story*, ed. Frederick W. Turner III [New York: Dutton, 1970].)
Geronimo, a Chiricahua Apache medicine man, is best known among the Apaches who resisted settlement on reservations. Here he gives his own account of his life.

Bartlett, John R. *Personal Narrative of Explorations and Incidents in Texas, New Mexico, California, Sonora, and Chihuahua Connected with the United States and Mexico Boundary Commission, During the Years 1850, '51, '52, '53.* 2 vols. New York: D. Appleton, 1854.
Personal account of explorations in the American Southwest shortly after the signing of the Treaty of Guadalupe Hidalgo.

Basso, Keith H., ed. *Western Apache Raiding and Warfare: From the Notes of Grenville Goodwin.* Tucson, University of Arizona Press, 1971.
See Goodwin below.

Begay, D. Y. "A Weaver's Point of View." In *All Roads Are Good: Native Voices on Life and Culture*, ed. Tom Hill and Richard W. Hill Sr. Washington, D.C.: Smithsonian Institution Press, 1994, 80–89.
A Navajo woman's perspective on weaving and the significance of weaving to Navajo life and culture come across clearly.

Begay, Shirley M. *Kinaalda: A Navajo Puberty Ceremony.* Rough Rock, Ariz.: Rough Rock Demonstration School, Navajo Curriculum Center, 1983.
The fullest documentation of the Girl's Puberty Ceremony from the Navajo point of view.

Bolton, Herbert E. *Anza's California Expeditions.* 5 vols. Berkeley: University of California Press, 1930.
Juan Bautista de Anza wrote thirteen diaries on his successful expedition of 1775–1776 that took 240 colonists from Tubac (presidio of Tucson) across the Colorado River to Monterey, California. These contain a wealth of ethnographic information, especially on the Quechan tribe, including the detailed autobiography of Quechan leader Salvador Palma, which is the earliest such document on record referring to Indians of the western United States.

Bourke, John G. *An Apache Campaign in the Sierra Madre.* New York: Charles Scribners's Sons, 1958.

———. *On the Border with Crook*. 1891; reprint, Alexandria, Va.: Time-Life Books, 1980.
  Captain John Bourke, who worked beside General George Crook in establishing an end to Chiricahua Apache resistance, agreed with Crook that
the blame did not rest with the Indians and that it was important to get the
Apache side of the story. When the Department of War made efforts between
1889 and 1894 to find a reservation for the Chiricahua Apaches, Crook and
Bourke held conferences with the Chiricahua regarding Fort Sill, Oklahoma
as a suitable location.

Brugge, Doug. *Memories Come to Us in the Rain and the Wind: Oral Histories
  and Photographs of Navajo Uranium Miners and Their Families*. Jamaica
  Plain, N.Y.: Red Sun Press, 1997.
  Heartrending accounts of the impact of uranium mining on Navajos and
their families.

Corbusier, William T. *Verde to San Carlos: Recollections of a Famous Army
  Surgeon and His Observant Family on the Western Frontier, 1869–1886*.
  Tucson: Dale Stuart King, 1969.
  Firsthand account of encounters with the Yavapai Indians.

Correll, J. Lee. *Through White Men's Eyes*. Vols. 1–6. Austin, Tex.: Dissemina-
  tion and Assessment Center for Bilingual Education, 1979.
  Accounts of such landmark events as the Navajo surrender at Fort Defiance, Arizona and their Long Walk to Bosque Redondo (Fort Sumner), New
Mexico.

Crook, George. *General George Crook: His Autobiography*. Ed. Martin F.
  Schmitt. 1946; reprint, Norman: University of Oklahoma Press, 1986.
  The army's foremost Indian fighter in the last quarter-century of hostilities,
General Crook also deeply sympathized with the Indians in their treatment by
the government and white settlers and had great insight into Indian thinking
and culture. In the Southwest, he led the Tonto Basin campaign in 1872–1873
and the Apache campaign in 1882–1886.

Cushing, Frank Hamilton. *My Adventures in Zuni*. 1882; reprint, Palo Alto,
  Calif.: American West, 1970.
  The first anthropologist to study a culture as a participant observer, Cushing
lived at Zuni Pueblo from 1879 to 1884, with the family of the Zuni governor.
He learned the Zuni language and was so accepted that he may have won ad-
mission to the Bow Priesthood.

——. "The Nation of the Willows." *Atlantic Monthly* 50 (1882): 362–375, 541–559. (Reprinted in Flagstaff by Northland Press, 1965).
Vivid account of Cushing's trip to the floor of the Grand Canyon in the early 1880s to visit the Havasupai Indians.

Frisbie, Charlotte J. and David P. McAllester, eds. *Navajo Blessingway Singer: The Autobiography of Frank Mitchell 1881–1967.* Tucson: University of Arizona Press, 1980.
Well-written and well-documented autobiography of a respected Navajo singer and leader.

Gatewood, Charles B. *Lieutenant Charles B. Gatewood, 6th U.S. Cavalry, and the Surrender of Geronimo.* Comp. Major C. B. Gatewood. Ed. Edward S. Godfrey. Baltimore: N.p., 1929.
Lieutenant Gatewood played an instrumental role in convincing Geronimo and Naiche to surrender after their flight into Mexico. His account of this experience makes fascinating reading.

Goodwin, Grenville. *Among the Western Apaches: Letters from the Field.* Ed. Morris E. Opler. Tucson: University of Arizona Press, 1973.
Grenville Goodwin, born in 1907, became a trader's assistant in Bylas, Arizona on the San Carlos Apache Reservation in 1930 because of his strong interest in Apache culture. Native Americans suffered more than many segments of the population from the Great Depression, and many Apaches exchanged their handiwork for credit or necessities at the trading post.

Gregg, Josiah. *Commerce of the Prairies.* Norman: University of Oklahoma Press, 1954.
Personal narrative of a trader's experiences in the Southwest as well as other areas.

Hackett, Charles W., ed. "Historical Documents Relating to New Mexico, Nueva Vizcaya and Approaches Thereto, to 1773." Comp. Adolph F.A. Bandelier and Fanny R. Bandelier. 3 vols. *Carnegie Institution of Washington Publication* 330 (2) (1923–1937).
This compilation of historical documents relate to the Spanish exploration and administration of New Mexico until 1773.

Hammond, George P. and Agapito Rey, ed. and trans. *Narratives of the Coronado Expedition, 1540–1542.* Albuquerque: University of New Mexico Press, 1940.

——. *Don Juan de Oñate, Colonizer of New Mexico, 1595–1628.* 2 vols. Albuquerque: University of New Mexico Press, 1953.

——. *The Rediscovery of New Mexico, 1580–1594: The Explorations of Chamuscado, Espejo, Castano de Sosa, Morlete, and Leyva de Bonilla and Humana.* Albuquerque: University of New Mexico Press, 1966.
This series of compilations and translations of accounts provides insights into the perspective of Spanish explorers as they saw New Mexico for the first time.

House, Conrad. "The Art of Balance." In *All Roads Are Good: Native Voices on Life and Culture.* Ed. Tom Hill and Richard W. Hill Sr. Washington, D.C.: Smithsonian Institution Press, 1994, 90–101.
Personal essay of how a Navajo artist balances traditional Navajo culture with the modern world.

Howard, Oliver O. *My Life and Experiences Among Our Hostile Indians.* 1907; reprint, New York: Da Capo Press, 1972.
——. *Famous Indian Chiefs I Have Known.* New York: The Century Company, 1916.
Known as the one-armed "praying general," Howard brought a keen social consciousness to his military career. In the Southwest, he is known for his successful negotiations in 1872 that ended ten years of hostility with Cochise's Chiricahua Apaches. He wrote extensively of his experiences with Indians.

Iliff, Flora Gregg. *People of the Blue Water: My Adventures Among the Walapai and Havasupai Indians.* New York: Harper and Brothers, 1954.
Recollections of Flora Gregg, who went to teach at a day school for the Hualapai Indians in 1900. Later she became superintendent of the Havasupai Indians. Her book contains a wealth of personal experiences and friendships.

Kelly, Jane Holden. *Yaqui Women: Contemporary Life Histories.* Lincoln: University of Nebraska Press, 1978.
Yaqui women tell the stories of their lives and those of their families.

Kino, Eusebio F. *Historical Memoir of Pimeria Alta: A Contemporary Account of the Beginnings of California, Sonora, and Arizona, by Father Eusebio F. Kino, S.J. Pioneer Missionary Explorer, Cartographer, and Ranchman, 1683–1711. Published for the First Time from the Original Manuscript in the Archives of Mexico.* Ed. and trans. Herbert E. Bolton. 2 vols. in 1. 1948; reprint, New York: AMS Press, 1976.

Dedicated to the welfare of the indigenous peoples of northwestern New Spain, Father Kino became a Jesuit in 1665 and accepted a missionary assignment in the New World. After work in California, he was sent to the O'odham Indians in Sonora and Arizona. Through his knowledge of the O'odham language and culture, he introduced cattle raising and more varied agriculture and stayed for twenty-four years, exploring and directing the construction of mission complexes in addition to ministering to the O'odham.

Laird, Carobeth. *Encounters with an Angry God: Recollections of My Life with John Peabody Harrington.* Banning, Calif.: Malki Museum Press, 1975.
A classic memoir. Once the wife of famed linguist John Peabody Harrington, Laird left him to marry his Chemehuevi consultant.

Manuel, Frances and Deborah Neff. *Desert Indian Woman: Stories and Dreams.* Tucson: University of Arizona Press, 2001.
The life history and reflections of Tohono O'odham Frances Manuel.

Matthews, Washington. "The Night Chant, A Navaho Ceremony." *Memoirs of the American Museum of Natural History* 6 (May 1902).
Washington Matthews spent eight years in residence in Navajo country as an army doctor and attended many ceremonies. He first witnessed the last night of the Night Chant ceremony in 1880 and worked with Navajo chanters to record its myths, prayers, songs, sandpaintings, and procedures.

Mitchell, Emerson Blackhorse and T. D. Allen. *Miracle Hill: The Story of a Navaho Boy.* Norman: University of Oklahoma Press, 1967.
Heartwarming autobiography of a Navajo boy born in a hogan and how he grows up within two cultures.

Moises, Rosalio, Jane Holden Kelley, and William Curry Holden. *The Tall Candle: A Personal Chronicle of a Yaqui Indian.* Lincoln: University of Nebraska Press, 1971.
Personal reflections by a Yaqui Indian whose family had to flee their homeland in Mexico as political refugees.

Qoyawayma, Polingaysi. *No Turning Back: A True Account of a Hopi Girl's Struggle to Bridge the Gap Between the World of Her People and the World of the White Man.* Albuquerque: University of New Mexico Press, 1964.
A classic book telling how a Hopi woman adjusts to Anglo and Hopi cultures.

Reichard, Gladys. *Spider Woman: A Story of Navajo Weavers and Chanters.*
    1934; reprint, Glorieta, N.M.: Rio Grande Press, 1971.
    A pioneer anthropologist's personal account of living among the Navajo and
being taught to weave.

Savala, Refugio. *Autobiography of a Yaqui Poet.* Ed. Kathleen Sands. Tucson:
    University of Arizona Press, 1980.
    The Yaqui author's name reflects his history: the Yaqui people settled in
Arizona after fleeing Mexico as political refugees.

Seowtewa, Ken. "Adding a Breath to Zuni Life." *Native Peoples* 5, no. 2 (1992):
    10–19.
    A Zuni artist whose family painted the murals of Zuni religious practices in
Our Lady of Guadalupe Church at Zuni writes about what they mean to his
family and the people.

Sequaptewa, Helen. *Me and Mine: The Life Story of Helen Sequaptewa.* Tuc-
    son: University of Arizona Press, 1969.
    This touching autobiography remains a classic in its field.

Shaw, Anna Moore. *A Pima Past.* 1974; reprint, Tucson: University of Arizona
    Press, 1994.
    Born in a traditional brush dwelling on the Gila River Indian Reservation
in 1898, Anna Moore Shaw served her tribe in many capacities throughout her
life. She writes about her family, her parents' generation, and how events have
unfolded in her life and in the lives of her people as they have had to integrate
Pima (Akimel O'odham) customs with Anglo-American culture.

Stephen, Alexander. "Hopi Journal." *Columbia University Contributions to An-
    thropology* 23 (2 parts). New York: Columbia University Press, 1936.
    An invaluable source of reference for Hopi ceremonial leaders and all stu-
dents of Hopi culture and life. A systematic recording of the daily life and ceremonies of the people of First Mesa between about 1881 and 1894.

Talayesva, Don. *Sun Chief: The Autobiography of a Hopi Indian.* New Haven,
    Conn.: Yale University Press, 1942.
    A classic autobiography.

Tapahonso, Lucy. "The Kaw River Rushes Westward." In *A Circle of Nations:
    Voices and Visions of American Indians.* Ed. John Gattuso. Hillsboro,
    Ore.: Beyond Words Publishing, 1993, 106–117.

Based on her experiences, one of the foremost Navajo poets creates work that is powerful and moving. .

TeCube, Leroy. *Year in Nam: A Native American Soldier's Story.* Lincoln: University of Nebraska Press, 1999.
A gripping and moving memoir by a Jicarilla Apache who served as an infantryman in Vietnam.

U.S. Congress, Senate, Committee on Indian Affairs. "Pascua Yaqui Tribe Extension of Benefits: Hearing Before the Committee on Indian Affairs." 103rd Congress, 2nd sess., 27 January 1994, 11.
The Yaquis testify before the Senate on their presence in Arizona.

Webb, George. *A Pima Remembers.* 1959; reprint, Tucson: University of Arizona Press, 1994.
George Webb writes about his father's experiences farming along the river on the Gila River Indian Reservation, as well as a life transition that gradually transforms but doesn't destroy the old ways. He was born around 1893 and attended a boarding school and public high school, then worked as a ranch hand until he was appointed as a farm overseer by the Indian agent at Sacaton.

4. ORAL TRADITIONS

The following volumes represent southwestern Indian oral literature in printed form. Oral literature is significant because it records what is most important in tribal histories and how each tribe ordered its physical/spiritual universe.

Benally, Clyde. *Dineji Nákéé Nááhane: A Utah Navajo History.* Monticello, Utah: San Juan School District, 1982.
A Utah Navajo writes an account of Navajo creation and history.

Between Sacred Mountains: Navajo Stories and Lessons from the Land. Tucson: Sun Tracks and University of Arizona Press, 1982.
A beautifully written book with many stories and recollections created by Navajo elders and young people from the Rock Point School in Rock Point, Arizona.

Cushing, Frank Hamilton. "Outlines of Zuni Creation Myths." In *13th Annual Report of the Bureau of American Ethnology for the Years 1891–1892* (Washington, 1896), 321–447.

Zuni thoughts on the origins of the cosmos, corn, and the deities from one of the first ethnologists to study Zuni mythology and to live with the Zuni people.

Evers, Larry, ed. *The South Corner of Time: Hopi, Navajo, Papago, Yaqui Tribal Literature*. Tucson: University of Arizona Press, 1980.
Origin stories and other important oral traditions.

Evers, Larry and Felipe Molina. *Yaqui Deer Songs Maso Bwikam: A Native American Poetry*. Tucson: Sun Tracks and University of Arizona Press, 1987.
The Deer Song tradition lies at the heart of Yaqui culture, and the authors write eloquently about that culture as revealed in the songs.

Fewkes, Jesse Walter. "Tusayan Migration Traditions." In *19th Annual Report of the Bureau of American Ethnology for the Years 1897–98*, Pt. 2 (Washington, 1900), 573–634.
Initiated into the Antelope and Flute religious societies of Walpi, Fewkes witnessed, recorded, and participated in the kiva preparations and ceremonials between 1890 and the 1920s. He is one of the most distinguished of American ethnologists.

Goddard, Pliny Earle. "Jicarilla Apache Texts." *Anthropological Papers of the American Museum of Natural History* 8, no. 1 (1911).
Goddard's work is invaluable.

——. "San Carlos Apache Texts." *Anthropological Papers of the American Museum of Natural History* 24, no. 3 (1918).

——. "Myths and Tales from the White Mountain Apache." *Anthropological Publications of the American Museum of Natural History* 24, no. 2 (1919).

——. "White Mountain Apache Texts." *Anthropological Publications of the American Museum of Natural History* 24, no. 4 (1920).

Goodwin, Grenville. "Myths and Tales of the White Mountain Apache." *Memoirs of the American Folklore Society* 33 (1939).
Oral literature recorded by a respected anthropologist.

Harrington, John P. "A Yuma Account of Origins." *Journal of American Folklore* 21, no. 82 (1908): 324–348.

Yuman origin stories by one of the most prolific scholars and collectors of linguistic and cultural material from California and southwestern tribes.

Harrison, Mike and John Williams. "How Everything Began and How We Learned to Live Right." In *The Yavapai of Fort McDowell: An Outline of Their History and Culture*, ed. Sigrid Khera. Fort McDowell, Ariz.: Fort McDowell Mohave-Apache Indian Community, 1977, 40–46.
Yavapai oral traditions.

Hinton, Leanne and Lucille Watahomigie, eds. *Spirit Mountain: An Anthology of Yuman Story and Song*. Tucson: Sun Tracks and University of Arizona Press, 1984.
A collection of stories and songs in Yuman languages with English translations provides the best introduction to Yuman oral literature and culture.

Hirst, Stephen. *Havsuw 'Baaja: People of the Blue Green Water*. Supai, Ariz.: Havasupai Tribe, 1985.
This moving chronicle of the fight for the expansion of the reservation includes accounts by Havasupai storytellers; the book is recommended by the Havasupai tourism office.

Kaczkurkin, Mini Valenzuela. *Yoeme: Lore of the Arizona Yaqui People*. Tucson: Sun Tracks and University of Arizona Press, 1977.
A Yaqui scholar and educator provides insights into the stories and culture of her people.

Kroeber, Alfred. "Seven Mohave Myths." *University of California Anthropological Records* II (1948): 1–70.
The preeminent ethnologist of his time recorded myths from the Mojave (Mohave).

Laird, Carobeth. *Mirror and Pattern: George Laird's World of Chemehuevi Mythology*. Morongo Indian Reservation, Banning, Calif.: Malki Museum Press, 1984.
George Laird was the primary Chemehuevi "informant" for linguist John Peabody because of the depth of his knowledge of Chemehuevi culture.

Levy, Jerrold E. *In the Beginning: The Navajo Genesis*. Berkeley: University of California Press, 1998.
Navajo myths about the underworlds, the Emergence, the present world, and tricksters.

Luckert, Carl W. *The Navajo Hunter Tradition.* With field assistance and transla-
    tions by John Cook, Victor Beck, and Irvy Goossen, and additional transla-
    tion by Father Berard Haile. Tucson: University of Arizona Press, 1975.
An extensive collection of texts regarding Navajo hunter mythology.

——. "A Navajo Bringing-Home Ceremony: The Claus Chee Sonny Version of
    Deerway Ajilee." *American Tribal Religion Series* 3. Flagstaff: Museum of
    Northern Arizona Press, 1978.
The Deerway Ceremonial with its accompanying myth by Navajo chanter
Claus Chee Sonny.

Nequatewa, Edmund. *Truth of a Hopi: Stories Relating to the Origin, Myths,
    and Clan Histories of the Hopi.* Flagstaff, Ariz.: Northland Press, in co-
    operation with the Museum of Northern Arizona, 1993. (Originally pub-
    lished by the Museum of Northern Arizona in 1936 as *Museum of North-
    ern Arizona Bulletin* No. 8.)

O'Bryan, Aileen. "The Dine: Origin Myths of the Navaho Indians." *Bureau of
    American Ethnology Bulletin* 163. 1956; reprint, New York: Dover, 1993.
Creation stories of the Navajo.

Schwarz, Maureen Trudelle. *Navajo Lifeways: Contemporary Issues, Ancestral
    Knowledge.* Norman: University of Oklahoma Press, 2001.
This book demonstrates how oral history informs Navajo understandings of
contemporary problems or situations such as the hanta virus outbreak of 1993,
a visitation by the Navajo Holy People in 1996, the Navajo-Hopi Land Dispute,
uranium mining, and problem drinkers who, in extreme cases, become socially
equivalent to those who are dead.

Shaw, Anna Moore. *Pima Indian Legends.* Tucson: University of Arizona Press,
    1968.
Oral literature from her own people.

Smithson, Carma Lee and Robert C. Euler. *Havasupai Legends: Religion and
    Mythology of the Havasupai Indians of the Grand Canyon.* Salt Lake
    City: University of Utah Press, 1994.
Oral literature of the Havasupais.

Tedlock, Dennis, trans. *Finding the Center: Narrative Poetry of the Zuni Indians,
    by Andrew Peynetsa and Walter Sanchez.* New York: Dial Press, 1972.
Oral literature of the Zunis.

Underhill, Ruth, Donald Bahr, B. Lopez, J. Pancho, and D. Lopez. "Rainhouse and Ocean: Speeches for the Papago Year." *American Tribal Religions* 4. Flagstaff, Ariz.: Museum of Northern Arizona, 1979.
Tohono O'odham ritual oratory.

Wright, Barton. *The Mythic World of the Zuni*. Albuquerque: University of New Mexico Press, 1994.
A museum curator and scholar edited and illustrated Cushing's classic work in a style that makes these stories come alive.

Yazzie, Ethelou. *Navajo History*. Many Farms, Ariz.: Navajo Community College Press, 1971.
Yazzie's work, as well as other publications from Navajo Community College Press (now Diné College, at Tsaile, Arizona), specializes in publishing Navajo oral traditions.

Zepeda, Ofelia, ed. *When It Rains: Papago and Pima Poetry*. Tucson: University of Arizona Press, 1982.
Oral tradition from the O'odham edited by the foremost scholar of her people's language and culture.

Zolbrod, Paul. *Diné Bahane: The Navajo Creation Story*. Albuquerque: University of New Mexico Press, 1984.
Based largely on Washington Matthews's classic account, this lively rendering brings much of the oral storytelling experience to the page in a manner accessible for undergraduates and general readers.

5. ARCHAEOLOGICAL STUDIES

The volumes in this section represent the most recent and best interpretations of the archaeological record for southwestern Indians. *All* are excellent sources.

Adams, E. Charles. *The Origin and Development of the Pueblo Katsina Cult*. Tucson: University of Arizona Press, 1991.

Bernardini, Wesley. *Hopi Oral Tradition and the Archaeology of Identity*. Tucson: University of Arizona Press, 2005.

Cheek, Lawrence W. A.D. 1250, *Ancient Peoples of the Southwest*. Phoenix: Arizona Department of Transportation, 1994.

Colwell-Chanthaphonh, Chip and T. J. Ferguson. *Collaboration in Archaeological Practice: Engaging Descendant Communities*. Lanham, Md.: AltaMira Press, 2007.

Cordell, Linda S. and George J. Gummerman, eds. *Dynamics of Southwest Prehistory*. Washington, D.C.: Smithsonian Institution Press, 1989.

Crown, Patricia L. *Ceramics and Ideology: Salado Polychrome Pottery*. Albuquerque: University of New Mexico Press, 1994.

Ferguson, T. J. *Historic Zuni Architecture and Society: An Archaeological Application of Space Syntax. Anthropological Papers of the University of Arizona*, no. 60. Tucson: University of Arizona Press, 1996.

——. "Native Americans and the Practice of Archaeology." *Annual Review of Anthropology* 25 (1996): 63–79.

——. "Archaeological Cultures and Cultural Affiliation: Hopi and Zuni Perspectives in the Southwest" (with Kurt E. Dongoske, Michael Yeatts, and Roger Anyon). *American Antiquity* 62, no. 4 (1997): 600–608.

——. "Native American Oral Tradition and Archaeology, Issues of Structure, Relevance, and Respect" (with Roger Anyon, Loretta Jackson, Lillie Lane, and Philip Vicenti). In *Native Americans and Archaeologists: Stepping Stones to Common Ground*, ed. Nina Swidler, Kurt Dongoske, Roger Anyon, and Alan Downer. Walnut Creek, Calif.: AltaMira Press, 1997, 77–87.

Ferguson, T. J. and Chip Colwell-Chanthaphonh. *History Is in the Land: Multivocal Tribal Traditions in Arizona's San Pedro Valley*. Tucson: University of Arizona Press, 2006.

Ferguson, T. J. and Barbara Mills. "Archaeological Ethics and Values in a Tribal Cultural Resource Management Program." In *Handbook of Ethics and Values in Archaeology*, ed. Ernestine Green. New York: The Free Press, 1984, 224–235.

Greenberg, Joseph H., Christy Turner II, and Stephen L. Zegura. "The Settlement of the Americas: A Comparison of the Linguistic, Dental, and Genetic Evidence." *Current Anthropology* 27, no. 5 (1986): 447–497.

Gummerman, George J., ed. *Exploring the Hohokam: Prehistoric Desert Peoples of the American Southwest*. Albuquerque: University of New Mexico Press, 1991.

Haury, Emil W. *Mogollon Culture in the Forestdale Valley, East-Central Arizona*. Tucson: University of Arizona Press, 1985.

Matson, R. G. *The Origins of Southwestern Agriculture*. Tucson: University of Arizona Press, 1991.

McGuire, Randall H. and Michael B. Schiffer, eds. *Hohokam and Patayan: Prehistory of Southwestern Arizona*. New York: Academic Press, 1982.

Mills, Barbara J., ed. *Alternative Leadership Strategies in the Prehispanic Southwest*. Tucson: University of Arizona Press, 2000.

——. "Recent Research on Chaco: Changing Views on Economy, Ritual, and Society." *Journal of Archaeological Research* 10, no. 1 (2002): 65–117.

Mills, Barbara J. and Patricia L. Crown. *Ceramic Production in the American Southwest.* Tucson: University of Arizona Press, 1995.

Mills, Barbara J., Sarah A. Herr, and Scott Van Keuren. *Living on the Edge of the Rim: Excavations and Analysis of the Silver Creek Archaeological Research Project, 1993–1998.* Tucson: University of Arizona Press, 1999.

Plog, Stephen. *Ancient Peoples of the American Southwest.* London: Thames and Hudson, 1997.

Reid, J. Jefferson and Stephanie Whittlesey. *The Archaeology of Ancient Arizona.* Tucson: University of Arizona Press, 1997.

Sheridan, Thomas E. *Arizona: A History.* Tucson: University of Arizona Press, 1995.

Vivian, R. Gwinn. *The Chacoan Prehistory of the San Juan Basin.* New York: Academic Press, 1990.

Whiteley, Peter M. "Archaeology and the Oral Tradition: The Scientific Importance of Dialogue." *American Antiquity* 67, no. 3 (2002): 405.

Woodbury, Richard B. *Sixty Years of Southwestern Archaeology: A History of the Pecos Conference.* Albuquerque: University of New Mexico Press, 1993.

6. GENERAL AND COMPARATIVE STUDIES

Bahti, Tom and Mark Bahti. *Southwestern Indians.* Las Vegas: KC Publications, 1997.

A beautifully illustrated guide to the arts of the Indians of the Southwest by a father and son greatly respected by Indians and non-Indians in the buying and selling of Indian arts.

Brody, J .J. *Indian Painters and White Patrons.* Albuquerque: University of New Mexico Press, 1971.

Deals primarily with the Santa Fe area; a classic on the development of the market for Indian painting.

Champagne, Duane, ed. *Native America: Portrait of the Peoples.* Detroit: Visible Ink Press, 1994.

A good overall reference that covers a wide range of topics, including regional and national issues, by Native American scholars.

——, ed. *Contemporary Native American Cultural Issues.* Walnut Creek, Calif.: AltaMira Press, 1999.

A series of well-documented articles on issues such as gender, Native identity, media, health, and environment.

——. *Social Change and Cultural Continuity Among Native Nations.* Lanham,
  Md.: AltaMira Press, 2007.
  Drawing from historical context, including the legacy of colonial domination, indigenous institutional change, and globalization, these essays analyze how
American Indian people have sought to maintain or restore political and cultural
autonomy. Includes a selection of impressive case studies demonstrating the complexity of issues of self-determination that goes beyond current social change theories. Excellent treatment of economic, political, social, and cultural issues.

Davis, Mary B., ed. *Native America in the Twentieth Century: An Encyclopedia.*
  New York and London: Garland, 1994.
  Contains shorter articles than those in *The Handbook of North American
Indians* and is somewhat less scholarly, but offers a wealth of valuable information about every tribal group in the United States and a wide range of topics,
such as associations, government policy, law, religion, and art. Many entries are
written by tribal members.

Debo, Angie. *A History of the Indians of the United States.* Norman: University
  of Oklahoma Press, 1970.
  A historical survey of relations between the European and Anglo-American
intruders and American Indian peoples that covers over 400 years and weaves
together people, policies, and events in a single volume. Debo is a respected
historian who has been writing about American Indian cultures since 1924.

Fontana, Bernard L. *A Guide to Contemporary Southwest Indians.* Tucson:
  Southwest Parks and Monuments Association, 1999.
  A guide to points of interest on each reservation in the Southwest, written for
the layperson by a well-known southwestern scholar.

Griffin-Pierce, Trudy. *Native Peoples of the Southwest.* Albuquerque: University
  of New Mexico Press, 2000.
  History, environmental adaptation, linguistic affiliation, social organization,
worldview, and spiritual beliefs and practices of each southwestern tribe. Native Americans express their views on contemporary as well as historic issues;
the living, dynamic nature of American Indian cultures is emphasized. Each
chapter is devoted to a tribe or group of related tribes and lists extensive biblio-
graphic material at the end.

Hall, Thomas D. *Social Change in the Southwest, 1350–1880.* Lawrence: University Press of Kansas, 1989.

Rigorous anthropological perspective on American Indian, Mexican, and American histories. A sweeping survey of social change intended for scholars.

Hoerig, Karl A. "'Here, Now, and Always.' Museum of Indian Arts and Culture, Santa Fe, New Mexico, Permanent Installation." *American Anthropologist* 100, no. 3 (1998): 768–769.
A review of an exhibit at the new Museum of Indian Arts and Culture in Santa Fe that includes Native American voices and perspectives.

——. "'This Is My Second Home': The Native American Vendors Program of the Palace of the Governors, Santa Fe, New Mexico." Ph.D. diss, University of Arizona, 2000.
Based on extensive interviews, an insightful study of the artists who sell their work in front of the Palace of the Governors and how this program has evolved over time.

Johansen, Bruce E. and Donald A. Grinde Jr. *The Encyclopedia of Native American Biography.* New York: Henry Holt, 1997.
Six hundred biographies, many of southwestern Indians, that range in length from several paragraphs to a couple of pages.

Johnson, Troy R., ed. *Contemporary Native American Political Issues.* Walnut Creek, Calif.: AltaMira Press, 1999.
Series of well-documented articles on such issues as sovereignty, economic development, repatriation, law and justice, and activism.

Leacock, Eleanor B. and Nancy Oestreich Lurie, eds. *North American Indians in Historical Perspective.* Prospect Heights, Ill.: Waveland Press, 1988.
A series of insightful articles about change in Native American cultures in response to European and American cultures by scholars in their fields.

Malinowski, Sharon, ed. *Notable Native Americans.* New York: Gale Research, 1995.
This edited volume contains biographies of many southwestern Indians, listed alphabetically by tribal group/nation and then by occupation/tribal role, along with a subject index for reference to other individuals, battles, treaties, movements, and organizations.

McCool, Daniel. *Native Waters: Contemporary Indian Water Settlements and the Second Treaty Era.* Tucson: University of Arizona Press, 2003.

Thorough treatment of an important conflict between Indians and non-Indians over a vital resource in a desert environment.

McCubbin, Hamilton, Elizabeth Thompson, Anne Thompson, and Julie Fromer, eds. *Resiliency in Native American and Immigrant Families.* Thousand Oaks, Calif.: Sage, 1998.
Contemporary perspective on family and cultural resilience among Native Americans and other groups. Well-documented material with statistical data.

McGuire, Thomas, William Lord, and Mary Wallace, eds. *Indian Water in the New West.* Tucson: University of Arizona Press, 1993.
Collection of essays on Indian water rights from lawyers, federal officials, engineers, ecologists, economists, professional mediators, an anthropologist, and a Native American tribal leader. Valuable for its diverse perspectives on a complex issue that will only intensify in the future.

Melendez, A. Gabriel, M. Jane Young, Patricia Moore, and Patrick Pynes, eds. *The Multicultural Southwest: A Reader.* Tucson: University of Arizona Press, 2001.
Historians, anthropologists, fiction writers, poets, sociologists, and geographers portray the cultural and ecological diversity of the Southwest.

Nabokov, Peter and Robert Easton. *Native American Architecture.* New York: Oxford University Press, 1989.
Even though this book is not limited to the Southwest, it is included here because it has a wealth of information on southwestern architectural forms.

Oppelt, Norman T. *The Tribally Controlled Indian College: The Beginnings of Self-Determination in American Indian Education.* Tsaile, Ariz.: Navajo Community College Press, 1990.
A brief account of American Indian higher education from the seventeenth century through the present describing why and how early education efforts failed tribal groups. Building on these experiences, two centuries later the tribally controlled Indian college movement began. This book examines each Indian-controlled college that has been established since the early 1960s.

Ortiz, Alfonso, ed. *Handbook of North American Indians: The Southwest.* Vol. 9 (1979, Puebloan tribes); vol. 10 (1983, all other Southwestern tribes). Washington, D.C.: Smithsonian Institution Press.

Classic ethnographic overviews of all southwestern tribes, with extensive bibliography. Not for the general audience, this series uses primary sources and each chapter is written by a scholar who has worked with the tribal people about whom he or she is writing.

Parman, Donald L. *Indians and the American West in the Twentieth Century.* Bloomington and Indianapolis: Indiana University Press, 1994.

Good review of governmental policy in the western states, including the relationships between economic interests and the government in dealing with Native Americans. Part of a series intended to provide the general public and scholars with an understanding of key issues in the recent past of the American West.

Sheridan, Thomas E. and Nancy J. Parezo, eds. *Paths of Life: American Indians of the Southwest and Northern Mexico.* Tucson: University of Arizona Press, 1996.

Related to the exhibit of the same name at the Arizona State Museum, University of Arizona, this series of essays covers a wide range of topics related to tribes of the American Southwest and northern Mexico.

Smithsonian Institution. *All Roads Are Good: Native Voices on Life and Culture.* Washington, D.C.: Smithsonian Institution Press, 1994.

Essays by a series of Native artists who reflect on their cultures and the integral role of art and spirituality in Indian cultures.

Spicer, Edward H. *Perspectives in American Indian Culture Change.* Chicago: University of Chicago Press, 1961.

Although not as well known as *Cycles of Conquest,* this book is an excellent and thorough study.

——. *Cycles of Conquest: The Impact of Spain, Mexico, and the United States on the Indians of the Southwest, 1533–1960.* Tucson: University of Arizona Press, 1981.

A classic work on the peoples and cultures of the Southwest.

Stoffle, Richard, Kristine Jones, and Henry Dobyns. "Direct European Immigrant Transmission of Old World Pathogens to Numic Indians During the Nineteenth Century." *American Indian Quarterly* 19, no. 2 (Spring 1995): 181–203.

Key article with detailed statistical data whose interpretation verifies that Native Americans lost the West because communicable diseases transmitted by newcomer colonists drastically reduced Native numbers.

Tanner, Clara Lee. *Southwest Indian Craft Arts.* Tucson: University of Arizona Press, 1982.
   Written by a specialist who probably had more comprehensive knowledge of southwestern Indian art than any other scholar, this book provides a wealth of information about basketry, pottery, weaving, and other art forms.

——. *Southwest Indian Painting: A Changing Art.* Tucson: University of Arizona Press, 1980.
   Though easel painting was introduced to Native Americans, they had been practicing some form of painting for many centuries. Tanner traces the development of this art form over the course of time.

Trimble, Stephen. *The People: Indians of the American Southwest.* Santa Fe, N.M.: School of American Research Press, 1993.
   A nonanthropologist's vivid portrayal of southwestern Indians for the layperson with an emphasis on contemporary issues and Native voices.

Washburn, Wilcomb E., ed. *Handbook of North American Indians: History of Indian–White Relations.* Vol. 4. Washington, D.C.: Smithsonian Institution Press, 1988.
   Classic series with articles by respected scholars in their fields. Although it covers all Native American groups, a number of chapters relate to the Southwest.

7. TRIBAL STUDIES

Apaches

Adams, Alexander. *The Camp Grant Massacre.* New York: Simon and Schuster, 1976.
   An account of the famous massacre of an encampment of peaceful Apaches by Tucson citizens and Tohono O'odham Indians in 1871.

Ball, Eve. *In the Days of Victorio: Recollections of a Warm Springs Apache.*
   See under Published Primary Sources.
——. *Indeh: An Apache Odyssey.*
   See under Published Primary Sources.

Bartlett, John R. *Personal Narrative of Explorations and Incidents in Texas, New Mexico, California, Sonora, and Chihuahua Connected with the*

United States and Mexico Boundary Commission, During the Years
1850, '51, '52.
See under Published Primary Sources.

Basehart, Harry. "The Resource Holding Corporation Among the Mescalero
Apache." *Southwestern Journal of Anthropology* 23 (1967): 277–291.
——. "Mescalero Apache Band Organization and Leadership." *Southwestern
Journal of Anthropology* 26 (1970): 87–106.
Two contemporary accounts of political and economic systems among the
Mescalero Apaches of New Mexico.

The most respected contemporary ethnologist of Western Apache culture, Basso
explains the symbolism and social context of the Western Apache Girl's
Puberty Ceremony. His books and essays listed below speak eloquently of
the complexities of language, word play, and worldview, based on many
years of fieldwork and friendship with Western Apache people.

——. "Western Apache Witchcraft." *Anthropological Papers of the University of
Arizona* 15. Tucson: University of Arizona Press, 1969.

——. *The Cibicue Apache.* New York: Holt, Rinehart, and Winston, 1970.

——. "To Give Up on Words: Silence in the Western Apache Culture." *Southwestern Journal of Anthropology* 26 (1970): 213–230.

——. "Western Apache." In *Handbook of North American Indians: The Southwest,* vol. 10, ed. Alfonso Ortiz. Washington, D.C.: Smithsonian Institution Press, 1983, 462–488.

——. *Portraits of the "Whiteman": Linguistic Play and Cultural Symbols Among the
Western Apache.* Cambridge, Eng.: Cambridge University Press, 1994.

——. *Wisdom Sits in Places: Landscape and Language Among the Western
Apache.* Albuquerque: University of New Mexico Press, 1996.

Basso, Keith H. and Morris Opler. *Apachean Culture History and Ethnology.*
Tucson: University of Arizona Press, 1971.

Bellah, Robert. *Apache Kinship Systems.* Cambridge, Mass.: Harvard University Press, 1942.
A classic treatment of various Apache kinship systems.

Bourke, John. *On the Border with Crook.*
    See under Published Primary Sources.

Cole, D. C. *The Chiricahua Apache, 1846–1876: From War to Reservation.* Albuquerque: University of New Mexico Press, 1988.
    Good account of a crucial period in Chiricahua Apache history.

Debo, Angie. *Geronimo: The Man, His Time, His Place.* Norman: University of Oklahoma Press, 1976.
    Written for a popular audience, this book is probably the best known biography of Geronimo.

Dobyns, Henry F. *The Apache People.* Phoenix, Ariz.: Indian Tribal Series, 1971.

——. *The Mescalero Apache People.* Phoenix, Ariz.: Indian Tribal Series, 1973.
    This series presents a series of readable accounts with basic information of various tribal cultures in the Southwest.

Farrer, Claire R. "The Performance of Mescalero Apache Clowns." *Folklore Annual* 4–5 (1973): 135–151.
    Respected anthropologist Claire Farrer has worked more closely with the Mescalero Apache than any other contemporary scholar. Her deep ties with the Mescalero span several decades of friendship and fieldwork; the medicine man Bernard Second asked her to record valuable material for the tribe so that it would not be lost. The titles below identify their subject matter.

——. "Singing for Life: The Mescalero Apache Girls' Puberty Ceremony." In *Southwestern Indian Ritual Drama,* ed. Charlotte J. Frisbie. Santa Fe and Albuquerque: School of American Research and University of New Mexico Press; Santa Fe: School of American Research, 1980, 125–159.

——. *Living Life's Circle: Mescalero Apache Cosmovision.* Albuquerque: University of New Mexico Press, 1991.
    Based on the Girl's Puberty Ceremony but encompassing much more, this book details the cosmological beliefs and practices of the Mescalero Apache.

Farrer, Claire R. and Bernard Second. "Living the Sky: Aspects of Mescalero Apache Ethnoastronomy." In *Archaeoastronomy in the Amerias,* ed. Ray Williamson. *Ballena Press Anthropological Papers* 22. Los Altos, Calif.: Ballena Press; College Park, Md.: The Center for Archaeoastronomy, 1981, 137–150.

Ferg, Alan, ed. *Western Apache Material Culture: The Goodwin and Guenther Collections*. Tucson: University of Arizona Press, 1988.

Goodwin (see Published Primary Sources) collected a valuable body of data on pre-reservation Western Apache culture, and the Guenthers were resident missionaries who collected objects that were made specifically for sale to outsiders over a seventy-year period.

Goddard, Pliny Earle. "Jicarilla Apache Texts." Also "San Carlos Apache Texts," "Myths and Tales from the White Mountain Apache," and "White Mountain Apache Texts."
See under Oral Traditions.

Goodwin, Grenville. "Myths and Tales of the White Mountain Apache."
See under Oral Traditions.

——. *The Social Organization of the Western Apache*. 1942; reprint, Tucson: University of Arizona Press, 1969.
A classic study by a respected scholar.

Griffin-Pierce, Trudy. *Chiricahua Apache Enduring Power: Naiche's Puberty Ceremony Paintings*. Tuscaloosa: University of Alabama Press, 2006.

Focused on their twenty-seven-year prisoner-of-war period (1886–1913), this book details the Chiricahuas' diaspora, which continues today because they have never been permitted to return to their homeland. The book takes a perspective of agency and demonstrates how the Chiricahuas deployed forms of resistance and made strategic choices within limited options. Power remains the centering focus for contemporary Chiricahuas, as enacted in the Girl's Puberty Ceremony, which was depicted through Naiche's distinctive hide paintings.

Howard, Oliver O. *My Life and Experiences Among Our Hostile Indians*.
See under Published Primary Sources.

Lieder, Michael and Jake Page. *Wild Justice: The People of Geronimo vs. the United States*. New York: Random House, 1997.

Written by a lawyer and a southwestern author. After giving a brief history of surrender and twenty-seven-year incarceration, this book examines the claims brought by the Chiricahua Apaches before the Indian Claims Commission.

Opler, Morris. *An Apache Life-Way: The Economic, Social, and Religious Institutions of the Chiricahua Indians*. 1941; reprint, Lincoln: University of Nebraska Press, 1996.

The best known and most respected scholar of Apache culture, Opler laid the foundation for Apache studies. This is but one of his many published works about various Apache tribes.

Robinson, Sherry. *Apache Voices: Their Stories of Survival as Told to Eve Ball.* Albuquerque: University of New Mexico Press, 2000.
   Robinson, working from Eve Ball's unpublished papers, expands our understanding of what the Chiricahua Apache experienced.

Sonnichsen, C. L. *The Mescalero Apaches.* 1958; reprint, Norman: University of Oklahoma Press, 1973.
   A well-known historian traces Mescalero Apache culture and history from the tribe's arrival in the Southwest to the late 1950s.

Sweeney, Edwin. *Cochise: Chiricahua Apache Chief.* Norman: University of Oklahoma Press, 1991.
   The best known biography of Cochise.

TeCube, Leroy. *A Year in Nam.*
   See under Published Primary Sources.

Thrapp, Dan L. *Al Sieber: Chief of Scouts.* Norman: University of Oklahoma Press, 1964.
   Biography of chief of Western Apache Indian scouts under General George Crook in Arizona.

Tiller, Veronica E. Velarde. *The Jicarilla Apache Tribe: A History.* Lincoln: University of Nebraska Press, 1992.
   A well-known Jicarilla Apache records her tribe's history.

Navajos

Aberle, David F. "The Navajo." In *Matrilineal Kinship*, ed. David Schneider and Kathleen Gough. Berkeley: University of California Press, 1961, 96–201.
   Classic work on Navajo kinship by a respected scholar.

——. *The Peyote Religion Among the Navajo.* Chicago: Aldine Press, 1966.
   The key study of the history of the peyote religion (the Native American Church) among the Navajo.

——. "The Navajo Singer's Fee: Payment or Presentation." In *Studies in Southwestern Ethnolinguistics*, ed. Dell Hymes and W. E. Bittle. The Hague: Mouton, 1967, 15–32.
A significant article that demonstrates the Navajo concept of reciprocity in the fee that a ceremonial practitioner receives.

Adair, John. *The Navajo and Pueblo Silversmiths.* Norman: University of Oklahoma Press, 1944.
Classic study of silversmithing among the Navajo and Pueblos by a respected scholar who spent over fifty years in field research among the Navajo and other tribes.

Adams, William Y. "Shonto: A Study of the Role of the Trader in a Modern Navaho Community." *Bureau of American Ethnology Bulletin* 188. Washington, D.C.: Smithsonian Institution Press, 1963.
Classic in Navajo studies.

Alvord, Lori Arviso, M.D. and Elizabeth Cohen Van Pelt. *The Scapel and the Silver Bear.*
See under Published Primary Sources.

Amsden, Charles A. *Navaho Weaving: Its Technic and History.* 1934; reprint, Glorieta, N.M.: Rio Grande Press, 1971.
The classic work on the history and techniques used in Navajo weaving.

Bailey, Garrick and Roberta Bailey. *A History of the Reservation Years.* Santa Fe, N.M.: School of American Research Press, 1986.
An excellent historical account of the interacting forces that have helped make Navajo culture unique.

Bailey, Lynn R. *The Long Walk: A History of the Navajo Wars, 1846–1868.* Los Angeles: Westernlore Press, 1964.
All of Lynn Bailey's books are useful in understanding a crucial period of Navajo history.

——. *Indian Slave Trade in the Southwest: A Study of Slave-taking and the Traffic of Indian Captives.* Los Angeles: Westernlore Press, 1966.

——. *Bosque Redondo: An American Concentration Camp.* Pasadena, Calif.: Socio-Technical Books, 1970.

Bedinger, Margery. *Indian Silver: Navajo and Pueblo Jewelers.* Albuquerque: University of New Mexico Press, 1973.
A useful study of Navajo and Pueblo jewelry making.

Begay, D. Y. "A Weaver's Point of View."
See under Published Primary Sources.

Begay, Shirley. *Kinaaldá: A Navajo Puberty Ceremony.*
See under Published Primary Sources.

Benally, Clyde. *Dinéji Nákéé Nááhane: A Utah Navajo History.*
See under Oral Traditions.

——. *Between Sacred Mountains: Navajo Stories and Lessons from the Land.*
See under Oral Traditions.

Brugge, David M. *The Navajo-Hopi Land Dispute: An American Tragedy.* Albuquerque: University of New Mexico Press, 1994.
A respected scholar presents evidence in favor of the Navajo perspective.

Brugge, Doug. *Memories Come to Us in the Rain and the Wind: Oral Histories and Photographs of Navajo Uranium Miners and Their Families.*
See under Published Primary Sources.

Csordas, Thomas J. *Body/Meaning/Healing.* New York: Palgrave Macmillan, 2002.
By a respected medical anthropologist, this book explores therapeutic process and embodiment in several settings. Navajo culture is the focus of part II and includes three previously published chapters and one that was prepared for this volume. Ritual healing and identity politics interact on three levels in contemporary Navajo society in an epidemic of hanta virus and a serious drought. The use of traditional Navajo ceremonies, Native American Church meetings, and Navajo Christian faith healing are explored. How people experience and make sense of cancer is another topic.

Davies, Wade. *Healing Ways: Navajo Health Care in the Twentieth Century.* Albuquerque: University of New Mexico Press, 2001.
An account of the complex process the Navajo Nation and various individuals have undertaken to make Western medicine available to Navajos, with inadequate federal health care, funding difficulties, and cultural conflicts.

Dobyns, Henry and Robert Euler. *The Navajo Indians.* Phoenix, Ariz.: Indian Tribal Series, 1972.
  A basic ethnography for the general reader.

Downs, James. "Animal Husbandry in Navajo Society and Culture." *University of California Publications in Anthropology* 1. Berkeley: University of California Press, 1964.
  Anthropological study of the Navajo herding economy.

——. *The Navajo.* New York: Holt, Rinehart, and Winston, 1964.
  Basic ethnography but with focus on herding economy.

Dyen, Isidore and David Aberle. *Lexical Reconstruction: The Case of the Proto-Athapaskan Kinship System.* New York: Cambridge University Press, 1974.
  Detailed study from linguistic reconstruction of the probable kinship system of ancestors of Athapaskan speakers.

Farella, John. *The Main Stalk: A Synthesis of Navajo Philosophy.* Tucson: University of Arizona Press, 1984.
  A detailed study of Navajo philosophy drawn on interviews with four Navajo elders, and the work of Father Berard Haile.

Farris, James. *The Nightway: A History and a History of the Documentation of a Navajo Ceremonial.* Albuquerque: University of New Mexico Press, 1990.
  This thoroughly documented book is an excellent record of the history of a major Navajo tradition and includes the various branches of this complex ceremonial.

——. *Navajo and Photography: A Critical History of the Representation of an American People.* Albuquerque: University of New Mexico Press, 1996.
  An excellent study of how the Navajo people have been represented in photographic images over time.

Franciscan Fathers. *An Ethnological Dictionary of the Navajo Language.* St. Michael's, Ariz.: St. Michael's Press, 1910.
  Though dated and superseded by Young and Morgan's work, still contains much valuable information on Navajo culture and language.

Frisbie, Charlotte J. *Kinaaldá: A Study of the Navaho Girls's Puberty Ceremony.* Middletown, Conn.: Wesleyan University Press, 1967.
  The most definitive and complete treatment of the Girl's Puberty Ceremony.

——. "Ritual Drama in the Navajo House Blessing Ceremony." In *Southwestern Indian Ritual Drama*, ed. Charlotte J. Frisbie. Santa Fe and Albuquerque: School of American Research and University of New Mexico Press, 1980, 161–198.

An essay by a preeminent scholar of Navajo culture on the Blessingway ceremony as it is used to bless newly constructed dwellings or those about to be reinhabited.

——. *Navajo Medicine Bundles or Jish: Acquisition, Transmission, and Disposition in the Past and Present.* Albuquerque: University of New Mexico Press, 1987.

An exhaustive and definitive study based on historical and ethnographic fieldwork data gathered between 1963 and 1986.

——. *Tall Woman: The Life Story of Rose Mitchell, a Navajo Woman 1874–1977.* Albuquerque: University of New Mexico Press, 2006.

A compelling biography that blends historical context with a personal life history.

Frisbie, Charlotte J. and David P. McAllester, eds. *Navajo Blessingway Singer: The Autobiography of Frank Mitchell.* See under Published Primary Sources.

Gilpin, Laura. *The Enduring Navaho.* Austin: University of Texas Press, 1968.

Gilpin's classic photographs and texts present an excellent record of Navajo culture as it once was.

Gold, Peter. *Navajo and Tibetan Sacred Wisdom: The Circle of the Spirit.* Rochester, Vt.: Inner Traditions International, 1994.

An interesting comparison of Navajo and Tibetan religious beliefs and practices for the general reader.

Goodman, James. *The Navajo Atlas: Environments, Resources, People, and History of Diné Bikeyah.* Norman: University of Oklahoma Press, 1982.

Though dated, provides an excellent summary of the physical environment, the evolution of the reservation, and resources.

Griffin-Pierce, Trudy. "Navajo Ceremonial Sandpaintings: Sacred, Living Entities." *American Indian Art* (Winter 1991): 58–67, 88.

A Navajo perspective on the nature of sandpaintings used in healing ceremonies.

——. *Earth Is My Mother, Sky Is My Father: Space, Time, and Astronomy in Navajo Sandpainting*. Albuquerque: University of New Mexico Press, 1992.
An exploration of the spiritual world of the Navajo as it relates to ceremonials. Based on traditional accounts, interviews, and fieldwork with Navajo chanters and specialists.

——. "How Sandpaintings Accomplish the Work of Healing." *Viennese Ethnomedicine Newsletter* 9, no. 2–3 (February–June 2007): 3–16.
Using perspectives from biomedical anthropology, such as performance theory, Navajo sandpainting rituals are considered as a means of reestablishing order and balance in the lives of the patient and the audience.

——. "Navajo Religion: The Continuous Renewal of Sacred Relations." In *Native Religions and Cultures of North America: Anthropology of the Sacred*, ed. Lawrence E. Sullivan. Center for the Study of World Religions at Harvard University and New York: The Continuum International Publishing Group, 2000, 121–141.
An essay that stresses the dynamic and interconnected nature of Navajo spiritual beliefs and practices.

Haile, Father Berard. "Navaho Chantways and Ceremonials." *American Anthropologist* 40, no. 4 (1938): 639–652.
Father Berard Haile was one of the earliest and most prolific writers about Navajo religion and culture. He published some sixteen articles and books during his lifetime. Only a few of his major works are listed below; two more are listed under Oral Traditions.

——. "Soul Concepts of the Navaho." *Annali Lateranensi* 7 (1943): 59–94.

——. *Head and Face Masks in Navaho Ceremonialism*. St. Michael's, Ariz.: St. Michael's Press, 1947.

——. *A Stem Vocabulary of the Navaho Language, Navaho-English; English-Navaho*. 2 vols. St. Michael's, Ariz.: St. Michael's Press, 1950–1951.

Henderson, Eric. "Navajo Livestock Wealth and the Effects of Stock Reduction." *Journal of Anthropological Research* 45 (1989): 379–403.
Well-documented article on how stock reduction affected the Navajo by a respected scholar.

House, Conrad. "The Art of Balance."

See under Published Primary Sources.

House, Deborah. *Language Shift Among the Navajo: Identity Politics and Cultural Continuity.* Tucson: University of Arizona Press, 2002.
Based on over ten years of fieldwork, an excellent study on the ideological factors that intervene between the desire to maintain the Navajo language and linguistic practice.

Iverson, Peter. *Diné: A History of the Navajos.* Albuquerque: University of New Mexico Press, 2002.
This excellent and comprehensive narrative traces the history of the Navajos from their origins to the beginning of the twenty-first century. Based on extensive archival research, traditional accounts, interviews, historic and contemporary photographs, and firsthand observations.

——. *"For Our Navajo People": Diné Letters, Speeches and Petitions 1900–1960.* Albuquerque: University of New Mexico Press, 2002.
A corpus of well-documented material written by Navajo leaders that traces the history of the Navajo Nation's relationship with the federal government over the course of a crucial sixty-year period.

——. *The Navajos.* New York: Chelsea House, 1990.
Helpful overview of Navajo culture and history.

Jett, Stephen and Virginia Spencer. *Navajo Architecture: Forms, History, Distributions.* Tucson: University of Arizona Press, 1981.
This classic work presents extensive documentation of the Navajo hogan and other architectural forms.

Johnson, Broderick and Ruth Roessel. *Navajo Livestock Reduction: A National Disgrace.* Tsaile, Ariz.: Navajo Community College Press, 1974.
The Navajo perspective of the federal government's disastrous stock reduction program of the 1930s.

Kammer, Jerry. *The Second Long Walk: The Navajo-Hopi Land Dispute.* Albuquerque: University of New Mexico Press, 1980.
Most Navajos consider the Navajo-Hopi land dispute to be as traumatic as the Long Walk of 1864 when they were exiled to Bosque Redondo.

Kelley, Klara B. and Harris Francis. *Navajo Sacred Places.* Bloomington: Indiana University Press, 1994.

A valuable study of the sacredness of the Navajo landscape by an ethnologist who has worked with the tribe for nearly twenty years and a Navajo who is an American Indian cultural rights protection consultant.

Kelly, Lawrence C. *The Navajo Indians and Federal Indian Policy, 1900–1935.* Tucson: University of Arizona Press, 1968.
An excellent account of the impact of federal policy on the Navajo between 1900 and 1935.

Kluckhohn, Clyde. "Navaho Witchcraft." *Papers of the Peabody Museum of American Archaeology and Ethnology, Harvard University* 22, no. 2. 1944; reprint, Boston: Beacon Press, 1967.
A classic study by one of the pioneer ethnologists of Navajo culture.

Kluckhohn, Clyde, W. W. Hill, and Lucy Wales Kluckhohn. *Navaho Material Culture.* Cambridge, Mass.: Harvard University Press, 1971.
Extensive documentation of Navajo objects related to subsistence, shelter, clothing, ritual, and recreation with information about manufacture and use, knowledge, and belief associated with each object. The only study of its kind of the material culture of any southwestern tribe.

Kluckhohn, Clyde and Dorothea Leighton. *The Navaho.* Rev. ed. Garden City, N.Y.: Natural History Library, 1962.
Though dated, a classic ethnography by two of the best known anthropologists of Navajo culture.

Kunitz, Stephen. *Disease Change and the Role of Medicine: The Navajo Experience.* Berkeley: University of California Press, 1989.
Based on data collected during the author's long-term research on Navajo epidemiology, an insightful book about the role of Western medicine among the Navajo.

Kunitz, Stephen and Jerrold Levy. "Changing Ideas of Alcohol Use Among Navajo Indians." *Quarterly Journal of Studies on Alcohol* 35 (1974): 243–259.
Excellent study that presents evidence disproving stereotypes of Indian drinking patterns.

Lamphere, Louise. *To Run After Them: Cultural and Social Bases of Cooperation in a Navajo Community.* Tucson: University of Arizona Press, 1977.
This scholarly study of Navajo social networks was written by one of the most respected anthropologists of Navajo culture.

Lamphere, Louise, with Eva Price, Carole Cadman, and Valerie Darwin. *Weaving Women's Lives: Three Generations in a Navajo Family*. Albuquerque: University of New Mexico Press, 2007.

Through her forty-year relationship with Eva Price and her family, a renowned anthropologist examines the way that individuals, especially women, utilize traditional Navajo conceptions and beliefs while also including new practices and ideas from the larger U.S. economy and society in which the Navajos have been incorporated for 150 years.

Leighton, Dorothea. *Children of the People*. Cambridge, Mass.: Harvard University Press, 1947.

Although dated, a classic about traditional child-raising practices in Navajo culture.

Levy, Jerrold E. *In the Beginning: The Navajo Genesis*.
See Oral Traditions.

Levy, Jerrold E. and Stephen J. Kunitz. *Indian Drinking: Navajo Practices and Anglo-American Theories*. New York: Wiley-Interscience, 1974.

More extensive treatment of evidence that disproves stereotypes of Indian drinking practices.

——. *Navajo Aging: The Transition from Family to Institutional Support*. Tucson: University of Arizona, 1991.

Major contribution to social epidemiology that examines the effect of the modernization process on treatment of the elderly in Navajo society.

Levy, Jerrold E., Raymond Neutra, and Dennis Parker. *Hand Trembling, Frenzy Witchcraft, and Moth Madness: A Study of Navajo Seizure Disorders*. Tucson: University of Arizona Press, 1987.

Traditional Navajo belief holds that major epileptic seizure results from sibling incest; this extensive study follows Navajo patients and examines the cultural meaning of their disease.

Lewton, Elizabeth L. and Victoria Bydone. "Identity and Healing in Three Navajo Religious Traditions: *Sa'ah Naagháí Bik'eh Hózho*." *Medical Anthropological Quarterly* 14, no. 4 (2000): 476–497.

This insightful article demonstrates how the key Navajo philosophical principle orients individuals in the world using examples in three different Navajo healing practices, traditional Navajo religion, the Native American Church, and Pentecostal Christianity.

Luckert, Carl W. *The Navajo Hunter Tradition.*
    See under Oral Traditions.

——. "Navajo Mountain and Rainbow Bridge Religion." *American Tribal Religion Series* 1. Flagstaff: Museum of Northern Arizona Press, 1977.
    Luckert carries on the tradition of Leland Wyman in studies of Navajo ceremonialism.

——. "A Navajo Bringing-Home Ceremony: The Claus Chee Sonny Version of Deerway Ajiłee."
    See under Oral Traditions.

——. *Coyoteway: A Navajo Healing Ceremonial.* Tucson and Flagstaff: University of Arizona Press and Museum of Northern Arizona Press, 1979.

Mayes, Vernon and Barbara Bayless Lacy. *Nanise': A Navajo Herbal: One Hundred Plants from the Navajo Reservation.* Tsaile, Ariz.: Navajo Community College Press, 1989.
    A description of a hundred plants with their uses for food, medicine, and religion, based on interviews with Navajo herbalists and specialists.

McAllester, David P. "Shootingway, An Epic Drama of the Navajos." In *Southwestern Indian Ritual Drama*, ed. Charlotte J. Frisbie. Santa Fe and Albuquerque: The School of American Research and the University of New Mexico Press, 1980, 199–237.
    A moving account of the Male Shootingway ceremony by the most respected ethnomusicologist in Navajo studies.

McCarty, Teresa. *A Place to Be Navajo: Rough Rock and the Struggle for Self-Determination in Indigenous Schooling: Sociocultural, Political, and Historical Studies in Education.* Mahwah, N.J.: Lawrence Erlbaum, 2003.
    This is an outstanding book on the founding of Rough Rock Demonstration School, a bilingual/bicultural community school that established the standard for other schools. It tells the heartbreaking story of the trials and errors that dedicated administrators, faculty, staff, and community endured to establish it and to keep it going through decades of obstacles.

McNeley, James. *The Holy Wind in Navajo Philosophy.* Tucson: University of Arizona Press, 1988.
    A groundbreaking book on the principle of wind and breath that unite all living things.

McNitt, Frank. *Navajo Wars, Military Campaigns, Slave Raids and Reprisals.*
     Albuquerque: University of New Mexico Press, 1972.
   Excellent documentation of history of Navajo and Anglo conflict in the mid-
1800s, with a focus on the extensive capture of Navajos for slaves.

McPherson, Robert S. *Sacred Land, Sacred View: Navajo Perceptions of the
     Four Corners Region.*
   See under Native Relationships with the Land.

Mitchell, Emerson Blackhorse and T. D. Allen. *Miracle Hill: The Story of a
     Navaho Boy.*
   See under Published Primary Sources.

Newcomb, Franc Johnson. *Navajo Omens and Taboos.* Santa Fe: Rydal Press,
     1940.
   Newcomb was a trader's wife and, although not trained as an anthropologist,
was a skilled observer of Navajo culture and close friend to many Navajos.

———. *Hosteen Klah: Navaho Medicine Man and Sand Painter.* Norman: Univer-
     sity of Oklahoma Press, 1964.
   Biography of the best-known Navajo chanter, born in 1867 while his
mother was imprisoned at Bosque Redondo. The Wheelwright Museum in
Santa Fe was built to house Klah's ceremonial material and drawings of his
sandpaintings.

Newcomb, Franc Johnson and Gladys A. Reichard. *Sandpaintings of the Na-
     vajo Shooting Chant.* New York: J. J. Augustin, 1937.
   Newcomb attended many ceremonies and produced drawings of the sandpaintings she saw being made in ceremonies; these are housed at the Wheelwright Museum in Santa Fe. Reichard pioneered ethnographic work with the
Navajos.

Nielsen, Marianne O. and James W. Zion. *Navajo Nation Peacemaking.*
   See under Politics.

Niethammer, Carolyn. *"I'll Go and Do More": Annie Dodge Wauneka, Navajo
     Leader and Activist.* Lincoln: University of Nebraska Press, 2001.
   Probably the most outstanding female leader in Navajo history, Annie
Dodge Wauneka played a pivotal role in helping to control the epidemic of
tuberculosis among the Navajos by convincing her people that hospitals could
help cure the disease.

O'Bryan, Aileen. *Navaho Indian Myths.*
    See under Oral Traditions.

Parezo, Nancy. *Navajo Sandpainting: From Religious Act to Commercial Art.*
    Tucson: University of Arizona Press, 1983.
    Respected scholar traces the historical process of Navajo sandpaintings on
boards becoming commercial products as artists made subtle changes in design, coloration, and/or pictorial content to create commercial versions of sacred sandpaintings for sale.

Powers, Willow. *Navajo Trading: The End of an Era.* Albuquerque: University
    of New Mexico Press, 2001.
    This book explores the era of the trading post on the Navajo reservation.

Reichard, Gladys. "Social Life of the Navajo Indians." *Columbia University
    Contributions to Anthropology* 7 (1928).
    A pioneering anthropologist gives an account of Navajo society.

——. *Spider Woman: A Story of Navajo Weavers and Chanters.*
    See under Published Primary Sources.

——. *Navajo Medicine Man: Sandpaintings and Legends of Miguelito.* New
    York: J. J. Augustin, 1939.
    A visual and written account of sandpaintings in their cultural context as
interpreted by anthropologist Gladys Reichard from chanter Miguelito.

——. "Prayer: The Compulsive Word." *Monographs of the American Ethnologi-
    cal Society* 7. New York: J. J. Augustin, 1944.
    A monograph that analyzes the structure, content, and function of Navajo
prayers.

Schwarz, Maureen Trudelle. *Molded in the Image of Changing Woman: Na-
    vajo Views on the Human Body and Personhood.* Tucson: University of
    Arizona Press, 1997.
    An excellent study that relates anthropological perspectives on the body to
Navajo culture with fieldwork to support the theoretical perspective.

——. *Navajo Lifeways: Contemporary Issues, Ancient Knowledge.* Norman: Uni-
    versity of Oklahoma Press, 2001.
    An analysis of the many ways Navajo people reinterpret tradition to con-
front such challenges as unexplained illness, the effects of uranium mining,

problem drinking, and threats to their land rights and spirituality. Using interviews with a wide range of individuals, this book provides a thoughtful and insightful perspective.

———. *Blood and Voice: Navajo Women Ceremonial Practitioners.* Tucson: University of Arizona Press, 2003.
    Based on extensive interviews, an anthropologist focuses on the challenges faced by female ceremonial practitioners who are prohibited from ceremonial contexts during menstruation; furthermore, oral history dictates that men are to be the leaders in ceremonial matters.

Sherry, John W. *Land, Wind, and Hard Words: A Story of Navajo Activism.*
    See under Native Relationships with the Land.

Underhill, Ruth. *The Navajos.* Norman: University of Oklahoma Press, 1956.
    For the general audience, this book by a respected anthropologist is a good starting point for learning about Navajo culture.

Wheat, Joe Ben. *Blanket Weaving in the Southwest.* Ed. Ann Lane Hedlund. Tucson: University of Arizona Press, 2003.
    Ann Hedlund, one of Joe Ben Wheat's students who has become probably the most respected scholar in the field of Navajo textiles, continued work on this thoroughly documented book after Wheat's death.

White, Richard. *The Roots of Dependency: Subsistence, Environment, and Social Change Among the Choctaws, Pawnees, and Navajos.* Lincoln: University of Nebraska Press, 1983.
    Account of how each group became economically dependent as their subsistence patterns became intertwined with the market economy. Excellent treatment of Navajo society, demonstrating how their livestock economy enabled them to remain economically independent relative to other American Indian groups until the stock reduction program of the 1930s.

Witherspoon, Gary. *Navajo Kinship and Marriage.* Chicago: University of Chicago Press, 1975.
    A respected scholar of Navajo culture writes about patterns of kinship and marriage.

———. *Language and Art in the Navajo Universe.* Ann Arbor: University of Michigan Press, 1977.

This classic book is an excellent study of Navajo language as it relates to worldview.

Worth, Sol and John Adair. *Through Navajo Eyes: An Exploration in Film Communication and Anthropology.* Albuquerque: University of New Mexico Press, 1997 (with new introduction and afterword by Richard Chalfen).
A classic study that shows the contribution of the bio-documentary method to ethnography and the field of visual anthropology. In an effort to understand how people structure reality through film, Adair and Worth taught Navajos to use cameras so that they could film what was significant to them.

Wyman, Leland. *Blessingway.* Tucson: University of Arizona Press, 1970.
Written by the foremost scholar of sacred sandpaintings, who devoted his life to documenting sandpaintings and related myths of various chantways.

——. *Southwest Indian Drypainting.* Santa Fe and Albuquerque: School of American Research Press and University of New Mexico Press, 1983.
For general readers and scholars, an overview of drypainting (sandpainting, as it is called by the Navajos) in Navajo culture, with chapters on this practice in other cultures of the Southwest and around the world.

Young, Robert and William Morgan. *The Navajo Language: A Grammar and Colloquial Dictionary.* Albuquerque: University of New Mexico Press, 1980.
An enormous (1,069 pages) volume, the most exhaustive work on the Navajo language by two highly respected scholars of the Navajo language.

O'odham

Bahr, Donald. *Pima and Papago Ritual Oratory: A Study of Three Texts.* San Francisco: Indian Historian Press, 1975.
An eminent scholar of O'odham ritual worked extensively with O'odham ceremonial practitioners to document aspects of ritual orations and practice.

Bahr, Donald, Juan Gregario, David Lopez, and Albert Alvarez. *Piman Shamanism and Staying Sickness.* Tucson: University of Arizona Press, 1974.
O'odham ceremonial practitioners interpret shamanism and the O'odham theory of disease causation.

Bennett, P. H., T. A. Burch, and M. Miller. "Diabetes Mellitus in American (Pima) Indians." *Lancet* 2, no. 7716 (July 17, 1971): 125–128.

The O'odham suffer from the highest rate of diabetes in the world, and this medical article provides a good overview.

Castetter, Edward and Willis Bell. *Pima and Papago Agriculture*. Albuquerque: University of New Mexico Press, 1942.
Two well-known scholars give a classic account of traditional O'odham agricultural practices.

Dobyns, Henry. *The Pima-Maricopa*. New York: Chelsea House, 1989.
A respected scholar of southwestern Indian cultures writes about two groups who have long been allies and have lived together even though the Pimas are O'odham and the Maricopas are River Yumans.

Erickson, Winston P. *Sharing the Desert: The Tohono O'odham in History*. Tucson: University of Arizona Press, 2003.
The Tohono O'odham perspective on their history, written with assistance of the Tohono O'odham Nation Education Department and the Research Staff of the American West Center.

Fontana, Bernard. *Of Earth and Little Rain*. Tucson: University of Arizona Press, 1981.
A highly readable book by a respected ethnologist and key source on Tohono O'odham culture and life, who has lived most of his life near the edge of the Tohono O'odham Reservation at San Xavier.

Haefer, J. Richard. "O'odham Celkona: The Papago Skipping Dance." In *Southwestern Indian Ritual Drama*, ed. Charlotte J. Frisbie. Santa Fe and Albuquerque: School of American Research and University of New Mexico Press, 1980, 239–274.
Good information on the practice of O'odham ceremonies in the 1980s, with history and cultural background of the *celkona*, which has always been associated with entertainment but does have religious overtones.

Kozak, David and David Lopez. *Devil Sickness and Devil Songs: Tohono O'odham Poetics*. Washington, D.C.: Smithsonian Institution Press, 1999.
Linking ritual healing and poetics, this volume brings greater understanding of Tohono O'odham illness theory, healing practices, and language.

Kroeber, Clifton and Bernard Fontana. *Massacre on the Gila: An Account of the Last Major Battle Between American Indians, with Reflections on the Origin of War*. Tucson: University of Arizona Press, 1986.

One of the best books on the history and changes in River Yuman warfare.

Manuel, Frances and Deborah Neff. *Desert Indian Woman: Stories and Dreams.*
See under Published Primary Sources.

Moreillon, Judith Lynn. *Sing Down the Rain.* Santa Fe: Kiva Publishing, 1997.
Illustrated by Tohono O'odham artist Michael Chiago, this children's book tells the story of the Saguaro Wine Ceremony as practiced by the Tohono O'odham. Recommended for adults because of its treatment of an often misunderstood cultural practice.

Nabhan, Gary Paul. *Gathering the Desert.* Tucson: University of Arizona Press, 1993.
An insightful account of Tohono O'odham plant knowledge by a leading scholar.

——. *The Desert Smells Like Rain: A Naturalist in Papago Indian Country.* Tucson: University of Arizona Press, 2002.
An award-winning nature writer and scholar, Nabhan provides insights into the O'odham relationship with their natural and spiritual worlds.

National Institutes of Health (NIH). "The Pima Indians: Pathfinders for Health." National Institute of Diabetes and Digestive and Kidney Disease. *National Institutes of Health Publication* 95–3821 (1995).
Medical documentation on O'odham diabetes and related diseases and what is being done to treat them.

Russell, Frank. "The Pima Indians." In *26th Annual Report of the Bureau of American Ethnology for the Years 1904–1905.* 1908; reprint, Tucson: University of Arizona Press, 1975, 3–389.
Classic ethnography.

Shaw, Anna Moore. *Pima Indian Legends.*
See under Oral Traditions.

——. *A Pima Past.*
See under Published Primary Sources.

Smith-Morris, Carolyn. *Diabetes Among the Pima: Stories of Survival.* Tucson: University of Arizona Press, 2006.

Drawing on narratives of pregnant Akimel O'odham women and nearly ten years' work in this community, this book reveals O'odham perceptions of type 2 and gestational diabetes and how these understandings relate to biomedical, political, and economic factors.

Underhill, Ruth. *Singing for Power: The Song Magic of the Papago Indians of Southern Arizona.* 1938; reprint, New York: Ballantine, 1973.
Underhill's body of work is a key source for Tohono O'odham culture and life as it was during an earlier period of time.

——. "Social Organization of the Papago Indians." *Columbia University Contributions to Anthropology* 30 (1939).

——. "Papago Indian Religion." *Columbia University Contributions to Anthropology* 33 (1946).

——. *People of the Crimson Evening.* 1951; reprint, Palmer Lake, Colo: Filter Press, 1982.

——. *Papago Woman.* 1979; reprint, Prospect Heights, Ill.: Waveland Press, 1985.

Underhill, Ruth, Donald Bahr, B. Lopez, J. Pancho, and D. Lopez. "Rainhouse and Ocean: Speeches for the Papago Year."
See under Oral Traditions.

Webb, George. A *Pima Remembers.*
See under Published Primary Sources.

Zepeda, Ofelia. *Ocean Power: Songs from the Desert.* Tucson: University of Arizona Press, 1995.
A professor and MacArthur award winner, Zepeda is the foremost scholar of her people's language and culture.

——, ed. *When It Rains: Papago and Pima Poetry.*
See under Oral Traditions.

Papagos and/or Pimas

See O'odham.

Pueblos

Babcock, Barbara A. and Guy and Doris Monthan. *The Pueblo Storyteller: Development of a Figurative Ceramic Tradition.* Tucson: University of Arizona Press, 1992.
   Written by a scholar and based on many years of research, this book documents the figurative tradition in Pueblo Indian ceramics, with an emphasis on the work of Helen Cordero of Cochiti Pueblo.

Bandelier, Adolph. *The Delight Makers.* New York: Dodd, Mead, 1890.
   A classic study by a pioneer ethnologist who used oral traditions to hypothesize about the evolution of social organization.

Beaglehole, Ernest and Pearl Beaglehole. "Hopi of Second Mesa." *American Anthropological Association Memoir* 44 (1935).
   Classic ethnography.

Benedict, Ruth. *Patterns of Culture.* New York: Mentor Books, 1934.
   Based on fieldwork in the early 1930s, this key study developed the theory that every culture has its own distinctive pattern and initiated a new field of research in anthropology known as culture and personality studies.

Bernstein, Bruce and J. J. Brody. *Voices in Clay: Pueblo Pottery from the Edna M. Kelly Collection.* Oxford, Ohio: Miami University Art Museum, 2001.
   Remarkable dialogue of contemporary Pueblo potters and curators that emphasizes how Pueblo pottery traditions have adapted through time.

Brown, Donald N. "Dance as Experience: The Deer Dance of Picuris Pueblo." In *Southwestern Indian Ritual Drama*, ed. Charlotte J. Frisbie. Santa Fe and Albuquerque: School of American Research and University of New Mexico Press, 1980, 71–92.
   Excellent introduction to scant literature on Tewa dance and explication of the Picuris Deer Dance.

Bunzel, Ruth. *The Pueblo Potter: A Study of Creative Imagination in Primitive Art.* 1929; reprint, New York: Dover, 1972.
   Groundbreaking study of its time that explores individuality and range of variability in design principles among Zuni, Acoma, Hopi, and San Ildefonso potters, with detailed illustrations of design elements.

——. *Zuni Ceremonialism.* Albuquerque: University of New Mexico Press, 1992. (This volume contains three studies originally published in 1932 by the Smithsonian Institution: *Introduction to Zuni Ceremonialism, Zuni Origin Myths,* and *Zuni Ritual Poetry.*)
This classic work by an early anthropologist contains a wealth of detailed information based on extensive fieldwork.

Clemmer, Richard. *Roads in the Sky: Hopi Culture and History in a Century of Change.* Boulder, Colo.: Westview Press, 1995.
An anthropologist provides an excellent account of changing Hopi life.

Colton, Harold. *Hopi Kachina Dolls.* Albuquerque: University of New Mexico Press, 1959.
Written by a founder of the Museum of Northern Arizona, one of the classic books on Hopi Kachina dolls, based on many years of study and firsthand contact.

Courlander, Harold. *The Fourth World of the Hopi.* Albuquerque: University of New Mexico Press, 1971.
A detailed account of Hopi beliefs and practices by a folklorist and novelist who brings together traditional accounts of events from mythic to historical times.

Cushing, Frank Hamilton. *My Adventures in Zuni.*
See under Published Primary Sources.

——. "Outlines of Zuni Creation Myths."
See under Oral Traditions.

Dillingham, Rick and J. J. Brody. *Fourteen Families in Pueblo Pottery.* Albuquerque: University of New Mexico Press, 1994.
Accounts of the work and lives of fourteen Pueblo families who have handed down the pottery-making tradition for generations.

Dozier, Edward P. *Hano: A Tewa Indian Community in Arizona.* New York: Holt, Rinehart, and Winston, 1966.
A detailed account of Hano culture and history, including how Hano culture has been affected by Hopi culture and vice versa and how certain Tewa cultural aspects have remained untouched by contact with the Hopi over time.

——. *The Pueblo Indians of North America.* New York: Holt, Rinehart, and Winston, 1970.

An anthropologist from Santa Clara Pueblo examines how Pueblo cultures have adapted through time to changing socioeconomic and political environments. Although dated, this remains a classic study.

Dunn, Dorothy. *American Indian Painting of the Southwest and Plains Area.* Albuquerque: University of New Mexico Press, 1968.
Dunn helped establish the studio art program of the Santa Fe Indian School that fostered the work of many fine Pueblo artists, as well as those of other tribes.

Eggan, Fred. *Social Organization of the Western Pueblos.* Chicago: University of Chicago Press, 1950.
Dated, but remains a classic in the field.

Ferguson, T. J., and E. Richard Hart. *A Zuni Atlas.* Norman: University of Oklahoma Press, 1990.
A valuable reference that covers a wide range of topics related to Zuni archaeology, ethnography, and other issues by well-known scholars.

Fewkes, Jesse Walter. "Tusayan Migration Traditions."
See under Oral Traditions.

——. "Hopi Katcinas Drawn by Native Artists." In *21st Annual Report of the Bureau of American Ethnology for the Years 1899–1900.* 1903; reprint, Glorieta, N.M.: Rio Grande Press, 1969, 13–126.
The first in-depth study of Hopi Katcinas by a scholar who also relates them to their cultural context.

James, Harry C. *Pages from Hopi History.* 1974; reprint, Tucson: University of Arizona Press, 1994.
Written for general readers as well as scholars, Hopi history as viewed from the perspective of Hopi friends of the author who asked him to set down an account of the most significant events in their past.

Kealiinohomoku, Joann W. "The Drama of the Hopi Ogres." In *Southwestern Indian Ritual Drama*, ed. Charlotte J. Frisbie. Santa Fe and Albuquerque: School of American Research and University of New Mexico Press, 1980, 37–70.
By a respected scholar of Pueblo dance and culture.

Laird, David. *Hopi Bibliography.*
See under Bibliographies and Research Aids.

Lange, Charles H. *Cochiti: A New Mexico Pueblo, Past and Present.* Austin: University of Texas Press, 1959.
    Although dated, the classic, in-depth study of Cochiti Pueblo.

Loftin, John. *Religion and Hopi Life.* Bloomington: Indiana University Press, 1991.
    An somewhat idealized but detailed account of contemporary Hopi religion, based on field research by a scholar of religion.

Ortiz, Alfonso. *The Tewa World: Space, Time, Being, and Becoming in a Pueblo Society.* Chicago: University of Chicago Press, 1969.
    A penetrating analysis of the belief system of the Tewa by a well-known anthropologist from San Juan Pueblo.

——, ed. *New Perspectives on the Pueblos.* Albuquerque: University of New Mexico Press, 1972.
    Twelve essays that summarize results to date in the areas of ecology, prehistory, ethnohistory, linguistics, social organization, music, mythology, ritual drama, worldview, and demography. By leading scholars of their time.

Page, Suzanne and Jake Page. *Hopi.* New York: Abrams, 1982.
    Written at the request of the Hopi Tribal Council, this well-written and beautifully photographed book presents an excellent account of contemporary life at Hopi.

Parsons, Elsie Clews. *Pueblo Indian Religion,* vols. 1 and 2. 1939; reprint, Lincoln: University of Nebraska Press, 1996.
    Classic study of Pueblo social organization and religious beliefs and practices, based on over two decades of research and writing on the Pueblos, with attention to the historical development and other processes of change.

Qoyawayma, Polingaysi. *No Turning Back: A True Account of a Hopi Girl's Struggle to Bridge the Gap Between the World of Her People and the World of the White Man.*
    See under Published Primary Sources.

Sando, Joe S. *Pueblo Nations: Eight Centuries of Pueblo Indian History.* Santa Fe: Clear Light, 1992.
    An eminent scholar from Jemez Pueblo traces the ongoing history of the Pueblo peoples.

Secakuku, Alph H. *Following the Sun and Moon: Hopi Kachina Tradition.* Flagstaff, Ariz.: Northland Press, 1995.
Written by a Hopi motivated by the desire to preserve cultural information and to counteract misrepresentation through education.

Sekaquaptewa, Emory. "Hopi Indian Ceremonies." In *Seeing with a Native Eye,* ed. W. Capps. New York: Harper and Row, 1976, 35–43.
A Hopi professor and lawyer writes about Hopi ceremonies based on his own experiences.

——. "One More Smile for a Hopi Clown." *Parabola* 4 (1979): 6–9.
This short article conveys more about the significance of clowning to the Hopi than much longer, more scholarly essays.

Sekaquaptewa, Helen. *Me and Mine: The Life Story of Helen Sekaquaptewa.* See under Published Primary Sources.

Seowtewa, Ken. "Adding a Breath to Zuni Life." See under Published Primary Sources.

Silverberg, Robert. *The Pueblo Revolt.* 1970; reprint, Lincoln: University of Nebraska Press, 1994.
A thorough study of the 1680 Pueblo Revolt.

Simmons, Leo W. *Sun Chief: The Autobiography of a Hopi Indian.* See under Published Primary Sources.

Stephen, Alexander. *Hopi Journal.* See under Published Primary Sources.

Stevenson, James. "Illustrated Catalogue of the Collections Obtained from the Indians of New Mexico and Arizona." *2nd Annual Report of the Bureau of American Ethnology for the Years 1880–1881* (1883):307–422.
Material collected by Matilda Coxe Stevenson and James Stevenson as well as other ethnologists of the time.

Stevenson, Matilda Coxe. "The Zuni Indians: Their Mythology, Esoteric Fraternities, and Ceremonies." *23rd Annual Report of the Bureau of American Ethnology for the Years 1901–1902* (1904): 3–634.
A classic work written by one of the best known early anthropologists at Zuni.

Talayesva, Don. *Sun Chief: Autobiography of a Hopi Indian.*
    See under Published Primary Sources.

Tedlock, Barbara. *The Beautiful and the Dangerous: Encounters with the Zuni
    Indians.* New York: Viking, 1992.
    An eminent scholar of Zuni culture writes eloquently about her experiences at
Zuni by fusing anthropological data with life-story narratives, legends, and myths.

Tedlock, Dennis, trans. *Finding the Center: Narrative Poetry of the Zuni Indi-
    ans, by Andrew Peynetsa and Walter Sanchez.*
    See under Oral Traditions.

Teiwes, Helga. *Kachina Dolls: The Art of Hopi Carvers.* Tucson: University of
    Arizona Press, 1991.
    This contemporary study by a respected photographer traces recent develop-
ments in kachina carving through interviews with Hopi carvers.

Titiev, Mischa. "Old Oraibi: A Study of the Hopi Indians of Third Mesa." *Pa-
    pers of the Peabody Museum of American Archaeology and Ethnology* 22,
    no. 1 (1944).
    Although dated, this remains a classic ethnography.

Underhill, Ruth. *Life in the Pueblos.* Santa Fe: Ancient City Press, 1991. (Origi-
    nally published as *Workaday Life of the Pueblos* by the Bureau of Indian
    Affairs, 1946.)
    Overview of Pueblo life as it existed in the 1940s and before.

U.S. Claims Commission. *Commission Findings on the Pueblo Indians.* New
    York: Garland, 1974.
    Valuable document on Pueblo land and water rights.

White, Leslie. "The Pueblo of Santo Domingo." *Memoirs of the American An-
    thropological Association* 43 (1935).
    Although dated, a classic ethnography.

——. "The Pueblo of Santa Ana, New Mexico." *Memoirs of the American An-
    thropological Association* 60 (1942).
    Another classic ethnography by a major scholar.

Whiteley, Peter. *Deliberate Acts: Changing Hopi Culture Through the Oraibi
    Split.* Tucson: University of Arizona Press, 1988.

A respected scholar adds perspective to Hopi history and culture through his documentation of the division of Old Oraibi into two groups and the subsequent founding of New Oraibi.

—. *Rethinking Hopi Ethnography*. Washington, D.C.: Smithsonian Institution Press, 1998.
A scholarly contribution that examines how ethnographies about Hopi culture have been researched and recorded, with insights into the biases of the authors.

Wright, Barton. *Hopi Kachinas: The Complete Guide to Collecting Kachina Dolls*. 1977; reprint, Flagstaff: Northland Press, 1997.
For the general reader, a comprehensive guide with photographs by one of the major experts in this field.

—. *The Mythic World of the Zuni*.
See under Oral Traditions.

Young, M. Jane. *Signs from the Ancestors: Zuni Cultural Symbolism and Perceptions of Rock Art*. Albuquerque: University of New Mexico Press, 1988.
A well-known scholar of Zuni culture interprets Zuni rock art as perceived by the Zuni people, with great sensitivity.

—. "Permeable Boundaries: Ambiguity and Metaphor in Zuni Ceremonialism and Daily Life." *Southern Folklore* 48 (1998): 159–189.
Insightful treatment of subtleties in Zuni perceptions of the universe.

Quechans

See River Yumans.

River Yumans: Mojaves, Quechans (Yumas), Maricopas, Cocopahs

Bee, Robert. "Changes in Yuma Social Organization." *Ethnology* 2, no. 2 (1963): 207–227.
Bee's work provides the best introduction to the Quechan (Yuma) Indians.

—. *Crosscurrents Along the Colorado: The Impact of Government Policy on the Quechan Indians*. Tucson: University of Arizona Press, 1981.
By the foremost scholar on Quechan culture.

Castetter, Edward and Willis Bell. *Yuman Indian Agriculture.* Albuquerque: University of New Mexico Press, 1951.
　A classic study.

Crawford, James M. *Cocopah Dictionary.* Berkeley: University of California Press, 1989.

Dobyns, Henry. *The Pima-Maricopa.*
　See under O'odham.

Dobyns, Henry, Paul Ezell, Alden Jones, and Greta Ezell. "Thematic Changes in Yuman Warfare: Cultural Stability and Cultural Change." In the *Proceedings of the American Ethnological Society.* Seattle, 1957, 46–71.
　Noted scholars discuss how the motivations for and methods of River Yuman warfare changed over time.

Fontana, Bernard. "History of the Colorado River Reservation." In *Social and Economic Studies: Colorado River Reservation*, Report No. 2. Tucson: Bureau of Ethnic Research, Dept. of Anthropology, 1958, 1–66.
　Unusual because it is home to Indians from four distinct ethnic groups, the Colorado River Indian Tribes Reservation with its agricultural resources is extremely productive.

Forbes, Jack. *Warriors of the Colorado: The Yumas of the Quechan Nation and Their Neighbors.* Norman: University of Oklahoma Press, 1965.
　A good source on the Quechan and their relations with other River Yuman tribes.

Forde, Daryll. "Ethnography of the Yuma Indians." *University of California Publications in American Archaeology and Ethnology* 28, no. 4 (1931): 83–278.
　A pivotal reference on the Quechan (Yuma) Indians.

Fradkin, Philip. *A River No More: The Colorado River and the West.* New York: Knopf, 1981.
　Traces the history of the Colorado River. All River Yuman tribes practiced agriculture that was based on the annual flooding; after the Colorado River was dammed, their economies and cultures never fully recovered.

Gifford, Edward. "Yuma Dreams and Omens." *Journal of American Folk-lore* 39, no. 151 (1926): 58–69.

River Yuman peoples believed that all talents, skills, and achievements in life were derived from dreams, so this study by a scholar is of special importance to understanding River Yuman cultures.

Hackenburg, Robert and Bernard Fontana. *Aboriginal Land Use and Occupancy of the Pima-Maricopa Indians.* 2 vols. New York: Garland, 1974.
Detailed study of land use practices by the Pima and Maricopa Indians by two experts.

Harrington, John. "A Yuma Account of Origins."
See under Oral Traditions.

Hinton, Leanne and Lucille Watahomigie, eds. *Spirit Mountain: An Anthology of Yuman Story and Song.*
See under Oral Traditions.

Kelly, William. "Cocopa Attitudes and Practices with Respect to Death and Mourning." *Southwestern Journal of Anthropology* 5, no. 2 (1949): 151–164.
Probably the major ritual of the River Yumans, the mourning ceremony is a communal ritual that features songs, speeches, a mock battle, and the burning of images representing the dead.

——. "Cocopa Ethnography." *Anthropological Papers of the University of Arizona* 29. Tucson: University of Arizona Press, 1977.
A key source on Cocopah (Cocopa) culture.

Kroeber, Alfred. "Preliminary Sketch of the Mohave Indians." *American Anthropologist* 4, no. 2 (1902): 276–285.

——. "Handbook of the Indians of California." *Bureau of American Ethnology,* Bulletin 78, Washington, 1925.
A pioneer ethnologist writes about the Mojave (Mohave).

——. "Seven Mohave Myths."
See under Oral Traditions.

McNichols, Charles. *Crazy Weather.* New York: Macmillan, 1944.
Set at the beginning of the twentieth century, this novel is a fine evocation of Mojave life, including the impact of their 1857 defeat at the hands of the Akimel O'odham and Maricopas.

Spier, Leslie. *Yuman Tribes of the Gila River.* Chicago: University of Chicago Press, 1933.
Valuable ethnographic source by a respected scholar.

———. *Cultural Relations of the Gila River and Lower Colorado.* New Haven: Yale University Press, 1936.
Well-known ethnologist discusses relations between Maricopa who moved to the Gila River and other River Yuman tribes who stayed on the Colorado River.

Stewart, Kenneth. "An Account of the Mohave Mourning Ceremony." *American Anthropologist* 1947: 49, no. 1 (1947): 146–148.
Respected scholar writes about a key ceremony.

Southern Paiutes

Bunte, Pamela A. and Robert J. Franklin. *From the Sands to the Mountain: Change and Persistence in a Southern Paiute Community.* Lincoln: University of Nebraska Press, 1987.
A remarkably detailed history of the San Juan Southern Paiutes.

Euler, Robert C. *Southern Paiute Ethnohistory.* Salt Lake City: University of Utah Press, 1966.
A respected anthropologist presents history and ethnology.

———. *The Paiute People.* Phoenix, Ariz.: Indian Tribal Series, 1972.
A good overview of Paiute culture.

Franklin, Robert J. and Pamela A. Bunte. *The Paiute.* New York: Chelsea House, 1990.
Providing fine descriptions of contemporary Paiute life, this book is an excellent general source.

Holt, Ronald L. *Beneath These Red Cliffs: An Ethnohistory of the Utah Paiutes.* Albuquerque: University of New Mexico Press, 1992.
Carefully documented account of termination for the Utah Paiutes.

Kelly, Isabel T. *Southern Paiute Ethnography.* New York: Garland, 1976.
Provides basic historical and ethnographic details.

Knack, Martha C. *Life Is With People: Household Organization of the Contem-*

porary Southern Paiute Indians. Socorro, N.M.: Ballena Press, 1980.
Set in the 1970s, this book provides a glimpse of terminated communities.

Laird, Carobeth. *Encounters with an Angry God: Recollections of My Life with John Peabody Harrington.*
See Published Primary Sources.

——. *The Chemehuevis.* Banning, Calif.: Malki Museum Press, 1976.
The key ethnography on Chemehuevi culture.

——. "Behavioral Patterns in Chemehuevi Myths." In *Flowers of the Wind: Papers on Ritual, Myth, and Symbolism in California and the Southwest,* ed. Thomas Blackburn. Socorro, N.M.: Ballena Press, 1977, 97–119.
Insights from a well-respected scholar of Chemhuevi culture.

Sapir, Edward. "The Mourning Ceremony of the Southern Paiutes." *American Anthropologist* 14, no. 1 (1912): 168–169.
Influenced by River Yuman culture, many Southern Paiutes also practiced an elaborate mourning ceremony.

Southern Paiute Consortium and Bureau of Applied Research in Anthropology, University of Arizona. *ITUS, AUV, TE'EK (PAST, PRESENT, FUTURE): Managing Southern Paiute Resources in the Colorado River Corridor.* No. 4-FC-40–15260.
Report of work carried out under the Southern Paiute Consortium Cooperative Agreement with the Bureau of Reclamation to document the condition over time of cultural resources along the Southern Paiute region of the Colorado River and the surrounding land.

Stoffle, Richard W. and Michael J. Evans. *Kaibab Paiute History: The Early Years.* Kaibab Paiute Tribe, 1978.
This tribal history by an applied anthropologist was written for and with the tribe. An excellent example of how anthropologists and American Indian communities can work together in mutually beneficial ways.

Stoffle, Richard, Kristine Jones, and Henry Dobyns. "Direct European Immigrant Transmission of Old World Pathogens to Numic Indians During the Nineteenth Century."
See under General Works.

Upland Yumans: Hualapais, Havasupais, Yavapais

Barnett, Franklin. *Viola Jimulla: Indian Chieftess.* Yuma, Ariz.: Southwest
    Printers, 1968.
    Biography of a well-known leader of the Yavapai Prescott Indian Tribe from
1940 to 1966.

Braatz, Timothy. *Surviving Conquest: A History of the Yavapai Peoples.* Lincoln:
    University of Nebraska Press, 2003.
    Drawing on in-depth archival research and accounts recorded by a Yavapai
named Mike Burns, this book fills a major gap in the literature by providing a
detailed history of the four Upland Yuman–speaking peoples who have become
known collectively as the Yavapais.

Corbusier, William T. *Verde to San Carlos: Recollections of a Famous Army
    Surgeon and His Observant Family on the Western Frontier, 1869–1886.*
    See under Published Primary Sources.

Cushing, Frank Hamilton. "The Nation of the Willows."
    See under Published Primary Sources.

Dobyns, Henry F. and Robert Euler. "The Ghost Dance of 1889 Among the Pai
    Indians of Northwestern Arizona." *Prescott College Studies in Anthropol-
    ogy* 1 (1967).
    The Hualapai Indians were among the few tribes in the Southwest to adopt
the Ghost Dance, a revivalistic movement that began in Nevada with the Paiute Indians.

——. *Wauba Yuma's People: The Comparative Socio-Political Structure of the Pai
    Indians of Arizona.* Prescott, Ariz.: Prescott College Press, 1970.
    Excellent ethnographic background of the Hualapai and Havasupai.

——. *The Havasupai People.* Phoenix, Ariz.: Indian Tribal Series, 1971.
    Basic ethnography for the general reader.

——. *The Walapai People.* Phoenix, Ariz.: Indian Tribal Series, 1976.
    Basic ethnography for the general reader.

Gifford, Edward W. "The Southeastern Yavapai." *University of California Publi-
    cations in American Archaeology and Ethnology* 29, no. 3 (1932): 177–252.

——. "Northeastern and Western Yavapai." *University of California Publications in American Archaoelogy and Ethnology* 34, no. 4 (1936): 247–354.
    Gifford's works are classic ethnographies of the Yavapai.

Harrison, Mike and John Williams. "How Everything Began and How We Learned to Live Right."
    See under Oral Traditions.

Hinton, Leanne. "Vocables in Havasupai Song." In *Southwestern Indian Drama*, ed. Charlotte J. Frisbie. Santa Fe and Albuquerque: School of American Research and University of New Mexico Press, 1980, 275–306.
    Vocables are syllables that form part of the song text and are common in North American Indian music. This in-depth study of vocables in Havasupai songs also includes a good introduction to Havasupai ceremonies.

Hinton, Leanne and Lucille Watahomigie, eds. *Spirit Mountain: An Anthology of Yuman Story and Song.*
    See under Oral Traditions.

Iliff, Flora Gregg. *People of the Blue Water: My Adventures Among the Walapai and Havasupai Indians.*
    See under Published Primary Sources.

Iverson, Peter. *Carlos Montezuma and the Changing World of the American Indians.* Albuquerque: University of New Mexico Press, 1982.
    Biography of outstanding Yavapai doctor and activist, written for the general public by a respected historian.

Khera, Sigrid, ed. *The Yavapai of Fort McDowell: An Outline of Their History and Culture.* Fort McDowell, Ariz.: Fort McDowell Mohave-Apache Indian Community, 1977.
    History and culture of the Fort McDowell Yavapai by a respected ethnologist.

Khera, Sigrid and Patricia Mariella. "Long-Term Resistance to Relocation in an American Indian Community." In *Involuntary Resettlement and Migration*, ed. Art Hansen and Anthony Oliver-Smith. Denver: Westview Press, 1979, 159–178.
    Efforts to relocate a Yavapai community and their resistance over time.

Kniffen, Fred, Gordon MacGregor, Robert McKennan, Scudder Mekeel, and Maurice Mook. "Walapai Ethnography." Ed. Alfred Kroeber. *Memoirs of the American Anthropological Association* 42 (1935).
    Classic ethnography.

Ruland-Thorne, Kate. *Yavapai: The People of the Red Rocks, the People of the Sun.* Sedona: Thorne Enterprises Publications, 1993.
    Written for the general public.

Smithson, Carma Lee and Robert C. Euler. *Havasupai Legends: Religion and Mythology of the Havasupai Indians of the Grand Canyon.*
    See under Oral Traditions.

Spier, Leslie. "Havasupai Ethnography." *Anthropological Papers of the American Museum of Natural History* 29, no. 3 (1928): 81–392.
    Classic ethnography by respected anthropologist.

Watahomigie, Lucille and Akira Y. Yamamoto. "Linguists in Action: The Hualapai Bilingual/Bicultural Education Program." In *Collaborative Research and Social Change: Applied Anthropology in Action*, ed. Donald Stull and Jean Schensul. Boulder: Westview Press, 1987, 77–98.
    Account of the innovative Hualapai bilingual/bicultural program that has helped save Hualapai language and culture, by Watahomigie, who helped found the program.

Whiting, A. F. *Havasupai Habitat: A. F. Whiting's Ethnography of a Traditional Indian Culture.* Ed. Steven Weber and David Seaman. Tucson: University of Arizona Press, 1985.
    A wealth of ethnographic information about the Havasupai from material collected in the 1940s.

Yaquis

Evers, Larry and Felipe Molina. *Yaqui Deer Songs Maso Bwikam: A Native American Poetry.*
    See under Oral Traditions.

Hu-DeHart, Evelyn. *Missionaries, Miners, and Indians: Spanish Contact with the Yaqui Nation of Northwestern New Spain, 1533–1820.* Tucson: University of Arizona Press, 1981.
    Valuable history.

——. *Yaqui Resistance and Survival: The Struggle for Land and Autonomy, 1821–1910.* Madison: University of Wisconsin Press, 1984.
Continuation of previous book.

Kaczkurkin, Mini Valenzuela. *Yoeme: Lore of the Arizona Yaqui People.*
See under Oral Traditions.

Kelley, Jane Holden. *Yaqui Women: Contemporary Life Histories.*
See under Published Primary Sources.

McGuire, Thomas R. *Politics and Ethnicity on the Rio Yaqui: Potam Revisited.* Tucson: University of Arizona Press, 1986.
A noted scholar goes to one of the Yaqui's original towns before their diaspora.

Moises, Rosalio, Jane Holden Kelley, and William Curry Holden. *The Tall Candle: A Personal Chronicle of a Yaqui Indian.*
See under Published Primary Sources.

Painter, Muriel Thayer. *With Good Heart: Yaqui Beliefs and Ceremonies in Pascua Village.* Tucson: University of Arizona Press, 1986.
Based on firsthand observations over the course of four decades, a detailed account of the beliefs and ceremonies of the Yaqui Indians whose faith is a synthesis of pre-Christian and Christian beliefs.

Savala, Refugio. *Autobiography of a Yaqui Poet.*
See under Published Primary Sources.

Spicer, Edward H. *Pascua: A Yaqui Village in Arizona.* Chicago: University of Chicago Press, 1940.
Spicer's work provides a thorough introduction; he was the best known non-Yaqui scholar of Yaqui culture and history.

——. *The Yaquis: A Cultural History.* Tucson: University of Arizona Press, 1980.

——. *The People of Pascua.* Tucson: University of Arizona Press, 1988.

Trujillo, Octaviana Valenzuela. "A Tribal Approach to Language and Literacy Development in a Trilingual Setting." In *Teaching Indigenous Languages,* ed. J. Reyhner. Flagstaff: Northern Arizona University Press, 1997, 10–21.
A former chair of the Pascua Yaqui Tribe of Arizona, Trujillo is one of the foremost Yaqui scholars, especially in linguistic studies.

Yumas

See River Yumans.

8. ARTISTIC PRODUCTION

Bahti, Tom and Mark Bahti. *Southwestern Indians: Arts and Crafts, Tribes, Ceremonials.* Las Vegas: KC Publications, 1997.
Written to introduce readers to southwestern Indians' contributions to the field of crafts and fine arts, this book emphasizes the important fact that art, ways of life, and religion are inseparable parts of the whole for Native Americans. Both authors—a father and son—spent many years with the people on the reservations and have worked with Indian communities to provide educational and economic development opportunities for reservation and urban Indian groups.

Tanner, Clara Lee. *Southwest Indian Painting: A Changing Art.* 1957; Tucson: University of Arizona Press, 1980.
Written by the best-known scholar of southwestern Indian art, based on her continuous research and extensive knowledge. Many contemporary artists, obviously, are not mentioned, but the book provides an excellent foundation for understanding the history of Southwest Indian painting.

——. *Southwest Indian Craft Arts.* Tucson: University of Arizona Press, 1968.
Although somewhat dated, this is the classic book on the arts of southwestern Indians by the most respected scholar in this field in her lifetime. Also includes a list of references for further research.

9. INDIAN–NON-INDIAN INTERACTION

Biolsi, Thomas and Larry Zimmerman. *Vine Deloria, Jr., and the Critique of Anthropology.* Tucson: University of Arizona Press, 2005.
A collection of essays by Indian and non-Indian scholars who examine how the relationship between anthropology and Indian people has changed over the quarter century since Vine Deloria Jr.'s controversial book, *Custer Died for Your Sins,* which criticized the anthropological community for its impersonal dissection of living American Indian cultures.

Bordewich, Fergus M. *Killing the White Man's Indian: Reinventing Native Americans at the End of the Twentieth Century.* New York: Doubleday, 1996.

An exploration of the fallacies and myths that surrounded Native Americans (not just those in the Southwest) in the 1990s that shows how Indian people are shaping their own destinies.

Castile, George Pierre. *To Show Heart: Native American Self-Determination and Federal Indian Policy, 1960–1975.* Tucson: University of Arizona Press, 1998.
  Written by an anthropologist who worked for Lyndon B. Johnson in the Office of Economic Opportunity; the author was part of efforts to introduce programs with a greater degree of self-determination than those previously administered by the Bureau of Indian Affairs.

———. *Taking Charge: Native American Self-Determination and Federal Indian Policy, 1975–1993.* Tucson: University of Arizona Press, 2006.
  An exploration of federal Indian policy in the Carter, Reagan, and first Bush administrations, tracing developments triggered by executive and congressional action and inaction and focusing on the dynamics of self-determination.

Hall, Thomas D. *Social Change in the Southwest, 1350–1880.* Lawrence: University Press of Kansas, 1989.
  See under General Works.

Spicer, Edward H. *Cycles of Conquest: The Impact of Spain, Mexico, and the United States on the Indians of the Southwest, 1533–1960.* 1962; Tucson: University of Arizona Press, 1981.
  See under General Works.

Stoffle, Richard W., Maria Nieves Zedeno, and David B. Halmo, eds. *American Indians and the Nevada Test Site: A Model of Research and Consultation.* Washington, D.C.: U.S. Government Printing Office, 2001.
  A detailed account of the Department of Energy Nevada Operations Office American Indian Program regarding the Yucca Mountain Site Characterization Office and its interaction with sixteen tribes, three official Indian organizations, and one urban pantribal organization, representing three ethnic groups and four states.

Washburn, Wilcomb E., ed. *Handbook of North American Indians: History of Indian–White Relations.* Vol. 4. Washington, D.C.: Smithsonian Institution Press, 1988.
  Although it covers all Native American groups, a number of chapters relate to the Southwest. Articles by respected scholars as well as a 161-page list of references for further research.

10. LANGUAGE

Brandt, Elizabeth. "Native American Attitudes Toward Literacy and Recording in the Southwest." *Journal of the Linguistic Association of the Southwest* 4, no. 2 (1981): 185–195.
This journal is valuable for anyone seeking more information about languages and related issues in the Southwest.

———. "Applied Linguistic Anthropology and American Indian Language Renewal." *Human Organization* 47, no. 4 (1988): 322–329.
A valuable article that documents the continued prohibition by some fundamentalist churches against members' speaking their native languages or even attending any event at which these languages are spoken.

Goddard, Ives, ed. *Handbook of North American Indians: Languages.* Vol. 17. Washington, D.C.: Smithsonian Institution Press, 1996.
Classic series with articles by respected scholars in their fields. Subjects relate to the languages of all Native American groups, not just those in the Southwest, but a sketch of the Zuni language is included. The chapter by Michael Foster on the languages of North America includes descriptions of those spoken in the Southwest, and references for further research are cited within the text.

Zepeda, Ofelia and Jane Hill. "The Condition of Native American Languages in the United States." In *Endangered Languages*, ed. R. H. Robbins and E. M. Uhlenbeck. Oxford, England: Berg, 1991, 135–155.
Although it deals with languages throughout the United States, this book by two respected linguists (one of whom is Tohono O'odham) presents a description of the current state of southwestern Indian languages, which is one of language loss and extinction.

11. LITERATURE: NATIVE AMERICAN VOICES

Evers, Larry, ed. *The South Corner of Time: Hopi, Navajo, Papago, Yaqui Tribal Literature.* Tucson: University of Arizona Press, 1981.
Excellent collection of literature from several southwestern tribes that includes text in both Native languages and English.

———. *Spirit Mountain: An Anthology of Yuman Story and Song.* Tucson: University of Arizona Press, 1984.

Literature presented bilingually in the Indian languages and in English that includes historical accounts, stories, thoughts on education, and songs from Upland, River, and Delta Yuman peoples.

Lobo, Susan and Steve Talbot, eds. *Native American Voices: A Reader.* New York: Addison-Wesley Longman, 1998.

A varied collection of scholarly articles, journalistic selections, oral history, songs, poetry, and other documents primarily by Native American authors who cover topics such as racism, history, stereotypes, family relations, education, and spirituality. Includes authors from but is not limited to the Southwest.

Momaday, N. Scott. *House Made of Dawn.* New York: Harper and Row, 1968.

Winner of the Pulitzer Prize for Fiction in 1969, this novel is widely credited as leading the breakthrough of Native American literature into the mainstream. Like the main character, Momaday grew up on the reservation and lived both inside and outside mainstream society. Many major American Indian novelists (e.g., Leslie Marmon Silko, Gerald Vizenor, James Welch, Sherman Alexie, and Louise Erdrich) have cited this novel as a major inspiration for their own work.

Zepeda, Ofelia. *Ocean Power: Poems from the Desert.* Tucson: University of Arizona Press, 1995.

Respected scholar and poet Ofelia Zepeda centers poems on her perceptions as a contemporary Tohono O'odham woman in this first written creative work by an individual in Tohono O'odham and English, a landmark in Native American literature.

12. NATIVE RELATIONSHIPS WITH THE LAND

Basso, Keith. *Wisdom Sits in Places: Landscape and Language Among the Western Apache.* Albuquerque: University of New Mexico Press, 1995.

Demonstrates how contemporary Western Apache people use particular features of the landscape as repositories of ancient wisdom. Important historical tales with moral force are deliberately attached to particular places so that these disciplinary tales comfort or rebuke, providing guidance on how to live properly.

Evers, Larry, ed. *The South Corner of Time: Hopi, Navajo, Papago, Yaqui Tribal Literature.*

See under Literature: Native American Voices.

———. *Spirit Mountain: An Anthology of Yuman Story and Song.*
See under Literature: Native American Voices.

Kelly, Klara Bonsack and Harris Francis. *Navajo Sacred Places.* Bloomington
and Indianapolis: Indiana University Press, 1994.
Stories that Navajos tell about places that anchor the ways of Navajo life as
well as stories about the origins and the correct pursuit of those ways.

McPherson, Robert S. *Sacred Land Sacred View: Navajo Perceptions of the Four
Corners Region.* Salt Lake City: Signature Books, 1992.
Stories and underlying philosophy about the Navajo sacred geography of the
Four Corners area.

Sherry, John W. *Land, Wind, and Hard Words: A Story of Navajo Activism.*
Albuquerque: University of New Mexico Press, 2002.
An account of the founding, activities, and evolution of Diné CARE (Citizens Against Ruining Our Environment), whose original mission was to protect the Navajo forest from the ravages of industrial logging. This is a vivid
rendering of the aftermath of the mysterious death of Leroy Jackson, from an
anthropologist who was living with Jackson and Adella Begaye, the leaders of
this organization.

13. POLITICS

Deloria, Vine. "Trouble in High Places: Erosion of American Indian Rights to
Religious Freedom in the United States." In *The State of Native America:
Genocide, Colonization, and Resistance,* ed. M. Annette Jaimes. Boston:
South End Press, 1992, 267–290.

Johnson, Troy R., ed. *Contemporary Native American Political Issues.*
See under General Works.

McCool, Daniel. *Native Waters: Contemporary Indian Water Settlements and
the Second Treaty Era.* Tucson: University of Arizona Press, 2003.
Treatment of a hotly contested issue as the demands on current water sources increase in the arid Southwest.

Nielsen, Marianne O. and James W. Zion, eds. *Navajo Nation Peacemaking: Living Traditional Justice.* Tucson: University of Arizona Press,
2005.

An account of the origins, history, context, and contributions of a traditional form of conflict resolution as it is being used in the Navajo Nation justice system. Peacemaking practices rooted in Navajo culture have been modified to take into account present-day issues and resources.

Peregoy, Robert, Walter Echo-Hawk, and James Botsford. "Congress Overturns Supreme Court's Peyote Ruling." *Native American Rights Fund Legal Review* 20, no. 1 (1995): 1, 6–25.
   The use of peyote as a sacrament in the Native American Church continues to be challenged.

Washburn, Wilcomb E., ed. *Handbook of North American Indians: History of Indian–White Relations.*
   See under General Works.
   See also titles under each tribe/nation.

14. RELIGION

Painter, Muriel Thayer. *With Good Heart: Yaqui Beliefs and Ceremonies in Pascua Village.* Tucson: University of Arizona Press, 1986.
   Along with the work of Edward Spicer, this is the most detailed study of the Easter ceremony that stands at the heart of Yaqui culture.

Parsons, Elsie Clews. *Pueblo Indian Religion.* 2 vols. 1939; reprint, Lincoln: University of Nebraska Press, 1996.
   Major contribution by a respected scholar of her day to the study of Pueblo religion.

Reichard, Gladys A. *Navaho Religion: A Study of Symbolism.* Bollingen Series XVIII. 1950; reprint, Princeton: Princeton University Press, 1974.
   Although dated, a classic study that breaks Navajo religion into categories such as ritual, pantheon of supernaturals, and symbolic content.
   See also entries under each tribe/nation.

15. WARFARE

Fried, Morton, Marvin Harris, and Robert Murphy, eds. *War: The Anthropology of Armed Conflict and Aggression.* Garden City, N.Y.: Natural History Press, 1968.

Useful anthropological perspectives on war; not specifically about the Southwest.

Goodwin, Grenville. *Western Apache Raiding and Warfare.* Ed. Keith Basso. Tucson: University of Arizona Press, 1971.
Account of Western Apache raiding and warfare with detailed description of the distinction between these two categories.

Kroeber, Clifton B. and Bernard L. Fontana. *Massacre on the Gila: An Account of the Last Major Battle Between American Indians, with Reflections on the Origin of War.* 1986; reprint, Tucson: University of Arizona Press, 1992.
Account of River Yuman warfare, which was unique among American Indian cultures because it appeared to be without economic or political motivation.

Nettleship, Martin A., ed. *War: Its Causes and Correlates.* The Hague and Paris: Mouton, 1975.
Though not about the southwestern Indians, this book presents useful perspectives on the causes of war.
See also entries under each tribe/nation, with particular attention to River Yumans.

16. FILMS

Allan Houser Haozous: The Lifetime Work of an American Master. Santa Fe: Allan Houser, Inc., n.d.
Moving account of the life, beliefs, and art of the Chiricahua Apache sculptor, with much cultural background about the Chiricahua people. Houser was the first Chiricahua born after their captivity ended in 1914.

Broken Rainbow. Mario Florio and Victorio Mudd, writers and producers. Los Angeles: Direct Cinema, 1986.
Narrated by Martin Sheen, this film tells the heartbreaking story of the Navajo-Hopi land dispute and relocation, from the Navajo perspective.

"A Clash of Cultures." Part I of *How the West Was Lost.* Bethesda, Md.: Discovery Communications, 1993.
A compelling account of the Long Walk in the 1860s when the Navajos were exiled to Bosque Redondo, New Mexico. The story is told from the Navajo

perspective, through interviews with descendants of those who went through this ordeal.

The Heard Museum: Native Cultures and Art. Phoenix, Ariz.: The Heard Museum, 1995.
A behind-the-scenes view of the Heard Museum and its programs, with interviews from Native Americans who design exhibits and display their works.

Hopi Songs of the Fourth World. Wayne, N.J.: New Day Films, 1984.
An outstanding film that portrays Hopi culture and life.

In the Heart of Big Mountain. Sandra Sunrising Osawa, writer, producer, narrator. Seattle: Upstream Productions, 1988.
The story of the Navajo relocation resisters.

Kinaaldá: Navajo Rite of Passage. Lena Carr. New York: Women Make Movies, 2002.
A documentation of the Navajo Girl's Puberty Ceremony.

Navajo. Flagstaff: Museum of Northern Arizona, 1982.
Life in a Navajo family with attention to tribal history, culture, and spiritual practices.

Pride and the Power to Win. Tucson, Ariz.: Presidio Film Group, 1990.
Moving account of how Baboquivari High School on the Tohono O'odham reservation evaluated and improved the quality of its education and the performance of its students through community involvement based on their traditional culture. Filmed in the late 1980s.

Ritual Clowns. Victor Masayesva, director. IS Productions. New Television Workshop, 1988.
A short film by the best-known Hopi filmmaker who uses graphics and technological devices to portray the role of clowns in Hopi ceremonial life.

Seasons of a Navajo. Tempe, Ariz.: KAET, PBS Video, 1997.
Narrated by Navajos Chauncey and Dorothy Neboyia, who share their life over the course of a year, including their children and grandchildren, who live in tract homes and attend public schools.

Southwest Indian Pottery. Mesa, Ariz.: Eager Outdoor Video Productions, n.d.

Potters from Santa Clara, San Ildefonso, Tesuque, Zuni, and Zia Pueblos and a Navajo potter demonstrate and discuss the process of pottery making. Although not quite of professional quality, this video is charming in its naturalness.

The Sunrise Dance. Gianfranco Norelli, director. Educational Resources, 1994.

An excellent video of the Western Apache Girl's Puberty Ceremony, or Sunrise Dance, on the White Mountain Apache Reservation, with interviews of the participants, who explain what the ceremony means to them.

Weave of Time: The Story of a Navajo Family 1938–1986. Los Angeles: Direct Cinema, 1981.

This outstanding film, based on the work of anthropologist John Adair, provides a moving and accurate portrayal of Navajo life from just before World War II to modern times.

17. MUSEUMS AND SITES

Arizona

Amerind Foundation, Dragoon
Arizona Historical Society, Tucson
Arizona State Museum, University of Arizona, Tucson
Besh-Ba-Gowah, Globe
Canyon de Chelly, Chinle
Casa Grande National Monument, Coolidge
Colorado River Indian Tribes Museum, Parker
Fort Bowie National Historic Site, 13 miles south of Bowie
Gila River Indian Museum, Sacaton
Grand Canyon National Park
The Heard Museum, Phoenix
Hopi Cultural Center and Museum, Second Mesa
Kinishba Pueblo, Whiteriver
Montezuma Castle National Monument, south of Flagstaff
The Museum of Northern Arizona, Flagstaff
Navajo Nation Museum, Library, and Visitor's Center, Window Rock
Navajo National Monument, northwest of Tuba City
Ned Hatathli Cultural Center, Diné College, Tsaile
Oraibi Pueblo, southeast of Tuba City
Pipe Spring National Monument, Pipe Spring

Pueblo Grande Museum, Phoenix
San Xavier del Bac Mission, Tucson
The Tohono O'odham Museum and Cultural Center, Topawa, near Sells,
     60 miles west of Tucson
Tonto National Monument, northwest of Globe
Tumacacori National Historical Park, 48 miles south of Tucson
Tuzigoot National Monument, northwest of Cottonwood
Walnut Canyon National Monument, southeast of Flagstaff
Walpi Pueblo, southeast of Tuba City
Wupatki National Monument, northeast of Flagstaff

New Mexico

Abo State Monument, southeast of Albuquerque
Anthropology Museum, Eastern New Mexico University, Portales
A:shiwi A:wan Museum and Heritage Center, Zuni
Aztec Ruins National Monument, Aztec
Bandelier National Monument, Los Alamos
Blackwater Draw Museum, north of Portales
Chaco Canyon National Monument, Bloomfield
Coronado State Monument, Bernalillo
El Morro National Monument, El Morro
Fort Sumner Memorial
Gallup Museum of Indian Arts, Gallup
Gila Cliff Dwellings National Monument, Gila Hot Springs
Gran Quivira National Monument
Indian Pueblo Cultural Center, Albuquerque
Institute of American Indian Arts Museum, Santa Fe
Jemez State Monument, southwest of Los Alamos
Jicarilla Apache Tribal Museum, Dulce
Kwilleylekia Ruins Monsument, Cliff
Laguna Pueblo
Maxwell Museum of Anthropology, The University of New Mexico, Albuquerque
Mescalero Apache Cultural Center, Mescalero
Miles Museum, Eastern New Mexico University, Portales
Millicent Rogers Museum, Taos
Museum of Indian Arts and Culture, Santa Fe
New Mexico State University Museum, New Mexico State University,
     Las Cruces
The Palace of the Governors, Santa Fe
Pecos National Monument, Pecos

Picuris Pueblo
Poeh Cultural Center, Santa Fe
Puye Cliff Ruins, Santa Clara Indian Reservation
Red Rock Museum, Church Rock
Salmon Ruins Museum, west of Bloomfield
San Ildefonso Pueblo Museum, Santa Fe
San Juan Pueblo
Sandia Man Cave, northeast of Albuquerque
Santa Clara Pueblo
Sky City Cultural Center and HAAK'U Museum (Acoma Pueblo)
Taos Pueblo
Walatowa Visitors Center, Jemez Pueblo
The Wheelwright Museum of the American Indian, Santa Fe
Zia Pueblo

18. TRIBAL NEWSPAPERS AND NEWSLETTERS

Jicarilla Chieftain (Jicarilla Apache)
Navajo-Hopi Observer
The Navajo Times
Qua'Toqti: The Eagle's Call (Hopi)
The Runner (Tohono O'odham)
Tutuveni (Hopi)
The Yaqui Bulletin

19. INDIAN TRIBES AND NATIONS IN THE SOUTHWEST

Acoma Pueblo
P.O. Box 309
Acomita, NM 87034
(505) 552–6604

Administration of Indian Affairs
Bureau of Indian Affairs
1849 C Street, NW
Washington, DC 20240–0001

Ak-Chin Indian Community
42507 W. Peters and Nall Rd.

Maricopa, AZ 85239
(623) 568–2618

Bureau of Indian Affairs
Public Inquiries
Phoenix, AZ
(602) 379–6780

Chemehuevi Indian Tribe
P.O. Box 1976
Chemehuevi Valley, CA 92362
(760) 858–4301

Cochiti Pueblo
P.O. Box 70
Cochiti, NM 87072
(505) 465–2245

Cocopah Tribe
Ave. G and Co. Fifteenth
Somerton, AZ 85350
(928) 627–2061

Colorado River Indian Tribes
Rt. 1
Box 23-B
Parker, AZ 85344
(928) 669–9211

Fort Apache Agency
P.O. Box 700
Whiteriver, AZ 85941
(928) 338–4346

Fort McDowell Yavapai Tribe
P.O. Box 17779
Fountain Hills, AZ 85269
(480) 837–5121

Fort Mojave Indian Tribe
500 Merriman Ave.
Needles, CA 92363
(760) 326–4591

Fort Yuma Quechan Tribe
P.O. Box 11352
Yuma, AZ 85366
(928) 572–0213

Gila River Indian Community
P.O. Box 97
Sacaton, AZ 85247
(480) 562–3311

Havasupai Tribe
P.O. Box 10
Supai, AZ 85435
(928) 448–2731

Hia C-ed O'odham Program
Sells, AZ 85634
(520) 383–4780

Hopi Tribe
P.O. Box 123
Kykotsmovi, AZ 86039
(928) 734–2441

Hualapai Tribe
P.O. Box 179
Peach Springs, AZ 86434
(928) 769–2216

Isleta Pueblo
P.O. Box 1270
Isleta, NM 87022
(505) 869–3111

Jemez Pueblo
P.O. Box 100
Jemez, NM 87024
(505) 834–7359

Jicarilla Apache Tribe
P.O. Box 507
Dulce, NM 85728
(505) 759–3242

Kaibab Paiute Tribe
HC 65
Box 2
Fredonia, AZ 86022
(928) 643–7245

Laguna Pueblo
P.O. Box 194
Laguna, NM 87026
(505) 552–6654

Mescalero Apache Tribe
P.O. Box 227
Mescalero, NM 88340
(928) 671–4494

Nambé Pueblo
Route 1
Box 117-BB
Santa Fe, NM 87501
(505) 455–2036

Navajo Nation
P.O. Box 9000
Window Rock, AZ 86515
(928) 871–6352

Pascua Yaqui Tribe
7474 S. Camino De Oeste
Tucson, AZ 85746
(520) 883–1052

Picuris Pueblo
P.O. Box 127
Penasco, NM 87533
(505) 587–2519

Pojoaque Pueblo
Route 11
Box 71
Santa Fe, NM 87501
(505) 455–2278

Salt River Pima-Maricopa Indian Community
Route 1
Box 216

Scottsdale, AZ 85256
(480) 941–7277

San Carlos Apache Tribe
P.O. Box "O"
San Carlos, AZ 85550
(928) 475–2361

San Felipe Pueblo
P.O. Box 4339
San Felipe, NM 87001
(505) 867–3381

San Ildefonso Pueblo
Route 5
P.O. Box 315-A
Santa Fe, NM 87501
(505) 455–2273

San Juan Pueblo
P.O. Box 1099
San Juan, NM 87566
(505) 852–4400

San Juan Southern Paiute Tribe
P.O. Box 1989
Tuba City, AZ 86045
(928) 283–4589

Sandia Pueblo
P.O. Box 6008
Bernalillo, NM 87004
(505) 867–3317

Santa Ana Pueblo
2 Dove Rd.
Bernalillo, NM 87004
(505) 867–3301

Santa Clara Pueblo
P.O. Box 580

Espanola, NM 87532
(505) 753-7330

Santo Domingo Pueblo
P.O. Box 99
Santo Domingo, NM 87072
(505) 465-2214

Taos Pueblo
P.O. Box 1846
Taos, NM 87571
(505) 758-9593

Tesuque Pueblo
Route 5
Box 360-T
Santa Fe, NM 87501
(505) 983-2667

Tohono O'odham Nation
  Cultural Affairs Office
P.O. Box 837
Sells, AZ 85634
(520) 383-4769; 383-2221

Tonto Apache Tribe
#30 Tonto Apache Reservation
Payson, AZ 85541

(928) 474-5000

White Mountain Apache Tribe
Fort Apache Indian Reservation
P.O. Box 700
Whiteriver, AZ 85941
(928) 338-4346

Yavapai-Apache Nation
3435 Shaw Ave.
P.O. Box 1188
Camp Verde, AZ 86322
(928) 567-3649

Yavapai-Prescott Indian Tribe
530 E. Merritt
Prescott, AZ 86301
(928) 445-8790

Zia Pueblo
General Delivery
San Ysidro, NM 87053
(505) 867-3304

Zuni Pueblo
P.O. Box 339
Zuni, NM 87327
(505) 782-4481

20. INTERNET SOURCES

Ak-Chin Indian Community
  www.itcaonline.com/Tribes/akchin.htm
Bureau of Indian Affairs
  www.doi.gov.bureau-indian-affairs.html
Chemehuevi Tribe
  www.csusm.edu/bbiggs/loc/rezinfo/chemehuevi
Cocopah Tribe
  www.cocopah.com
Colorado River Indian Tribes
  Members.tripod.com/~CRIT/

Fort McDowell Mohave-Apache Indian Community
    www.ftmcdowell.org
Fort Mojave Tribe
    www.itcaonline/Tribes/mojave.htm
Gila River Indian Community
    www.gilariver.com
Havasupai Tribe
    www.itcaonline.com/Tribes/havasupa.htm
Hopi Tribe
    www.hopi.nsn.us
Hualapai Tribe
    www.itcaonline.com/Tribes/hualapai.htm
Index of Native American Resources on the Internet
    http://hanksville.phasts.umass.edu/misc/Naresources.html
NativeWeb
    www.nativeweb.org
Navajo Nation
    www.navajo.org
Pascua Yaqui Tribe
    www.itcaonline.com/Tribes/pascua.htm
Quechan Tribe
    www.itcaonline.com/Tribes/quechan.htm
Salt River Pima-Maricopa Indian Community
    www.saltriver.pima-maricopa.nsn.us
San Carlos Apache Tribe
    www.itcaonline.com/Tribes/sancarl.htm
San Juan Southern Paiute Tribe
    www.itcaonline.com/Tribes/sanjuan/htm
Tohono O'odham Nation
    www.itcaonline.com/Tribes/tohono.htm
Tonto Apache Tribe
    www.itcaonline.com/Tribes/tonto.htm
White Mountain Apache Tribe
    www.wmat.nsn.us
Yavapai-Apache Tribe
    www.yavapai-apache-nation.com
Yavapai-Prescott Tribe
    www.itcaonline.com/Tribes/yavapai.htm
Zuni Tribe
    www.zuni.org.hk

INDEX

Field Peas to Foie Gras

Southern Recipes with a French Accent

Jennifer Hill Booker

Photography by

Deborah Whitlaw Llewellyn

PELICAN PUBLISHING COMPANY
Gretna 2014

The word "Pelican" and the depiction of a pelican are
trademarks of Pelican Publishing Company, Inc., and are
registered in the U.S. Patent and Trademark Office.

ISBN: 9781455619726
E-book ISBN: 9781455619733

Produced by Pinafore Press / Janice Shay
Food styling by Jennifer Hill Booker
Index by Sara LeVere
Additional editing by Cameron Spencer
and Michelle Menner

Photographs on pages 63, 83, 92, and 149 were taken at the
Community of Serenbe, near Newnan, GA

Printed in China

Published by Pelican Publishing Company, Inc.
1000 Burmaster Street, Gretna, Louisiana 70053

This book is dedicated with love and admiration to:
Ida Belle, Bessie Lee, and LaVerne,
three of the best cooks I know;
and to
Jenelle, Regine, Derrick, and Evette,
my daily motivators;
and, of course, to
Fifi, Erin, and Chelle—
thank you for years of dishwashing, hauling boxes,
and helping me fulfill my dreams.

I love you all.

Contents

Getting Here from There

This book is inspired by my childhood on my family's farm in Charleston, Mississippi, and, later, by my Le Cordon Bleu culinary training in Paris, France. I found surprising similarities between the Southern food I grew up with and classical French cuisine, such as the use of every part of the pig to flavor soups, stews, salads, and greens; preferring to use fresh, local, farm-raised ingredients; and slow-cooking meats such as venison or rabbit with wine to bring out the flavor. These recipes are sprinkled with my memories of growing up on a farm, then living and studying in Europe.

My Southern heritage gave me a very strong foundation in growing, harvesting, and cooking, while my formal French culinary training allowed me to expand my palate and present food in a more aesthetically pleasing way. These combined experiences have added to and greatly benefited my culinary career and have contributed to the many home recipes in this book.

My path to Paris and a career as a personal chef and culinary educator was fueled by a lifelong passion for cooking. As a child, I watched as my grandmother cooked traditional Southern dishes and my mother cooked all sorts of regional and ethnic foods. I tuned in to Julia Child's television show every Sunday—our version of *Top Chef*. I began checking out cookbooks and feeding our family in my early teens, and my sister Naomi still complains about the amount of dishes she had to wash after one of my meals!

A high school graduation trip to Paris opened my senses to the smells, flavors, and beauty of French food, and I looked for some connection to the Southern food I had grown up with and knew so well. Discovering that the French sourced their food locally and ate seasonally just as we did on the farm gave me the courage to go to culinary school to learn to cook the incredible dishes I had experienced in Europe. While studying culinary arts at Oklahoma State University, I was delighted that my teachers were French and Swiss. After graduation, I married a military man and we moved to Germany. I decided to be a personal chef there as a way to continue my culinary career while living in Germany. I cooked

American food for the couples on base who missed the food back home, and taught German families how to cook American dishes. They raved about my food to friends, and I got a lot of business and an unofficial start as a culinary educator. It gave me a creative outlet for the times my husband was deployed, which was often. I began to keep a database of recipes, which led to writing many of these recipes. When we were moved to Heidelburg, I applied for a continuing education scholarship and received it. I saved all I could and applied to Le Cordon Bleu in Paris and was accepted. I remember arguing with the admissions director that I should start in the intermediate courses, but she insisted that I had to start at the beginning. I'm glad I did! The lectures and demonstrations were taught in French, and by the time I left, I was fluent in the language.

There is an assumption, more often than not, that because I am a black chef I must only know how to cook Southern food, and that I have no culinary training. Neither assumption is true. Southern food has a rich history that is firmly rooted in tradition and, yes, originally cooked by blacks, both slaves and Freemen. But I did not set out to strictly be a Southern chef and do not make my living cooking only Southern food. I would, however, be remiss if I didn't acknowledge the huge influence African food has had on Southern cuisine. Okra, black-eyed peas, yams—these all came to us from Africa. I grew up enjoying traditional Southern black dishes, such as hoe cakes, cracklin' bread, hog head cheese, chicken feet, and fried squirrel (all are included in this cookbook). Although these dishes are not part of French cuisine, they are my culinary heritage, and I have attempted to refine them by making them healthier and using modern cooking techniques. Thankfully, we don't need to cook hoe cakes on a hoe heated on the open fire anymore!

Interestingly, I found that any prejudice in commercial kitchens is more about gender than color. My Paris Le Cordon Bleu instructors were especially tough on women, letting us know that they thought of us as housewives and felt we had no place in their kitchens. After a particularly tough critique, I would sometimes go to the bathroom to cry—I didn't want to be perceived as an emotional

female, so I never let them see me cry. At the beginning of the classes, there were a large number of female American students, but almost all dropped out eventually, due in large part to the rigorous schedule.

When I graduated, I received top honors for *base de cuisine*, and I was determined to be a woman in the kitchen, regardless of the prevailing sentiment. I live in Atlanta now, and things have changed a lot in the food world. I am proud to stand with a spectacular group of female chefs. In 2012, I had the honor of being inducted into the prestigious Atlanta chapter of Les Dames d' Escoffier International (LDEI), an elite group of women in the culinary profession that includes chefs, business owners, authors, and farmers. We promote education and philanthropy for our communities. I also co-chair Green Tables, a farm and garden philanthropic initiative of LDEI. Its purpose is to provide a link between urban and rural farmers, to promote the planting of gardens in urban communities, and for schools, restaurants, and kitchen tables.

In 2004, I was hired to teach at the new Le Cordon Bleu campus in Atlanta, Georgia. Within six months, I was promoted to lead chef instructor and given my own classroom for *garde manger*, which means "keeper of the food." I taught the traditional methods of canning, preserving, cheese and sausage making, terrines, cold soups, and salads. This teaching job led to a directorship of the culinary arts program at Grayson High School in Atlanta, which became the first accredited culinary high school program in the state of Georgia.

I was recently honored by being chosen as one of four Georgia Grown Executive Chefs—and the only black female chosen by the Georgia Commission of Agriculture and the Georgia Restaurant Association. I have come full circle back to my Southern roots, and when I teach or give cooking demonstrations, I often use the staples of Southern food to show students similarities to French cooking techniques.

This cookbook, I hope, reflects the best of both cuisines. The recipes are culled from my childhood and my culinary experiences, working and teaching, and our favorite family meals. I hope you enjoy them as much as I do!

(Clockwise fromt top left) The author at age 3; At the Seine river in Paris, France, 2008; Big Mama (great grandmother Ida Belle Metcalf) with her infant son, Tommy Lee, 1910; Eiffel Tower, Paris, 1998.

Glossary

French Terms for Southern Cooks

Baguette: a long, thin loaf of French bread.

Braise: to cook tough cuts of meat in liquid after browning it in oil.

La Boucherie: a butcher shop.

Le Chocolat Chaud: hot chocolate, or cocoa.

Charcuterie: turning meats, usually pork, into bacon, sausages, hams, and other cured meats.

Chantilly Cream: whipped cream that has been flavored with vanilla and sweetened with powdered sugar.

Compote: stewed fruit with water and spices added; served with biscuits, rolls, and as a topping for ice cream.

Croquette: a round meat patty coated in breadcrumbs or corn meal, and fried in oil. Can be made of meat, fish, or mashed potatoes.

Croissant: similar to a crescent roll, but made of many buttery, flaky layers.

Crudités: Raw vegetables, cut up and served as a snack or appetizer, usually with a dip or sauce.

Foie Gras: a fattened goose or duck liver, quickly seared in a hot pan and served on toasted bread.

Galette: a free-formed pie made on a cookie sheet instead of in a pie pan.

Herbs de Provence: a mixture of dried herbs used in cooking, usually containing savory, marjoram, rosemary, thyme, oregano, and lavender leaves. Used in stews, meats, and on fish.

Lardon: bacon cut into strips or cubes, cooked, and used in soups, stews, and on salads.

Meringue: whipped egg whites and sugar, used to top a pie or pudding; can also be baked into a light, crisp cookie.

Nappé: a sauce or gravy thick enough to coat the back of a spoon without running.

Roux: used to make gravies and thicken sauces; made of lard, bacon grease, or butter and flour.

Ragout: a stew made of well-seasoned meat or vegetables, cooked in a thick sauce.

Terrine: a pork meatloaf served cold or room temperature, usually with crackers.

Vinaigrette: a quick salad dressing made with oil, vinegar, fresh herbs, and a pinch of salt.

Jellies, Jams, And Preserves

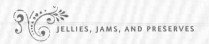
A Basic Guide to Canning and Preserving

Canning, or jarring, started as a way of preserving foods so they could be kept and eaten later, usually during the winter months when particular foods were scarce. Adding sugar, salt, and acids, like lemon juice and vinegar, helped the foods last longer. Pickles, preserves, jellies, and relishes are just a few of the fruits and vegetables we continue to preserve, not out of necessity, but because we've grown to love their taste. On a farm, preserving foods is a way of life. When crops were harvested, part of it was used to feed the family, part stored to feed the livestock, and the rest was cooked and placed in ceramic crocks or packed into glass jars, processed in boiling water and kept in a cool, dark place until needed. Produce in season is at the peak of flavor and nutritional value, and generally less expensive than at any other time of year. Canning fresh produce to enjoy again later—turning apples into applesauce, berries into compote, pears into preserves—is an easy, fun process with a few simple rules.

Cleaning and Sterilizing

The two most important steps in canning and preserving are Cleaning & Sterilizing and Processing. An important point to remember is that all jams, jellies, and pickled products that have been processed less than 10 minutes should be stored in sterile empty jars. Follow these simple rules to clean and sterilize your jars.

Cleaning

Wash empty jars, lids, and rings in hot water with detergent and rinse well, either by hand, or in a hot dishwasher. These washing methods do not sterilize jars, but you must begin with a well-cleaned jar before the sterilizing step.

Sterilization of Empty Jars

To sterilize the cleaned jars, set them right-side-up on the rack in a boiling-water canner pot, or on a towel inside a large stockpot.

Fill the pot and the jars with hot, but not boiling, water to cover the tops of the jars by 1 inch. Bring the pot to a boil and boil for 10 minutes. At altitudes of more than 1,000 feet, boil 1 additional minute for each additional 1,000 feet elevation. Using sterile tongs, remove and drain the hot sterilized jars and allow them to cool on a clean cooling rack or towel.

Processing

In this step, the sterilized jar is filled with food; leaving ½-inch empty space, or head space, inside the top of the jar; all air bubbles are removed by pressing the food down and re-moving them with a Bubble Remover or chopstick; then the jar is sealed with the lid and collar, and placed in a pot of water that is slowly heated to boiling for a specified time (see chart on the opposite page). This destroys any microorganisms that are naturally present in food and may have entered the jars when filling. Boiling also allows gases and air to vent from the jar, creating an airtight vacuum seal. As the filled jars cool, this step prevents your canned items from being re-contaminated. Whether you use a hot water canner or a stockpot with a lid, you must place a rack or thick towel in the bottom of the pot to keep the jars away from direct heat.

All high-acid foods like fruit jams, jellies, and preserves, marmalades, chutneys, fruit butters, and anything pickled with vinegar, such as pickles and relish, must go through this hot-water processing bath to create a vacuum and kill off any potentially harmful bacteria.

Low acid foods, such as non-pickled vegetables (except tomatoes), dried beans, meats, and poultry, must be processed in a pressure canner.

When canning in boiling water, more processing time is needed for most raw-packed foods and for quart jars than is needed for hot-packed foods and pint jars.

To destroy microorganisms in acidic foods processed in a boiling-water canner, you must process jars for the correct number of minutes in boiling water and cool the jars at room temperature on a cooling rack or thick towel. The food may spoil if you fail to add processing time for lower boiling temperatures at altitudes above 1,000 feet. Process for fewer minutes than specified, or cool the jars in cold water.

Allow the jars to cool for 12 to 24 hours, then remove the screw bands and test the seals. To loosen a ring band that sticks, cover it with a hot, damp cloth, or run the lid under hot water for 1 to 2 minutes.

You can test the seals in one of the following ways: Press the middle of the lid with your finger; if the lid remains firm when you release your finger, the lid is sealed. You can also tap the lid with the bottom of a teaspoon. If it makes a ringing, high-pitched sound, the seal is tight. Finally, you can hold the jar at eye level and look across the top. The lid should be concave, curving slightly down in the center, to ensure a proper seal. If a lid fails to seal properly, you should remove the lid and check both the lid and the lip of the jar for tiny nicks or scratches

If a small amount of liquid has been lost from sealed jars do not open them to replace it. If the jar is sealed and the liquid is only slightly below the level of the food, the food is safe. Plan to use these jars first, as the food may discolor. If a large amount of liquid has been lost, refrigerate and use the product in 2 to 3 days, freeze and use within one month, or reprocess the contents. To reprocess, empty the contents of the jar into a saucepan and bring to a boil. Fill clean, hot jars and process according to the prescribed method for the full length of time recommended. Use these jars first, as the quality will be lower than those processed only once.

Preventing Spoilage

Although sugar helps preserve jellies and jams, molds can grow on the surface of these products. Research now indicates that the mold which people usually scrape off the surface of jellies may not be as harmless as it seems. Mycotoxins have been found in some jars of jelly with surface mold growth. Mycotoxins are known to cause cancer in animals, but their effect on humans is still being researched.

Because of possible mold contamination, paraffin or wax seals are no longer recommended for any sweet spread, including jellies.

Indications of food spoilage include: **broken seals, seepage, mold growth, yeast growth, gassiness, fermentation, spurting liquid when the jar is opened, sliminess, cloudiness, and/or disagreeable odors.**

Storage

Properly canned food stored in a cool, dry place will retain optimal quality for at least 1 year. Canned food stored in a warm place, such as near hot pipes, a range, a furnace, or in direct sunlight, may lose some of its taste quality in a few weeks or months, depending on the temperature. Dampness may corrode metal lids and cause leakage that will spoil the food, so it's best to store in a cool, dark place.

Tips for Success

1. Use only peak produce; cut off and discard soft or discolored parts of the fruit or vegetable.
2. Fill jars with same-sized food pieces for even processing.
3. Keep workspace and equipment very clean to reduce the risk of contamination in your food jars.
4. Do not over-tighten the bands. Over-tightening can prevent air venting from the jars, resulting in buckled lids or seal failure.

Basic Canning Equipment

A large, tall pot
A rack to fit inside the pot or thick kitchen towel
Canning jars with lids and bands
A timer
Jar lifter or tongs
Long handled spoons
Rubber spatulas
Jar funnel
Bubble Remover or chopstick

Processing Times

For altitudes of 0–3000 feet, using pint and quart jars

Applesauce: 20 minutes /25 minutes
Berries: 20 minutes/25 minutes
Plums: 25 minutes/ 30 minutes
Peaches: 30 minutes/35 minutes
Fruit Purees and Compotes: 20 minutes/20 minutes
Pears: 25 minutes/30 minutes
Figs: 50 minutes/55 minutes
Oranges: 15 minutes/15 minutes
Fruit Jellies, Jams and Syrups: 10 minutes/10 minutes
Pickles: 15 minutes/20 minutes
Pickled Green Tomato Relish: 15 minutes/20 minutes
Pickled Beets: 35 minutes/35 minutes
Hot Pepper Relish: 15 minutes/15 minutes
Pickled Peppers: 10 minutes/10 minutes

Applesauce

Yields 4 pints, or 8 cups

Some of my favorite smells: fresh apples, spicy cinnamon, and fragrant lemon—that's exactly what this recipe
tastes like. Applesauce tastes best paired with something salty, such as Fresh Pork Sausage (recipe, p. 125).

6 pounds apples, peeled, cored,
    and coarsely chopped
2 tablespoons fresh lemon juice
1 cup light brown sugar, firmly
    packed
1 teaspoon cinnamon

Combine the apples, lemon juice, brown sugar, and cinnamon
with 1 cup water in a large stockpot over medium heat. Bring to
a simmer and cook for 25 minutes, stirring occasionally. Taste
and adjust the sweetness with additional sugar, if needed.

Ladle the hot applesauce into hot sterilized jars (see Cleaning
and Sterilizing, p. 16), leaving ½-inch headspace. Wipe the rims
clean, add lids, and secure the bands until the fit is fingertip tight.

Process the jars in boiling water (see Processing, p. 16), then remove
and let cool. Jars may be stored in a cool, dark place for up to 1 year.

Blackberry Sauce

Yields 4 pints, or 8 cups

4 pounds fresh blackberries
3 cups sugar
¼ cup fresh lemon juice
1 teaspoon finely grated
    lemon zest

Bring the blackberries and sugar to simmer in a large saucepan
over medium-high heat, and simmer for 15 minutes, stirring often.
Skim off any foam that gathers on top of the berries. Stir in the
lemon juice and zest and cook an additional 5 minutes.

Ladle the blackberry sauce into hot sterilized jars (see Cleaning
and Sterilizing, p. 16), leaving ½-inch headspace. Wipe the rims
clean, add lids, and secure the bands until the fit is fingertip tight.

Process the jars in boiling water (see Processing, p. 16), then remove and let cool. Jars may be stored in a cool, dark place for up
to 1 year.

Use Blackberry Sauce as a topping for ice cream, pound cakes,
or as a filling for cobblers and pies.

Peaches in Syrup

Yields 4 pints, or 8 cups

Peaches preserved in syrup taste as close to fresh as you can get. Use what's called a "non-melting" or firm-fleshed peach for this recipe. The hard flesh stays firm and crispy even when fully ripe. You can turn these peaches into cobblers, add them to ice cream, and use them to garnish cakes for a fresh-from-the-tree taste.

4 pounds fresh peaches

¼ cup fresh lemon juice

4½ cups sugar

Fill a large stockpot half full of water and bring to a rolling boil over high heat.

In a large bowl, stir together 1 quart ice water and the fresh lemon juice.

Using a slotted spoon, submerge a whole peach into the boiling water for about 30 seconds, then drop it into the iced lemon water to loosen the skin. Carefully remove the peach from the ice water and slide the skin off. Repeat this for all the peaches. Halve the peaches, remove their pits, and scrape away any red fibers from around the pit. These red fibers can cause the jarred peaches to discolor. Return the peeled peach halves to the lemon water.

Combine the sugar and 4½ cups water in a large saucepan and bring to a boil over high heat, stirring until the sugar is dissolved. Skim the foam from the top if necessary. Reduce the heat to low to keep the syrup warm, but not hot enough to let the syrup brown.

Drain the peaches, pat dry, and pack them, cut-side down, into hot sterilized jars (see Cleaning and Sterilizing, p. 16), leaving ½-inch headspace. Wipe the rims clean, add lids, and secure the bands until the fit is fingertip tight.

Process the jars in boiling water (see Processing, p. 16), then remove and let cool. Jars may be stored in a cool, dark place for up to 1 year.

Cranberry Orange Relish

Yields 2 pints, or 4 cups

This relish is easy to make and delicious year-round. Serve it as a condiment with grilled sausages, as a topping on fresh baked biscuits and rolls, and, of course, as a side with roasted turkey and dressing.

1 cup fresh cranberries, rinsed

1 cup dried, unsweetened cranberries

½ cup sugar

½ cup light brown sugar

¾ cup freshly squeezed orange juice

2 oranges, peeled and segmented

1 teaspoon orange zest

4 teaspoons fresh lemon juice

1 pinch sea salt

Combine the fresh and dried cranberries, the sugars, orange juice, and ¾ cup water in a medium-sized, heavy-bottom stainless steel saucepan. Over high heat, bring the pot just to boil, then reduce the heat to low and simmer for 15 minutes, stirring occasionally.

When the fresh cranberries burst, add the orange segments, orange zest, lemon juice, and salt and continue to simmer for an additional 15 minutes, until the compote thickens and the orange segments begin to break down. Remove from heat and allow the relish to cool in the pan.

If you plan to use the relish within a week, pour it into airtight containers and store in the refrigerator.

Otherwise, ladle the relish into hot sterilized jars (see Cleaning and Sterilizing, p. 16), leaving ½-inch headspace. Wipe the rims clean, add lids, and secure the bands until the fit is fingertip tight.

Process the jars in boiling water (see Processing, p. 16), then remove and let cool. Jars may be stored in a cool, dark place for up to 1 year.

My daughter Jenelle's first garden on my mother's farm in 2000.

Fresh Fig Compote

Yields 2 pints, or 4 cups

2 pounds fresh figs, cut into
  quarters
6 tablespoons dark brown sugar
6 tablespoons local honey
2 tablespoon fresh lemon juice
1 pinch sea salt

Combine the figs, brown sugar, honey, lemon juice, and salt with ½ cup water in a heavy-bottomed stainless steel saucepan. Cook over medium heat for 10 to 20 minutes, stirring frequently, until the compote begins to bubble.

The compote is done when the syrup has thickened, is amber in color, and the figs are glossy. Be careful not to overcook, or the mixture will harden when it cools. Ladle the compote into hot sterilized jars (see Cleaning and Sterilizing, p. 16), leaving ½-inch headspace. Wipe the rims clean, add lids, and secure the bands until the fit is fingertip tight.

Process the jars in boiling water (see Processing, p. 16), then remove and let cool. Jars may be stored in a cool, dark place for up to 1 year.

Peach Bourbon Sauce

Yields 3 pints, or 6 cups

3 pounds peaches, peeled,
  pitted, and coarsely chopped
½ cup sugar
½ cup unrefined sugar
½ cup Tupelo honey
2 tablespoons fresh lemon juice
1 large pinch sea salt
1½ cups good quality bourbon,
  your choice brand

Combine all ingredients, except the bourbon, in a large heavy-bottomed stainless steel stockpot over high heat. Bring to a boil, then reduce the heat to low and simmer 45 to 60 minutes, stirring occasionally, until the sauce thickens.

Add the bourbon, and remove from the heat. Allow to cool before you adjust the taste with salt and honey.

Ladle the sauce into hot sterilized jars (see Cleaning and Sterilizing, p. 16), leaving ½-inch headspace. Wipe the rims clean, add lids, and secure the bands until the fit is fingertip tight.

Process the jars in boiling water (see Processing, p. 16), then remove and let cool. Jars may be stored in a cool, dark place for up to 1 year.

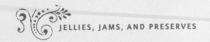

Fig Jam

Yields 2 pints, or 4 cups

6 pounds fresh figs, washed
    and stemmed

4 cups sugar

¼ cup fresh lemon juice

1 tablespoon lemon zest

In a large stainless steel saucepan, combine the figs, sugar, lemon juice, and zest. Bring to a simmer over medium-low heat, stirring constantly. Cover, reduce the heat to low, and simmer for 1 hour, stirring occasionally.

After 1 hour, remove the cover and continue to simmer for 15 minutes, stirring constantly, until the mixture thickens and gels, or "sets up" when a small amount is cooled. The melted and cooked sugar is what causes the preserves to set up as it thickens and cools.

Ladle the fig jam into hot sterilized jars (see Cleaning and Sterilizing, p. 16), leaving ½-inch headspace. Wipe the rims clean, add lids, and secure the bands until the fit is fingertip tight.

Process the jars in boiling water (see Processing, p. 16), then remove and let cool. Jars may be stored in a cool, dark place for up to 1 year.

Warm Berry Compote

Yields 2 pints, or 4 cups

1 cup fresh strawberries,
    stemmed and quartered

1 cup fresh blackberries

1 cup freshly squeezed orange
    juice

1 teaspoon orange zest

1 tablespoon lemon juice

1 pinch sea salt

In a medium stainless steel saucepan over medium-high heat, combine all the ingredients with 1 cup water. Bring just to a boil, then reduce the heat to low and simmer for 15 minutes, stirring occasionally, until the compote thickens.

Remove from the heat and allow the compote to cool in the pan.

Ladle the compote into hot sterilized jars (see Cleaning and Sterilizing, p. 16), leaving ½-inch headspace. Wipe the rims clean, add lids, and secure the bands until the fit is fingertip tight.

Process the jars in boiling water (see Processing, p. 16), then remove and let cool. Jars may be stored in a cool, dark place for up to 1 year.

Frost Plum Jelly

Yields 4 pints, or 8 cups

The wild plums that grew around the farm were called "frost plums." They were small and oval, and had skin that was a deep, reddish-purple color on the side that faced the sun, and a bright red color on the sides that were in the shade. But the real reason we called them frost plums was that they were completely covered with a thin blue bloom that looked like frost.

5½ pounds plums, halved and pitted
1¾ ounces powdered fruit pectin
7½ cups sugar

Place the plums and 4 cups cold water in a large stainless steel stockpot over medium heat and simmer 30 minutes, or until the plums are tender.

Line a sieve with 4 layers of damp cheesecloth and place it over a large bowl. Pour the plum mixture into the lined sieve, then cover the sieve with 2 additional layers of cheesecloth and let it stand for 30 minutes, occasionally pressing gently with a ladle, until all the plum juice has drained through the cheesecloth.

Measure out 5½ cups of plum juice and return this to the stockpot. Stir the pectin into the stockpot and bring to a boil over medium-high heat. Stir in the sugar and slowly bring to a full rolling boil. Boil for 1 minute, stirring constantly, then remove the pot from the heat, and skim off any foam.

Ladle the plum jelly into hot sterilized jars (see Cleaning and Sterilizing, p. 16), leaving ½-inch headspace. Wipe the rims clean, add lids, and secure the bands until the fit is fingertip tight.

Process the jars in boiling water (see Processing, p. 16), then remove and let cool. Jars may be stored in a cool, dark place for up to 1 year.

Muscadine Jelly

Yields 4 pints, or 8 cups

In certain places in the South, you can walk through the woods and see wild grapevines with clusters of large round grapes so dark purple they almost look black. These are Muscadine grapes, also known as Scuppernongs in North Carolina. They have a thick skin, and a juicy, sweet flavor with a tart finish, making it one of my favorite grapes to use for jelly. If you're not down South you can substitute purple or Concord grapes for this recipe.

3½ pounds Muscadine grapes

2 teaspoons fresh lemon juice

3 ounces liquid pectin

7 cups sugar

In a large stainless steel stockpot, crush the grapes using a potato masher, or a muddler. Be careful not to break the seeds. Add 1½ cups cold water to the crushed grapes and slowly bring to a boil over medium heat. Cover, reduce the heat to medium-low, and simmer for 10 minutes.

Line a sieve with 4 layers of damp cheesecloth and place it over a large bowl. Pour the grape mixture into the lined sieve, then cover the sieve with 2 additional layers of cheesecloth and let it stand for 30 minutes, occasionally pressing gently with a ladle, until all the grape juice has drained through the cheesecloth. Discard the solids.

Return the grape juice to the stockpot and add the lemon juice and pectin. Bring to a boil over medium-high heat, stirring constantly. Stir in the sugar and return to a boil, stirring constantly. Boil for 1 minute, stirring constantly, then remove the pot from the heat, and skim off any foam.

Ladle the compote into hot sterilized jars (see Cleaning and Sterilizing, p. 16), leaving ½-inch headspace. Wipe the rims clean, add lids, and secure the bands until the fit is fingertip tight.

Process the jars in boiling water (see Processing, p. 16), then remove and let cool. Jars may be stored in a cool, dark place for up to 1 year.

Strawberry Preserves

Yields 4 pints, or 8 cups

5 pounds fresh strawberries,
   hulled, and quartered
¼ cup fresh lemon juice
6 tablespoons pectin
7 cups sugar

Combine the strawberries and lemon juice in a large stainless steel saucepan over medium heat, and gradually stir in the pectin. Slowly bring the mixture to a full rolling boil, stirring constantly.

Pour in all the sugar at one time, stirring constantly until it dissolves. Return the presesrves to a full rolling boil, and boil for 1 minute, stirring constantly. Remove from the heat and skim any foam from the top.

Ladle the preserves into hot sterilized jars (see Cleaning and Sterilizing, p. 16), leaving ½-inch headspace. Wipe the rims clean, add lids, and secure the bands until the fit is fingertip tight.

Process the jars in boiling water (see Processing, p. 16), then remove and let cool. Jars may be stored in a cool, dark place for up to 1 year.

Spiced Pear Preserves

Yields 3 pints, or 6 cups

6 cups (about 4 pounds) firm
   pears, peeled, cored, and sliced
1 tablespoon fresh lemon juice
2 cups sugar
½ cup light brown sugar, firmly
   packed
½ teaspoon allspice
½ teaspoons ground nutmeg

In a large saucepan, combine the pears, lemon juice, and sugar with 1 cup water. Slowly bring to a boil over medium heat, stirring to dissolve the sugar, then reduce the heat and simmer for 1 to 1½ hours, or until the pear preserve is thick and glossy. Stir occasionally to prevent the mixture from sticking to the bottom of the pan.

Remove from the heat, and stir in the brown sugar, allspice, and nutmeg. Ladle the pear preserves into hot sterilized jars (see Cleaning and Sterilizing, p. 16), leaving ½-inch headspace. Wipe the rims clean, add lids, and secure the bands until the fit is fingertip tight.

Process the jars in boiling water (see Processing, p. 16), then remove and let cool. Jars may be stored in a cool, dark place for up to 1 year.

Pickles, Peppers, And Hot Sauce

Pickling, as a way to preserve foods, is a practice shared around the world. Traditionally, it was used as a way to preserve foods to be eaten when they were out-of-season, although most pickled food today are eaten because people enjoy the sour, salty taste.

Technically any food that has been preserved in a brine or vinegar can be called a pickle. Pickles in France include beets, pearl onions, and tiny whole cucumbers called cornichons. In the United States, pickles are cucumbers, whole or sliced, that have been preserved in vinegar or brine. Everything else has its own distinct name, especially in the South, where we still have a strong tradition of pickling foods.

Walk into any grocery store down South and you'll find pickled foods ranging from pickled eggs colored with beet juice, crunchy pickled okra, and spicy hot peppers, to sour watermelon rind, garlicky sausages, and even jellied pickled pig feet. You'll even find a jar of pickled green tomatoes and cabbage called chow-chow—or as we call it in my family, Cha Cha.

There are two popular ways to pickle foods: the first is to ferment the food in a brine of salt and water; the second method is to pack the food in a vinegar and water solution. Foods that are totally submerged in a salt water brine produce lactic acid, and fermentation occurs. Lactic acid is what gives foods like cucumbers their sour taste. Storing foods in a vinegar and water solution also gives the food a sour taste, but it is a much quicker process than fermentation, and preserves the food longer. Whatever process you choose to make your pickled foods, consider adding dried or fresh herbs— like dill, black pepper, or tarragon—to the pickling solution for added aroma and flavor.

Pickling Spice

Yields 1 cup

2 tablespoons mustard seeds

1 tablespoon whole allspice berries

2 teaspoons coriander seeds

2 tablespoons black peppercorns

1 teaspoon dried mace

1 tablespoon cardamom

1 teaspoon red pepper flakes

1 teaspoon dried ginger

2 dried bay leaves, crumbled

2 cinnamon sticks, crushed

6 whole cloves

Combine all ingredients in a glass jar with a tight-fitting lid.

Seal tightly and shake to combine.

This spice mixture will last 3 months when stored in a cool, dark place.

Herbs de Provence

Yields 2 cups

2 tablespoons dried rosemary

1 tablespoon fennel seed

2 tablespoons dried savory

2 tablespoons dried thyme

2 tablespoons dried basil

2 tablespoons dried marjoram

2 tablespoons dried lavender
    flowers

2 tablespoons dried Italian parsley

1 tablespoon dried oregano

1 tablespoon dried tarragon

1 teaspoon ground bay leaf

Using a mortar and pestle, grind the rosemary and fennel seed together and transfer to a medium bowl.

Add the savory, thyme, basil, marjoram, lavender, parsley, oregano, tarragon, and the ground bay leaf, and stir until well mixed.

Store in an air-tight container for up to 6 months.

Use the Herbs de Provence to add a hint of that freshness to soups and stews, roasted and grilled meats, fresh fish, and pickled goodies such as Pickled Tarragon Eggs (recipe, p. 32).

Apple Cider Vinaigrette

Yields 1½ cups

3 shallots, minced

1 clove garlic, minced

2 teaspoons Dijon mustard

1 teaspoon honey, to taste

⅓ cup apple cider vinegar

1 tablespoon freshly squeezed
orange juice

1 tablespoon fresh lemon juice

1 tablespoon lime juice

1 cup extra virgin olive oil

Sea salt, to taste

Freshly ground black pepper

In a small bowl, combine the shallots, garlic, mustard, honey, vinegar, and fruit juices.

Slowly pour the oil into the bowl in a steady stream, whisking constantly as you pour. The vinaigrette should be thick. If the oil settles on the top, continue to whisk until well combined.

Add salt and pepper to taste, and additional honey if the dressing is too tart.

Use this vinaigrette on green salads, sliced tomatoes, and add a bit to fruit salad to bring out the sweetness of the fruit.

Champagne Vinaigrette

Yields 1½ cups

You can make your own Champagne vinegar by placing leftover Champagne in a jar, cover with layers of cheesecloth, and store for 4 to 6 months. Check it monthly, and use it when it has the tartness of vinegar.

1 tablespoon French mustard,
course grain

1 large clove garlic, minced

Sea salt and freshly ground
pepper, to taste

½ cup Champagne vinegar

¾ cup extra virgin olive oil

1 teaspoon honey (optional)

Place the mustard, garlic, salt, and pepper in a medium bowl.

Whisk in the vinegar. Add the oil all at once, and whisk until well combined.

The vinaigrette will thicken as you whisk.

Adjust the taste with salt, pepper, and, for sweetness, add the honey.

Pickled Beets
with Shallots & Garlic

Yields 12 pints

Southern and French cuisines have a lot of foods in common and pickled beets is an example. Shallots add a mild onion flavor to the beets and the garlic gives this dish a little heat. I make jars of these for gifts, they are so pretty. If you are only making these for yourself and don't need 12 pints, you may halve the recipe.

5 pounds fresh small beets,
    stems removed

12 large cloves garlic, peeled

12 medium shallots, peeled

1 cup sugar

2 cups cider vinegar

1½ teaspoons pickling salt

Sterilize your jars and lids (see Cleaning and Sterilizing, p. 16).

Place the beets in a large stockpot with enough water to cover the beets by 2 inches.

Bring to a boil over medium-high heat, and cook 15 minutes, or until the beets are fork tender. Drain, reserving 2 cups of the beet water. Allow the beets to cool, then peel and cut them into quarters.

Tightly pack each sterilized jar with the beet quarterss, then add 1 whole garlic clove, and 1 shallot to each jar.

In a large stainless steel saucepan over high heat, combine the sugar, reserved beet water, vinegar, and pickling salt. Bring to a rapid boil and pour the hot brine into the jars with the beets, garlic and shallots, leaving ½-inch headspace.

Wipe the rims clean, add lids, and secure the bands until the fit is fingertip tight.

Process the jars in boiling water (see Processing, p. 16), then remove and let cool. Jars may be stored in a cool, dark place for up to 1 year.

Pickled Tarragon Eggs

Yields 6 eggs

This pickling process was traditionally used to preserve eggs for the winter months when chickens didn't lay. The added beet juice adds a little sweetness to the eggs, while turning them into a beautiful ruby-colored garnish for any salad. The tarragon adds a mild, fresh licorice taste and aroma to the eggs.

1 large beet, peeled and coarsely
    chopped in 1- to 2-inch pieces
1 cup beet juice
6 hardboiled eggs, peeled
½ cup cider vinegar
½ cup tarragon vinegar
1 small onion, sliced
½ cup sugar
2 sprigs fresh tarragon
1 teaspoon mustard seeds
1 teaspoon Herbs de Provence
    (recipe, p. 28)

In a saucepan over medium-low heat, bring the chopped beets and 1 cup water to a simmer, and continue to simmer for 30 to 40 minutes, until tender. Strain and reserve 1 cup of the beet juice.

Peel the eggs and place them in the bottom of a clean, 1-quart glass jar.

In a medium saucepan, add the beet juice, the vinegars, onion, sugar, and spices and bring the mixture to a boil over high heat. Reduce the heat to medium-low and simmer for 5 minutes, or until the sugar has dissolved and the onions are translucent. Remove the saucepan from the heat, add the tarragon sprigs, and allow the mixture to cool in the pan for 10 minutes.

Pour the vinegar/onion mixture over the eggs in the jar, covering the eggs completely. Cover with the lid, seal tightly, and refrigerate for up to 1 month.

The pickled eggs will be ready to eat after a few days but the longer the eggs pickle, the more the pickling brine will penetrate the eggs and add to the taste.

Red Hot Pepper Relish

Yields 8 pints, or 16 cups

Better than store-bought since it uses only the freshest ingredients, I use this relish in place of hot sauce and eat it with fried fish, greens, and, of course, Pig Ear & Pig Tail Sandwiches (recipe, p. 124).

20 red chili peppers, such as cayenne or cherry, finely chopped

20 green chili peppers, such as jalapeños or habañeros, finely chopped

4 pounds (6 to 8 medium) onions, finely chopped

1 tablespoon pickling salt

2 cups cider vinegar

1 cup white vinegar

2½ cups sugar

Sterilize your jars and lids (see Cleaning and Sterilizing, p.16).

Place the chili peppers, onions, and pickling salt in a large stainless steel stockpot and cover with 2 quarts boiling water. Be careful not to inhale the fumes. Let the pot stand for 10 minutes. This step reduces some of the pepper's heat, so omit it if you want a really hot pepper relish. Strain the peppers and onions, discarding the liquid, and return them to the stockpot.

Stir both vinegars and the sugar into the mixture. Bring to a boil over medium-high heat, then reduce the heat to low and simmer for 20 minutes.

Ladle the pepper relish into sterilized pint jars, pressing down as you pack the chili mixture so that the cooking liquid completely covers the relish. Add additional cooking liquid to fill the jar, leaving ½-inch headspace. Wipe the rims clean, add lids, and secure the bands until the fit is fingertip tight.

Process the jars in boiling water (see Processing, p. 16), then remove and let cool. Jars may be stored in a cool, dark place for up to 1 year.

My cousin, Michelle, age 3, in a field of wildflowers in 1982.

Green Tomato Cha Cha

Yields 8 to 10 pint jars

Chow-chow, or Cha Cha as my family fondly calls it, has its beginnings in France, and was brought to the South by the Acadians by way of Novia Scotia. Although it may have started in France, it has been claimed by Southern- ers as our own. My grandmother used her ChaCha to add a crisp, sweet-tart bite to greens, beans, and even potato salad, making this recipe a family favorite.

4 large yellow onions, coarsely chopped

1 large cabbage, cored and chopped into ¼-inch pieces

4 cups green tomatoes, cored and coarsely chopped

3 large green bell peppers, chopped into ¼-inch pieces

3 large red bell peppers, chopped into ¼-inch pieces

6 large cloves garlic, minced

½ cup pickling salt

6 cups sugar

2 cups cider vinegar

2 cups white vinegar

½ cup Pickling Spice (see recipe, p. 28)

Sterilize your jars and lids (see Cleaning and Sterilizing, p. 16).

In a large bowl, combine the onions, cabbage, green tomatoes, green and red bell peppers, garlic, and the pickling salt. Cover the bowl with a clean cloth and let stand at room temperature overnight, or at least 12 hours.

The next day, drain the vegetables using a colander or sieve lined with cheesecloth, and allowing up to 2 hours to drain.

Place the vegetables in a large stainless steel stockpot over medium heat and add the sugar, vinegars, 2 cups water, and the pickling spice. Bring to a simmer and cook for 20 minutes, stir- ring frequently.

Ladle the Cha Cha into hot sterilized jars (see Cleaning and Ster- ilizing, p. 16), leaving ½-inch headspace. Wipe the rims clean, add lids, and secure the bands until the fit is fingertip tight.

Process the jars in boiling water (see Processing, p. 16), then remove and let cool. Jars may be stored in a cool, dark place for up to 1 year.

Sweet & Sour Pickles

Yields 6 pint jars

Similar in taste to bread and butter pickles, these pickles are sweet, sour, and crunchy. This recipe relies on refrigeration to preserve the pickles. It allows you to skip the hot-water processing step, and results in a crisper, fresher tasting pickle in less time.

2 ½ pounds cucumbers, sliced into ¼-inch rounds

1 pound white onions, thinly sliced

3 large cloves garlic, sliced

¼ cup pickling salt

1½ cup white distilled vinegar

1 cup cider vinegar

2 cups sugar

1 tablespoon mustard seeds

1 teaspoon crushed red pepper flakes

¾ teaspoon celery seeds

1 cinnamon stick

6 allspice berries

6 whole cloves

½ teaspoon turmeric

Place the cucumbers, onions, garlic, and pickling salt in a large bowl and stir to coat evenly. Cover with a clean tea towel and refrigerate for at least 4 hours.

Rinse the cold cucumbers, onions, and garlic slices thoroughly, drain, and repeat the rinsing process. Set aside.

In a large stainless steel stockpot, bring the vinegar, sugar, and all of the spices to a rolling boil over medium-high heat, stirring constantly. When the sugar has dissolved, set aside.

Pack the cucumber-onion-garlic mixture into sterilized jars, leaving 1 inch of headspace in the jar. Pour the hot vinegar to cover the vegetables to ½-inch from the rim. Be sure the vinegar covers the vegetables.

Remove any air bubbles using a bubble remover, or a chopstick. Wipe the rim clean, seal tightly with the jar lid, and store in the refrigerator for at least 1 month before eating to allow the flavors to be absorbed into the cucumbers.

These pickles can be kept, refrigerated, for up to 1 year.

Dill Pickles

Yields 3 pounds

This recipe uses a traditional fermentation process by placing the cucumbers in a saltwater brine instead of vinegar. This process produces a cucumber that is tart and crunchy, with less of the acidic taste you get with pickles made with vinegar.

½ cup pickling salt

1 tablespoon black peppercorns

1 tablespoon red pepper flakes

4 large cloves garlic, crushed

1 teaspoon dill seed

1 large bunch fresh dill

3 pounds cucumbers, 4- to 6-inches long

In a 1-gallon ceramic crock, combine the pickling salt and 3½ quarts cold water, and stir until the salt has dissolved.

Add the peppercorns, pepper flakes, garlic, dill seed, and fresh dill, and stir to combine.

Rinse the cucumbers under cool running water and trim both ends. Add the cucumbers to the crock of salt water and spices, and place a saucer or small bowl on top of the cucumbers to weight them down. Make sure that all the cucumbers are completely covered with brine. Cover the crock with 3 sheets of cheesecloth, secured with a large rubber band or twine.

Leave the crock in a cool, dry place for 3 days, then check to see if bubbles are rising to the top of the crock. If so, fermentation has begun.

For each of the next 7 days of the fermentation process, skim off any scum that forms, replacing the cheesecloth over the crock each time. Fermentation is complete when the pickles taste sour and bubbles no longer rise to the top of the crock.

Cover the crock with fresh cheesecloth and place it in the refrigerator for another 3 days, skimming the top as needed.

The crock of dill pickles may be refrigerated for up to 2 months. Skim the top as needed.

Discard all pickles if any of the pickles should become soft, discolored, or have an off odor.

Infused Chili Oil

Yields 2 cups

Boasting olive oils ranging in taste from mild and sweet to bold and tart, France produces some of the best olive oils I've tasted. While in Paris, I made a point of cooking with the olive oils I bought at spice shops and markets, and found that each had a different color and taste. You can change an oil by heating it and adding fresh or dried herbs and spices, which infuses the oil with the color, flavor, and aroma of that herb or spice.

2 cups extra virgin olive oil

3 fresh chilis, such as cayenne, serrano, or Fresno chili pepper, stems removed

1 tablespoon dried chili flakes

Always work in a well-ventilated area when infusing oils.

Heat the extra virgin olive oil in a saucepan over medium heat until you see tiny bubbles form in the bottom of the pan. Turn the heat off before the oil begins to smoke. Immediately add the fresh chilies and dried chili flakes to the oil. The chilies will sizzle or "cook," and will diffuse their heat into the oil.

Allow the mixture to cool to room temperature. At this point, you may strain the oil, or leave the chilies in the oil longer for more heat.

Pour the strained oil into a clean, sterilized glass jar, or bottle with a tight-fitting lid and store, refrigerated, up to 3 weeks.

Discard the oil if it begins to look cloudy or shows evidence of bacterial growth.

Drizzle the Infused Chili Oil on soups for an added burst of heat, or use it to make a spicy vinaigrette.

(Left to right) My cousin Peal (age 7), Aunt Honey (age 5), and my mother, LaVerne (age 7), out walking their dolls in 1956.

Tarragon Vinegar

Yields 2 cups

A popular French herb, tarragon has a mild licorice aroma and taste. This fragrant vinegar can be used in vinaigrettes to brighten up salads, and added to mayonnaise for a unique taste. Simply add fresh springs of tarragon to ordinary vinegar and turn it into a sophisticated, French-style vinegar..

1 cup fresh sprigs tarragon

2 cups white wine vinegar

1 cup additional fresh tarragon
  sprigs, optional

Gently rinse the tarragon in a bowl of cold water and pat dry.

Place the tarragon sprigs in a 1-pint sterilized jar, and gently bruise the tarragon by pressing down on the sprigs with a wooden spoon.

Add enough vinegar to cover, seal the jar tightly with a lid, and store in a cool, dark place for 2 to 3 weeks to let the flavor develop.

Strain and discard the old tarragon and add additional fresh tarragon at this point, if desired. New tarragon will add a more pronounced licorice taste to the vinegar.

This is the perfect time to transfer your Tarragon Vinegar to a more decorative bottle if you wish to display it, or give it as a gift.

Tarragon Vinegar can be stored in a cool place for up to 6 months without losing its flavor.

My daughters, Regine
(seated, age 12) and
Jenelle (standing, age 14),
and my niece, Evette
(kneeling, age 9).

Fresh from the Garden

We enjoy a very long growing season here in the South. From April until late fall we grow, harvest and enjoy a variety of vegetables from our gardens that are cooked into delicious meals. It's not uncommon to see four or five different garden-fresh vegetables—including beans, salads, and greens—on the table at both dinner and supper. Imagine how pleased I was to see that same love of fresh vegetables while studying in France. One of the differences I noticed between French and Southern cooking is that here in the South we tend to overcook our foods—especially vegetables. Greens, yellow squash, and string beans might taste delicious with so much cooking, but they lose their vibrant color. Using French techniques, I like to keep vegetables vibrant by either par-cooking them and then adding them back to the dish at the end, or by cutting the vegetable in uniform pieces so that they cook quickly and retain their color.

Black-Eyed Pea Salad

Serves 6

Black-eyed peas are a big part of Southern cuisine; they are usually served hot, as a side dish. Serving this dish cold gives an unexpected twist to a Southern staple and highlights the flavor and texture of the peas. I recommend cooking the black-eyed peas until firm, then adding the vinaigrette to them while they are still hot. This allows the peas time to absorb all the great flavors in the salad dressing as they cool down. Any leftover salad lasts up to a week, refrigerated, and actually gets better-tasting each day.

4 cups black-eyed peas, cooked
   (*see recipe, p. 66, and omit the
   salt pork*)

2 cloves garlic, minced

1 teaspoon fresh thyme,
   chopped

1 tablespoon fresh parsley,
   chopped

1 tablespoon honey

¼ teaspoon red chili flakes

1 teaspoon sea salt

1 teaspoon freshly ground black
   pepper

½ cup apple cider vinegar

1 cup extra virgin olive oil

¼ cup diced yellow onion

¼ cup diced red bell pepper

¼ cup diced green bell pepper

Prepare the black-eyed peas (recipe, p. 66). Set aside

In a large bowl, combine the garlic, thyme, parsley, honey, red pepper flakes, salt, black pepper, and cider vinegar. Slowly whisk in the olive oil. Adjust the seasoning with salt and pepper.

Add the cooked black-eyed peas, the onion, and the red and green bell peppers.

Mix well, cover, and refrigerate for at least 4 hours before serving.

Root Vegetable Mash

Serves 6

Similar to mashed potatoes, this recipe uses cream and butter, but substitutes parsnips and rutabagas—vegetables popular in French cooking—for the potatoes. Infusing the hot cream with fresh herbs gives this dish a depth of flavor not found in ordinary mashed potatoes.

1½ pounds assorted seasonal root vegetables (such as carrots, parsnips, turnips, and rutabagas), peeled and coarsely chopped

4 cloves garlic

1 teaspoon sea salt

1½ cups heavy cream

¼ cup unsalted butter

3 fresh thyme sprigs

1 fresh sprig rosemary

1 bay leaf

Sea salt and freshly ground black pepper, to taste

½ cup fresh chives, chopped

Drizzle extra virgin olive oil

Place the root vegetables and garlic in a large pot with enough cold water to cover, and add the sea salt. Bring to a boil over medium-high heat, then reduce the heat to medium-low and simmer for 30 minutes, or until the vegetables are fork-tender.

In the meantime, combine the cream, butter, thyme, rosemary and bay leaf in a small stainless steel saucepan over low heat. Cook for 10 to 15 minutes, allowing the butter to slowly melt and infuse the cream with the aroma and flavor of the fresh herbs. Do not let the cream boil.

Remove the pan from the heat, cover, and let the herbs steep in the cream while you perform the next step.

Drain the vegetables and transfer them to a large mixing bowl. Mash, using a potato masher, or an electric mixer with a paddle attachment. Strain the cream into the mashed vegetables, discarding the bay leaf and herbs.

Return the vegetables to the large pot and cook over low heat for 10 minutes, stirring until the cream is absorbed and the vegetables are smooth.

Adjust the seasoning with salt and pepper. Garnish with chopped chives and a drizzle of olive oil.

Cucumber, Tomato, & Onion Salad

Serves 8

When my grandmother made this salad, the ingredients came directly from our garden, still warm from the sun.

2 medium cucumbers, thinly
  sliced
5 medium tomatoes, cut in wedges
1 small yellow or white onion,
  thinly sliced
⅓ cup apple cider vinegar
¼ cup olive oil
Sea salt and cracked black pepper

In a large bowl, toss the cucumbers, tomatoes, and onions.

Combine the vinegar, oil, salt and pepper to taste, and set aside ¼ cup for later.

Toss the veggies with the remaining dressing and allow the salad to stand at room temperature for about 30 minutes.

Toss again just before serving and be sure to pass the remaining dressing around the table.

Gram's Coleslaw

Serves 8

1 cup mayonnaise
½ cup milk
⅓ cup sugar
¼ cup cider vinegar
Sea salt and freshly ground
  black pepper, to taste
1 small head green cabbage,
  shredded
1 medium carrot, shredded
1 small yellow onion, peeled
  and shredded

In a large bowl, whisk together the mayonnaise, milk, sugar, vinegar, salt, and pepper until thick and creamy.

Add the cabbage, carrot, and onion, and mix well. Refrigerate before serving.

Watermelon Salad
with Apple Cider Vinaigrette

Serves 6

Summertime in the South wouldn't be complete without a sweet, juicy watermelon. I used to eat them by the slice, without benefit of plate or fork. This recipe has become my favorite way to eat watermelon. The crisp watercress and tangy vinaigrette seem to make the watermelon sweeter, and the combination turns a simple slice of watermelon into an elegant salad.

3 tablespoons sesame seeds

6 cups seeded watermelon, cut into 1-inch cubes

¼ cup Italian or flat leaf parsley leaves

½ cup whole scallions, or green onions, sliced

½ cup fresh chervil tops

1 to 1½ cups Apple Cider Vinaigrette (recipe, p. 29)

6 cups watercress leaves (1 large bunch), stems removed

In a small sauté pan over very low heat, toast the sesame seeds for 5 to 10 minutes, or until golden brown. Shake the pan occasionally to stir the sesame seeds. Sesame seeds have a high oil content, so you do not need to add oil to the pan. Let cool.

In a large bowl, toss 1½ tablespoons toasted sesame seeds, the watermelon, parsley, scallions, and chervil with the Apple Cider Vinaigrette.

Divide the watercress between 6 chilled salad plates and place a portion of the watermelon salad on each plate. Sprinkle with the remaining sesame seeds and serve immediately.

Southern Fried Corn

Serves 6

The best way to get corn kernels off the cobb is to use the sharp edge of a chef or butcher knife to slice them off, then use the back of the knife to scrape out the juice, or "milk." A cast-iron skillet is a must when making this dish. It heats evenly and helps the corn fry and thicken in a way that stainless steel just can't match.

6 ears corn, shucked

2 tablespoons bacon fat

2 tablespoons unsalted butter

2 tablespoons flour

Salt and freshly ground black
    pepper, to taste

Slice the corn from the cobb into a bowl, scraping downward to capture the "corn milk," and any remaining kernels left on the cobb.

Heat a heavy cast-iron skillet over medium-high heat and add the bacon fat and butter. When the bacon fat is hot and the butter has melted, add the corn, corn milk, salt, and pepper. Continue to cook for 15 to 20 minutes, stirring often. Stir in the flour, one teaspoon at a time, and cook an additional 20 minutes after all the flour has been incorporated.

Adjust the seasoning with salt, and pepper, and serve hot.

Baked Sweet Potatoes

Serves 4

*Baked sweet potatoes are superior to boiled ones for pie fillings, muffins, and tarts.
Their flavor and sweetness is intensified, instead of being lost in the boiling process.*

4 medium sweet potatoes

1 tablespoon vegetable oil, or
    lard

4 tablespoons unsalted butter

Scrub the sweet potatoes under cool water and blot dry.

Brush each sweet potato with oil and place on a sheet pan. Bake for 45 minutes to 1 hour, or until the sweet potatoes are fork tender.

Cut a 2- to 3-inch slit in the top of each potato and, holding the potato at each end, press towards the middle until some of the baked potato pops out. This slit makes it easier to get into the skin of your potato and is a perfect spot to put the butter.

Top with butter and serve piping hot.

Making Hominy

Hominy is dry corn that has been removed from the cobb, and then cooked in an alkaline or lye solution to remove the hulls. The process is known as nixtamalization and it improves the nutritional value of corn, removes fungal-mycotoxins from stored corn, and improves the corn's taste in the process. There are several steps in making this dish, and making a lye solution is the first one. The best and safest recipe for making hominy uses Pickling Lime (also known as CAL or Food Grad Like, aka CAL, or Food Grade Lime), available in the canning section of many grocery stores.

Yields 1 quart hominy

Combine ¼ cup Pickling Lime and 2½ quarts water in a large cast-iron pot or Dutch oven over medium-high heat, and stir with a non-reactive spoon. Slowly bring to a boil and continue to boil for 10 minutes.

Remove from the heat, cover, and let rest at room temperature for 5 hours.

Once cooled, there will be a skin formed on top of the water and white solids on the bottom. You want to use the clear liquid in between for the hominy. Remove the skin using a non-reactive spoon and strain the clear liquid through 5 layers of cheesecloth.

Return the clear liquid to the cleaned pot, add 1 quart dried corn kernels to the pot, and bring to a boil over medium heat. Reduce the heat to a simmer and cook for 30 minutes, stirring often.

Remove the pot from the heat and allow the corn to steep in the lye solution for 12 hours, or overnight.

Next, strain, rinse the corn kernels, and transfer the corn to a large ceramic bowl or crock with 2 gallons cold water.

Gently rub the kernels of corn between the palms of your hands. This will release the corn hulls and they will float to the top of the bowl. Use a slotted spoon to skim the hulls from the water. Repeat the process until all of the corn hulls have been removed and discarded. Strain the kernels a second time, rinse, and discard the water.

Add the corn and 1 gallon clean cold water to a large stockpot over medium heat and simmer gently for 1 hour, or until the corn has doubled in size. This is now hominy. Stir occasionally, and skim off any remaining corn hulls.

At this point you can steam the hominy, or add it to soups and stews. My grandmother liked to cook it with a bit of rendered salt pork, seasoned simply with butter, salt, and pepper.

Tomato & Okra Gravy

Serves 4

I use to watch, mortified, as my grandfather would use fresh biscuits to sop up his tomato and okra gravy. I wondered how something as slimy as okra could give him such obvious pleasure. It wasn't until decades later that I grew to appreciate this summertime dish. Okra pods become tough and stringy as they age, so it's best to use small tender ones for this dish. And the riper the tomato, the better, since ripe tomatoes have more juice and the juice is what gives this gravy its beautiful color.

3 tablespoons bacon drippings

1 small onion, chopped

1 tablespoon flour

½ cup chicken stock, or water

5 medium garden fresh tomatoes,
   cored and sliced

1 pound tender young okra, cut
   into ½-inch pieces

Sea salt, to taste

Freshly cracked black pepper

Pinch cayenne pepper

In a medium skillet over low heat, warm the bacon drippings. Add the onion and cook 3 to 5 minutes, until soft, but do not brown. Add the flour, and stir for 5 minutes, or until it is well incorporated.

Whisk the stock into the skillet, and simmer for 10 minutes, whisking occasionally, until the gravy is thick and smooth.

Add the tomatoes and okra to the gravy, increase the heat to medium, and bring it to simmer again, stirring frequently. Cook 20 minutes, or until the okra softens and the tomatoes begin to break down, thickening the gravy.

Add salt, pepper, and cayenne pepper, and continue to simmer another 10 to 15 minutes, until the okra has cooked through. The exact time will depend on how tender your okra is.

Adjust the taste with salt and pepper. Serve the Tomato & Okra Gravy over white rice, or with Buttermilk Biscuits (recipe, p. 98).

Baked Tomatoes

Serves 4

Tomatoes are at their peak of flavor in late summer and early fall, especially when picked straight from a garden. You can usually find a neighbor or your local farmer's market with garden fresh tomatoes, if you don't garden. By using garden fresh tomatoes in this recipe, their natural sweetness really shines through and makes this simple dish a perfect start to any meal.

¼ cup melted butter

¼ cup extra virgin olive oil

3 large tomatoes, sliced in
    1-inch rounds

1 tablespoon chopped fresh basil

1 teaspoon chopped fresh thyme

1 teaspoon chopped fresh
    rosemary

2 large cloves garlic, minced

¼ teaspoon red chili pepper
    flakes

1 pinch sea salt

Freshly ground black pepper,
    to taste

Preheat the oven to 350° F.

Butter the sides and bottom of an 8 x 8 x 2-inch baking dish.

In a large bowl, combine the olive oil, tomato, basil, thyme, rosemary, garlic, chili pepper flakes, salt, and pepper. Toss to coat the tomato slices evenly.

Layer the tomatoes in the prepared baking dish and be sure to scrape any oil and herbs left in the bowl into the dish.

Bake uncovered for 20 to 30 minutes, or until the tomatoes are bubbly and lightly browned on top.

Serve with fresh baked bread, or over white rice.

My grandmother's tomato and herb garden at her "in-town" house in Charleston, Mississippi, around 1989.

Poke Salad

Serves 6

This truly Southern vegetable is full of protein, iron, and calcium, making it a nutritional powerhouse. My grand-mother would serve it hot, sautéed with onions and scrambled eggs. I've reinvented this dish by adding lardons, or thickly cut bacon, and chopped boiled eggs instead of scrambled. However you decide to cook it, just remember to take special care when preparing the poke weed. It is important to use only the thick, succulent new growth (3 to 4 inches of the leaf tips). The rest of the plant contains so much vitamin A that it must be boiled in fresh water 3 separate times to leech out most of the potentially poisonous vitamin.

2 pounds pokeweed, rinsed well, found at your farmer's market

6 to 8 slices thick cut bacon, cut into lardons (¼-inch strips)

1 large onion, diced

Salt and pepper, to taste

3 hardboiled eggs, chopped

1 small spring onion, green stem only, sliced

Place the pokeweed in a large, high-sided saucepan, or a stockpot over high heat, with enough cold water to cover. Bring to a rapid boil and continue to boil for 20 minutes. Drain and rinse with tepid water.

Repeat this boiling and rinsing process two more times, then drain and rinse with cold water. Set aside to drain completely.

In a cast-iron skillet over medium heat, fry the lardons until crisp and brown. Transfer them to paper towels to drain, leaving the drippings in the pan.

Add the pokeweed to the drippings, along with the onion, 1/4 cup water, and salt and pepper to taste.

Cook 15 to 20 minutees, or until the onions are sautéed and all the water has cooked out.

Serve hot, garnished with hard-boiled egg, lardons, and sliced spring onions.

Wild Mushroom Ragout

Serves 4

Wild mushroom ragout, or stew, can be made with just one type of mushroom, or an assortment of what's on hand. To prepare the mushrooms for cooking, simply brush the caps with a dry towel to remove any dirt. Do not wet or wash the mushrooms since any dampness causes debris to stick to the mushroom. If you're using mushrooms with dark colored "gills" — the thin lines under the mushroom cap — scrape them off with a spoon and discard. The gills won't hurt the flavor of the ragout, by may discolor the cream. Remove the stems, and slice or quarter the mushroom caps before cooking.

2 tablespoons unsalted butter

2 pounds assorted mushrooms (such as morels, chanterelles, shitake, and porcini)

½ teaspoon sea salt

½ teaspoon freshly cracked black pepper

2 cloves garlic, minced

⅓ cup Marsala wine, or red table wine

½ cup chicken stock, or vegetable stock

1 cup heavy cream

1 tablespoon chopped fresh thyme

Heat the butter in large sauté pan over medium-high heat for 5 minutes, until it starts to foam. Add all the mushrooms, then stir in salt and pepper, reduce the heat to medium-low, and simmer until all of the liquid has cooked out of the mushrooms.

Once the liquid has cooked out, continue to sauté the mushrooms for 5 to 7 minutes, or until they have browned. Stir in the garlic and sauté for 1 minute. Add the Marsala wine and cook for 1 minute more.

Stir in the chicken stock, cream, and chopped thyme and cook an additional 3 to 5 minutes, or until the sauce thickens.

Salt and pepper to taste and serve hot.

Winter Pumpkin Soup
with Parmesan Croutons & Bacon Chips

Serves 4

Any type of winter pumpkin or squash, such as Sugar Pie pumpkin or butternut squash, can be used for this soup. Just remove the seeds, cut it into wedges, drizzle with olive oil, and roast in a 350° F oven. The roasting softens the vebetable and reinforces its natural sweetness. The addition of stock and cream gives the soup a velvety smoothness, and the croutons and bacon chips add a nice crunch.

2 tablespoons olive oil

6 slices of Hickory smoked
   bacon, cut into 1-inch strips

2 sprigs fresh rosemary

1 tablespoon unsalted butter

½ medium white onion, diced

1 clove garlic, minced 2 cups
   roasted pumpkin, mashed,
     or unsweetened pumpkin
     puree

2½ cups chicken stock

Sea salt and freshly ground
   black pepper, to taste

½ cup heavy cream

2 cups stale bread, cut into
   1-inch cubes

1 tablespoon extra virgin olive oil

¼ cup grated Parmesan cheese

¼ teaspoon red chili flakes

Freshly ground black pepper

In a large stockpot over medium heat, add 2 tablespoons of olive oil. Add the bacon and cook for 5 to 6 minutes, then add the rosemary and cook an additional 4 to 5 minutes, or until the bacon is golden and crispy and the rosemary leaves are lightly browned.

Drain the bacon and rosemary on a paper towel. Remove the rosemary leaves from the stems and roughly chop the leaves, discarding the stems. Set the rosemary aside. Discard all but 1 tablespoon bacon grease from the stockpot. Set the bacon chips aside while you make the pumpkin soup.

Add the butter, onion, and garlic to the bacon grease in the stockpot and cook over medium-low heat for 15 minutes, or until the onion is translucent. Stir often to loosen any browned bits from the bottom of the pan. Add the mashed pumpkin and the chicken stock, and season lightly with salt and pepper.

Bring to a simmer, reduce the heat to low, and cook 15 to 20 minutes. Stir in the heavy cream just before you serve; do not let the soup boil once the cream has been added.

Preheat the oven to 400° F.

To make the parmesan croutons, toss the bread, olive oil, cheese, chili flakes, and black pepper together in a large bowl. Spread the bread mixture onto a sheet pan and bake 5 to 6 minutes, or until the bread cubes are golden brown.

Serve the soup in warm bowls topped with croutons, bacon chips, and the chopped rosemary.

Potato & Egg Salad

Serves 8

Southern potato salad is generally a mixture of boiled potatoes, mayonnaise, pickle relish, and boiled eggs, garnished with paprika. It's really up to the cook how much of each ingredient goes in the salad, as well as any additions—such as the mustard and bell pepper in this recipe. We put lots of boiled eggs in ours, which prompted my youngest daughter to sometimes call it "egg salad." So this is our version of a Southern potato salad, with lots of boiled eggs. I enjoy this salad warm, but it's also great served cold.

6 large potatoes, peeled and quartered

1½ to 2 cups mayonnaise

3 tablespoons yellow mustard

1 tablespoon sugar

2 ribs celery, finely chopped

⅓ cup yellow onion, finely chopped

3 green onions, white and green parts, chopped

6 hard-boiled eggs (4 chopped, and 2 sliced)

3 heaping tablespoons Green Tomato Cha Cha (recipe, p. 34), or your choice sweet pickle relish

Sea salt and freshly ground black pepper, to taste

Paprika, for garnish

Boil the quartered potatoes in enough water to cover until they are fork tender. Drain and transfer them to a large bowl. Add the mayonnaise, mustard, and sugar, and mash with a potato masher until smooth.

Add the celery, yellow onion, green onion, 4 chopped eggs, pickle relish, salt, and pepper to taste. Stir well and garnish with 2 sliced eggs and a sprinkling of paprika.

Serve hot or cold.

Sautéed Garlic & Kale

Serves 6

I've changed the boiled kale recipe I grew up eating into this sautéed version. I figured if the French could improve something as basic as greens, then so could I. Cooking the kale in a pan of hot oil, then steaming with stock or water, makes them tender; the lemon juice keeps the color bright green; and the garlic compliments the kale's slight sweetness.

3 tablespoons olive oil

2 cloves garlic, finely sliced

2 pounds young kale, stems and
   leaves coarsely chopped

1 teaspoon red chili flakes

½ cup vegetable stock, or water

2 tablespoons fresh lemon juice

Sea salt and freshly cracked
   black pepper, to taste

Heat the olive oil in a large sauté pan over medium heat. Add the garlic and cook 3 minutes, until it softens, but do not brown.

Add the kale and chili flakes and toss to combine. Add the stock, cover, and continue to cook for 5 minutes.

Remove the cover and continue to cook, stirring, about 15 minutes, or until all the liquid has evaporated. Add the lemon juice and season with sea salt and pepper to taste.

Crook Neck Squash & Onions

Serves 8

This recipe and its ingredients are simplicity at its best. The fresh squash is layered with sweet onion and spiced with a pinch of cayenne pepper. The end result is a perfect combination of flavor and color.

6 large yellow squash, sliced
   into ¼-inch rounds

1 medium sweet onion, chopped

3 tablespoons bacon grease

⅛ teaspoon cayenne pepper

Sea salt and freshly ground
   black pepper, to taste

Melt the bacon grease in large cast-iron skillet over medium heat. Add the squash and onions in 3 layers, sprinkling salt and pepper lightly between each layer. Reduce the heat to low, cover, and cook 20 minutes, or until the vegetables are tender.

Remove the lid, and cook 5 to 10 minutes longer, or until most of the liquid has cooked off. Add salt and pepper to taste.

Glazed Turnips
with Pearl Onions & Brown Butter

Serves 4

I grew up eating turnips boiled with turnip greens and salt pork. So the first time I tasted glazed turnips in Paris, it was love at first bite. It took me a few tries to get the turnips just right, but, while practicing, I learned that the longer vegetables cook the sweeter and more caramelized they become.

4 tablespoons unsalted butter

1 pound baby turnips, peeled
    and diced

1 pound pearl onions, peeled
    and trimmed

1 cup chicken stock, or
    substitute water

⅓ cup light brown sugar

1 tablespoon apple cider vinegar

Sea salt

Freshly ground black pepper

¼ cup fresh parsley, chopped

In a large sauté pan, melt the butter over medium heat. When the butter begins to foam and turn a golden brown, add the turnips and onions and toss to coat.

Stir the chicken stock, brown sugar, and apple cider vinegar into the pan and cover with a tight-fitting lid. Increase the heat to high and bring the mixture to a boil, then reduce the heat to medium-high and cook for 10 minutes.

Remove the lid and continue to cook 7 to 10 minutes more, until the sauce is thickened and shiny and the vegetables are tender.

Remove from the heat and season with salt and pepper to taste. Garnish with the parsley.

Beans, Greens, And Pot Likker

Pot Likker is the liquid that is left behind after boiling greens such as collard, mustard, or turnip greens. My family always cooks our greens with pieces of salt pork, hog jowls, bacon, or sometimes smoked ham hocks, so the pot likker has both the pungent bite of cooked greens and the richness of simmered pork. If you've never tried it, you should know that pot likker is considered to be not only good tasting, but good for you! It contains essential vitamins and minerals, including iron and vitamin C, as well as a lot of vitamin K, which aids in blood clotting. So the next time you cook your greens, pour yourself a big cup of the pot likker, add a wedge of Cracklin' Corn Bread, or a crumbled Hoe Cake, and enjoy some real down-South cuisine.

Garden Vegetable Soup

Serves 8

This is my mother's favorite soup. She uses vegetables straight from her garden, and serves it with a big green salad and lots of hot buttered bread. I've taken her recipe and added a French accent by cutting the vegetables in uniform pieces, adding lots of fresh herbs, and reducing the cooking time. These small changes make for a fresher tasting soup, full of bright, tender vegetables.

2 tablespoons olive oil

2 tablespoons unsalted butter

2 cups chopped leeks (white part only), or 1 cup diced yellow onion

3 large cloves garlic, minced

Sea salt

2 cups carrots, peeled and chopped into rounds

2 cups potatoes, peeled and diced

2 cups fresh green beans, cut into ¾-inch pieces

2 quarts vegetable stock

2 bay leaves

3 sprigs fresh thyme

1 sprig fresh rosemary

4 cups tomatoes, seeded and chopped

2 ears sweet corn, kernels only

Freshly ground black pepper

¼ cup fresh parsley leaves, finely chopped

Heat the olive oil and butter in large, heavy-bottomed stockpot over medium-low heat. Add the leeks, garlic, and a pinch of sea salt and cook 7 to 8 minutes, or until the leeks begin to soften and release their aroma.

Add the carrots, potatoes, and green beans and continue to cook for another 4 to 5 minutes, stirring occasionally.

Stir in the stock, bay leaves, and thyme. Increase the heat to high, and bring the soup to a simmer. Once simmering, add the tomatoes, corn, and black pepper to taste. Reduce the heat to low, cover, and cook 25 to 30 minutes, or until the vegetables are fork tender.

Adjust the seasoning with salt and pepper. Remove from the heat and sprinkle with fresh parsley. Serve piping hot.

Black-Eyed Peas

Serves 8

Black-eyed peas, also known as cow peas, have a rich history. They are thought to have originated in North Africa and were introduced to the New World by Spanish explorers and African slaves. In the South, it is considered good luck to eat black-eyed peas on the first day of the New Year..

2 pounds dried black-eyed peas

8 ounces salt pork, with rind

1 large onion, coarsely chopped

1 small dried cayenne pepper

Sea salt, to taste

Freshly ground black pepper

In a colander, pick over the peas and discard any misshapen or discolored peas, and rinse well. Transfer the peas to a large bowl and fill with enough cold water to completely cover the peas. Soak overnight.

When you are ready to cook the peas, drain and place them into a large stock pot.

Slice the fat off the salt pork down to the rind, leaving the fat and rind attached. Do not discard the fat.

Add the salt pork, chopped onion, the dried red pepper, and 6 cups cold water. Add more water as needed to just cover the peas.

Over medium-high heat, bring the peas to a boil, then reduce the heat to low, cover tightly, and simmer slowly for 2 hours, or until the peas are tender.

Season with salt and pepper to taste. Do not skim off any fat.

Serve with Cha Cha (recipe, p. 34) and Buttermilk Cornbread (recipe, p. 88).

Black-Eyed Peas

Butter Beans & Hog Jowlss

Purple Hull Peas

Butter Beans & Hog Jowls

Serves 8

Hog jowl comes from the cheek area of the hog and is usually found in the pork section of your grocery, next to the ham, or at a butcher shop. Although it tastes similar to bacon, it has a texture that remains firm during long cooking times. You can use it fresh, cured, or smoked to add richness and flavor to any pot of beans, peas, or greens.

2 pounds fresh, or dried butter
    beans (soak overnight)

1 large ham bone

1 (8-ounce) hog jowl, diced

1 large yellow onion, chopped

2 cloves garlic, minced

1 dried red chili pepper

1 teaspoon salt, to taste

¼ teaspoon freshly ground
    black pepper, to taste

Place the beans in a large stockpot and add 6 cups water, the ham bone, hog jowl, onion, garlic, and chili pepper. Slowly bring to a boil over medium-high heat. Reduce the heat to low, cover tightly, and simmer for 40 to 60 minutes, stirring occasionally. If the beans look dry, add enough water to keep them covered by 1 inch water. The longer the beans simmer, the thicker the broth will become. Do not skim off the fat.

Salt and pepper to taste.

Serve with Buttermilk Cornbread (recipe, p. 88).

Cooking Beans

Beans and greens are a huge staple in Southern cuisine and cooked in much the same way here as they are in French cuisine. Whether the beans you use are fresh, frozen, or dried they are cooked the same way—by adding a liquid, a cured or smoked piece of meat for flavoring, and seasoning. Although fresh and frozen greens can be cooked the same way as dried beans, they are more versatile and can be sautéed with oil and garlic, or even steamed with apples and sausage.

  I always cook a double portion of the bean and greens recipes I make. This way I can serve half and freeze the other half for a future meal. To freeze your cooked beans or greens, simply allow them to cool thoroughly,

place in a freezer safe container or freezer bag, and place in your freezer. Beans can be kept frozen for 6 months, and greens for 3 months without losing their taste or quality.

Dried Beans

Fresh, frozen, or even dried beans and peas can be used in these recipes. If using dried beans, place the beans in a large bowl and cover with cold water. Allow them to soak in the water overnight; then drain, rinse, and follow the recipe for fresh or frozen beans and peas.

Purple Hull Peas

Serves 8

*Imagine my surprise to find fresh Purple Hull Peas for sale at the local farmer's market in Paris!
We grew up sitting on the front porch, shelling them by the bushel. I bought a double handful of the peas and
cooked them with the smoked hog jowl I bought at the La Boucherie next door, and had them for dinner
that night — with a double helping of childhood memories!*

2 pounds fresh Purple Hull
    peas, shelled

8 ounces hog jowl, coarsely
    chopped

1 large onion, coarsely chopped

1 dried red chili pepper

6 cups cold water

Salt, to taste

Freshly ground black pepper

Place the peas in a large saucepan with the hog jowl, onion, chili pepper, and 6 cups water, or enough to cover the peas. Cover and bring to a boil over medium-high heat. Reduce the heat to medium-low and simmer for 1 hour, or until the peas are tender.

Salt and pepper to taste.

Serve with Cucumber, Tomato & Onion Salad (recipe, p. 45) and Hoe Cakes (recipe, p. 84).

My sisters, Erin (age 2) and Fifi (age 7), sitting in our great-grandmother's wheelchair on Mitchell Lake at a 1979 family reunion.

Great Northern Beans & Ham

Serves 8

1 pound dried Great Northern
   beans
1 large ham bone
2 cups diced ham
1 large yellow onion, chopped
2 cloves garlic, minced
1 dried red chili pepper
1 bay leaf
Salt, to taste
Freshly ground black pepper,
   to taste

In a colander, pick over the peas and discard any misshapen or
discolored peas, then rinse well. Transfer the peas to a large bowl
and fill with enough cold water to completely cover the peas.
Soak overnight.

When you are ready to cook, drain the beans, and place them in a
large stockpot. Add 6 cups cold water, the ham bone, ham, onion,
garlic, chili pepper, and bay leaf and slowly bring to a boil over
medium-high heat. Cover and reduce the heat to medium-low.
Simmer for 6 to 8 hours, stirring occasionally. Add additional
water as needed to keep the beans covered by 2 inches of water.

Salt and pepper to taste.

Serve with Buttermilk Cornbread (recipe, p. 88).

String Beans with New Potatoes

Serves 6

3 pounds fresh string beans,
   ends removed, and snapped
   in half
¼ pound salt pork, with rind
12 small red potatoes
1 small dried cayenne pepper
Freshly ground black pepper,
   to taste
Sea salt, as needed

Place the string beans in a colander and rinse with cold water.
Set aside to drain.

Slice the fat part of the salt pork down to the rind. Leave the fat
and rind attached. Trim the white part off the salt pork, from the
edge to just before the brown rind. You want the white fat to stay
attached to the rind, so do not cut through the rind. It will look
like an unzipped zipper.

In a large cast-iron Dutch oven, combine the string beans, salt
pork, potatoes, cayenne, and black pepper. Add 3 cups water, or
enough to cover the vegetables.

Cover the pot and cook over medium-low heat for 25 to 30 minutes,
or until the beans and potatoes are tender. Salt and pepper to taste.

Pinto Beans & Ham Hocks

Serves 6

The longer you cook your pinto beans, the thicker the sauce or "gravy" will become. I find it best to cook them a day or two before you plan to serve them, and refrigerate until you are ready to reheat and serve. This guarantees a thick, rich pot of beans.

1 pound dried pinto beans

1 large smoked ham hock

1 large yellow onion, finely chopped

2 cloves garlic, minced

2 dried red chili peppers

1 teaspoon salt

¼ teaspoon freshly ground black pepper

6 small spring onions, chopped

Place the beans in a bowl or stockpot with enough water to cover, and soak overnight.

When you are ready to cook, drain the beans, rinse and discard any misshapen or discolored beans, and them put them in a stockpot with 12 cups cold water. Add the ham hock, onion, garlic, and chili peppers. Season with salt and pepper.

Bring to a boil over medium-high heat, then cover and reduce the heat to medium-low. Simmer for 3 hours, stirring occasionally, or until the beans are tender and the ham falls from the bone. For a thicker and richer broth, you may choose to simmer on low heat for 6 hours.

You may remove and discard the bone, or leave it in the beans for added flavor. Adjust the seasonings to taste.

Garnish with chopped fresh spring onions and serve with Cracklin' Bread (recipe, p. 86).

Fresh Field Peas & Snap Beans

Serves 8

I grew up eating field peas and years later in culinary school I found out that field peas and Crowder peas are the same pea. I also learned that it doesn't matter if you start with fresh, frozen, or dried field peas, they always turn a muddy color when they're cooked. It made me realize that my grandmother always added snap beans (or string beans) to her pot of peas to provide a bright spot of color.

2 pounds fresh Crowder peas

2 cups fresh snap beans, trimmed and cut in half

8 ounces salt pork

1 large onion, coarsely chopped

1 dried red chili pepper

Salt, to taste

Freshly ground black pepper

In a colander, pick over the peas and discard any misshapen or discolored peas. Rinse well and transfer to a large saucepan.

Add the salt pork, chopped onion, dried chili pepper, and 6 cups cold water. Add more water as needed to cover the peas. Cover tightly, bring to a boil over medium-high heat, reduce the heat to low, and simmer for 40 minutes. Add the snap beans and cook for another 15 to 20 minutes, or until the peas and snap beans are tender.

Do not skim off the fat. Season with salt and pepper to taste.

Serve with Green Tomato Cha Cha (recipe, p. 34) and Buttermilk Cornbread (recipe, p. 88).

Mustard & Turnip Greens

Serves 4

These greens can simmer all afternoon if you have the time. The longer they cook, the better they taste, because greens can often be bitter and long, slow cooking softens the bitterness. Mustard greens are peppery and turnip greens have a slight bitter taste, but, surprisingly, they complement each other when cooked together. The cooking liquid, or pot likker as it's sometimes called in the South, is often eaten with cornbread or drunk alone to aid digestion.

1 big bundle (about 8 cups)
    mustard greens

1 big bundle (about 8 cups)
    turnip greens

2 small turnips, peeled and cut
    into wedges

¼ pound salt pork

⅓ cup bacon drippings

1 dried red chili pepper

1 tablespoon apple cider vinegar

Sea salt, to taste

Freshly ground black pepper,
    to taste

Cut or strip the mustard and turnip greens from their stems. Wash them at least 3 times, then drain in a colander.

Transfer the greens to a large stockpot. Add the turnips, salt pork, bacon drippings, chili pepper, vinegar, and 4 cups cold water and bring to a boil over medium-high heat. Reduce the heat to medium-low and simmer the greens for 2 hours, or for 3 to 4 hours on low heat.

Season the greens with salt and pepper to taste. Serve with a helping of the pot likker and a slice of Buttermilk Cornbread (recipe, p. 88).

My niece, Evette (age 9), holding a
fresh bunch of collard greens.

How to Clean Greens

Fill your sink or a large bowl with cold tap water.
Submerge a double handful of greens in this water
and agitate them, using an up and down motion, to
remove all the sand and any bugs. Repeat this process
until all of the greens have completed this first
wash. Transfer the greens to a clean bowl.

Rinse the sink or bowl well to rid it of the dirt and
debris that has settled on the bottom, then refill
with cold tap water and repeat the cleaning process.
Repeat the process a third time so that your greens
are clean enough to begin cooking. If the greens are
really dirty, a fourth and fifth washing may be necessary. Use your eyes and your good judgment to
make sure the greens are completely clean.

I was a grown woman with of family of my own
when I discovered that not everyone cleans their
greens the same way my family does. While visiting
a friend during the holidays, I was keeping her company in the kitchen as she was getting dinner ready.
Her daughter was removing the leaves of the greens
from their hard stems—and doing a mighty fine job
for a five-year-old!—and my friend was getting
ready to wash them. I was sitting in a nearby chair,
catching up with her on gossip when I stopped mid-
sentence. She had squirted a stream of dishwashing
liquid into the sinkful of water that held the greens!
My face must have showed my surprise because she
asked, "Don't you wash your greens with dish liquid?" When I didn't immediately respond, she went
on to say that the women in her family have always
used soap to wash their greens. We both chuckle
about that to this day—and I always have second
helpings of her greens.

Smoked Sausage
with Cabbage, Apples, & Onion

Serves 8

This recipe is a perfect combination of the tastes, textures, and colors of the farm! Pick cabbages with lots of dark green leaves to add a nice 'bite' to the dish. Use both green and red apples to give your dish lots of color, smoked sausage to impart a rich and smoky flavor, and the onion as a compliment to all the other ingredients.

2 tablespoons bacon drippings

2 pounds smoked sausage, cut into 2-inch pieces

1 yellow onion, thinly sliced

1 large unpeeled Red Delicious apple, cored and thinly sliced

1 large unpeeled Granny Smith apple, cored and thinly sliced

1 large head of green cabbage, cut into 2-inch strips

¼ teaspoon red pepper flakes

Sea salt, to taste

Freshly ground black pepper, to taste

Heat the bacon drippings in a large cast-iron skillet over medium heat.

Add the sausage and onion, and cook until the sausage has browned and the onion softens and turns a caramel brown color.

Stir in the apples, cabbage, and ½ cup water. Cover with a tight-fitting lid, and cook 25 minutes, or until the cabbage is soft.

Add the red pepper flakes, and adjust the seasoning with salt and pepper.

Breads

Cornbread is to Southerners as a baguette is to the French—an expected part of every meal. Down South, cornbread may take the form of a traditional cast-iron skillet of buttermilk cornbread, a hot griddle of hoe cakes, or even a platter stacked high with rich cracklin' bread.

Butter Roll

Serves 6

My grandmother made so many truly delicious breads and rolls that it's almost impossible for me to pick a favorite; but if I did, I would have to choose her Butter Roll. This French-style dough is similar to croissant dough in that it is full of fresh creamy butter, then folded, rolled, and folded again. But my grandmother went further and baked the dough in a rich, fragrant vanilla sauce. A piece of this sweet bread is a great way to start the day, but many have been known to enjoy it for dessert as well.

½ cup shortening, cold

2 cups self-rising flour

½ cup, plus 2 cups whole milk, divided

½ cup unsalted butter, room temperature, divided

¼ cup, plus ⅔ cup sugar, divided

1 teaspoon cinnamon

1 vanilla bean, seeds removed and saved

Preheat the oven 350° F.

Butter an 8 x 8-inch ceramic baking dish.

In a large bowl, use a pastry cutter, or 2 butter knives, to cut the shortening into the flour until it has the consistency of cornmeal. Stir in ½ cup milk. Place the dough on a lightly floured surface and form it into a ball.

Roll out the dough ball to a rectangle shape, about 7 x 10 inches, and spread ¼ cup butter on the dough. Fold the dough in half lengthwise and roll it out again into a rectangle shape. Spread the remaining ¼ cup butter on top and sprinkle with ¼ cup sugar and the cinnamon.

Fold the dough in thirds by folding ⅓ the width of the dough on top and ⅓ the dough under the bottom of the rolled dough. The dough will now have 3 connected layers; one on top, one in the middle, and one on the bottom. Place the folded dough into the buttered baking dish and set aside.

In a medium stainless steel saucepan over medium heat, combine the whole milk, ⅔ cup sugar, the vanilla bean, and vanilla seeds. Cook for 10 minutes, stirring constantly, until the mixture begins to gently bubble. Remove the vanilla bean and pour the sauce over the butter roll.

Bake for 30 to 40 minutes, or until the roll turns lightly brown on top. Allow the butter roll to sit for a few minutes at room temperature. This will allow the rolls to soak up more of the sauce.

Spoon sauce from the baking dish over each serving.

Cinnamon & Spice Rolls

Yields 1 dozen rolls

*Growing up, cinnamon rolls were made for special occasions and considered a real treat—and they still are!
It's the browned butter that made them so special, giving the rolls a nutty caramel taste.*

¾ cup melted unsalted butter,
  plus 2 tablespoons to grease
  the baking dish

1 cup pecan halves, toasted

½ cup whole milk

½ cup sugar

1½ teaspoon salt

2 (.25-ounce) packages active
  dry yeast

2 large eggs, beaten

4½ cups all-purpose flour

1 cup firmly-packed brown sugar

1 tablespoon cinnamon

¼ teaspoon allspice

1 cup dark brown sugar

2 cups confectioners' sugar

¾ cup heavy whipping cream

Butter a 9 x 13-inch baking dish with 2 tablespoons butter. Set aside.

To make the brown butter, heat 8 tablespoons butter in a small saucepan over medium heat until the butter stops foaming and turns a golden brown, with a nutty aroma. Set aside.

Place the pecans in an oil-free sauté pan over low heat and cook 10 minutes, stirring occasionally, until the nuts have browned.

Scald the milk in a stainless steel saucepan by bringing it just to a boil and immediately removing it from the heat. Stir in the sugar, salt, and ¼ cup butter. Set aside and allow the mixture to cool to room temperature.

Combine ½ cup warm water (105° to 115° F) and the yeast in a large bowl, and stir until the yeast is dissolved. Add the scalded milk mixture, the beaten eggs, and half the flour to the bowl of dissolved yeast and beat until smooth. Gradually mix in the remaining flour. The dough should be elastic and slightly stiff, but not dry. More or less flour may be needed to achieve this consistency.

Turn the dough out onto a floured board or work surface, and knead it for 8 to 10 minutes, or until it is smooth and very elastic.

Butter the inside of a large mixing bowl, then add the dough and turn several times to coat it with the butter. Cover the bowl with a clean dish towel and place it in a warm place to rise for 1 hour, or until it doubles in size.

In a small bowl, combine the brown sugar, cinnamon, and allspice and set aside.

Once the dough has doubled in size, punch it down using your fists, turn it out onto a lightly floured board, and roll the dough into a large rectangle, about 18 x 10 inches.

Brush the dough with the melted brown butter, sprinkle it with the brown sugar mixture and the toasted pecans, leaving a 1-inch border along each side of the dough.

Tightly roll the dough up, starting at the long side and pressing the edges to seal. Slice into 1- to 1½-inch wide rolls.

Place the rolls cut-side down in the buttered baking dish, cover, and let rise a second time for 1 hour, or until they have doubled in size.

Preheat the oven to 350° F.

Bake the cinnamon rolls for 25 to 30 minutes, until lightly browned.

Hoe Cakes

Yields 16 cakes

1 cup self-rising flour

1 cup self-rising cornmeal

2 large eggs

2 teaspoons sugar

⅓ cup water

¾ cup buttermilk

¼ cup bacon grease

Bacon grease for frying

In a large bowl, add all the ingredients, except the bacon grease, and mix well.

Place a large cast-iron skillet or griddle over medium heat, add enough bacon grease to cover the bottom of the pan and heat until very hot. Test the temperature of the oil by adding a bit of batter to the hot oil—it will sizzle when the oil is hot enough.

Drop the batter by scant half-cups into the hot pan. Cook as many as the pan can hold without letting the sides of the hoe-cakes touch.

Fry each hoecake for 5 minutes, until the edges are brown and small bubbles appear in the center of the cake. Turn with a spatula and cook another 5 minutes to brown the other side. Lower the temperature of the skillet if the hoe cakes brown too quickly.

Serve hot, with bacon and fresh cream butter.

Hoe Cake History

Growing up, my sisters and I would spend our summers down South with our grandparents on their farm in Mississippi. I was always excited to go because my grandmother would make all our favorite foods. Although I loved everything she made, my favorite was what she called "hoe cakes." They were a mixture of corn meal, flour, and water cooked in a little bit of bacon fat in a cast-iron skillet on top of the stove. Every morning she would bake fresh biscuits for my grandfather and sisters and I would beg her to make a hoe cake for me, which she did, serving them up piping hot and slathered with fresh cream butter.

She would always chuckle to herself when she made them. When I finally thought to ask her what was so funny, she told me that it was funny that I loved "slave food" so much. I asked my grandmother how something as delicious as a hoe cake could be slave food. She explained to me that her mother; my great grandmother; who, though she died a free woman, had been born a slave, made them in the cotton fields. My grandmother went on to explain that when the field slaves were given a break after working in the fields all morning, they made themselves some dinner. Since they didn't have an oven or a skillet to cook their bread in, they used their garden hoe instead. The slaves would heat the flat metal hoe in the fire, add a bit of pork fat, and cook their corn bread batter on it. This was what they called a hoe cake.

My great-grandmother taught my grandmother how to make them and when she got married she continued to make them, but in a skillet instead of on a hoe. This story has always made me respect the resourcefulness of my ancestors and the belief that every family recipe has some history mixed into it.

Cracklin' Bread

Serves 8

This is my favorite way to eat cracklin's. My grandmother would always make a pan just for me whenever we came to visit. Crackling—or cracklin' as we call it in the South—are the bits of cooked skin and meat left over from rendering pork fat for lard. Once they have floated to the top of the hot lard, skim them from the lard and drain on a towel. When cool enough to handle, salt lightly and either eat as a snack, or use to flavor breads, beans, and greens. The key to soft, moist Cracklin' Bread is to make sure you don't overcook the cracklin's.

2 cups cornmeal

½ cup all-purpose flour

½ teaspoon salt

½ teaspoon baking soda

½ teaspoon baking powder

1 cup cracklings, chopped into
    ¼-inch pieces

1 tablespoon butter

2 tablespoons lard, or bacon
    grease

1½ cup buttermilk

2 eggs, beaten

Preheat the oven to 400° F.

Sift the cornmeal, flour, salt, baking soda, and baking powder together into a large bowl.

Add the cracklings to the cornmeal mixture and stir to coat. Coating the crackling with this mixture will ensure that they do not fall to the bottom of the skillet while baking.

Add the butter and lard to a 9-inch cast-iron skillet and place it in the oven for 10 minutes to melt the fat and heat the skillet.

Pour the melted fat, buttermilk, and eggs into the cornmeal and crackling mixture. Stir until well combined.

Spoon the batter into the hot skillet and bake for 30 minutes.

Serve hot with a cold glass of milk.

Buttermilk Cornbread

Serves 8

Like the baguette is to the French, cornbread is to the South—a comforting mainstay. Cornbread can be served sweet or plain, for lunch or dinner, with butter, molasses, or even honey, so long as it's served. I've found that baking cornbread in a cast-iron skillet helps the bread cook more evenly. Once you've seasoned your skillet, your cornbread will bake perfectly every time.

½ cup, plus 1 tablespoon lard,
   or bacon fat, melted

⅓ cup sugar

2 large eggs

1 cup buttermilk

½ teaspoon baking soda

1 cup cornmeal

1 cup all-purpose flour

½ teaspoon salt

In a large bowl, mix the warm lard and the sugar together. Add the eggs and beat until well blended.

In a separate bowl, combine the buttermilk and baking soda, and pour into the bowl with the egg mixture. Stir well. Next, stir in the cornmeal, flour, and salt until well blended. Only a few lumps should remain.

Heat 1 tablespoon lard or bacon fat in a 8-inch cast-iron skillet over medium heat for 5 minutes, or until the fat has melted and the skillet is hot. Pour the batter into the hot skillet.

Bake for 30 to 40 minutes, or until a toothpick inserted in the center comes out clean.

Serve with Dry Rubbed Smoked Pork Shoulder (recipe, p. 122) and Gram's Coleslaw (recipe, p. 45).

My Big Mama (Ida Belle Metcalf Collins) with her husband, Lane Collins, and his brother, Uncle Love (L. Moore Collins), and his wife, Hannah Collins, around 1950.

Nana's Sweet Yeast Rolls

Yields 1 dozen rolls

These rolls are fragrant, soft, and slightly sweet. Here are a few tips to ensure your breadmaking is a success: Temperature matters, so invest in a kitchen thermometer to make sure the milk is not too hot; be sure to measure all of the ingredients and use the right amount of yeast; and resist the urge to over-knead your dough.

½ cup whole milk

½ cup sugar

1½ teaspoon salt

¼ cup unsalted butter, melted, plus ½ cup additional butter for coating bowls and brushing on rolls

2 (.25 ounce) packages active dry yeast

2 large eggs, beaten

4½ cups all-purpose flour

Butter a 9 x 13-inch baking dish.

Scald the milk in a stainless steel saucepan by bringing it just to a boil, then immediately removing the pan from the heat. Stir in the sugar, salt, and butter. Set aside to cool to room temperature.

Combine ½ cup warm water (105° to 115° F) and the yeast in a large bowl and stir until the yeast is dissolved. Add the scalded milk mixture, the beaten eggs, and half the flour to the bowl of dissolved yeast. Beat until smooth. Gradually mix in the remaining flour. The dough should be elastic and slightly stiff, but not dry. More or less flour may be needed.

Turn the dough out onto a floured board and knead it for 8 to 10 minutes, until it is smooth and very elastic.

Butter the inside of a large mixing bowl, add the dough, and turn it several times to coat with the butter. Cover the bowl with a clean dish towel and place it in a warm place to rise for 1 hour, or until it doubles in size.

Once the dough has doubled in size, use your fists to punch it down, then turn it out onto a lightly-floured board. Pinch off a 2- to 3-tablespoon-size chunk of dough and shape it into a ball. Repeat until you have 12 balls of dough. Place them in the buttered baking dish, barely touching, cover with a kitchen towel, and leave in a warm place to rise a second time for 1 hour, or until the rolls have doubled in size and are touching.

Preheat the oven to 375° F.

Bake the rolls for 20 to 25 minutes, until golden brown. Remove from the oven and brush the tops of the rolls with melted butter. Allow them to sit for 10 minutes before serving.

Sweet Potato Muffins

Yields 1 dozen muffins

I was so excited the first time I made these Sweet Potato Muffins with sweet potatoes leftover from dinner! What I discovered is that sweet potatoes baked in their skin don't lose any of their flavor the way peeled and boiled potatoes can. The muffins came out moist and had an intense caramelized flavor you just don't get when using boiled potatoes.

1¼ cups firmly-packed dark
    brown sugar

½ cup melted butter, plus 1
    tablespoon for greasing
    the muffin tin

2 teaspoons vanilla extract

2 large eggs, room temperature

2 cups all-purpose flour

2 teaspoons baking powder

1 teaspoon ground cinnamon

1 teaspoon freshly grated nutmeg

½ teaspoon ground allspice

½ teaspoon salt

4 cups baked sweet potato,
    mashed

½ cup raisins, optional

1 cup walnuts chopped into
    small pieces, optional

Grease a 12-cup muffin tin with 1 tablespoon butter.

Whisk together the brown sugar, butter, vanilla, and eggs in a small bowl, until light and creamy.

In a separate bowl sift together the flour, baking powder, spices, and salt. Stir the mashed sweet potato into the flour mixture. Make a well in the center of the sweet potato dough and pour in the egg mixture. Stir to combine, then stir in the raisins and walnuts.

Spoon the batter into the muffin tins, filling each muffin cup three-quarters full. Bake for 25 to 30 minutes, or until a tooth-pick inserted into the middle comes out clean. Remove from theoven and let the pan cool on a wire rack for 10 minutes, then invert the muffin tin and gently tap the bottom of each cup to release the muffins.

Serve hot with fresh cream butter, and store any leftover muffins in an airtight container. They will last 3 to 5 days, unrefrigerated, and 1 week in the refrigerator. These muffins also freeze well when triple-wrapped in plastic wrap, and can be kept in the freezer for up to 1 month.

Rise And Shine

Breakfast is considered the most important meal of the day, and this definitely holds true in the South. A big country breakfast is needed to give you the energy to go out and work the fields, hunt, fish, and take care of the livestock. Some of my favorite childhood recipes, such as Buttermilk Biscuits with Blackstrap Molasses, Mackerel Croquettes, and Smothered Squirrel, are in this chapter. Other recipes are inspired by my time in France.

While in Paris I found that breakfast wasn't as big a deal as it is back home, but what was served was taken very seriously. I've taken the fresh berries and egg soufflés often served at breakfast and given them a Southern twist, as in the Berries & Cream and Spring Omelet Roll recipes.

Whatever the differences, what's served for breakfast by both Southerners and the French uses the freshest produce available, fresh baked bread, creamy butter, farm raised eggs, strong hot coffee, and hand-cured meats.

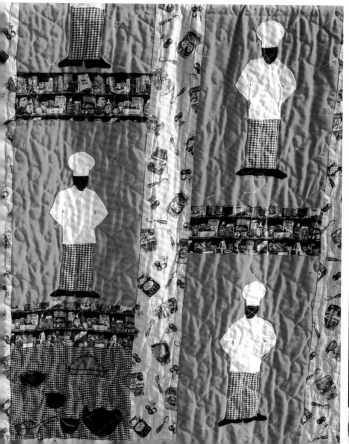

Pan-Fried 'Taters & Spring Onions

Serves 4

Potatoes or pommes de terre, *as they're called in France, are as popular there as they are here. The French often cook them with rendered lard or bacon drippings, reminding me of how we ate them on the farm. We liked to fry the potatoes in lard with spring onions and garnish the finished dish with paprika.*

3 tablespoons lard, or bacon
    drippings
6 medium potatoes, sliced into
    ⅛-inch thick rounds
3 large spring onions, thinly
    sliced, reserving the green
    tops as garnish
1 teaspoon salt, or to taste
Freshly ground black pepper,
    to taste
1 red bell pepper, diced
2 medium cloves garlic, minced
1 teaspoon paprika

Heat the lard in a large cast-iron skillet over medium high heat. Add the potatoes and the onions, season with salt and pepper, and toss to coat with oil.

Cover the skillet, reduce the heat to medium, and cook for 10 minutes, without stirring.

Remove the lid of the skillet and increase the heat to medium-high. Add the bell pepper and garlic and continue cooking for 15 minutes, stirring occasionally, until the potatoes and onions are browned.

Chop the reserved spring onion greens. Stir in the paprika, remove from heat, adjust seasoning with salt and pepper, and sprinkle with the spring onion tops.

Serve with Scrambled Eggs & Hog Brains (recipe, p. 106).

Seasoning & Cleaning Cast Iron

Seasoning is vegetable oil baked onto the iron at a high temperature. Traditional cast-iron skillets and pans are seasoned by coating the skillet with cooking oil and baking it in a 350° F oven for 1 hour. Seasoning creates the natural, easy-release properties of the pan. The more you cook, the better it gets, by reinforcing its non-stick coating. It will take several uses to get that shiny, black "seasoned" look.

Cooking in cast iron increases the iron content in your food. The longer the food is in contact with the skillet, the more iron is absorbed. Iron is a metal that's essential for life—it helps carry oxygen to the blood and regulate the growth of cells. Iron comes from the foods you eat, and any excess iron is stored for future use. Frying, baking, roasting, and even sautéing works great in cast-iron pans, but never boil water in your cast-iron pan or it will rust.

To best clean a cast-iron pan, rinse with hot water immediately after cooking. If you need to remove burned-on food, scrub the pan with coarse salt and a nonmetal brush—never use dishwashing soap.

If the pan gets a sticky coating or develops rust over time, scrub it with steel wool and then re-season it in the oven. To prevent rust, dry the skillet thoroughly, and lightly coat the cooking surface with cooking oil after each use. If you create, maintain, and repair the "seasoning," your cookware can last 100 years or more. I have two cast-iron skillets that I got from my mother, who got them from her mother. They are both seasoned beautifully, and nothing sticks on them—not even an egg.

Chicken & Apple Sausage

Yields 12 patties

Until I went to culinary school, I always made sausage from pork or venison. At school I discovered that you can make sausage out of most any type of meat, poultry, seafood, or fish. Using chicken makes a leaner sausage that is a great alternative to pork sausage. This chicken sausage recipe is garnished with apples and seasoned with onion and sage, and is a great addition to the breakfast table.

½ tablespoon olive oil

1 medium green, or tart, apple, cored and finely chopped

1 small onion, finely chopped

1 teaspoon rubbed sage

Sea salt and freshly cracked black pepper, to taste

1½ pounds ground chicken breast and thighs

1½ teaspoons Poultry Seasoning, (recipe, p. 147)

1 teaspoon sweet paprika

Heat the olive oil in a medium stainless-steel sauté pan over medium heat. Add the apple, onion, and sage, and season with salt and pepper. Cook for 10 minutes, until the mixture is soft and lightly browned. Remove from the heat and allow to cool at room temperature.

Place the ground chicken in a large bowl and season with additional salt and pepper. Stir in the poultry seasoning and paprika. Stir in the apple mixture until well combined.

Form the sausage into 12 small patties.

Heat a griddle pan or large cast-iron skillet over medium-high heat and cook the patties for 3 to 4 minutes on each side, until golden brown.

Serve on a warm platter.

Jenelle, Regine, and my mother LaVerne in the chicken coop on the farm in 2003.

Fresh Berries & Cream

Serves 4

Picture a table set with beautifull crystal bowls filled with fresh seasonal berries, and topped with a rich sweetened cream. This French-inspired dish is light, refreshing, and adds beauty and elegance to any breakfast table. Mix whatever berries are in season, and if fresh aren't available, you can substitute frozen.

10 whole egg yolks

1 cup sugar, divided

2 cups heavy whipping cream

1 vanilla bean, split lengthwise, seeds scraped and reserved

3 cups mixed fresh seasonal berries, such as blueberries, raspberries, strawberries, or blackberries

Whisk the egg yolks with ½ cup sugar in a large bowl for 5 minutes, until light and creamy. Set aside.

Combine the cream, the remaining sugar, and the vanilla bean and seeds in a medium stainless-steel saucepan over medium heat. Bring to a strong simmer, but do not boil. Remove from heat.

Slowly temper the egg mixture with the warm cream, stirring continuously as you drizzle the cream into the eggs. Note: if you add the warm cream to the eggs too quickly, your eggs will scramble.

Once all the cream has been stirred into the eggs, pour the mixture into the top of a double boiler (or a dry stainless-steel bowl fitted over a saucepan of simmering water). Cook over medium heat for 10 minutes, stirring gently and constantly as the egg/cream mixture slowly thickens and becomes *nappé* (meaning it runs slowly off the back of a spoon). If it starts to really thicken up, remove from the heat immediately.

Strain the cream through a sieve into a large glass or stainless-steel bowl set into a larger bowl of ice water, and stir to halt the cooking process and cool the cream.

Place the mixed berries into small bowls or glasses, and top with the cooled cream.

Buttermilk Biscuits

Yields 18 biscuits

My grandmother made buttermilk biscuits every morning for my grandfather. My sisters, cousins, and I would all vie for the biggest biscuit, the one we called the "Papa" biscuit, named in honor of our grandfather. Many Southerners believe that using buttermilk to make their biscuits insures that they will be light and fluffy. Buttermilk doesn't have any added butter, so it's actually the opposite—milk that has had all of the cream and butter churned out of it. Unlike unchurned or "sweet" milk, buttermilk is very tart due to its lactic acid. This acid reacts with the baking soda in biscuit dough and creates a gas that adds lightness to the biscuit.

3 cups unbleached all-purpose
    flour, plus ½ cup for dusting

½ teaspoon baking soda

1 tablespoon, plus 1 teaspoon
    baking powder

1 teaspoon salt

⅔ cup lard

1 cup, plus 2 tablespoons
    buttermilk

½ cup unsalted butter, melted

Preheat your oven to 450° F.

Sift the dry ingredients together in a large bowl.

Using a pastry cutter, cut the lard into the flour until it resembles cornmeal. Add the buttermilk and mix until just combined.

Turn the dough out onto a floured surface. Gently pat the dough out to a ½-inch thickness. Fold the dough 4 to 5 times, gently pressing the dough down to a 1-inch thick disc on the final turn.

Use a biscuit cutter to cut the dough into rounds. Gently knead the scraps together to make a few more biscuits, or 1 large one.

Place the biscuits on a cookie sheet so that they are touching. Bake for 10 to 12 minutes, until they are a light golden brown on both the top and bottom.

Serve hot with Blackstrap Molasses with Fresh Churned Butter (recipe, p. 100).

Blackstrap Molasses
with Fresh Churned Butter

The process of making molasses is part of the manufacture of sugar. The sugarcane plant is stripped of its leaves, and the juice is extracted from the cane by crushing or mashing, then boiled to concentrate it, which produces sugar crystals. The result of the first boiling and removal of the sugar crystals is called "first molasses" (mild) and is the sweetest tasting. The "second molasses" (dark) is created from a second boiling and removal of sugar crystals. "Blackstrap" is the result of a third boiling of the syrup. The darker molasses has a bittersweet taste.

8 tablespoons unsalted butter,
   room temperature
¼ cup blackstrap molasses
Pinch of sea salt

Whip the butter in a medium bowl until light and fluffy. Drizzle in the molasses and sprinkle in the salt, whipping until well mixed. Using a rubber spatula to scrape down the bowl, transfer the molasses butter to a small serving bowl, or a large ramekin.

Serve with hot Buttermilk Biscuits (recipe, p. 98), Hoe Cakes (recipe. p. 84), or even with Cracklin' Bread (recipe, p. 86).

Fried Salt Pork

Serves 6

Like bacon, salt pork is made from pork belly and has not been cured or smoked, simply heavily salted. This salt pork recipe is best served with something sweet, such as Blackstrap Molasses.

2 pounds salt pork, thinly sliced
½ cup flour
½ teaspoon freshly ground black
   pepper
¼ cup lard, for frying

Place the slices of salt pork and 4 cups cold water into a medium saucepan over high heat and bring to a boil. Continue to boil for 5 minutes, then drain the salt pork on paper towels and pat dry.

On a large plate, season the flour with black pepper, and dredge both sides of the salt pork in the flour.

Melt the lard in a cast-iron skillet over medium-high heat, and fry the salt pork for 5 minutes on each side, until golden brown. Drain on paper towels and serve with Buttermilk Biscuits (recipe, p. 98) and Blackstrap Molasses with Fresh Churned Butter.

Mackerel Croquettes

Serves 6

2 (12-ounce) cans mackerel, drained, or 1½ pounds fresh cooked mackerel

1 medium onion, finely chopped

2 large eggs

½ cup fresh breadcrumbs

½ cup flour

¼ cup yellow cornmeal

½ teaspoon paprika

Salt and black pepper

½ cup vegetable oil

¼ cup fresh lemon juice

1 small yellow onion, chopped

3 green onions, chopped

¼ cup capers

3 large garlic cloves, peeled

2 tablespoons horseradish

1 cup mayonnaise

3 tablespoons whole-grain mustard

2 tablespoons cane syrup

1 teaspoon hot sauce, or Hot Pepper Relish (recipe, p. 33)

3 tablespoons chopped parsley

¼ teaspoon cayenne pepper

1 teaspoon salt

⅛ teaspoon freshly ground black pepper

In a large bowl, add the mackerel and break into small pieces with a spoon or fork. If using fresh mackerel, use only the flesh, discarding the skin and bones.

Add the onion, eggs, breadcrumbs, flour, cornmeal, paprika, salt, and pepper and stir until well incorporated. Form the mixture mixture into patties and place them on a large plate or platter. Cover with plastic wrap and refrigerate for 30 minutes before cooking.

Heat the oil in a large cast-iron skillet over high heat until hot (350° to 375° F). Use a spatula to place the mackerel patties into the hot oil, and fry for 5 minutes on each side, or until golden brown. Remove and drain on paper towels.

To make the rémoulade sauce, combine the lemon juice, onions, green onions, capers, garlic, horseradish, mayonnaise, mustard, syrup, hot sauce, parsley, cayenne, salt, and pepper in the bowl of a food processor and process for 30 seconds. Use immediately or store, refrigerated, in an airtight container for 3 to 5 days.

Serve hot with Tomato & Okra Gravy (recipe, p. 50), or cold the next day with the rémoulade sauce.

Applesauce & Fried Ham Steak

Serves 4

You can find real ham steaks at your butcher shop. What I mean by "real" is a full slice from the ham that includes a slice of the ham bone in its center and the rind or skin outlining the ham slice. Serving it with applesauce — or thinly sliced apples cooked in the ham juice for about 5 minutes — makes the perfect start to any morning.

2 (¼-inch thick) ham steaks, with rind

3 teaspoons dark brown sugar

2 cups Applesauce (recipe, p. 18)

Score the fat on the ham rind by making small cuts in it. Do not remove the rind.

Sprinkle both sides of the ham steaks with the brown sugar and let sit for 10 minutes.

Heat a large cast-iron skillet over medium-low heat, add the ham steaks, and cook 5 minutes on each side, until browned. Reduce the heat if the sugar starts to burn. Transfer the ham steaks to a warm platter.

Use ½ cup water to deglaze the pan over medium-high heat, scraping the browned bits from the bottom of the pan. When the water is almost to a boil, stir in the applesauce.

Return the ham steaks, plus whatever juices have accumulated in the platter, to the skillet. Reduce the heat to low and simmer for 3 to 5 minutes.

Spring Omelet Roll

Serves 8

Similar to baked soufflé, this dish is whipped up light and fluffy and baked in a hot oven to trap the air in the egg mixture. What makes it special is that you can add different fillings, such as bacon, ham, onions, or cheese. Roll it up, slice it, and it still stays light and fluffy. Baking it in a jellyroll pan makes it easier to roll, and precooking the raw ingredients ensures that the omelet is cooked through.

2 tablespoons unsalted butter, melted, plus 2 tablespoons for greasing the pan

½ cup cream cheese, room temperature

2 tablespoons all-purpose flour

1 teaspoon sea salt, to taste

1 teaspoon freshly ground black pepper, to taste

¾ cup whole milk

12 medium eggs, well beaten

1 large green bell pepper, finely diced

½ cup finely diced red onion

2 tablespoons Dijon mustard

2½ cups sharp cheddar cheese, shredded

2 cups black pepper bacon, or other smoked bacon, cooked and drained (recipe, p. 110)

2 medium tomatoes seeded and diced

¼ cup green onion tops, chopped

Preheat the oven to 375° F.

Line the bottom of a jellyroll pan, or deep sheet pan, with parchment paper, and grease with 2 tablespoons butter. Set aside.

In a large bowl, beat the cream cheese, flour, salt, pepper, and milk until smooth. Stir in the beaten eggs.

Heat the melted butter in a large stainless-steel sauté pan over medium heat. Add the bell peppers and onion and cook for 10 minutes, or until translucent, being careful not to brown. Remove from the heat and allow the vegetables to cool in the pan.

Add the onions and peppers to the bowl with the egg mixture, and stir until well combined. Pour into the prepared jellyroll pan and bake for 30 to 35 minutes, or until the eggs have puffed up and are set in the center. Remove from the oven and immediately spread the mustard on top of the egg roll, and sprinkle with 1 cup cheese. Top with bacon and and an additional 1 cup cheese.

Roll the baked egg lengthwise, peeling the parchment paper away as you go. Return the rolled omelet to the pan, sprinkle the top with the remaining cheese, and bake an additional 3 to 4 minutes, until the cheese is melted. Remove from the oven and allow the egg roll to rest for 5 minutes. Cut into 2-inch slices and garnish with the diced tomatoes and chopped green onions.

Scrambled Eggs & Hog Brains

Serves 4

Eating brains is considered a delicacy around the globe, including inthe South. Eating hog brains is just another example of how similar the eating habits of the French are to those of Southerners—we eat every part of the pig. Hog brains have a distinctive texture similar to extra creamy, extra fluffy scrambled eggs. They are served, sautéed with brown butter and capers, as an individual dish in France, and mixed into scrambled eggs and served with breakfast in the South. For added crunch, they can be dipped in milk, rolled in cornmeal, and pan fried in lard. Whenever you make scrambled eggs, I suggest that you use farm fresh eggs, whether from your farm or your local farmer's market. Crack each fresh egg, one at a time, into a small bowl before adding this to your main mixing bowl. This insures that you don't mix in a partially formed chick into your dish.

½ pound hog brains, from your
    butcher

1 tablespoon cider vinegar

1 teaspoon salt

3 tablespoons bacon drippings

8 large eggs, beaten

Sea salt and freshly ground black
    pepper, to taste

Prepare the hog brains for cooking by placing them in a large bowl with the cider vinegar, salt, and enough cold water to totally cover the meat. This vinegar mixture will solidify the brains and loosen the thin membrane covering it. Refrigerate, covered, for 2 hours, then rinse with cool water and carefully remove the membrane surrounding the hog brain. Use your thumb and forefinger to peel away the membrane.

Place the brains in a large, high-sided saucepan with enough water to cover, and bring to a boil over high heat. Reduce the heat to medium-low, cover, and simmer gently for 15 minutes. The hog brains should form a firm greyish-white mass.

Drain the brains and rinse again with cool water. Pat dry and set aside.

In a large cast-iron skillet over medium heat, add the bacon drippings and the brains and mash with a fork. Pour in the beaten eggs, season with salt and black pepper, and stir until the eggs are firm, but still creamy.

Place on a warm platter and serve with Fried Salt Pork (recipe, p. 100) and Pan-Fried 'Taters & Spring Onions (recipe, p. 94).

Smothered Squirrel

Serves 6

Cooking rabbit in culinary school reminded me of cooking squirrel back home. The meat of both animals is dredged in flour, cooked in oil, and served with gravy. The two main differences were how we cooked the dish and where we got the rabbits and the squirrels. In culinary school, we made a roux in a separate pan and thickened it with stock to make the gravy. Back home we made the gravy in the same pan in which we fried the squirrel, and thickened it with milk. The rabbits in school were bought at the farmer's market or butcher shop. Back home, we hunted squirrels for this dish.

2 squirrels, each cut into 6 pieces

1 cup flour

1 teaspoon salt

½ teaspoon black pepper

½ teaspoon paprika

3 slices smoked bacon, chopped

½ cup butter

1 medium onion, diced

½ cup milk, or cold water

Cut up the squirrel by removing the front and hind legs, and then cutting the torso in half.

In a medium bowl, mix the flour, salt, pepper, and paprika. Dredge the squirrel pieces in the seasoned flour and set aside.

Render the fat from the bacon in a large cast-iron skillet over low heat for 5 to 10 minutes, stirring occasionally. Add the butter and onions to the rendered bacon and cook for 10 minutes, or until the butter foams and the onions begin to brown.

Place each piece of floured squirrel into the skillet along with the bacon, butter, and onions. Cook for 8 to 10 minutes, turning to brown both sides, then stir any of the remaining seasoned flour into the skillet and whisk in the water. Cover with a tight-fitting lid, reduce the heat to low, and simmer for 30 to 45 minutes.

Adjust the gravy's consistency and seasoning with milk, salt, and pepper, as needed.

Serve this recipe over white rice, or with Pan-Fried 'Taters & Spring Onions (recipe, p. 94).

What's for Supper?

Like many Southern women, my grandmother sat a beautiful dinner table. Silver salt and pepper shakers would flank her silver sugar dish on the crisp, ironed tablecloth. Her lazy-susan would be laden with jars of pickled cucumbers, hot pepper sauce, green tomato cha cha, jellies, jams, and preserves. The table would be piled high with field peas or snap beans, fried corn, and slices of fresh cucumbers, tomatoes, and spring onions. But the main dish would be the surprise we all awaited—it might be smothered rabbit, braised short ribs, oxtail stew, or another family favorite.

These supper recipes lean toward the Southern palate, with nods to a few French dishes that are "kissing cousins." And, I offer a complete primer on cooking the best Thanksgiving turkey you'll ever serve, complete with sage and cornbread dressing.

Black Pepper Bacon

Yields 3 to 4 pounds

Curing meat takes time and the right ingredients, one of which is Pink Curing Salt. This curing salt, also known as Prague Powder #1 and TCM, or tinted curing mix, is not to be confused with table salt. It is a mixture of sodium, nitrates, and nitrites that inhibit the growth of microorganisms that can cause food-borne illness. It is colored pink to help distinguish it from salt or sugar, and to blend better with the meats it's being used to cure. Curing salts can be ordered on-line or acquired from a butcher. No matter what its name, curing salt should be used sparingly, and due to its high nitrate and nitrite levels, never eaten alone.

¼ cup sea salt

1 cup dark brown sugar

2 tablespoons freshly ground
   black pepper

½ teaspoon ground bay leaf

1 teaspoon granulated onion

1 teaspoon granulated garlic

½ teaspoon ground thyme

2 teaspoons Pink Curing Salt,
   or Prague Powder #1

3 to 4 pounds fresh pork belly

Mix the salt, brown sugar, black pepper, bay leaf, onion, garlic, and thyme together and place in a large flat plastic container with a cover. Taste and adjust the seasoning before you add the Pink Curing Salt. Add the Pink Curing Salt and mix well.

Add the pork belly to the container and spread the cure mix over the entire pork belly, being sure to press the mix into all the cracks and crevices of the belly. Cover and refrigerate for 10 days, turning the pork belly after 5 days.

After day 10, remove the pork from the container and rinse with cold water; removing as much of the cure mix as possible. Discard the mix left in the container.

Pat the pork belly dry, place on a wire rack in a sheet pan, and refrigerate, uncovered, for 24 hours to form a pellicle, or sticky skin.

Preheat the grill or smoker to 300° F using a fire made of ⅔ hickory wood and ⅓ charcoal. Smoke the cured pork belly for 1 ½ hours per pound at 200° to 215° F, or until the internal temperature reaches 155° F.

Remove and let the bacon rest at room temperature for 30 minutes. Refrigerate the bacon before slicing to make it easier to cut.

Fry the bacon slices in a hot cast-iron skillet over medium heat for 5 minutes on each side, or until crisp.

Serve with Buttermilk Biscuits (recipe, p. 98), or Pan-Fried 'Taters & Spring Onions (recipe, p. 94).

Hog Killin' Time

My grandfather butchered our hogs in the fall, sometimes right before Thanksgiving. My grandmother would then rub huge amounts of salt all over the pork and stack the cuts in the refrigerator. He would bring in the hog's head and other bits and pieces that had been trimmed off. Grandmother would put those pieces into a washtub on the table, and place the hog's head in a huge pot on the stove filled with water, onions, garlic, and lots of herbs and spices. I would stand on a stool and watch the hog's head bob up and down in the pot, counting how many times the nose would pop out of the water, until my grandmother called me to help make the sausage. She would season the bits and pieces in that washtub with salt, red pepper, and lots of rubbed sage, mixing it around with her hands. Once she was done, I turned the handle of the meat grinder, which was clamped on the edge of the table. Magically (for a child), out came pork sausage! She would cook a little test patty and we would taste it to decide if the sausage needed more salt, red pepper, or sage.

Rendered Lard

Yields 1 quart

A big part of the hog-killing process is rendering lard from the pork fat. You must heat the pork fat slowly so that it melts and separates itself from any lean meat or skin attached to the fat. On the farm, this was done in a huge cast-iron kettle over a wood fire. I never got to stir the pot as a child, but I never stopped asking to do so!

4 pounds unsalted and uncured
   pork fat, fatback, or pork scraps

Types of Fat From a Hog

Back Fat or Fatback
This is the fat that comes from the back, shoulder, and rump of the animal. It's literally the layer of fat directly below the skin. It's usually sold in pieces and often with the skin still attached. This type of fat is best used for frying.

Belly
The pork belly is a rich, soft, firm fat layered with meat, used mostly to cure bacon. Because the meat is laced with fat, it provides added flavor to dishes such as beans and greens.

Leaf Lard
Leaf lard is the fat from around a pig's kidneys. This is the cleanest fat on the animal and, rendered properly, will produce a pure white, odorless lard to use for pastry. Leaf lard is used to make perfect, flaky pie crusts.

Cut the fat into 1-inch cubes. This will ensure that the pork renders evenly.

Put the pork and ½ cup water into a heavy-bottomed stockpot over medium-high heat. Stir constantly until the pork starts to melt, then reduce the heat to low and stir occasionally.

Remove and save any cooked pieces of fat and skin. This is called crackling, and it can be salted and eaten as a snack or added to cornbread to make Cracklin' Bread (recipe, p. 86).

Once all of the fat has melted, carefully strain the liquid through a sieve lined with a double layer of cheesecloth. Pour the lard into heavy plastic containers and allow to cool. Store the rendered lard for up to 3 months in the refrigerator, or up to 1 year in the freezer.

Bacon Jam

Yields 3 half-pint jars

Jam usually brings to mind visions of fresh fruit juice and sugar boiled together until thick enough to spread on biscuits, rolls, and hoe cakes. Bacon jam is pretty much the same—the meat is simmered with sugar, plus onions, vinegar, coffee, and bourbon. Spread baacon jam on biscuits, rolls, and hoe cakes.

1½ pounds smoked bacon, cut into ¼-inch pieces

2 medium onions, diced

3 large cloves garlic, minced

½ cup apple cider vinegar

½ cup firmly packed dark brown sugar

¼ cup molasses

6 tablespoons brewed coffee

6 tablespoons bourbon, your choice brand

Sea salt, to taste

Freshly ground black pepper, to taste

Cook the bacon in a large cast-iron skillet over medium-high heat for 20 minutes, stirring occasionally until the fat is rendered and the bacon is lightly browned and starting to crisp. Drain on paper towels and set aside.

Pour off all but 1 tablespoon of the rendered fat, then reduce the heat to low, and add the onions and garlic. Cook for 5 minutes, stirring, until the onions are soft and translucent.

Add the vinegar, brown sugar, molasses, coffee, and bourbon. Increase the heat to medium, bring the mixture to a boil, and cook for an additional 2 minutes, stirring, and scraping the browned bits from the bottom of the skillet.

Return the cooked bacon to the skillet and stir to combine. Lower the heat and simmer, uncovered, about 3½ to 4 hours, or until the liquid has reduced and the bacon jam has thickened slightly. Stir occasionally to keep the jam from sticking.

Adjust the seasoning with salt and pepper, allow to cool to room temperature, then transfer the jam to jars with tight-fitting lids. Bacon jam may be kept in the refrigerator for up to 1 month.

Serve with Hoe Cakes (recipe, p. 84), and Southern Fried Corn (recipe, p. 48).

Scotch Eggs with Mustard Sauce

Yields 6

Culinary school was the first time I ever heard of a Scotch Egg. When my chef instructor told us that we were going to boil eggs, peel them, pack ground sausage around them, bread them, and deep fry them, I couldn't understand why—until I tasted one. It was absolutely delicious. To this day I can't decide if it's the creamy egg yolk, the savory sausage, or the crunchy breading that is my favorite part of a Scotch egg. So I will have to keep making them to find out.

6 medium eggs

12 ounces ground pork sausage, sweet or Italian

1 tablespoon dried parsley, crushed

2 teaspoons (1 lemon) grated lemon zest

¼ teaspoon ground nutmeg

¼ teaspoon dried marjoram

Salt and pepper, to taste

1 egg, beaten

4 cups dry bread crumbs

2 quarts oil, for deep frying

1 medium egg

1 cup mayonnaise

¼ cup Dijon mustard

2 tablespoons brown sugar

Place 6 whole eggs in a saucepan, add enough water to cover, bring to a boil over high heat, and cook for 10 to 12 minutes. Drain the cooked eggs, let them cool enough to handle, then peel and set aside.

Combine the sausage in a bowl with the parsley, lemon zest, nutmeg, marjoram, salt, and pepper. Use your hands to work all the ingredients into the sausage, and divide it into 6 portions. With wet hands, work the sausage around the eggs to form an even coating. Repeat for each boiled egg.

Put the beaten egg in a small bowl and the bread crumbs in a separate bowl. Roll each sausage-coated egg in the beaten egg, then dredge in the breadcrumbs, and transfer to a small pan. Cover the pan and refrigerate the eggs at least 30 minutes before frying.

Heat the oil in a deep-fryer to 375° F.

Using a slotted spoon, carefully slide the eggs into the oil, and fry, 3 at a time, for 4 to 5 minutes, until they are deep golden brown. Turn the eggs as they cook so that they brown evenly. Remove with the slotted spoon, drain on paper towels, and repeat with the remaining 3 eggs.

To make the mustard sauce, crack 1 egg into a small saucepan. With the heat on low, stir in the mayonnaise, Dijon mustard, and brown sugar. When the mixture just reaches a boil, remove the pan from the heat and allow it to cool. Transfer the mustard sauce to a serving dish and refrigerate for at least 10 minutes.

Leftover eggs can be individually wrapped and refrigerated for up to 3 days, and the mustard sauce will keep, refrigerated, for 1 week.

Barbecue Pig's Feet

Serves 4

Excited wouldn't begin to describe how I felt the first time I saw pig's feet in Paris. I first spotted them in the case of a Le Boucherie (butcher shop), and later on several different restaurant menus around the city. The French cooked them a variety of ways: stuffed with ground pork; boiled, deboned, and turned into terrines; and even roasted until their skin was crispy. I tried them all, but my favorite way to eat pig's feet is barbequed. First, they're boiled, then baked or grilled to caramelize their skin, and finally slathered with spicy barbecue sauce. Delicious!

8 pig's feet, split in half

2 small onions, quartered

3 large cloves garlic, mashed

1 bunch fresh thyme

1 bunch fresh oregano

1 bay leaf

1 dried cayenne pepper

½ cup apple cider vinegar

1 tablespoon sea salt

1 teaspoon freshly cracked
  black pepper

2 cups barbecue sauce, your
  choice brand

Wash the pig's feet in cold water until the water runs clear. Remove any hair on the feet, paying special attention between the toes. Place them in a large stockpot along with the onions, garlic, thyme, oregano, bay leaf, cayenne pepper, vinegar, salt, and pepper, and cover with cold water.

Bring the pot to a rolling boil over high heat, then reduce the heat to low and simmer for 3 hours, or until tender. Add additional water to keep the feet covered during the cooking time.

When the meat is fork tender, remove the stockpot from the heat and refrigerate the feet overnight in their cooking liquid.

The next morning, preheat your oven to 350° F. (You can also cook them on the grill following the same cooking directions.)

Remove the pig's feet from their cooking liquid, which will be thick and gelatinous when cold, and place them in a large roasting pan, skin-side up. Bake for 1 hour, basting frequently with barbecue sauce.

Serve piping hot with Mustard & Turnip Greens (recipe, p. 74) and Cracklin' Bread (recipe, p. 86).

Barbecue Spareribs

Serves 4

I grew up watching my grandfather, great uncles, and my father cook ribs over an open-pit fire of hickory wood. It takes patience, because the best barbecue ribs are cooked "low and slow," meaning they are cooked over low heat for a long time. But the falling-off-the-bone tenderness and the smokiness of the meat is always worth the wait.

1 slab (4 pounds) pork spareribs

2 teaspoons sea salt

1 tablespoon freshly ground
   black pepper

2 tablespoons smoked paprika

1 pinch cayenne pepper

¼ cup dark brown sugar

2 cups barbecue sauce, your
   choice brand

1 lemon, juiced and quartered

1 large onion, chopped

3 cloves garlic, mashed

½ cup apple cider vinegar

Using a sharp paring knife, remove the membrane from the slab of ribs by making a cut across the top of the rib bone, grabbing the membrane with your thumb and index finger, and firmly pulling in a downward motion. Use the paring knife to trim excess fat from the slab of ribs, being careful not to over trim. (Remember, fat adds flavor.) Set aside.

Combine the salt, pepper, paprika, cayenne pepper, and brown sugar in a bowl and rub this onto both sides of the slab of ribs.

Wrap the ribs tightly with plastic wrap and refrigerate for 12 to 24 hours.

Using a mixture of hickory wood and charcoal, preheat your grill to 300° F.

Place the slab "curl" side up on the grill, away from the direct flame, using indirect heat to smoke them.

To make a wash, combine the lemon juice and quarters, the onion, garlic, vinegar, and 4 cups water.

Cook the slab for 2½ hours with the "curl" side up, then turn the slab over and cook 1 additional hour. Baste with the lemon wash throughout the cooking process to add flavor and help tenderize the ribs.

During the last 10 minutes of cooking, brush both sides with barbecue sauce. Remove from the grill and let the spareribs rest 15 minutes before slicing.

Serve with Gram's Cole Slaw (recipe, p. 45) and Mustard & Turnip Greens (recipe, p. 74).

Hog Head Cheese

Serves 8 to 10

Known as tête fromagée *(which translates as "cheesed head") in France, and as "souse" in the South, Hog Head Cheese is made from a hog's head, but it is not cheese. It is a tasty, gelatinous dish made of herbs, spices, and tender pieces of chopped pork from the cooked flesh of the hog's head, and then chilled in its cooking liquid, usually in a terrine or loaf pan. You can serve Hog Head Cheese with crackers as a snack, as coldcuts on a sandwich, or with toasted French bread as an hors d'ouvre.*

1 large hog head

3 large onions, quartered

3 large whole cloves garlic, plus
   3 cloves, minced

¼ cup sea salt, plus more to taste

1 tablespoon freshly ground black
   pepper, plus more to taste

2 teaspoons red chili pepper flakes,
   divided

1 cup apple cider vinegar

2 cups white wine, such as
   Chardonnay

2 teaspoons rubbed sage

Using a very sharp butcher or chef's knife, clean the hog's head by removing the eyes, ears, and brains, reserving the brains for Scrambled Eggs & Hog Brains (recipe, p. 106). Using a small saw, divide the head into 4 pieces. (You may also ask your butcher to do this for you.) You may boil the hog's head without cutting it into pieces, if you have a stock pot large enough to hold it.

In a large stockpot, add the pieces of the hog's head, the onions, whole cloves garlic, sea salt, black pepper, 1 teaspoon red chili pepper flakes, vinegar, Chardonnay, and enough cold water to cover, and bring to a rolling boil over high heat.

Reduce the heat to low and simmer for 3 hours, or until the meat is tender and falling off the bones. Allow the meat to cool in the cooking liquid long enough to handle with your bare hands, then strain, reserving the cooking liquid.

Pick the meat from the bones, discard the bones, and chop the meat, cooked onions, and garlic cloves into small, ¼-inch pieces. Place this mixture in a large bowl. Mix in the rubbed sage, the remaining red chili pepper, and enough of the cooking liquid—about 2 to 4 cups—to give the mixture a loose consistency. Season with additional salt and black pepper to taste. Using a rubber spatula, firmly pack the hog head cheese into several 8 x 4 x 6 (or larger) ceramic terrines. Any mixture that does not fit into the terrines can be packed into loaf pans or plastic containers. Cover the terrines (or other containers) with lids or plastic wrap, and refrigerate overnight.

When you are ready to serve, cut into slices and serve on toasted slices of baguette, or with crackers.

Hog Liver & Onions

Serves 4 to 6

Liver is one of those dishes you either love, hate, or simply tolerate. Whatever your opinion on liver, soaking it in milk at least an hour before cooking helps to remove some of the bitterness. Frying the liver in bacon grease and serving it with sweet onions also improves the taste, making this a dish you will love.

2 pounds beef liver, sliced in
    1-inch thick strips

1½ cups milk

2 cups all-purpose flour

¼ cup unsalted butter, divided

2 large Vidalia, or sweet onions,
    sliced

2 tablespoons bacon drippings,
    or lard

Sea salt, to taste

Freshly ground black pepper,
    to taste

Gently rinse the liver slices under cold water, place them in a medium bowl, add the milk, and let the liver soak for 2 hours.

Put the flour onto a large plate and season it with salt and pepper. Drain the milk from the bowl of liver, and coat each slice with the seasoned flour mixture. Set aside.

Melt half the butter in a large cast-iron skillet over medium heat and cook the onions for 10 minutes, or until they are soft. Set the cooked onions aside, and melt the remaining butter in the skillet over medium heat. When the butter stops foaming, add the bacon drippings and increase the heat to medium-high. Fry the coated liver slices in the hot drippings for 5 minutes, or until they are golden brown on the bottom, then turn each slice, add the reserved onions, and cook an additional 5 minutes, or until the other side has browned.

Adjust the seasoning with salt and pepper as needed and serve hot.

Brown Sugar-Cured Ham

Serves 10 to 12

Ham, from a Southern point of view, has always been made from the hind leg of the pig. It is cured with either salt or in a brine, then smoked or dried. This process was traditionally done in the fall, and it preserved the ham through the winter months when fresh meat was scarce. Molasses, brown sugar, or maple syrup were often used to add more flavor to the ham. If you've never cured your own ham, you'll love the results.

1 (10- to12-pound) uncured ham

1 cup sea salt

1 cup dark brown sugar

¼ cup blackstrap molasses

1 tablespoon freshly ground
   black pepper

¼ teaspoon ground cloves

1 teaspoon Pink Curing Salt,
   also known as Prague
   Powder #1, order on-line, or
   from your butcher

Bring 1 gallon water to a boil in a large stockpot.

Remove the pot from the heat and stir in the sea salt, sugar, molasses, pepper, cloves, and Pink Curing Salt until the sugar and salts have dissolved. Transfer the brine to a large plastic container and refrigerate to a temperature of 40° F before you add the ham. The brine must be chilled to reduce the chance of any bacteria growth. Add the raw ham to the chilled brine. If any parts of the ham bob above the surface of the brine when it is added to the container, place a ceramic plate on top of the ham to weight it down.

Place the container with the ham in the refrigerator, and let it brine for 1 day per every two pounds of ham (for example, a 10-pound ham should brine for 5 days). Turn the ham over halfway through the brining process, and once again make sure all parts are submerged.

When the brining period is done, rinse the ham under cold running water, and discard the brine. Place the ham in a clean container, cover with cold water, and refrigerate for another 24 hours.

Preheat the oven to 325° F.

Remove the ham from the container, pat dry, and bake 30 minutes per pound, or until the internal temperature reaches 150° F.

Allow the ham to rest 30 minutes before carving.

Dry-Rubbed Smoked Pork Shoulder

Serves 8 to 10

When slow-smoking a pork shoulder, you should figure 1½ hours per pound of pork. A 10-pound, bone-in pork shoulder takes a long time to cook, but for the majority of that time it is in the smoker. You can get it started right after breakfast and have it ready in time for dinner.

2 tablespoons kosher salt

2 tablespoons freshly ground
   black pepper

2 tablespoons sugar

3 tablespoons garlic powder

2 tablespoons onion powder

3 tablespoons paprika

1 tablespoon ground sage

2 teaspoons dried oregano

1 teaspoon dry mustard

1 teaspoon cayenne pepper

1 (8 to 10-pound) bone-in pork
   shoulder

Mix all the ingredients together in a bowl, and rub them thoroughly into the pork shoulder. Wrap the pork in plastic wrap and refrigerate for at least 8 hours.

Before smoking it, unwrap the pork shoulder and allow it to rest at room temperature for ½ to 1 hour.

Heat your smoker to a constant 225° F. This may require several additions of water-soaked wood to keep the smoke going. Add the pork shoulder when the temperature of the smoker has reached 225° F, close the lid, and adjust the vents so that the smoke flows freely throughout the smoker.

Cook 10 to 14 hours, or until the meat is tender and reaches an internal temperature of 185° to 195° F. Let the meat rest 30 minutes before slicing, pulling, or chopping the pork.

Serve with Gram's Coleslaw (recipe, p. 45), a splash of hot pepper sauce, or your favorite barbecue sauce.

Chitterlings in Pepper Sauce

Serves 8

In a sink or large bowl of cold water, rinse the chitterlings repeatedly by filling each intestine with water on one end and forcing it out the other end. Repeat this process several times until the water runs clear and free of debris. Using a sharp paring knife, trim the large pieces of fat off each chitterling, leaving enough to add flavor.

20 pounds chitterlings, thoroughly cleaned

2 large onions, diced

3 cloves garlic, chopped

2 dried cayenne peppers

2 tablespoons sea salt

1 tablespoon freshly cracked black pepper

½ cup apple cider vinegar

Place the chitterlings in a large stockpot, and cover with 2 quarts cold water. Bring to a full, rolling boil and add the onions, garlic, cayenne pepper, sea salt, pepper, and vinegar. Be sure the water is at a full boil before adding the seasoning or the chitterlings will be tough. Reduce the heat to low and simmer the chitterlings for 3 to 4 hours, or until they are tender but have a little "bite" left.

Serve them in a warm bowl with some of their cooking liquid, and a generous amount of hot pepper sauce.

Spicy Pig Ear & Pig Tail Sandwiches

Serves 8

2 pounds pig ears, whole or halved

1 pound pig tails

2 large onions, quartered

3 large cloves garlic, mashed

2 tablespoons pickling spice

3 tablespoons red chili flakes

¼ cup apple cider vinegar

1 tablespoon sea salt

1 tablespoon freshly ground black pepper

16 slices white bread

Wash the pig ears and tails in cold water until the water runs clear. Scrape them to remove any hair.

Place the pig ears and tails in a large stockpot with enough cold water to cover. Add the onion, garlic, pickling spice, chili flakes, vinegar, salt, and pepper, and bring to a boil over high heat, then reduce the heat to medium and simmer for 2 hours, or until tender.

Drain the ears and tails, discarding the cooking liquid, and serve between 2 pieces of white bread with Green Tomato ChaCha (recipe, p. 34) and Red Hot Pepper Relish (recipes, p. 33).

Fresh Pork Sausage

Yields 6 pounds bulk sausage

As a child, I loved turning the grinder when we made fresh sausage. That way, I knew I would get the first taste of the sausage patty we cooked. One of the great things about grinding your own sausage is that you are in control of the texture and taste. Like a richer sausage? Add more fat. Leaner? Add less fat. The same holds true for the taste—add whatever mixture of herbs and spices that appeal to you. So, make a batch, taste a sample, and go from there.

2 pounds fresh pork, from loin and shoulder, cut into ½-inch strips

3 pounds fresh pork belly (unsalted, uncured bacon), cut into ½-inch strips

¼ cup firmly-packed dark brown sugar

1 to 2 tablespoons sea salt

2 teaspoons freshly ground black pepper

2 teaspoons dried rubbed sage

½ teaspoon red pepper flakes

1 cup rock salt

Place the pork and pork belly in a large bowl with the sugar, salt, pepper, sage, and red pepper flakes. Mix thoroughly and place the bowl within a larger bowl that has been filled with the rock salt and 3 pounds of ice. This step is important to keep the pork cold so that it does not clog the grinder.

Feed the pork mixture through the meat grinder. Once all of the pork has been ground, make a small patty and fry it in a skillet to test for flavor. Add more seasoning to adjust the flavor as needed.

Form the ground sausage into 2-inch round patties, about ½-inch thick, and place on a wax (or parchment) paper-lined sheet pan. Cover the pan with plastic wrap. Refrigerate the pork sausage for 24 to 36 hours before cooking. This aging allows all of the flavors to come together and results in a superior taste.

At this point, the fresh pork sausage patties are ready to be cooked for breakfast, or you may choose to wrap each patty tightly in plastic wrap and freeze them for later use.

Seared *Foie Gras*

Serves 4

Foie gras, or, literally, "fat liver," is the enlarged liver of a fattened duck or goose and is considered a delicacy in France. Be sure to buy Grade A, the highest quality. Store for 1 week in the refrigerator, but never freeze.

4 sliced of French baguette, cut at an angle

1 tablespoon butter, room temperature

4 medallions of Grade A duck foie gras, 1-inch thick x 2 to 3 inches round, deveined (see Cook's Notes below) and chilled

Sea salt, to taste

2 tablespoons balsamic vinegar

Heat a cast-iron skillet over medium heat for 5 minutes, until hot.

Butter one side of each slice of bread and place them butter side down in the hot skillet. Cook for 2 minutes, or until golden brown. Remove the bread from the pan, and transfer the toast to a warm plate.

Wipe the skillet with a damp towel, and increase the temperature to high, heating the pan to very hot, but not smoking. If the pan starts to smoke, remove from the heat and allow to cool slightly.

Score the *foie gras* medallions in a cross-hatched pattern on both sides, then sear in the very hot pan for 1 to 1½ minutes per side. Working quickly, remove the medallions from the skillet, drain on paper towels, and immediately season with a pinch of sea salt.

Reduce the heat to medium and add 2 tablespoons balsamic vinegar to the fat left in the pan. Bring to a boil, allowing the vinegar to reduce slightly, for 5 minutes. Serve the foie gras on the toasted bread, drizzled with ¼ teaspoon of the balsamic reduction, and a side of Pickled Beets with Shallots & Garlic (recipe, p. 30).

Cook's Notes

Like all liver, *foie gras* should be deveined before cooking. To do this, let the foie gras sit at room temperature for 1 hour, until soft and pliable. Separate the 2 halves, or lobes, and, using your index finger, find the place where the veins surface on the underside of each lobe. With a small paring knife, gently pry the *foie gras* open and follow the major veins into the liver. Remove the veins by pulling gently, or using small kitchen pliers. Try not to break up the liver too much. Scrape away any red blood spots, rinse in cold running water, then pat dry. If the lobe becomes misshapen while deveining, reshape it by smoothing over the vein line with your finger. Repeat with the smaller lobe.

To slice *foie gras* into medallions, place on a cutting board with the round side facing you. Using a warm slicing knife (dip the knife blade in a pitcher of hot water, and dry before slicing), start at the narrow end of the liver and cut at an angle to make each medallion at least 1-inch thick and 2- to 3-inches wide.

Smoked Ham Hocks

Yields 10 pounds, or about 30 small ham hocks

Ham hocks, also known as pork knuckles, are made up of mainly tough skin, ligaments, and tendons. But once you brine and smoke this cast-off piece of pork, you have a flavorful addition to any pot of greens, beans, or soup. Growing up, we would brine all the ham hocks we butchered, then smoke them along with the hams and bacon. Once smoked, we stored them in the freezer until we were ready to use.

10 pounds ham hocks

1 cup sea salt

1 cup dark brown sugar

1 large onion, finely diced

3 cloves garlic, minced

1 tablespoon Pink Curing Salt, or Prague Powder #1

1 tablespoon freshly cracked black pepper

1 teaspoon red chili flakes

1 bay leaf

Rinse the ham hocks under cold running water. Pat dry and set aside.

In a large stockpot, bring 1 gallon water to boil over high heat .

Remove the pot from the heat and add the sea salt, brown sugar, onion, garlic, Pink Curing Salt, black pepper, chili flakes, and bay leaf, stirring to dissolve the salt and sugars. Transfer the brine to a large plastic container and chill to 40° F.

Submerge the ham hocks in the chilled brine, weighting them with a ceramic plate, if needed, to keep them fully submerged, and refrigerate, covered, for 3 days.

Remove the ham hocks from the brine, rinse for 5 minutes under cold running water, and soak in a pot of clean water for 2 to 3 hours.

Remove from the water, pat dry, and refrigerate, uncovered, for 24 hours to form a pellicle or sticky skin. This will help the smoke flavor stick to the ham hocks.

Using hickory wood, preheat the grill or smoker to 215° to 250° F.

Smoke the ham hocks for 3 to 5 hours, or until the internal temperature reaches 160° F, adding more wood to keep the temperature steady at 250° F.

Remove from the heat and allow to cool, uncovered, on a large sheet pan or roasting pan. Individually wrap the ham hocks in plastic wrap. They will last up to 2 weeks in the refrigerator and up to 1 year in the freezer.

Use the ham hocks to add richness and flavor to beans, greens, and soups.

Venison Stew

Serves 6

Wild game can be found on most farm tables in France and in the South, where hunting is still an accepted way to get meat for the table. Growing up, I would see my grandfather, great uncles, and my father hunt everything: squirrels, ducks, quail, rabbits, and deer. Once the game were cleaned and skinned, my grandmother would help butcher them, and salt or smoke the meat for later, cooking the choicest pieces for dinner that night.

¼ cup flour

1 tablespoon salt

1 tablespoon freshly cracked black pepper

1 teaspoon paprika

¼ teaspoon cayenne pepper

1 teaspoon dried oregano

1 teaspoon dried thyme

2 pounds venison, cut into ½-inch cubes

3 tablespoons olive oil

4 slices thick cut bacon, cut into ½-inch pieces

1 large onion, diced

3 celery stalks, diced

3 carrots, peeled and diced

3 large cloves garlic, minced

2 large tomatoes, diced

1 tablespoon chopped thyme

2 bay leaves

1 cup red wine, such as Pinot Noir

4 cups beef stock

In a large bowl, stir together the flour, salt, pepper, paprika, cayenne, oregano, and thyme. Add the venison and toss to coat the with the seasoned flour. Set aside.

Heat the oil in a large stockpot over medium-high heat, add the bacon and cook for 5 minutes, or until the bacon is crisp. Drain the bacon on paper towels.

Increase the heat to high and sear the floured venison for 2 to 3 minutes, stirring occasionally. Add the onions and sauté for 2 minutes; add the celery and carrots and sauté for an additional 2 minutes. Add the garlic, diced tomatoes, thyme, and bay leaves to the pan and season with salt and pepper to taste.

Deglaze the pan with the red wine, scraping the sides to get all the browned bits. Add the beef stock and the cooked bacon, and increase the heat to high. Bring the liquid to a boil, cover, and reduce the heat to low. Simmer the stew for 45 minutes to 1 hour, or until the meat is very tender. If the liquid evaporates, add a little more beef stock.

Serve in warm bowls with Buttermilk Cornbread (recipe, p. 88).

Hickory-Smoked Chicken Croquettes

Yields 8 (4-ounce) croquettes

Croquettes are very popular in French cuisine, made from your choice of meat, fish, seafood, and even leftover mashed potatoes. Their richness comes from the added cream and eggs; fresh herbs and lemon zest bring color and flavor; and the bread crumbs gives croquettes their croquer, *or crunch.*

1 cup heavy cream

2 eggs

4 slices white bread, cubed

1½ pounds raw boneless, skinless chicken breast, cut into large chunks

½ pound Hickory-smoked bacon, cut into 2-inch pieces

1 small yellow onion, quartered

2 cloves garlic

¼ cup fresh sprigs thyme

¼ fresh parsley leaves

1 tablespoon lemon zest

½ teaspoon sea salt

½ teaspoon white pepper

4 cups Panko breadcrumbs

Oil for frying

Whisk together the heavy cream and eggs. Add the bread to the egg mixture and set aside.

Combine the chicken, bacon, onion, garlic, thyme, parsley, lemon zest, salt, and white pepper together in a large bowl.

Working in small batches, coarsely grind the chicken mixture in a food processor or meat grinder.

Mix the egg mixture into the ground chicken until all ingredients are evenly distributed. (At this point, you may want to cook a small patty to check for seasoning and adjust with salt and pepper, if necessary.)

Pour the Panko breadcrumbs onto a large plate or baking sheet. Set aside.

Form the chicken croquette mixture into 8 (4-ounce) round patties and dredge in the breadcrumbs to cover the top, bottom, and sides of each patty. Transfer the patties to a parchment-lined sheet pan and refrigerate for at least 30 minutes. This will help the croquettes hold their shape during cooking.

Once the croquettes are chilled, heat enough oil over medium-high heat to cover the bottom of a skillet or deep sauté pan. Place a single layer of croquettes in the hot oil and cook 6 minutes on each side, until golden brown. Transfer the croquettes to drain on layers of paper towels.

Serve hot with Cranberry Orange Relish (recipe, p. 20).

Braised Short Ribs

Serves 6

6 bone-in short ribs (4 pounds)

Sea salt

Freshly ground black pepper

4 tablespoons all-purpose flour

¼ cup olive oil

8 ounces thick cut bacon, cut
   into ½-inch pieces

2 tablespoons unsalted butter

1 pound mushrooms, quartered

1 large onion, diced

2 carrots, peeled and diced

4 cloves garlic

2 cups ripe tomatoes, peeled
   and diced

2 cups full-bodied red wine,
   such as Burgundy or Bordeaux

3 cups beef stock

1 bay leaf

2 springs fresh thyme

Preheat oven to 325° F.

Pat each short rib dry and season liberally with sea salt and pepper. Dredge with flour and set aside, saving the remaining flour.

Heat ⅛ cup olive oil in a Dutch oven over medium heat, and sauté the bacon for 3 to 4 minutes, until lightly browned. Transfer to paper towels to drain.

Add the butter to the Dutch oven. As soon as butter has melted and the foam begins to subside, add the mushrooms, and cook 10 to 15 minutes, until lightly browned. (Do not overload the pot or the mushrooms will steam instead of brown.) Remove the mushrooms from the pot and set aside. Add the remaining olive oil to the pot, and heat just until the oil begins to smoke. Add the short ribs and brown for 5 minutes on each side. Remove and set the short ribs aside.

Reduce the heat to low and stir in the onion, carrots, garlic, diced tomatoes, and any remaining flour. Cook 10 minutes, until browned. Return the short ribs and bacon to the pot. Add the red wine, enough beef stock to cover the ribs, the bay leaf, and the thyme. Bring to a simmer, cover with a tight-fitting lid, and transfer the pot to the oven.

Simmer for 3 to 4 hours, or until the meat is tender. Remove the pot from the oven and set aside to allow the short ribs to rest in the braising liquid for 10 minutes at room temperature.

Increase the oven temperature to 425° F. Remove the short ribs from the Dutch oven, transfer to a greased sheet pan, and bake for 10 to 15 minutes until browned.

While the ribs are browning, skim the fat from the top of the braising liquid in the Dutch oven and remove the bay leaf, sprigs of thyme, and any bones. Add the mushrooms to the pot and reduce over medium heat for 20 minutes, or until the sauce thickens.

Return the short ribs to the Dutch oven and simmer 2 to 3 minutes longer. Adjust the seasoning with additional sea salt and pepper as needed before serving.

Fried Gizzards

Serves 4

Considered a delicacy in the South, fried chicken gizzards are both crunchy and chewy, making them a great snack. Tenderize them in a marinade of buttermilk and hot sauce, dredge in well-seasoned flour, and deep fry in hot oil.

1 cup buttermilk

2 tablespoons hot pepper sauce, your favorite brand

1 teaspoon sea salt

1 teaspoon ground black pepper

1 pound chicken gizzards, cleaned

1 cup flour

2 teaspoons paprika

1 teaspoon sea salt

1 teaspoon ground black pepper

Lard for frying

In a large bowl, combine the buttermilk, hot pepper sauce, salt, and pepper. Add the chicken gizzards to the bowl, cover, and marinate in the refrigerator for 8 to 12 hours, or overnight.

When you are ready to cook, drain the chicken gizzards on paper towels and set aside. Discard the remaining buttermilk marinade.

To make the breading, combine the flour, paprika, salt, and pepper in a medium bowl. Coat the gizzards evenly with flour.

Melt enough lard to reach 1 to 1½ inches up the sides of a large cast-iron skillet and heat over medium-high heat to a temperature of 350° to 375° F.

Fry the gizzards for 4 to 6 minutes, or until golden brown. (The chicken gizzards will cook quickly.)

Drain on a towel and serve piping hot with Green Tomato Cha Cha (recipe, p. 34).

Roasted Chicken & Dumplings

Serves 6 to 8

Southerners share this with the French: we both have a talent for stretching ingredients further than you would think possible. A good example of this is turning yesterday's roasted chicken into today's Roasted Chicken & Dumplings. Using up leftover chicken is what gives this dish an intensely rich taste, and this recipe is versatile enough to use other roasted meats, such as turkey, in place of the chicken.

2 cups flour

4 teaspoons baking powder

½ teaspoon sea salt

1 cup milk

¼ unsalted butter

1 cup chopped onion

1 cup chopped carrots

1 cup chopped celery

1 clove garlic, minced

¼ cup all-purpose flour

½ teaspoon fresh or dried oregano

¼ teaspoon fresh or dried thyme

¼ teaspoon fresh or dried rosemary

8 cups chicken stock

4 cups potatoes, peeled and cubed

1 teaspoon sea salt

1 teaspoon freshly ground black pepper

2 cups cubed roasted chicken

1 cup cream

1 tablespoon chopped parsley

To make the dumpling batter, sift the flour, baking powder, and salt together in a large bowl. Add the milk and stir to make a thick batter. Set aside.

In a large stockpot, heat the butter over medium-low heat and cook the onion, carrots, and celery for 10 minutes, until soft and tender. Add the garlic and cook 1 minute longer. Stir in the flour, oregano, thyme, and rosemary and cook until the flour turns light brown. Gradually whisk in the stock until smooth.

Add the cubed potatoes, salt, and pepper to the stockpot, increase the heat to medium-high, and bring to a boil. Reduce the heat to low, cover, and simmer for 20 minutes, or until the potatoes are fork tender. Add the diced chicken, increase the heat again to medium-high, and bring to a boil.

Drop double tablespoonfuls of the dumpling batter into the boiling chicken stew, using all the batter. Cover the pot, immediately reduce the heat to low, and simmer for an additional 10 to 15 minutes, stirring occasionally to keep the dumplings from sticking together. The dumplings will sink to the bottom of the pot and then float to the top when they are done.

Heat the cream in a small stainless-steel saucepan over medium heat and stir into the Roasted Chicken & Dumplings.

Garnish with chopped parsley just before serving.

Pan-Fried Round Steaks & Brown Gravy

Serves 6

When I was a child, we would often eat this lean, inexpensive cut of beef. My mother would simmer the tenderized round steaks in gravy after browning them in oil.

½ cup lard, plus more as needed

1 cup all-purpose flour

1 teaspoon sea salt, plus more to taste

2 teaspoons freshly ground black pepper, plus more to taste

3 pounds round, or cube, steak

2 tablespoons butter

1½ cup beef stock, or water

Heat the lard in a large cast-iron skillet over medium heat.

Mix together the flour, salt, and pepper in a large bowl.

Season both sides of the steaks with additional salt and pepper and dredge each piece in the seasoned flour mixture, pressing to coat well with flour. Set aside the remaining seasoned flour for later.

Melt the butter in the hot lard before adding the round steaks to the skillet. Do not crowd the pan; fry the steaks in batches if needed. Fry for 5 minutes, then turn and fry another 5 minutes, until the steaks are a deep golden brown. Transfer the steaks to a towel-lined plate to drain.

After cooking all the steaks, pour off all but 2 tablespoons of pan drippings. Return the skillet to medium heat and whisk in 3 table-spoons of the remaining seasoned flour. Gradually whisk in the stock and continue whisking until the gravy boils and thickens. Reduce the heat and simmer for 15 to 20 minutes.

Return the steaks to the skillet of gravy and bring just to a boil, adjust the seasoning with salt and pepper, and serve with white rice.

Southern Fried Chicken with Cream Gravy

Serves 4 to 6

Southern fried chicken is the best in the world. Batter-dipped or lightly dredged in well-seasoned flour, fried in boiling hot lard until it is crisp and juicy, and served piping hot. It doesn't get much better than this.

Lard for frying

1 whole chicken, cut into 12
    pieces (2 legs, 2 thighs, 2 wings,
      4 breast pieces, back, and neck)

2 teaspoons sea salt

2 teaspoons ground black pepper

1½ cups flour

1 tablespoon salt

2 teaspoons ground black pepper

1 tablespoon paprika

Drippings from fried chicken
    (can also use drippings from
    pork steak, or round steak)

3 tablespoons flour

½ teaspoon salt

¼ teaspoon black pepper

1½ cups whole milk, or
    Half-and-Half

Add enough lard to reach 1 to 1½ inches up the side of a large cast-iron skillet, and heat over medium-high heat until hot (between 350° to 375° F).

Season the chicken pieces with salt and pepper and set aside.

In a bowl, season the flour with additional salt, pepper, and paprika.

Dredge the chicken pieces through the seasoned flour. Carefully place the pieces in the skillet of hot lard, cover, and fry for 30 minutes, or until golden brown, turning once after 15 to 20 minutes.

Remove the lid and cook the chicken an additional 10 minutes to crisp up the skin. Transfer the chicken to a paper towel-lined platter to drain.

To make the cream gravy, pour off all but 2 tablespoons of pan drippings. Return the skillet to medium heat and whisk in the flour, salt, and pepper until smooth. Gradually add the milk, whisking continuously, until the gravy boils and thickens. Reduce the heat and simmer for 15 to 20 minutes.

Serve the Southern Fried Chicken with Cream Gravy and Hot Pepper Relish (recipe, p. 33), or your favorite hot sauce.

Oxtails & Rice

Serves 4

Once considered a cast-off piece of meat, oxtails are gaining popularity due to their gelatin-rich meat. Seared in oil and then braised until fork tender, oxtails create a thick, silky sauce. I like them served over white rice, but they also go great with Root Vegetable Mash (recipe, p. 44).

2 pounds beef oxtails, available from your butcher, or the meat section of a grocery

2 large cloves garlic, minced

1 large onion, diced

1 tablespoon sea salt, plus more to taste

1 teaspoon freshly cracked black pepper, plus more to taste

¼ teaspoon dried thyme

¼ teaspoon dried basil

¼ teaspoon dried marjoram

¼ teaspoon smoked paprika

2 tablespoons bacon drippings, or lard

2 tablespoons all-purpose flour

White rice, your choice brand

Place the oxtails, garlic, onion, salt, pepper, thyme, basil, marjoram, and paprika in a large stockpot. Fill with enough water to cover the meat, and bring to a boil over high heat. Cover, and reduce the heat to medium-low. Cook for 2 ½ to 3 hours, or until the meat is fork tender.

Remove the pot from the heat, and reserve 2 cups of the broth.

Heat the bacon drippings in a large stainless-steel saucepan over medium heat.

Stir in the flour, and cook for 3 minutes, stirring constantly. Stir in the reserved broth and season to taste with salt and pepper. Cook for 15 minutes, stirring constantly, until the gravy thickens.

Transfer the oxtails to the sauté pan, and stir to coat with gravy. Cook over medium-low heat for 5 minutes, stirring occasionally. Serve hot over white rice.

Chicken Liver Stuffed Figs

Serves 4 to 6

I decided to take a very French approach to chicken liver for this recipe and make a chicken liver paté. It's a paste made with chicken, calf, hog, or duck livers—highly seasoned, lightly fried, and bursting with flavor from aromatics like onion and parsley. It owes its richness to fresh butter, and a subtle sweetness to a splash of Cognac. This is a very basic chicken liver paté, stuffed into dried figs, and cooked with a little chicken stock and a touch more Cognac. The end result is a dish that elevates the ordinary chicken liver, and pairs beautifully with toasted walnuts.

1 pound chicken livers, trimmed
    and cleaned

Sea salt

Freshly ground black pepper

4 tablespoons unsalted butter,
    room temperature, plus more
    to grease a casserole

2 small onions, minced

1 tablespoon chopped flat leaf
    parsley

Pinch allspice

1 teaspoon lemon zest

20 large dried figs

2 cups chicken stock

½ cup Cognac, or brandy

1 tablespoon chopped fresh chives

½ cup toasted walnuts, chopped

1 baguette, sliced and toasted

Preheat the oven to 350° F.

Pat the chicken livers dry, and season them with salt and pepper. In a large skillet over medium heat, melt 2 tablespoons butter and cook the onions 5 to 10 minutes, stirring, until they are softened but not brown. Transfer to a bowl and set aside.

Add the remaining butter to the pan and cook over medium-high heat until the foam subsides. Add the chicken livers and sauté for 2 minutes, until they are just browned on the outside, and pink inside. Remove them from the pan and add to the bowl of onions.

Stir the parsley, allspice, lemon zest, and salt and pepper to taste into the bowl. Place the mixture into a food processor and pulse until the mixture is well combined, but still slightly coarse.

With a sharp knife, make a slit in the stem end of each fig, and use your finger to force it open. Stuff each fig carefully with a small amount of the chicken liver mixture.

In a well-buttered casserole dish, place the figs stem-side up in a single layer. Pour the chicken stock and Cognac (or brandy) over the stuffed figs, and cover tightly.

Bake in the preheated oven for 15 to 20 minutes, or until the sauce has reduced and thickened. (If the sauce has not thickened, remove the cover and continue to bake an additional 5 to 10 minutes.)

Place the Chicken Liver Stuffed Figs on a warmed platter. Drizzle with their sauce and garnish with the chives and walnuts. Serve with toasted baguette slices.

Braised Chicken Feet

Serves 6

Waste not, want not — and on the farm, chickens are no exception. We eat their eggs, their meat, and even their feet! Admittedly there isn't much to eat on a chicken foot, since most edible tissue on the feet consists of skin and tendons with no muscle. However, being mostly skin, chicken feet are very gelatinous, adding a velvety thickness to a dish when stewed or braised.

2 pounds (about 24) chicken feet

2 teaspoons sea salt, plus more
   to taste

1 teaspoon ground black pepper,
   plus more to taste

1 cup flour

½ cup lard

2 onions, coarsely chopped

3 large cloves garlic

1 teaspoon dried chili flakes

1 bay leaf

Wash the chicken feet thoroughly in cold water and blot dry with paper towels. Use kitchen shears to clip off the toenails. In a large bowl, season the chicken feet with salt and pepper and toss with the flour.

Melt the lard in a stainless-steel stockpot over medium-high heat until very hot. Add the chicken feet and cook for 15 minutes, turning occasionally, until they have browned on both sides.

Add the onions, garlic, and chili flakes and continue to cook 5 to 10 minutes, stirring occasionally until the onions are tender and light brown.

Add 4 cups cold water and the bay leaf, then turn the heat to high and bring to a boil. Reduce the heat to low, cover the pot, and simmer 2 hours, or until the chicken feet are tender.

Adjust the seasoning with salt and pepper and serve over white rice with Hot Pepper Relish (recipe, p. 33)

Smothered Rabbit

Serves 6

Imagine walking into your kitchen and seeing a rabbit on the counter looking back at you! That was my experience the first time we cooked rabbit at Le Cordon Bleu. Luckily I had grown up cooking and eating squirrel and that experience prepared me for that day. Since the size and meat of rabbit and squirrel are similar, I knew exactly how to cook it — low and slow.

3 slices smoked bacon, chopped

½ cup butter

5 shallots, minced

1 cup flour

1 teaspoon salt

1 teaspoon black pepper

½ teaspoon paprika

2 rabbits, each cut into 6 pieces

½ cup heavy cream

Render the bacon in a large cast-iron skillet over medium heat until crisp.

Add the butter and shallots and cook for 5 to 10 minutes, until the butter foams and the shallots begin to brown.

In a large bowl, season the flour with the salt, pepper, and paprika. Dredge the rabbit in the seasoned flour and place each piece in the skillet with the bacon, butter, and shallots, and brown the meat on both sides.

Remove the browned rabbit from the skillet, and whisk in any remaining seasoned flour, plus the cream and ½ cup cold water. Continue to whisk until the sauce is thick and creamy.

Return the rabbit to the pan and cover with a tight-fitting lid. Reduce the heat to low and simmer for 30 to 45 minutes.

Adjust the seasoning with salt and pepper, and serve hot over white rice.

Stewed Hen with Vegetables

Serves 8

Think of a hen as an older chicken: a little fatter, a little tougher, and—some feel—a little tastier. Keeping those differences in mind, the main thing to remember is that it's best to stew or braise a hen in a chicken or vegetable stock until the meat is falling-off-the-bone tender, and then thicken the sauce using heavy cream or a roux.

1 celery rib, diced

1 small leek, trimmed, bulb split, and chopped

1 carrot, peeled and chopped

1 medium onion, chopped

2 cloves garlic, minced

3 cups red wine, such as Cabernet Sauvignon or Pinot Noir

1 large hen, cut into 8 pieces

2 tablespoons olive oil

1 tablespoon unsalted butter

10 slices thick bacon, cut into ¼-inch strips

2 teaspoons all-purpose flour

12 pearl onions, peeled

2 celery ribs, chopped diagonally

2 tablespoons Muscadine Jelly (recipe, p. 24)

1 cup heavy cream

To marinate the hen, combine the celery, leek, carrot, onion, garlic, and wine in a large bowl. Place the hen pieces in the marinade, cover, and refrigerate overnight.

When you are ready to cook, preheat the oven to 325° F.

Remove the hen from the marinade and pat dry. Strain the marinade into a bowl and reserve the vegetables in a separate bowl.

Heat the oil, butter and sliced bacon in a large Dutch oven over medium heat. Add the hen pieces and brown for 10 minutes on both sides. Remove the browned pieces and set aside, leaving the bacon in the pot.

Add the reserved marinated vegetables to the pot with the bacon and stir to coat with the oil left in the pan. Sprinkle in the flour and cook for 3 minutes, stirring, until the flour is golden brown and smells toasted. Whisk in the reserved marinade, bring to a boil, and reduce the heat to medium-low.

Return the browned hen to the pot, cover, and braise in the oven for 1 to 1½ hours, until the chicken is tender. Transfer it to a serving plate and keep warm.

Strain the braising liquid through a fine sieve. Pour the strained liquid into a large stainless-steel sauté pan. Add the pearl onions and celery, bring to a boil, then reduce the heat to low and simmer for 15 minutes, or until the vegetables are tender.

Stir in the Muscadine jelly and the cream. Add the hen and any juice from the platter to the sauce, and cook over low heat for 10 minutes. Do not boil or the cream will separate.

Serve on a warm platter with Nana's Yeast Rolls (recipe, p. 89).

Deep-Fried Mississippi Catfish

Serves 6 to 8

I remember the wonderful fried catfish at our annual family reunions in Charleston, Mississippi, to celebrate Big Mama's birthday. The celebration was kicked off the Friday before Labor Day with a huge fish fry. Big cast-iron pots full of bubbling hot lard would be filled with catfish, brim, perch, buffalo, and French fries. Big Mama told me she always fried in lard because it got hotter and cooked crisper than any other oil—and she was right. We would eat the piping-hot fried fish on slices of white bread with hot pepper sauce and mustard.

1 quart lard

5 pounds catfish fillets, perch,
   brim, or buffalo, skin removed

3 cups cornmeal, finely ground

1½ cups flour

2 tablespoons salt, divided

2 tablespoons freshly ground
   black pepper, divided

¼ cup paprika

Heat enough lard to cover the fish in a large cast-iron pot over medium-high heat, until hot (350° F).

While the lard is heating, combine the cornmeal, flour, 1 tablespoon salt, 1 tablespoon pepper, and paprika and set aside.

Season the fish with the remaining salt and pepper, and dredge the fillets in the seasoned cornmeal mixture.

Carefully drop the fillets, 3 or 4 at time, in the hot lard and cook 10 to 12 minutes, turning once, until the fillets float. If you are frying small whole fish, cook until the fish pulls away from the bone at the thickest point.

Use a large slotted spoon to remove the fillets. Drain on a paper towel-lined platter.

Serve piping hot.

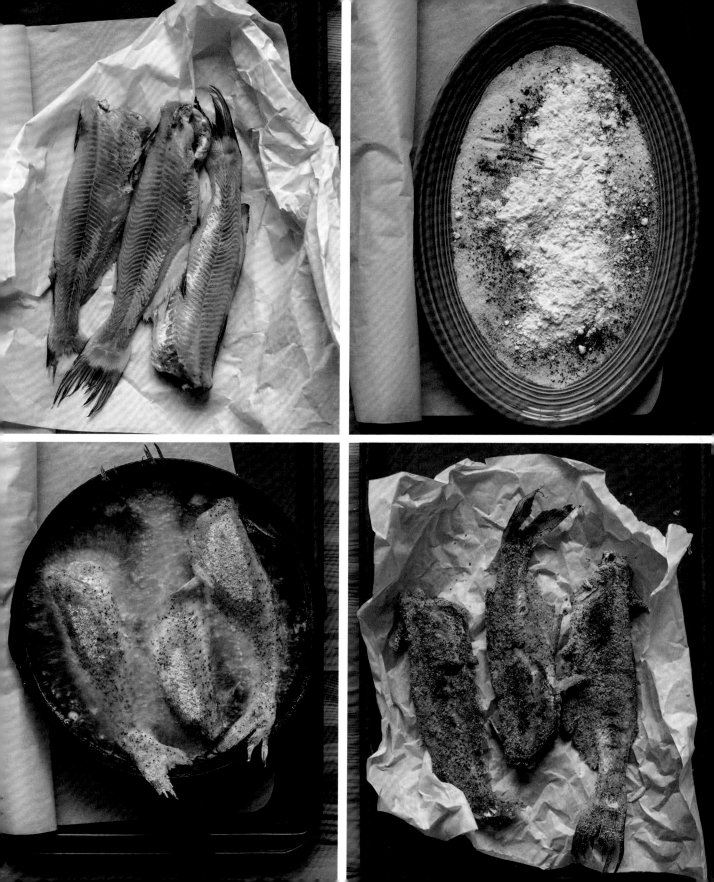

Cooking the Perfect Thanksgiving Turkey

Roasting a turkey seals in the juices, crisps the skin, and fills the house with the aroma of good things to come. Last year, I bit the bullet and bought an organic, free-range turkey. It was the moistest, most flavorful turkey I have ever cooked or eaten. No matter what type of turkey you decide to cook for your holiday dinner, here are some tips for cooking the perfect Thanksgiving turkey.

Turkey Brine

1 cup kosher salt
½ cup light brown sugar
1 gallon vegetable stock
1 tablespoon black peppercorns
1½ teaspoons allspice berries
1½ teaspoons chopped candied ginger

Combine the salt, brown sugar, vegetable stock, peppercorns, allspice berries, and candied ginger in a large stockpot over medium-high heat. Stir occasionally and bring to a boil, then remove from the heat, and allow the brine to cool to room temperature.
Combine the brine and 1 gallon heavily-iced water in a 5-gallon bucket. Place a thawed turkey breast-side down in the brine. If necessary, weight the bird down to ensure it is fully immersed, then cover, and refrigerate, or set in a cool area (like an insulated cooler) for 8 to 16 hours, turning the bird halfway through the brining.
When you are ready to cook, remove the bird from the brine and rinse it inside and out with cold water. Discard the brine. Place the bird on a roasting rack inside a half-sheet pan and pat dry with paper towels.

Turkey Rub

2 teaspoons sage, crumbled
1 teaspoon leaf thyme, crumbled
½ teaspoon marjoram
1 teaspoon black pepper
3 tablespoons sea salt
1 tablespoon garlic powder
1½ teaspoons basil
1 teaspoon paprika

Combine all ingredients in a bowl. Rub liberally over the entire turkey, as well as in the cavity, and under the skin of the breast, before roasting.

Roasted Turkey

Begin roasting your turkey, uncovered, in a pre-heated 425° F oven for 30 minutes. Loosely cover the breast with aluminum foil, and reduce the temperature to 325° F for the remainder of the cooking time. This guarantees a turkey that is crisp outside and juicy inside.

Serves 12 to 16

1 (12- to 16-pound) turkey
½ cup Turkey Rub
¼ cup salted butter, room temperature

Preheat the oven to 425° F.
Mix the turkey rub with the butter and set aside.
Remove the giblets and neck from the turkey's cavity and reserve. Rinse the turkey well and pat dry.
Loosen the skin of the turkey breasts by gently working your hand between the skin and the meat. Liberally rub the Turkey Rub mixture over the entire turkey, as well as in the cavity, and under the skin of the breast.
Rub the herb butter under the skin of the turkey.
Roast the turkey on the lowest rack of the oven at 425° F for 30 minutes. Cover the turkey breast with aluminum foil and reduce the oven temperature to 350° F.
Bake the turkey to an internal temperature of 165° F. (A 14- to 16-pound turkey will need 3 to 3½ hours of cooking time.)
Remove from the oven and stuff the roasted turkey with the Sage & Cornbread Dressing.

Poultry Seasoning

An all-purpose seasoning of dried herbs and spices complements the flavor of most poultry, such as chicken and turkey.

2 cups dried parsley
1 cup rubbed sage
½ cup dried rosemary, crushed
½ cup dried marjoram
2 tablespoons sea salt
1 tablespoon freshly ground black pepper
2 teaspoons onion powder
½ teaspoon ground sage

Combine all ingredients and mix very well.
Store the Poultry Seasoning in a glass jar with a tight fitting lid. Store in a cool dark place for up to 1 year. Shake well before using.

Sage & Cornbread Dressing

1 (9-inch) skillet Buttermilk Cornbread
    (recipe, p. 88), crumbled
6 day-old Buttermilk Biscuits (recipe, p. 98),
    or 12 heels white bread
¾ cup butter
3 large stalks celery, chopped
2 large onions, chopped
1 large bell pepper, diced
2 large garlic cloves, minced
4 cups turkey stock
1 cup turkey pan drippings, from the
    cooked turkey
1 tablespoon Poultry Seasoning
1 tablespoon rubbed sage
2 teaspoons sea salt
½ teaspoon freshly ground black pepper

Preheat the oven to 350° F.
Crumble the cornbread and biscuits, or h eels of bread, into a very large mixing bowl.

Heat the butter in a large cast-iron skillet over medium heat, and add the celery, onion, bell pepper, and garlic and sauté until the onions and bell pepper are soft and the onion is transparent.
Add the sautéed vegetables to the bowl of crumbled bread and mix well. Add the turkey stock and turkey pan drippings, and mix well. Season with the poultry seasoning, rubbed sage, salt and pepper, and mix thoroughly.
Return the mixture to the skillet and cook over medium heat for 15 minutes.
Remove from heat and spoon the dressing around the turkey in the roasting pan and into the cavity of the fully cooked turkey.
Cover and bake for 1 hour. Remove from the oven and let rest 15 minutes before carving.

Giblet Gravy

Simmered in water or roasted alongside the bird, the giblets—which are the neck, hearts, liver, and gizzards from the turkey—are what adds flavor and a meaty texture to the gravy.

3 tablespoons turkey drippings from the
    roasting pan
3 tablespoons all-purpose flour
2 ½ cups turkey stock
½ cup cooked turkey giblets, (turkey heart,
    liver, and gizzard), chopped
1 cooked turkey neck, meat removed, and
    bones discarded
½ tablespoon chopped fresh sage
½ teaspoon ground black pepper
Salt, to taste

Heat the pan drippings in a large cast-iron skillet over medium heat. Gradually whisk in the flour and stir 10 minutes, until the gravy is golden brown. Slowly whisk in the turkey stock until blended and smooth. Stir in the giblets and season with sage, pepper, and salt.
Bring to a boil, reduce heat, and simmer for 8 to 10 minutes, or until thickened. Add salt and pepper as needed.

Pies, Cakes, And Cobblers

The sheer volume and variety of confections in a Parisian pastry shop are almost overwhelming. In Paris, I saw everything from heart-shaped cookies called *palmiers*, made out of puff pastry and sprinkled with sugar, to fruit tarts topped with Chantilly cream, and beautiful chocolate cakes called *gateaux* filling the display cases. I wanted to try everything I saw. Luckily, walking to and from culinary school allowed me to indulge in many of the pastries I saw in the shops. One of my favorite cakes was a cheesecake made out of goat's milk. Goat cheese, which is naturally tart, was mixed with sugar, lemon juice, and lemon zest to achieve the perfect balance between sweet and tart. I also fell in love with the beauty of the desserts; it seemed as though the pastry chef made each one just for me.

There are some amazing sweets to be had in the South, too. The main difference between the desserts in Paris and those down South is the size of the serving. Even the French cakes can't compare to the size of our Southern cakes. Southerners like to make desserts that are not only pretty and delicious, but can also be shared with family and friends.

This chapter features some Southern favorites like Caramel Cake and Peach Cobbler, and some French favorites—Meringue Cookies and Lavender Cake—along with Christmas Coconut Cake and Hand-Churned Vanilla Ice Cream, my family's favorites.

Apple Turnovers

Yields 8 turnovers

This recipe is a traditional Southern recipe with a French twist, combining puff pastry dough — a French staple — with a Southern-style apple pie filling.

2 tablespoons fresh lemon juice

4 tart Granny Smith apples, peeled, cored and sliced

2 tablespoons butter, plus 1 tablespoon for the pan

1 cup dark brown sugar

1 teaspoon ground cinnamon

1 tablespoon flour

1 Puff Pastry sheet (recipe, p. 151)

1 cup confectioners' sugar

1 tablespoon milk

1 teaspoon vanilla extract

Place the lemon juice, 4 cups cold water, and the sliced apples into a large bowl. The lemon water will keep them from browning.

In a large skillet over medium heat, melt the butter.

Drain the water from the sliced apples, pat dry with paper towels, and place them into the hot skillet. Cook for 2 minutes, stirring constantly. Add the brown sugar and cinnamon, and cook for another 2 to 3 minutes.

Meanwhile, stir together the flour and 1 tablespoon cold water in a cup, and add to the skillet, stirring to mix well. Cook until the sauce has thickened, then remove the pan from the heat and allow to cool to room temperature.

Unwrap a sheet of puff pastry, and cut it into 8 equal squares. Spoon cooled apple mixture onto the center of each square. Fold the puff pastry over from corner to corner, making a triangle shape, and press the edges together to seal the dough.

Place the turnovers on a greased baking sheet, leaving about 1 inch between them. Bake for 25 minutes, or until the dough is puffed and lightly browned.

Transfer from the oven to a cooling rack and allow the turnovers to cool completely.

Mix the confectioners' sugar, milk, and vanilla together in a small bowl, and drizzle the glaze over the cooled turnovers.

Puff Pastry

Yields 1 (16 x 16-inch) sheet puff pastry

Puff pastry is a light, flaky dough that turns into thin delicate layers as it bakes, making it perfect for breakfast pastries like the Apple Turnovers. Each time the butter-filled dough is folded and rolled, it compounds the layers the crust will have once it is baked. This pastry is versatile enough to be used for cookies and pastries, snacks such as cheese straws, and savory dishes like wild mushroom tarts.

5 cups bread flour

2½ teaspoons salt

2 cups (1 pound) unsalted butter, room temperature

Sift the flour and salt together in a large bowl. Gradually stir in 2 cups cold water until the dough holds together enough to pull cleanly away from the sides of the bowl. (You may not need the full amount of water). Shape the dough into a flat ball, and let it rest at room temperature for at least 10 minutes.

Place the butter between two pieces of plastic wrap and use a rolling pin to roll into a flat disc. Refrigerate 20 minutes, until firm.

On a lightly-floured work surface, roll the dough out into a large rectangle about ½ inch thick. Place the disc of chilled butter on the right side of the dough and fold the left side of the dough over the butter as if closing a book. Make sure that the butter is completely encased in dough. Roll the dough out again to a ½-inch thickness, taking care not to let the butter break through the dough. Fold the dough in thirds by folding ⅓ the width of the dough on top and a second ⅓ of the dough under the bottom of the rolled dough. This "turn" will give you a piece of dough with 3 connected layers; one on top, one in the middle, and one on the bottom.

Turn the dough so that it is length-wise on your work station, and using additional flour if needed to keep the dough from sticking, roll the dough out into a rectangle, and fold into thirds again. By this time the butter is starting to warm up.

Place the dough on a sheet of plastic wrap and use a finger to mark it with two pokes (signifying 2 turns). Wrap the dough in plastic and refrigerate for at least 30 minutes.

Repeat the rolling out and refrigeration process 2 more times, making a total of 6 turns. Wrap with plastic wrap and refrigerate after each turn. The dough will then be ready to roll out and use.

Meringue Cookies

Yields 1 dozen

Following in the footsteps of French desserts like a Pavlova, these cookies are light and crisp, and put me in mind of a crispy marshmallow. They can also be shaped flat, baked, and topped with fresh fruit and whipped cream for a light, elegant dessert.

2 large egg whites

¼ teaspoon cream of tartar

1 teaspoon clear vanilla extract or other clear extracts, like almond or rum

½ cup sugar

Preheat the oven to 225° F.

In a small stainless-steel bowl, beat the egg whites with the cream of tartar and vanilla until foamy. Add the sugar, 2 tablespoons at a time, beating constantly until the sugar is dissolved and the whites are glossy and form stiff peaks.

Drop the meringue by rounded teaspoons, or pipe through a pastry tube, onto a parchment-lined cookie sheet.

Bake 1 hour, or until firm. Turn off the oven and leave the cookies in the oven with the oven door closed for at least 1 additional hour, or until the cookies are cool, dry, and crisp.

Store the Meringue Cookies in a tightly sealed container. To crisp up older cookies, bake in a preheated 200° F oven for 15 to 20 minutes.

Caramel Cake

Serves 12

The boiled caramel icing for this recipe combines fresh cream butter, farm fresh eggs, and rich dark brown sugar. Making the caramel takes patience and a strong arm. Let the sugars come to a boil over low heat, but don't rush it. When it's ready, quickly beat in the confectioners' sugar until the icing is thick and glossy—then it's ready to pour over your cake.

3 cups cake flour, plus 3 tablespoons for the cake pans

3 teaspoons baking powder

½ teaspoon salt

1 cup unsalted butter, softened, plus 3 tablespoons for the cake pans

2 cups sugar

4 large eggs

1 cup milk

1 teaspoon vanilla extract

2 tablespoons unsalted butter

1 cup heavy cream

2¼ cups firmly packed dark brown sugar

Pinch salt

2 teaspoons vanilla extract

1 (16-ounce) box confectioners' sugar

Preheat the oven to 350° F degrees.

Butter 3 (9-inch) cake pans, coat the with flour, and remove excess flour by turning the pans upside down and tapping. In a large bowl, sift together the cake flour, baking powder, and salt. Set aside.

Cream the butter until light and smooth. Add the sugar, ¼ cup at a time, beating well after each addition. Add the eggs, one at a time, mixing well. Add the flour mixture and milk alternately, starting and ending with the flour. Add the vanilla and mix well. Divide the batter between the three pans and tap to level the batter. Bake 20 to 25 minutes, shifting the pans on the racks halfway through baking. The cakes are done when a toothpick inserted into the center of the cake comes out clean. Let them cool in the pan for 10 minutes, then turn them out onto a rack to cool completely.

To make the caramel icing, mix the butter, cream, brown sugar, and salt in a small stainless-steel saucepan. Bring to a boil over low medium-high heat, stirring constantly, then remove from the heat and add the vanilla. Beat in the confectioners' sugar gradually until the icing is thick and glossy.

If the icing is too thick, stir in a few drops of cream for a workable consistency. Place 1 layer of cake on a cake plate, top side down, and spread with one-third the icing. Stack the second cake layer on top of the first, top side up, and spread another one-third of the icing on top. Add the last cake layer, top side up, pour the remaining icing in the center, and spread it over the top and sides, working quickly. If the icing becomes too thick to spread, return it briefly to very low heat and add additional cream, stirring until smooth.

Allow the iced cake to set for at least 1 hour before slicing. Store, covered, at room temperature.

Lavender Cake with Fresh Lemon Glaze

Serves 12

Most people believe that lavender is a flower, but it's actually an herb. Widely used in French cuisine, it infuses each dish, whether savory or sweet, with an ever-so-slight minty taste and the smell of summer. Although delicate in appearance, a little goes a long way, so go easy when using lavender to flavor dishes.

8 ounces unsalted butter,
    plus 1 tablespoon for the pan
12 ounces cake flour, plus
    1 tablespoon for the pan
1 teaspoon baking powder
½ teaspoon baking soda
½ teaspoon salt
2 teaspoons dried lavender
    flowers, plus 1 tablespoon
8 ounces Caster sugar
7 ounces sour cream
4 medium eggs, well beaten
¼ cup whole milk

3 tablespoons fresh lemon juice
1 cup confectioners' sugar
Zest of one lemon
2 tablespoons dried lavender
    flowers, for garnish

Preheat oven to 350° F.

Butter and flour 2 (8-inch) cake pans, then turn upside down and tap to remove any excess flour. Set aside.

Sift the flour, baking powder, baking soda, and salt together. Stir in 2 teaspoons lavender flowers.

Using the blade attachment of your food processor, or a mortar and pestle, grind the Caster sugar and 1 tablespoon of lavender flowers together until the buds are in very small pieces.

In a separate bowl, cream together the butter and the lavender sugar until light and fluffy. Stir in the sour cream. Mix in the sifted flour mixture in increments of ⅓ at a time, then the beaten eggs, and milk, mixing well after each addition.

Divide the cake batter equally between the prepared cake pans and gently tap the sides of the pans to release any air bubbles. Bake for 35 minutes, or until a toothpick inserted into the center of the cake comes out clean. Transfer the cakes to a wire rack to cool for 10 minutes, then turn them out onto the wire rack to cool completely.

While the cakes are cooling, make the Fresh Lemon Glaze icing. Mix the lemon juice and confectioner's sugar together until smooth, adding small amounts of cold water as needed to make the glaze thick but pourable.

Place one cake layer upside down on a cake plate, pour half the lemon glaze in the center and spread over the layer. Stack with second layer, top side up, and spread the remaining glaze on top. Garnish with the freshly grated lemon zest and the lavender flowers.

Coconut Christmas Cake

Serves 12

Our family has many traditional family recipes that have been handed down from generation to generation. One of my favorites is this Coconut Christmas Cake. The creamy white icing and grated coconut always remind me of fresh snow. If using fresh coconut instead of packaged coconut, carefully crack it open with a heavy knife or meat cleaver, drain the coconut water from inside, then grate the white flesh of the coconut.

¾ cup unsalted butter, room temperature, plus 2 tablespoons for the cake pans

2 cups sugar

5 extra-large eggs, room temperature

1½ teaspoons vanilla extract

1½ teaspoons almond extract

3 cups all-purpose flour, plus 2 tablespoons for the cake pans

1 teaspoon baking powder

½ teaspoon baking soda

½ teaspoon salt

1 cup milk

4 ounces shredded coconut

½ cup unsalted butter, room temperature

¾ teaspoon vanilla extract

¼ teaspoon almond extract

1 pound confectioners' sugar, sifted

8 ounces shredded coconut

Preheat the oven to 350° F.

Butter 2 (9-inch) round cake pans and dust lightly with flour.

Cream the butter and sugar until light yellow and fluffy. Beat in the eggs, 1 at a time, scraping the sides and bottom of the bowl as you go. Add the vanilla and almond extracts and mix well.

In a separate bowl, sift together the flour, baking powder, baking soda and salt. Add the dry ingredients and the milk alternately to the batter, beginning and ending with the dry ingredients. Mix until just combined. Fold in 4 ounces shredded coconut.

Divide the batter evenly between the 2 pans, and smooth the tops with a knife. Bake in the center of the preheated oven for 45 to 55 minutes, until the tops are browned and a toothpick inserted into the center of the cake comes out clean. Transfer the pans to a cooling rack for 30 minutes, then turn the cakes out onto the rack to finish cooling.

To make the icing, beat the butter, vanilla, and almond extract in a bowl until smooth and creamy. Add the confectioners' sugar and mix until just smooth. Do not overmix.

Place 1 cake layer on a serving plate, top side down, and spread the top with icing. Sprinkle with half the coconut. Place the second layer on top of the first, top side up, and spread the top and sides with the remaining icing. Sprinkle the top with coconut and lightly press more coconut onto the sides of the cake.

Lemon Chevre Cheesecake
with a Cookie Crumb Crust

Serves 12

French for goat cheese, chevre *gives balance to what can often be an overly sweet cheesecake. The addition of lemon zest and citrus juices makes this a very light dessert; and using cookies for the crust gives it a crisper crust, than the traditionally-used graham crackers.*

1 tablespoon unsalted butter

7 ounces tea cookies, or
ginger snaps

2 tablespoons, plus 1 teaspoon
finely grated fresh lemon zest
(about 3 lemons)

1 cup sugar, divided

12 ounces mild goat cheese

10 ounces cream cheese

1½ tablespoons fresh lemon
juice, divided

1 teaspoon finely grated orange
zest

½ cup sour cream

1 teaspoon vanilla

2 eggs

8 to 10 medium strawberries,
stemmed

Preheat oven to 325° F.

Butter an 8-inch springform pan.

Crumble the cookies into a food processor and pulse until they are finely ground.

In a medium bowl, toss 2 tablespoons lemon zest with 1½ tablespoons sugar. Add the cookie crumbs and mix well. Press the cookie mixture into the bottom of the springform pan—not on the sides—and bake for 15 minutes. Remove from the oven and let the crust cool in the pan.

Lower the oven temperature to 275° F.

Beat the goat cheese and cream cheese together in a large bowl until light and fluffy. Add the remaining lemon zest, 1 tablespoon lemon juice, the orange zest, ¾ cup sugar, sour cream, and vanilla and beat well, scraping the bowl. Add the eggs one at a time, beating well after each addition. Pour the batter into the prebaked, cooled crust and bake for 1 hour, or until the batter has set around the edges but is still jiggly in the center. Turn the oven off, crack the oven door, and let the cheesecake cool slowly in the oven for 2 hours.

Remove and let the cheesecake cool completely. Then refrigerate, covered, at least 2 hours, or overnight.

Run a thin knife between the cake and the rim of the springform pan to remove. Garnish with thinly sliced strawberries tossed with the remaining 2½ tablespoons sugar and lemon juice. Drizzle the top with any juice left in the bowl.

Old-Fashioned Sweet Potato Pie

Serves 8

My grandmother always grew sweet potatoes in her late summer garden so that we could have them baked, mashed, and made into pies in the fall. The great thing about sweet potatoes, besides their taste and versatility, is that you can bake and freeze them to have whenever you're in the mood for this old-fashioned pie.

1 unbaked Deep Dish Pie Crust
 (recipe, p. 166)

4 medium sweet potatoes,
 baked in their skins

½ cup unsalted butter, softened

¼ cup sugar

¾ cup brown sugar

3 eggs, beaten

1 teaspoon vanilla extract

½ teaspoon cinnamon

⅛ teaspoon nutmeg

⅛ teaspoon ginger

⅛ teaspoon allspice

½ teaspoon salt

¾ cup heavy cream

Preheat oven to 350° F.

Prepare and bake the pie crust for 10 minutes. Remove from the oven and place the pan on a wire rack to cool.

Remove the sweet potato pulp from their skins and transfer to a large bowl. Using a potato masher, mash the pulp until smooth.

In another large bowl, beat together the butter, sugar, and brown sugar until creamy. Add the eggs, one at a time. Mix in the vanilla, cinnamon, nutmeg, ginger, allspice, and salt. Stir in the heavy cream and add the mashed sweet potatoes. Beat together until smooth and creamy. Adjust the taste with additional spices if you like a spicier or sweeter pie.

Pour into the prebaked and cooled pie shell. Bake on the bottom rack of the oven for 1 hour, or until center of pie is firm.

Serve warm with Chantilly Cream (recipe, p. 167).

Hand Churned Vanilla Ice Cream

Yields 1½ quarts

I grew up eating my Aunt Sis' delicious vanilla ice cream — cold, creamy, and flavored with real vanilla bean. When I was in culinary school in Paris, I was surprised to find out that the custard we made from fresh eggs, cream, and sugar — what the French called crème Anglaise, *or egg custard — was, to me, simply ice cream.*

8 whole large egg yolks

3 cups Half-and-Half

2 cups sugar

1 whole vanilla bean, split
  lengthwise, seeds removed
  and set aside

Pinch sea salt

3 cups heavy cream

In a large bowl, whisk the egg yolks until thick and pale yellow. Set aside.

In a large, stainless-steel saucepan over low heat, combine the Half-and-Half, sugar, vanilla bean, and the vanilla seeds. Heat to just before boiling, when you can see tiny bubbles along the edge of the pan. Temper the egg yolks by slowly adding 1 cup of the hot half-and-half mixture, whisking constantly.

Pour the tempered egg yolks, along with 1 cup of the hot Half-and-Half mixture, into the pan containing the remaining Half-and-Half. Cook over low heat, stirring constantly, until the custard thickens. Be careful not to overheat or the egg yolks will scramble in the custard.

Strain the custard through a fine mesh strainer.

In a large bowl, stir together the strained custard with the heavy cream. Cover and refrigerate for at least 8 hours.

Add the custard to a hand-churn or electric ice cream maker and follow the instructions until the ice cream has thickened, then transfer to a freezer to harden for an additional 8 hours.

Peach Cobbler

Serves 6 to 8

Pastry shops in Paris boasted all kinds of beautiful pastries, cookies, candies, and cakes, but I never saw one cobbler. To surprise my favorite culinary instructor at Le Cordon Bleu, I made a small peach cobbler for him. After he tasted it, he said he thought it well-prepared and delicious—deserved praise for this Southern dish, indeed!

2 tablespoons butter

6 large ripe peaches (about 6 cups), peeled, pitted, and thickly sliced

1 cup firmly packed dark brown sugar

1 tablespoon cornstarch

1 tablespoon fresh lemon juice

½ teaspoon cinnamon

½ teaspoon nutmeg

1½ cups all-purpose flour

¼ cup, plus 1 tablespoon sugar

1 tablespoon baking powder

½ teaspoon salt

¼ cup unsalted butter, chilled

½ cup milk

½ teaspoon vanilla extract

Preheat the oven to 375° F.

Butter a 2-quart baking dish.

Combine the peaches, brown sugar, cornstarch, lemon juice, cinnamon, and nutmeg in a large saucepan. Mix gently, and cook over low heat for 10 minutes, until the peaches are just tender and the syrup has thickened. Pour the filling into the prepared baking dish.

To make the topping, stir together the flour, ¼ cup sugar, baking powder, and salt in a large bowl. Using two knives or a pastry cutter, cut in the butter until the mixture has the consistency of coarse crumbs or cornmeal. Add the milk and vanilla, and quickly blend using a spatula. Drop heaping tablespoons of the dough on top of the peaches, covering the fruit completely. Sprinkle with the remaining 1 tablespoon sugar.

Bake for 25 to 30 minutes, until the top is golden and the dough is cooked through.

Let the cobbler stand for 5 minutes before serving.

Peach Cobbler

Apple, Peach, & Pecan Galette

Blackberry Cobbler

Pralines

Apple, Peach, & Pecan Galette

Serves 8

This freeform tart, also known as a French galette, is elegant and easy to make. Simply roll out a pie crust into a 12-inch round, fill the center with the apples, peaches, and pecans. Then gently fold the edges of the crust back over the fruit, and bake. You can use whatever fruit is in season, so let your taste buds lead the way.

1¼ cups all-purpose flour

¼ teaspoon salt

1 teaspoon sugar

7 tablespoons cold unsalted
    butter, cut into chunks

4 to 5 medium apples, such as
    Honey Crisp, Gala, or
    Granny Smith, peeled, cored
    and cut in ½-inch thick slices

1 cup dark brown sugar

1 cup dried peaches

1 large egg, beaten

2 tablespoons sugar

½ cup toasted pecans, chopped

¼ cup confectioners' sugar

Sift together the flour, salt, and sugar. Cut the cold butter into the flour mixture until the mixture resembles coarse cornmeal. Add 3 tablespoons cold water, one tablespoon at a time, and stir until the mixture comes together into a loose ball.

Turn the dough out onto a lightly floured surface and shape into a disc. (You won't roll the dough out until it has chilled.) Wrap tightly in plastic wrap and refrigerate at least 30 minutes. This dough can also be made, wrapped, and refrigerated 2 days ahead.

In a large bowl, combine the apples and brown sugar and set aside.

In a small saucepan over medium-high heat, combine the dried peaches and 2 cups water. Bring to a boil, then reduce the heat and simmer for 10 minutes, or until the peaches are plump and tender. Remove from the heat, let cool slightly, then drain the peaches, reserving ¼ cup of the liquid. Add the cooked peaches to the apple mixture along with the reserved liquid and mix until well combined.

Remove the dough from the refrigerator and let it sit at room temperature for 10 to 20 minutes to temper it. Tempering the dough makes it easier to roll without cracking. When it has tempered, remove the plastic wrap and place on a sheet of lightly floured parchment paper. Roll out the dough, shaping it into a 12-inch round disc.

Brush the excess flour from the dough and parchment paper and transfer the dough and parchment paper to a baking sheet. Spoon the apple mixture into the center of the dough disc and fold the edges up around the fruit filling. Do not try to cover the fruit completely with the dough—keep a 6-inch circle of fruit showing at the top of the galette. Brush the dough with the beaten egg mixture, sprinkle it with the 2 tablespoons sugar, and bake for 30 minutes, or until the fruit mixture is bubbling and the crust is golden brown. Garnish with chopped pecans and a dusting of confectioners' sugar.

Blackberry Cobbler

Serves 4

Blackberries were one of the berries I didn't see much in Paris. I saw lots of strawberries and raspberries, but blackberries were definitely under-represented. I ended up making cobblers with the berries I could find, but Blackberry Cobbler remains my favorite. I think the fresh tartness of the berries balances the sweetness of the sugar and pairs perfectly with the cinnamon. But if you love other berries, feel free to substitute them for the blackberries in this recipe. It will still be delicious—and more French!

1 tablespoon butter, room
   temperature
4 cups fresh blackberries
¼ cup sugar, plus 1 tablespoon
2 cup all-purpose flour
3 tablespoons sugar
1 tablespoon baking powder
½ teaspoon salt
½ cup cold butter

½ cup whole milk
1 teaspoon cinnamon
2 cups Blackberry Sauce
   (recipe, p. 18)

Preheat an oven to 350° F.

Butter a 12 x 8 x 2–inch baking dish with 1 tablespoon butter.

Place the blackberries in a small bowl, sprinkle them with ¼ cup sugar, and set aside.

Combine the flour, sugar, baking powder, and salt in a mixing bowl. Cut in the cold butter using a pastry cutter or fork until the mixture has the consistency of coarse cornmeal. Add the milk and mix well. Divide the dough into two unequal size portions—about ⅔ and ⅓. On a lightly floured surface, roll the larger piece of dough out to a ⅛-inch thickness. Place the dough into the prepared baking dish and top with the berries.

Roll out the remaining smaller dough ball to a rectangle large enough to cover the dish, and place it on top of the berries in the baking dish, tucking in the outer edges to completely cover the berries. Pour 1½ cups boiling water over the dough and berries in the dish.

Combine the cinnamon with 1 tablespoon sugar and sprinkle over the top crust of the cobbler. Bake for 35 minutes, or until the crust is golden brown. The blackberries may bubble up to the top during baking—this is okay.

Top individual servings of the cobbler with hot Blackberry Sauce and serve with Chantilly Cream (recipe, p. 167).

Deep Dish Pie Crust

Yields 1 (9 1/2-inch) pie crust

Lard is perfect for making pastry . When the lard is cut into the flour and baked, the flour cooks between the fat crystals of the lard, making for a crisp, flaky pastry. At Le Cordon Bleu, we were taught to make our pie crust out of lard, but over the years I have come to like a crust made with half lard and half butter. I found that using both gives the best of both worlds —a crisp flaky crust that bakes golden brown and also tastes of sweet cream butter. Do not overmix your pie dough, or the butter and lard will become too warm and your dough will be too soft.

4 tablespoons unsalted butter

5 tablespoons lard

¾ cup cake flour

¾ cup all-purpose flour

1 teaspoon sugar

½ teaspoon salt

⅛ teaspoon baking powder

1 egg yolk

2 teaspoons distilled white
    vinegar

In a small bowl, cut the butter and lard into small pieces and freeze for about 20 minutes.

Sift together the cake flour, all-purpose flour, sugar, salt, and baking powder into a separate bowl. Using a pastry cutter or two butter knives, cut the cold butter and lard into the flour mixture until it is the consistency of peas. Do not overmix.

Beat the egg yolk and vinegar in another bowl, then add 3 ice cubes and ½ cup cold water, and let it sit for 3 to 4 minutes.

Sprinkle up to 5 tablespoons of this egg mixture into the flour mixture, a little at a time, and mix gently with a fork, until the dough comes together to form a ball. Do not overmix the dough. You do not want a wet dough, either. Shape the pie dough into a flat disc, wrap with plastic wrap, and refrigerate for 20 minutes.

Remove the dough from the refrigerator and roll out into a 9½-inch circle on a lightly floured work surface. Gently press the dough into a 9½-inch pie pan and reserve for your pie filling.

Chantilly Cream

Yields 2 cups

1 cup heavy whipping cream

3 tablespoons confectioners' sugar

½ teaspoon vanilla extract

In a small, chilled copper or glass bowl, beat the cream until it begins to thicken.

Add the confectioners' sugar and vanilla extract and beat until soft peaks form.

Deep Dish Pecan Pie

Serves 8

1 unbaked Deep Dish pie crust, (recipe, p. 166)

1½ cups dark corn syrup

4 large eggs, beaten

1 cup sugar

3 tablespoons unsalted butter, melted

1 teaspoon vanilla extract

2 cups pecan halves

Preheat the oven to 350° F.

Line a pie pan with a pie crust and prebake the crust for 10 minutes. Remove from the oven and set aside to cool at room temperature.

Beat the corn syrup, eggs, sugar, melted butter, and vanilla together in a large bowl. Stir in the pecan halves. Pour the filling into the cooled, prebaked pie crust and place the pie pan on a cookie sheet.

Bake on the center rack of the oven for 60 to 70 minutes. The center of the pie should be soft to the touch and bounce back when pressed. Do not overbake.

Remove from the oven and cool on a wire rack for at least 2 hours before serving.

Serve topped with Chantilly Cream.

Fresh Fig Cookies

Yields 2½ dozen

1 cup sugar

1 cup light brown sugar

1 cup unsalted butter, softened

2 eggs, well beaten

4 cups all-purpose flour

2 teaspoons baking soda

2 teaspoons baking powder

1 teaspoon salt

½ teaspoon cloves

½ teaspoon cinnamon

2 cups chopped fresh figs

1 cup chopped walnuts

Preheat the oven to 350° F.

Cream the sugars and butter together until creamy and light. Mix in the beaten egg until well combined.

In a separate bowl, sift together the dry ingredients and add this to the egg mixture in three parts, stirring to combine. Fold in the chopped figs and nuts.

Drop by heaping spoonfuls onto a greased cookie sheet and bake for 15 to 20 minutes.

Allow to cool on a cookie rack before serving.

These cookies will keep well in an airtight container for up to 2 weeks.

Pecan Pralines

Yields 1 dozen

1 cup dark brown sugar

½ cup sugar

½ cup heavy cream

¼ teaspoon cream of tartar

1 cup pecan halves, or pieces

2 tablespoons cold unsalted butter

½ teaspoon vanilla extract

¼ teaspoon sea salt

Combine the sugars, cream, and cream of tartar in a heavy saucepan, and cook over low heat until the sugar dissolves, scraping the crystals from the sides of the pan with a rubber spatula.

Increase the heat to medium and continue to cook for 15 minutes, or until the mixture reaches the "softball stage" (234° to 240° F on a candy thermometer), and when the candy forms a soft ball when dropped into a cup of cold water. Add the pecans and cook, stirring constantly, for another 2 minutes. Remove the pan from the heat and beat in the butter, vanilla, and salt, until the mixture looks creamy around the edges of the pan.

Drop by spoonfuls onto sheets of waxed paper. Allow the pralines to cool completely before you remove them from the paper.

My Best Lemon Pound Cake

Serves 12

A well-made pound cake is a sign of the Southern baker's talent in the kitchen. It should be moist and dense, without being heavy, and baked to a golden brown so that the crust tastes like the cake, only intensified.

1 cup unsalted butter, room
    temperature, plus 1
    tablespoon for coating the
    cake pan
2 cups unbleached flour, plus 1
    tablespoon for dusting the
    cake pan
¼ teaspoon salt
1⅔ cups sugar
2 teaspoons finely grated
    lemon zest
1 tablespoon fresh lemon juice
1 tablespoon vanilla extract
5 eggs

Preheat an oven to 325° F.

Butter and lightly flour a bundt pan.

Sift together the flour and salt. Set aside.

In a large mixing bowl, beat the butter and sugar until pale and creamy. Beat in the lemon zest, lemon juice, and vanilla. Add the eggs, 1 at a time, beating until just combined after each addition.

Fold in the flour mixture in 2 batches, mixing after each addition, until the batter is smooth. Be careful not to overmix.

Spoon the batter into the bundt pan and bake for 45 to 55 minutes, or until a toothpick inserted into the cake comes out clean. If the crust browns too quickly, cover the pan loosely with aluminum foil.

Remove the cake from the oven and transfer the pan to a cooling rack for 10 minutes, then turn the cake out onto a wire rack to cool completely.

Drinks And Cocktails

The art of making small batch wines and spirits is alive and well in the South. This chapter offers a taste of family recipes for making seasonal wines, artisan cocktails, and fruit brandies. I have taken the liberty of adding some French-inspired techniques that I learned while living in France and have been tweaking ever since. Several of the cocktails are classics, some are my favorites, and a few I've come up with by using herbs like basil, mint, and lavender from the garden; and peaches, strawberries, winter pears, and even pomegranate seeds to give these drinks a unique flavor. Use your favorite brand of alcohol when making these drinks, or try a new one. You'll also find that many of these cocktails can be enjoyed without any alcohol and still be delicious.

-My grandmother Bessie Lee's brothers: (left to right) Spencer, Eugene, Earnest, Robert, and Willie, circa 1940.

Lavender Lemonade

Yields 2 drinks

Lavender is big in French cooking, but I grew up thinking it was something used to add fragrance to lotions and bath salts — until I ate a dish seasoned with Herbes de Provence (recipe, p. 28), in which lavender was one of the main ingredients. That experience encouraged me to use it my cooking, too. It wasn't until recently that I started adding it to drinks. This lemonade still has the sweet-tart flavor you would expect, but the addition of fresh lavender softens the lemon and adds a beautiful aroma.

4 ounces vodka, your choice brand

2 ounces Lavender Simple Syrup

1 teaspoon fresh lavender flowers

2 ounces fresh lemon juice

4 ounces seltzer water, or club soda

2 slices lemon

Pour the vodka and simple syrup into a cocktail shaker. Add the lavender flowers and lemon juice. Muddle until the lavender flowers are broken into small pieces.

Add 1 cup crushed ice and shake for 10 seconds.

Strain into a chilled martini glass, top with the seltzer water, and garnish with a slice of lemon.

Lavender Simple Syrup

Yields 1½ cups

Lavender lends its aroma and subtle floral flavor to this simple sweetener. This Syrup may be covered and kept, refrigerated, for 2 weeks. Make it ahead of time so that a spoonful or two is always ready to brighten up the taste of a classic cocktail.

1½ cups fresh lavender flowers

1 cup sugar

In a saucepan over medium-high heat, bring the lavender, sugar, and 1 cup water to a boil. Stir until the sugar is dissolved. Allow the syrup to simmer, undisturbed, for 2 minutes.

Strain the syrup through a fine sieve, pressing hard on the lavender, then allow the syrup to cool to room temperature.

Basil Martini

Yields 2 cocktails

Crisp and fresh is the best way to describe this martini. The traditional olives are replaced with key lime juice and muddled basil leaves, adding an enticing aroma, a pleasant tartness, and a beautiful color to this elegant drink. Enjoy it ice cold, made with your favorite gin or vodka, and wwith fresh basil from your herb garden.

4 ounces dry gin, your choice brand

1 ounce Simple Syrup

5 small (or 3 large) basil leaves

1 ounce Key lime juice

4 ounces seltzer water, or club soda

2 sprigs fresh basil

Pour the gin and simple syrup into a cocktail shaker, add the basil leaves, and lime juice. Muddle the basil leaves to break them into small pieces.

Add 1 cup crushed ice and shake 10 seconds.

Pour into 2 chilled martini glasses, top with seltzer water, and garnish with a sprig of basil.

Simple Syrup

Yields 1⅓ cups

Sweet tea is the unofficial official drink of the South. Hot or cold, simple syrup sweetens it quickly and without having to add tons of sugar, or stirring forever to get the sugar to dissolve. It is also great to keep on hand for a touch of sweetness when mixing hand-crafted cocktails.

1 cup sugar

In a medium saucepan over medium-high heat, combine the sugar with 1 cup water. Bring to a boil, stirring until the sugar has dissolved.

Allow to cool to room temperature.

Use in the the Basil Martini or the Cranberry Sparkler cocktail (recipe, p. 185). The remaining syrup may be kept, refrigerated, for 2 weeks.

Gingersnap Martini

Yields 1 cocktail

Inspired by childhood memories of gingerbread houses, orange spiced cider, and Christmas carols, this martini tastes like Christmas in a glass. If you like your gingersnaps sweeter, then use a sparkling wine in place of the Champagne, or add another teaspoon of simple syrup to your martini.

1½ ounce orange-flavored vodka, your choice brand

1 ounce ginger liqueur

1 teaspoon Simple Syrup (recipe, p. 174)

1 ounce brut Champagne

Orange peel

1 sliver fresh ginger

Fill a cocktail shaker with crushed ice. Add the vodka, liqueur, and simple syrup.

Shake vigorously and strain into a chilled martini glass.

Top with Champagne and garnish with an orange peel and a sliver of ginger.

Old Fashioned

Yields 1 cocktail

Some French believe that bourbon has an ancient connection with their House of Bourbon, but Southerners know that origins of the popular liquor are closer to Kentucky and our Southern distilleries. Made from at least 51% corn and aged in charred oak barrels, bourbon has long been the cornerstone of American cocktails.

1 tablespoon simple syrup (recipe, p. 174)

1 thin slice of orange peel

2 dashes Angostura bitters

2 ounces bourbon, your choice brand

Muddle the simple syrup and orange peel into a lowball glass. Add the bitters and bourbon and stir. Add ice cubes and serve.

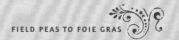

Peppermint Hot Chocolate

Yields 4 cups

In Paris I fell in love with le chocolat chaud, *or hot chocolate. I make mine with cream, but you can use milk instead. Adding a few drops of peppermint oil gives a fresh mint flavor that pairs beautifully with the creamy chocolate .*

3 cups heavy cream

3 cups milk

½ cup sugar

1 pinch salt

12 ounces bittersweet chocolate, chopped

6 drops peppermint oil

8 tablespoons Chantilly Cream (recipe, p. 167)

4 peppermint candy canes, crushed or whole

Combine the cream, milk, sugar, and salt in a stainless-steel saucepan over medium-low heat, and cook until the milk begins to steam.

Add the chopped chocolate and peppermint oil and stir constantly until the chocolate has completely melted. While on low heat, whisk for 5 to 10 minutes to thicken the hot chocolate. Remove from heat if it begins to stick to the bottom of the pan.

Pour into hot mugs and garnish with Chantilly cream, and crushed or whole candy canes.

Pomegranate Gimlet

Yields 1 cocktail

Imagine my surprise when I discovered two pomegranate trees growing in my front yard! By early fall I could see that these big ruby-colored fruits were pomegranates. They are in season in the Southeast from September through February, the perfect time to make your Pomegranate Brandy .

2 ounces gin, your choice brand

1 ounce fresh lime juice

1 ounce Pomegranate Brandy (recipe, p. 181)

1 ounce Simple Syrup (recipe, p. 174)

1 wedge lime

Fill a highball glass with crushed ice and add the gin, lime juice, Pomegranate Brandy, and simple syrup.

Stir and garnish with a lime wedge.

Spiced Wine

Serves 6

Springtime in Paris is beautiful. The crisp sunny weather is ideal for walks along the city streets. Winter in Paris is a different story. It can to be cold, wet, and windy, making walking anywhere the last thing I wanted to do. That's why spiced wine makes a perfect winter drink. You can make it ahead of time with whatever red wine you have on hand. Add a bit of brown sugar, some warm spice, heat, and enjoy. I serve it during holiday parties and family gatherings, and on cold, rainy days.

1 bottle full-bodied red wine, your choice brand

½ cup dark brown sugar

Zest of 1 orange

Zest of 1 lemon

3 black peppercorns, crushed

2 cardamom pods, crushed

1 cinnamon stick

2 cloves

½ cup kirsch, a clear cherry brandy

6 cinnamon sticks

In a large saucepan over medium heat, combine the red wine, sugar, orange and lemon zests, peppercorns, cardamom pods, 1 cinnamon stick, and cloves. Bring the wine to a low simmer, stirring to dissolve the sugar.

Remove from the heat, strain to remove the zest and spices, and stir in the kirsch.

Ladle the spiced wine into heatproof glasses, garnish each glass with 1 cinnamon stick, and serve hot.

Spiced Wine

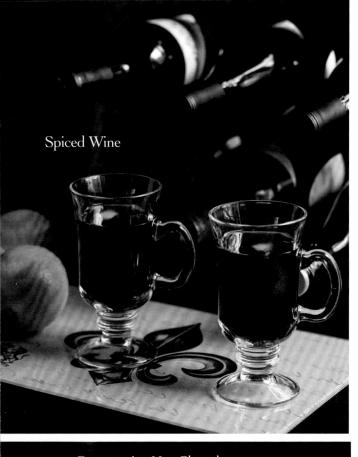
Peppermint Hot Chocolate

Pomegranate Gimlet

The Hot Toddy

Serves 1

When I had the sniffles or a cough, my mother would make me a hot toddy with lots of honey, lemon, and a shot of whiskey added. This recipe is a modern spin on that old classic, and perfect for a cold winter night.

½ teaspoon orange blossom honey

1 teaspoon dried green tea leaves

1½ ounces Peach Brandy
   (recipe, p. 182)

1 ounce apple schnapps

½ teaspoon clove-flavored
   liqueur, your choice of brand

½ teaspoon fresh lemon juice

1 strip orange peel, studded with
   1 clove

Place the honey and tea-filled infuser into a teapot. Pour in ½ cup boiling water, cover, and steep for 5 minutes.

Remove the tea infuser and add the brandy, schnapps, liqueur, and lemon juice.

Stir to mix and pour into a warm mug.

Garnish with the clove-studded orange peel.

Holiday Punch

Serves 8

½ cup Mint Syrup (recipe, p. 172)

1 (750-ml) bottle brut Champagne,
   chilled

1 cup white rum

1 cup Pomegranate Brandy
   (recipe, p. 181)

1 lemon, thinly sliced

1 cup frozen cranberries

1 bunch fresh mint leaves

Combine the mint syrup, Champagne, rum, and pomegranate brandy in a punch bowl filled with 1 quart crushed ice.

Stir in the lemon slices, frozen cranberries, and fresh mint leaves.

Serve in chilled Champagne glasses.

Pomegranate Brandy

Yields 3 quarts

The ruby jewel tones of pomegranate juice is what inspired me to make this brandy—that, and the fact that fresh pomegranates are available through fall and most of the winter, which is a best time to make brandy. This is a simple recipe made of fresh pomegranates, sugar, and a little yeast to get the fermentation process started. The outer skin of a pomegranate is very tough, so be careful when cutting them.

3 quarts (6 pounds) ripe
   pomegranates, cut into quarters
4 pounds sugar
2 tablespoons active dry yeast
6 cups lukewarm bottled water

Put the quartered pomegranates in a sterilized 2 gallon ceramic crock or glass pitcher. Pour the sugar on top of the cut pomegranates.

Dissolve the yeast in 1 cup warm water (110° to115° F) and pour over the top of the pomegranates and sugar. Stir until well combined, then pour the bottled water on top of the pomegranate-sugar yeast mixture and mix well. The water should fully cover the pomegranates. Add additional bottled water if necessary to fully cover the fruit. Be sure to leave at least 2 inches from the top of the fruit to the lip of the container for the fermentation process to bubble up.

Cover the crock with a plate, or a clean unbleached towel secured with twine or a rubber band, and place in a cool, dark place for 1 week. The brandy will bubble up during the fermentation process, so be sure to put a larger tray or platter beneath the crock to catch any of the juice that overflows.

After a week, stir the mixture with a long-handled spoon, cover, and let it sit for another week. Repeat this process each week for 4 to 6 weeks. As the pomegranates ferment, they will begin to break down and settle to the bottom of the container.

After 6 weeks, strain the mixture through several layers of cheesecloth and discard the pomegranate pulp and seeds. Return the brandy to the container and allow the remaining sediment to settle to the bottom of the container overnight, then strain through layers of cheesecloth a second time.

Using a funnel, pour the Pomegranate Brandy into sterilized, dry bottles. Cover tightly and store in a cool, dark place for at least 4 months for optimum taste.

Peach Brandy

Yields 3 quarts

My grandmother did not approve of drinking, especially for women, so it was a big shock the first time I saw one of my great aunts having a "thimbleful" of peach brandy. She said it was for medicinal purposes.

3 quarts (6 pounds) ripe peaches

4 pounds sugar

2 tablespoons active dry yeast

6 cups bottled water

Wash the peaches and cut each one into 4 to 5 pieces, leaving the peel on and the pits intact. Put the quartered peaches in a sterilized 2 gallon ceramic crock or glass pitcher. Pour the sugar on top of the cut peaches and mix.

Dissolve the yeast in 1 cup warm water (110° to 115°F) and pour over the top of the peaches and sugar. Stir until well combined then pour the bottled water on top of the peaches and sugar-yeast mixture, and mix well. The water should fully cover the peaches. Add additional bottled water if necessary to fully cover the fruit. Be sure to leave at least 2 inches from the top of the fruit to the lip of the container for the fermentation process to bubble up.

Cover the crock with a plate, or a clean unbleached towel secured with twine or a large rubber band and place the crock in a cool, dark place. The peach brandy will bubble up during the fermentation process, so be sure to put a larger tray or platter beneath the crock to catch any of the juice that overflows.

After 1 week, stir the brandy with a long-handled spoon, cover, and let it sit for 4 to 6 weeks, stirring once each week. As the peaches ferment, they will begin to break down and settle to the bottom of the container.

After 6 weeks, strain the mixture through 5 layers of cheesecloth and discard the peach pulp and pits. Transfer the brandy to a clean, sterilized container and allow the remaining sediment to settle to the bottom of the container overnight.

Strain a second time through 5 layers of cheesecloth.

Using a funnel, pour the Peach Brandy into sterilized, dry bottles. Cover tightly and store in a cool, dark place for at least 4 months for optimum taste.

Serve at room temperature, or slightly chilled.

Papa's Holiday Eggnog

Serves 8

Eggs, milk, and cream were always on hand on the farm, and what better way to use them than in this decadent eggnog? It is delicious with or without the alcohol, but adding it does make for a festive atmosphere. The key to making this drink is to chill it for several hours so it thickens before you add the whipped cream and egg whites.

12 eggs, separated

1½ cups sugar

1 cup bourbon

1 cup brandy

¾ cup dark rum

2½ cups heavy cream

6 cups milk

2 teaspoons freshly ground
   nutmeg

1 teaspoon cinnamon

In a large bowl, beat the egg yolks and sugar together until the mixture is firm and the color of butter. Slowly beat in the bourbon, brandy, and rum, ½ cup at a time.

Once all the alcohol has been added, refrigerate the mixutre for at least 4 hours.

Thirty minutes before serving the eggnog, beat the cream in a bowl until it forms stiff peaks.

In a separate bowl, beat the egg whites until stiff peaks form.

Stir the milk into the chilled egg yolk and alcohol mixture. Stir in the ground nutmeg and gently fold in the egg white mixture. Lastly, gently fold in the cream.

Ladle the Holiday Eggnog into cups and garnish each cup with a sprinkle of cinnamon.

Serve cold.

Strawberry Sparkler

Yields 2 cocktails

Imagine picking strawberries fresh from the berry patch and transforming them into a grownup strawberry lemonade. That's exactly what this cocktail recipe does. Crushed strawberries, fresh lemon juice, and your favorite vodka will make this a summertime favorite.

4 ounces vodka, your choice brand

2 ounces Simple Syrup (recipe, p. xx)

2 teaspoons fresh lemon juice

4 large strawberries, stems removed, plus 2 for garnish

4 ounces seltzer water, or club soda

2 lemon slices

Pour the vodka, simple syrup, and lemon juice into a cocktail shaker. Add 4 strawberries and muddle until they are broken into small pieces.

Add 1 cup crushed ice and shake for 10 seconds.

Pour into a chilled martini glass, top with club soda, and garnish each drink with a slice of lemon and a strawberry.

Cranberry Sparkler

Yields 4 cocktails

2 cups unsweetened cranberry juice

1 cup fresh orange juice

½ cup apple flavored liqueur, your choice brand

2 tablespoons Simple Syrup (recipe, p. 174)

2 cups seltzer water

4 fresh sprigs mint

12 fresh cranberries

In a large pitcher, combine the cranberry juice, orange juice, apple liqueur, simple syrup, and 4 cups crushed ice.

Strain into 4 chilled champagne flutes, top with seltzer water, and garnish with mint sprigs and 3 fresh cranberries.

Muscadine Wine

Yields 3 to 4 bottles

Just as sweet tea is the unofficial 'official' drink of the South, wine is the official drink of France. It was such a fun learning experience trying different wines, learning about grape varieties, and seeing firsthand the French winemaking process. This recipe is similar to the French process. It uses locally grown grapes, crushed and fermented, then bottled and aged.

3 pounds ripe Muscadine
   grapes, stems removed
3 pounds sugar
1 ounce active dry yeast

Rinse the grapes in cold water 3 to 4 times, until the rinse water runs clear. Using your hands, or a mortar and pestle, crush the grapes and place them into a sterilized 2 gallon ceramic crock or glass pitcher.

In a large stockpot over high heat, bring 1 gallon cold water to a rolling boil. Add the sugar and bring to a second boil, stirring to dissolve the sugar. Remove the pot from the heat, allow it to cool for 10 minutes, then pour the hot sugar water over the crushed grapes. Allow the mixture to cool to room temperature.

Dissolve the yeast into 1 cup warm water (110° to 115°F), and add to the grape mixture, stirring until well combined.

Cover the container with a clean tea towel secured with twine or a rubber band. The muscadine wine will bubble up during the fermentation process, so be sure to put a larger tray or platter beneath the container to catch any of the juice that overflows.

Place in a cool, dark place to ferment for 3 weeks, or until the fermentation process is complete, stirring the wine twice each week. The wine will bubble during the fermentation process. There will be no bubbles once fermentation is complete.

Strain the wine through a triple layer of cheesecloth. Using a small funnel, pour the wine into sterilized wine bottles. Cover the bottles with cheesecloth for 3 days to allow for any last minute fermentation.

After 3 days, seal the wine bottles tightly with corks and store on their sides in a cool, dark place. Allow the wine to age at least another 6 weeks before drinking.

Winter Pear Wine

Yields 3 to 4 bottles

Grapes aren't the only fruit that can be made into wine. Most fruits can be used, and winter pears are no exception. The winemaking process starts with ripe seasonal fruits, sugar, and yeast. These three ingredients, plus time and patience will result in a tasty fruit wine. The most important ingredient of wine is the fruit. Use whatever fruits are in season, and remember that the fruit doesn't have to be pretty — only fresh.

6 pounds winter pears

2 pounds sugar, divided

12 raisins, divided

1 teaspoon active dry yeast

Wash and cut each pear into 3 to 4 pieces, leaving the skin on and the seeds intact. Place half the chopped fruit into a sterilized 2-gallon ceramic crock. Pour half the sugar and raisins over the pears. Add the remaining fruit, sugar, and raisins on top of the first layer. Do not stir.

Bring 5 quarts cold water to a rolling boil over high heat and pour the boiling water over the fruit. There should be at least 2 inches of room at the top of the container to allow the mixture to bubble up during the fermentation process. Stir the mixture until the sugar is dissolved. Cover the container with a clean tea towel and allow the mixture to cool overnight.

The next day, dissolve the yeast in 1 cup of warm water (110° to 115° F) and stir into the fruit mixture. Cover again with the tea towel, this time securing it with twine or a large rubber band. The mixture will start bubbling immediately after adding the yeast and will continue to bubble up during the fermentation process, so be sure to put a larger tray or platter beneath the crock to catch any of the juice that overflows.

Place the container in a cool, dark place for 6 weeks to allow the fermentation process, stirring once weekly.

Strain the wine through 5 layers of cheesecloth. Using a funnel, pour the wine into sterilized wine bottles. Cover the bottles loosely with cheesecloth and let stand for another 3 days to allow for any last minute fermentation.

After 3 days, seal the bottles tightly with corks and store on their sides in a cool, dark place. Allow the wine to age at least another 6 weeks for optimum taste.

Mulled Cider

Serves 6

Growing up, the kids drank cider without the spices, while the grownups added cinnamon, allspice, cloves, and star anise, then warmed the cider and topped it off with a splash of spiced rum.

1 quart apple cider

1 (1-inch) piece fresh ginger, peeled

1 fresh lemon, cut in quarters

1 fresh orange, cut in quarters

2 cinnamon sticks

Pinch of allspice

2 whole cloves

1 cup spiced rum, your choice brand

6 whole star anise

Combine the apple cider, ginger, lemon, orange, cinnamon sticks, allspice, and cloves in a stainless-steel saucepan over medium heat and bring to a boil. Reduce the heat to low and simmer for 15 minutes.

Strain the mixture, add the spiced rum, and serve hot in mugs.

Garnish with the star anise.

A 1950 family portrait of my Grandfather Green, Grandmother Bessie Lee, Uncles Lawrence and Jimmy (the baby), my mother LaVerne, and Aunt Honey.

Acknowledgments

There is a saying that it takes a village to raise a child, and I feel the same about writing this cookbook. I have been inspired and motivated by so many people along the way, and it humbles me to know that they've cared enough to help me fulfill my dream of writing this book.

Dianna, thank you for your unwavering years of love and support—and for yanking my coattails when I try to fly too close to the sun.

Mickie (Crockett), who knew that this culinary thing would actually pay off—your boundless energy and determination to "have it all" keeps me motivated to do more than I think I can. Thank you for that.

I appreciate you, Matthew Raiford, for teaching me the Three R's and talking me off the ledge whenever I'd try to give up.

Chef Joe Randall and Chef Glenn Butler: you two gentleman have given me the blueprint of what it takes to stay true to yourself in this crazy world we cook in, and for that I am ever grateful.

Pier, over the years we have shared so much, thank you for many words of wisdom, never judging me, and being a true friend.

Maurietta Amos, I can always count on you to take me one step closer to the finish line, either by leading the way, walking by my side, or by carrying me for a bit of the journey.

A special thanks to Virginia and Mary Eva for your support, and for always telling me how great I am—you're the best cheerleaders I could hope for.

Thanks to MFH Group and Chef Connie for my beautiful custom-made chef's coat.

Thanks to Atlanta stylist Annette Joseph for the loan of some beautiful photo props.

And finally, thanks to all the students I have taught along the way. You helped me learn more about cooking (and life) than you realize.

Index